# RESEARCH METHODS
# IN PSYCHOLOGY

# RESEARCH METHODS IN PSYCHOLOGY

*edited by*

## Glynis M. Breakwell, Sean Hammond and Chris Fife-Schaw

SAGE Publications

London · Thousand Oaks · New Delhi

Editorial arrangement © Glynis M. Breakwell,
Sean Hammond and Chris Fife-Schaw 1995
Chapters 1, 2 and 15 © Glynis M. Breakwell 1995
Chapter 3 © Martyn Barrett 1995
Chapters 4, 7, 8, 12 and 23 © Chris Fife-Schaw 1995
Chaper 5 © Alyson Davis 1995
Chaper 6 © Sarah L. Wilson 1995
Chapter 9 © Ian Donald 1995
Chapter 10 © David Rose 1995
Chapter 11 © Paul Barrett 1995
Chapters 13 and 24 © Sean Hammond 1995
Chapter 14 © Jill Wilkinson 1995
Chapter 16 © Adrian Coyle 1995
Chapter 17 © Margaret Wilson 1995
Chapter 18 © Lynne Millward 1995
Chapter 19 © Glynis M. Breakwell and Peter Wood 1995
Chapter 20 © David Uzzell 1995
Chapter 21 © Jonathan Chase 1995
Chapter 22 © Peter Simpson 1995
Chapter 25 © Peter Wood 1995

First published 1995   Reprinted 1995

SAGE Publications Ltd
6 Bonhill Street
London EC2A 4PU

SAGE Publications Inc
2455 Teller Road
Thousand Oaks, California 91320

SAGE Publications India Pvt Ltd
32, M-Block Market
Greater Kailash - I
New Delhi 110 048

**British Library Cataloguing in Publication data**

A catalogue record for this book is
available from the British Library.

ISBN 0 8039 7764 6
ISBN 0 8039 7765 4 (pbk)

**Library of Congress catalog card number 94–061391**

Typeset by Photoprint, 9–11 Alexandra Lane, Torquay
Printed in Great Britain by Redwood Books, Trowbridge,
Wiltshire

# Contents

## PART IV

# Contributors

**Martyn Barrett** is a Reader in Psychology at the University of Surrey. He obtained his degrees at Cambridge and Sussex in the 1970s. His principal research interests are in the development of children's cognitive representations of objects, events, people and places. He has worked extensively on children's language acquisition, looking at the representations that underlie lexical and early syntactic development. He has also worked on the development of children's drawings, their understanding of television and on children's memory for events. He is currently investigating, within a cross-national framework, children's knowledge of, and attitudes to foreign peoples and foreign countries and the development of regional and national identities in children. He is the reviews editor for *First Language*, the UK Coordinator for the Child Language Data Exchange System and a member of the Executive Committee of the International Association for the Study of Child Language.

**Paul Barrett** is a Lecturer in Psychology at the University of Canterbury, Christchurch, New Zealand. He is also a visiting senior lecturer at the University of Surrey. His research interests are in electrophysiological correlates of personality and intelligence, and both theoretical and applied psychometrics. His main overall area of interest is individual differences psychology.

**Glynis M. Breakwell** is Professor of Psychology and Head of the Department of Psychology at the University of Surrey. She conducts research in identity dynamics and social representations; political and economic socialisation; attitudes towards science and technology; sexual attitudes and activity; and processes of environmental change. Her most recent research concerns the relationship between risk evaluation and decision making. Most of her research has been funded by the Economic and Social Research Council (ESRC) but also latterly by the EU and various government departments. She has published 17 books and more than 100 articles in social psychology. She edits a series on social psychology for Academic Press/Surrey University Press and co-edits a series on personal and professional development for the British Psychological Society.
In 1993, the British Psychological Society (BPS), in recognition of her contribution to social psychological knowledge, gave her the Myers Award, one of the Society's highest honours.

**Jonathan Chase** is a Lecturer in Psychology at the University of Surrey. He obtained a masters degree in social psychology and also his Ph.D. from the London School of Economics and Political Science before taking up his current post in the Department. He has research interests in psychological aspects of social dilemmas, economic psychology and decision making. He has recently obtained research funding for a large-scale international study of the psychological determinants of environmental action and another for an investigation into nurses' patient-related decision-making strategies.

**Adrian Coyle** is a Lecturer in Department of Nursing and Midwifery at the University of Surrey. He obtained his degree in psychology from University College Dublin and his Ph.D. from the University of Surrey. Before taking up his present post, he worked in HIV/AIDS research, counselling and education. His research interests include identity, the psychosocial aspects of HIV/AIDS and the use of qualitative methods in psychology. He has recently obtained funding from the Department of Health to study experiences of the HIV test.

**Alyson Davis** is a Lecturer in Psychology at the University of Surrey. She obtained her degree in psychology from Sussex before taking a PGCE. Her Ph.D., awarded by the University of Birmingham, was completed before taking up a lectureship in Educational Psychology at the same institution. She was then appointed to a lectureship in Child Psychology at the Institute of Education before taking up her current post in the Department. She has research interests in children's representations (drawing, writing and number) and in the relationship between early mathematical thinking and education.

**Ian Donald** is a Lecturer in Psychology at the University of Surrey. He has an M.Sc. in Environmental Psychology from Surrey and a Ph.D. in Organisational and Environmental Psychology from the University of Aston Management School, where he was also Visiting Lecturer in Applied Psychology. He has researched in a wide variety of areas in social, environmental and organisational psychology, and has recognised expertise in the areas of office design, human behaviour in emergencies and disasters, and facet theory. His principal research interests at present are in the relationship between organisational factors and environmental design and experience, safety and human and organisational behaviour, place evaluation and the social psychology of disasters. Ian Donald has published in many areas of environmental and organisational psychology including personnel selection, organisational climate and culture, place evaluation, office design, behaviour in fires, and facet theory.

**Chris Fife-Schaw** is a Lecturer in Psychology at the University of Surrey. He obtained his degrees at Newcastle, Strathclyde and Sheffield Universities in the late 1970s/early 1980s. His Ph.D. was concerned with the notion of rationality in voting decisions. Since 1984 he has worked in the Department on several research projects concerned with young people. The first about young people's attitudes to new technology, the second on the political and economic socialisation of young people and the third on the impact of HIV/AIDS on the general population of young people. He now lectures in social psychology and research methods and his research interests are in political psychology and developing alternative measures of attitudes that do not involve questionnaires. He is a member of the Editorial Board of the *British Journal of Social Psychology*.

**Sean Hammond** is a Lecturer in Psychology at the University of Surrey. He obtained his degrees from London, Leicester and Surrey Universities in the late 1970s and 1980s. His primary interests are in psychometrics and multivariate statistics and he has a particular interest in individual differences and health psychology. Current work involves an assessment of ipsative procedures in personality assessment, the measurement of pro-environmentalism, the assessment of mentally disordered offenders and an evaluation of cross-cultural psychometric strategies. He has been a research and psychometrics consultant to a number of companies and health authorities and is an Honorary Reader at Broadmoor Hospital.

**Lynne Millward** is a Lecturer in Psychology at the University of Surrey. She obtained her degrees from Exeter and Kent Universities and her Ph.D. was concerned with identity processes, group formation and change and the relationship between cognition and affect. Prior to joining the Department she worked as an occupational psychologist in a management consultancy practice in London where she specialised in the design and implementation of selection, training and assessment procedures. Her current research interests include the social psychology of work, group processes, identity dynamics, sexuality and the relationship between thoughts, feelings and behaviour.

**David Rose** is a Lecturer in Psychology at the University of Surrey. He is interested in wide areas of brain research, visual perception, cognition, philosophy of mind and the philosophy of science. His research currently centres mainly on visual psychophysics, but he also has experience in neurophysiology, neuropharmacology, neurochemistry, quantitative neural modelling, epilepsy, memory, hemisphere differences, time perception and computer methods for generating theories. He has undertaken consultancy work for the government on the automatisation of television image assessment and the ergonomics of aircraft safety. In addition to his research at Surrey he has worked in universities in Cambridge, Bristol, Brunel, Chicago, Nashville, Bozeman and Boston, supported by funds from the Wellcome Trust, the Science and Engineering Research Council (SERC), the Medical Research Council (MRC), the National Institute of Health (NIH), the National Science Foundation (NSF) and the Royal Society among others. He has edited two books, *The Artful Brain* and *Models of the Visual Cortex*, is on the Editorial Board of the *Journal of Intelligent Systems* and is a consultant referee for *Vision Research* and *Perception*.

**Peter Simpson** is a Lecturer in Psychology at the University of Surrey. He obtained degrees from Leeds, Sussex and Cambridge Universities. He has carried out research on visual attention and recognition, and problem solving in science and engineering education. He has contributed work to the design of computer interface languages for the European Space Agency (ESA) and has researched musical acoustics and skills. He is currently investigating factors in the auditory location of speech and the provision of synthetic speech aids for the disabled.

**David Uzzell** is a Senior Lecturer in Psychology at the University of Surrey. He is a social and environmental psychologist specialising in applied research in urban planning, environmental, health and civic education; social representations of the past; environmental interpretation; museum and exhibition evaluation; attitudes and behaviours in environmental planning and global environmental change. He has many years' experience of undertaking research and acting as a consultant to government departments and major environmental, heritage and tourism agencies in Britain and overseas. David Uzzell is regularly invited to give seminars and papers throughout the world, and is a member of the Editorial Board of the *Journal of Environmental Psychology* and *Publics et Musées*.

**Jill Wilkinson** is a Lecturer in Psychology at the University of Surrey. She is a counselling psychologist who holds a half-time appointment in the Department and also runs her own clinical practice. Her particular interests are in social behaviour in schizophrenia both from a research perspective and in terms of therapeutic implications, and in the psychological effects of ill health. She has been very active in the development of Counselling Psychology within the British Psychological Society and her teaching includes Counselling, Interviewing and Assessment.

**Margaret Wilson** is an Associate Lecturer in Psychology and Research Fellow at the University of Surrey. She has an M.Sc. in environmental psychology and a Ph.D. in psychology from the University of Surrey. She has worked in several areas of applied social psychology, as well as undertaking theoretical and methodological research. Her research interests are in social, environmental and investigative psychology. She is also interested in facet theory and qualitative research methods, and has been instrumental in developing the use of open-ended sorting procedures.

**Sarah L. Wilson** is a Lecturer in Psychology at the University of Surrey. She graduated from Swansea and studied for her Ph.D. at the Institute of Psychiatry. She is a neuropsychologist and since 1980 has been engaged in research involving severely physically disabled and brain-injured people. Areas of research include computer-based assessment, the role of psychological factors in rehabilitation, recovery from very severe brain injury and, most recently, the treatment of patients in vegetative state.

**Peter Wood** is a Lecturer in Psychology at the University of Surrey. He graduated in psychology from Manchester University and received his Ph.D. from Loughborough University. A large part of his earlier career was spent at Loughborough in the Department of Ergonomics, subsequently in the Department of Social Sciences undertaking research in vehicle ergonomics, consumer safety and behaviour in fires. He also spent three years in industry working for the Ford Motor Company on vehicle safety systems. Over more recent years his interests have broadened into the general area of Occupational and Organisational Psychology.

# PART I

# 1 Introducing Research Methods in Psychology

*Glynis M. Breakwell*

## Contents

## 1.1 Objectives of the book

The purpose of this book is to offer students at the undergraduate and postgraduate levels a reasonably comprehensive introduction to the research methods which can be used in the exploration of psychological processes. Like any science, psychology is concerned with identifying how processes operate. A process here is defined as a series of changes. The task of the psychological researcher is to plot patterns of changes in any one variable and to describe the relationships between changes in that variable and changes in others. Theories essentially specify the principles or rules which predict these relationships. The variables which interest theorists in psychology lie at intraindividual, interpersonal and societal levels of analysis. They range from the biochemical and genetic, through the physiological, to the cognitive and affective, and beyond to inter-personal networks and communication, and further still to social power hierarchies and ideologies. Insofar as the psychological processes they study are influenced by the material context or physical environment, many psychologists see these also as a target of their analysis. Such diversity of subject matter requires a diversity of research methods. Students of psychology are therefore usually subjected to research methods training which is simultaneously both broader and more intensive than in virtually any other science.

This book is designed to provide the basic information a student might need about each of the common research strategies used to examine psychological processes. How to conduct experiments and the nature of quasi-experimental designs for data collection are described. Classic methods of direct observation are depicted. Psychophysical and psychophysiological procedures are catalogued. Survey techniques are presented. Questionnaire design, psychometric techniques and interviewing are all reviewed. Ethnography and action research are introduced. Alongside these popular and well-rehearsed approaches, others that are less frequently used or that are relatively new and little understood, are also represented. These include single case experimental designs, discourse analysis, focus groups, diary techniques, simulation and historical analysis. We have included such a wide range of approaches because we believe that it is only by knowing most, if not all, of what could be used to address a particular research problem that the researcher can make appropriate methodological choices.

In presenting these approaches, we have tried to be value-neutral: we do not play favourites; there are no methodological heroes or design villains. Each approach is presented as fairly as possible and there is no attempt to proselytise any one in particular. In fact, the assumption underlying this collection of approaches is that the usefulness of any method can only be judged against the properties of the research question that you wish to answer. More importantly, it is assumed that all methods have weaknesses and limitations. Therefore, it is argued that theorists will want to have recourse to a variety of methods and will implement them in an integrated fashion (see Chapter 2).

## 1.2    Structure of the book

Each chapter attempts to present a practical guide to the research approach it covers. The object is to demythologise where necessary, to systematise and summarise succinctly relevant information, and to offer advice which will be useful when you try to use the approach yourself. Each chapter should provide you with enough information so that you can judge whether that approach will be any use to you in addressing a particular research problem. Typically, the chapters are structured so as to introduce the approach, illustrate its potential and the details of using it, identify its weaknesses (where possible showing how they can be overcome), and suggest exercises or projects which can be used to acquire a better understanding of it. Each chapter also provides a list of further reading about the approach.

As is evident from the contents pages, the book is divided into four unequal parts. The first describes the issues surrounding the relationship between theory-building concerning psychological processes and research methodology. It also provides a thorough examination of the practical and ethical issues involved in planning and executing any research. The second part focuses upon how to structure data collection, presenting both the principles which need to be understood when trying to measure a psychological variable and the prime types of research design which can be employed. This segment also includes a chapter on facet theory which in reality is not a theory but a metatheoretical approach which hopes to show how researchers can be more systematic in defining their hypotheses and operationalising variables. The third and largest part of the book contains the descriptions of what might be called data elicitation techniques. Mostly, these include details of the types of data which the technique yields and what forms of data analysis are necessary to make sense of them. The final part of the book explains the nature of the assumptions underlying bivariate, multivariate and meta-analytic statistical approaches. The purpose of this segment is not to provide detailed explanations of specific statistical tests. The object is to explain the logic which should dictate which statistical test you should choose to use and what this sort of test is capable of telling you about your data. A basic understanding of statistical assumptions is often slow to mature and can be delayed by dealing too soon with the mathematical details of specific tests. Here, the student is introduced to these fundamental statistical assumptions in a way which shows how they are linked to types of research design and levels of measurement and, perhaps, this makes them more comprehensible. Readers needing detailed information on specific statistical tests are directed to appropriate alternative texts.

Given the variety of approaches covered in this book, we expect that it will prove useful throughout the course of an individual's research training. Chapters which are not used at an undergraduate level may well be central to a postgraduate course or be valuable later when considering further research activity. Effectively, the book can be used in modules and progress towards a thorough understanding and skilled use of these various approaches can be achieved in easy stages. As a reference text for more experienced researchers, the book has been written as far as possible so as to incorporate current and recent developments. This is done in the hope that this book can be used as a resource in the process of continuing professional development.

# 2 Research: Theory and Method

*Glynis M. Breakwell*

## Contents

## 2.1 Theory-building and theory-testing

Why do we do research? Once the cynical retorts to this question, such as 'to keep a job' or 'to get good coursework marks', are out of the way, the serious answer would be: 'we do research to find out what has happened, how it happened, and, if possible, why it happened'. I use 'happened' rather than 'happening' because by the time we have recorded something it is inevitably in the past.

Research is not inevitably tied to formal theory-building or theory-testing. Some researchers self-consciously eschew the construction of theory for metaphilosophical reasons. They use their research to describe in detail specific happenings without any attempt to use these as instances to illustrate or test some general underlying explanatory framework. Other researchers ignore theory because they do their research for purely practical reasons. They need to know what has happened in order to decide what they (or their clients) should do next.

It could be argued, of course, that even those researchers who have no time for formal theories are working with implicit theories. A theory, after all, is merely a set of propositions which posit the nature of the relationships between predefined constructs (or variables). At an informal level, we build theories all the time. In fact, George Kelly (1955), when he developed the theory of personal constructs to explain personality and cognitive processes, based his argument on the metaphor of 'man the scientist'. Kelly suggested that we all behave as scientists insofar as we are inveterate constructors of theories. They help us to navigate in the social world by letting us explain to ourselves what we think is happening and why it is happening. Informal theories of this type are particularly valuable because we often use them as the basis for predicting what will happen next. So, for instance, I might observe events which lead me to conclude that men in their late teens or early twenties are more likely than other people to drive their cars aggressively and erratically, with their windows open, with heavy bass music blaring, on sunny days. From this I might generate an informal theory that attributes their driving behaviour to their age or possibly some interaction of their age with the music and the sunshine. As a naïve scientist, I am not obliged to test my theory. I can go ahead to predict from it that young men, playing audible music on sunny days are more likely to be a danger to me as another road user and adjust my own behaviour accordingly. Theory-building of this sort has survival value, though when it goes wrong it also has the capacity to seriously endanger you. Such theories can mislead you, directing you to cues in the situation which are irrelevant. My sunny day, music-loving bad driver theory is only really valuable if it turns out that in the rain young men are at least as good as any other driver. However, Kelly pointed out that the erroneous theory is usually just a staging post to a better version. As naïve scientists, we are mostly willing to refine our theories on the basis of new information which proves the earlier versions wrong.

The implicit theories which inform some research have the same sort of power to both aid and hinder survival. Even while they remain unmentioned, these implicit theories direct the attention of the researcher to focus on some things rather than others, to use certain research approaches rather than others, and to try this rather than that form of analysis. In most cases, it would be better if the researcher did articulate these implicit theories. By doing so, it is possible to analyse their logical weaknesses (for example, inconsistencies) and their substantive weaknesses (for example, omission of important variables). Some researchers resist making their implicit theories explicit because they do not see their task as theory-building. Yet this is actually a poor excuse. It does not really preclude the need to specify which theoretical assumptions underlie your work. Since these assumptions will inevitably affect what you do, they should be described so that other researchers can judge how far your research activities and findings are influenced by them. Researchers who do try to lay bare these underlying assumptions often find that the discipline needed to articulate them has the effect of bringing about for themselves a new understanding of their research problem. Essentially, whether you see yourself as a theory-builder or not, it is always useful to examine the implicit theories which affect your research.

The process of formal theory-building is supposed by some philosophers of science to proceed in an orderly manner from description, to taxonomy, and thus to testable causal propositions. This would mean that the first task of the theorist is to thoroughly and systematically describe the phenomena of interest. The next task is to categorise phenomena, showing how specific instances are characterised by common attributes which make them capable of being treated in some sense as equivalent to each other. Such categorisation is one way of ordering the plethora of data which are generated whenever descriptions are not prestructured. The categories can be labelled as a theoretical construct. Learning theory has categorised phenomena to generate two very salient constructs: stimuli and responses. To the behaviourist, all phenomena at any one moment can be categorised as either a stimulus or a response. By this act of definition, suddenly the multitudinous social world is dichotomised, order is imposed and it is the relationship between these two which is to be explained.

Once the taxonomy is complete, the theorist's next task entails stating how one category of phenomena is related to another. The description of a single set of relationships between phenomena does not become a theory unless general principles about the relationships of similar phenomena are formulated. To say: 'The woman kicked the dog after he bit her and he was never found to bite her again' is a description of a pattern of events, it is not a theory. But if one were to say: 'The woman punished the dog for biting and he never did it again' there remains only one further step towards generalisation before a theory comes into being: 'Punishment of a behaviour leads to the diminution of that behaviour'. The result is a recognisable basic tenet of learning theory (to be much qualified later by statements about the frequency or punishment, the temporal relationship of the punishment to the behaviour and the availability of alternative rewards for the behaviour). Theories are basically sets of what might be called **relational rules**. The relational rule specifies how variation in one theoretical construct is related to variation in one or more others.

An explanation can be of two sorts: the mechanistic or process variety or the functional variety. The **mechanistic or process explanation** accounts for a phenomenon in terms of phenomena which are its precursors. It is usually in the form: if A and B occur, then C will follow. The **functional explanation** accounts for a phenomenon in terms of the consequences it has. It is usually in the form: A occurs in order that B will follow. The functional explanation assumes that the phenomenon to be explained is purposive or intentional (occurs to achieve some goal).

Another way of talking about the distinction between the mechanistic and functional types of explanation would be to say that the former is concerned with causes and the latter with reasons. Psychological theories use both types of explanation. Some theorists use both explanatory forms to account for a single psychological process. For instance, in studying altruism (helping or pro-social behaviour) researchers have found that people are less likely to offer someone help if they perceive the person to be in need because they have made too little effort, not used their own ability and not chosen to get out of the difficulty when they had it in their control to do so. One explanation of helping suggests that people see the need for assistance then assess whether the individual is responsible for his or her own predicament. If they are responsible this leads to anger and no helping but, if they are deemed not to be responsible this leads to sympathy and helping. This is clearly a mechanistic explanation. Another explanation of helping suggests that people are unwilling to help those unfortunates whom they see to be the origin of their own fate because they wish to punish the miscreant for failures of effort or judgement. In this explanation the punishment (that is, failure to help) serves the function in some way of extracting restitution and may warn others that such slack behaviour is unacceptable and not rewarded with help. It should be noted that these two explanations of the same phenomenon are not mutually exclusive. The functional explanation may serve to account for the anger, so central to the mechanistic explanation, which is aroused when the needy are shown not to have tried to help themselves.

This mixing of mechanistic and functional explanations is common in psychological theories. It may emanate, in part, from the way psychological processes and thus psychological theories often traverse many levels of analysis. I would argue (Breakwell, 1994) that psychologists should be building theories which encompass processes at the intrapsychic (i.e. cognitive, affective and oretic) level, the interpersonal level and the societal level of analysis. But we are currently a long way away from the grand theory in psychology. We have low- or middle-range theories designed to explain relatively narrow bands of phenomena. Thus, for instance, we have theories of aggression distinct and separate from theories of altruism when common sense might think them to be in some way connected. These low-level theories, while they may offer a detailed mechanistic explanation of their target phenomena, tend to rely upon what Israel (1972) called 'stipulative statements' that concern assumptions about the nature of Man, the nature of society and the nature of the relationship between Man and society. These stipulative statements are often functionalist (for example, a variety of Social Darwinism as illustrated in the theory of altruism described above). This results in a strange mélange of explanatory types being moulded together in many psychological theories; made more strange by the fact that some significant element of the explanation remains unsaid. Those elements which lie at a different level of analysis from that of the main theory will reside at the margin; unexamined and untested. Another example of such stipulative statements would be the assumption of the rational model of Man.

Just as mechanistic and functional explanations are not so simple to keep apart, the distinction between theories built from induction and theories developed through deduction is not easy to maintain in practice. **Induction** entails inferring of a general law from particular instances. **Deduction** entails drawing from the general an inference to the particular. In practice, theory-building is a messy, iterative process. Relational rules that seem to be valid are usually crafted by successive approximation. This process of approximation will involve both deductive and inductive reasoning. I may well, for instance, set off in developing a theory of how identity processes which concern self-esteem affect memory capacity by cataloguing the range of examples of instances where memory capacity has been shown to be greater for self-relevant information and where it has been proven to be more accurate for information which is positive about the self. From this I might induce a generalisation: the memory for self-evaluative information will be greater and more accurate if that information is positive than if it is negative. From this generalisation, I might go on to deduce that memory for exam results will be better if they are the individual's own results and especially if they were good results. Essentially, the process of induction allows us to produce theoretical generalisations; the process of deduction allows us to derive specific propositions from those generalisations. Deduction is as important as induction in theory-building because a theory can only be tested through examining whether the specific propositions that have been derived from it can be supported empirically.

Induction is based on evidence about a range of specific instances. One reason for doing research is to collect this evidence. Deduction generates specific propositions. Another reason for doing research is to test these propositions.

A theory can be evaluated along several dimensions which are reasonably independent. It can be assessed in terms of its parsimony: a theory should not include constructs which do not add to its explanatory power. It can be evaluated in terms of its ease of communication and the stimulus it provides for new insights. It can be judged in terms of its responsiveness to new evidence and its flexibility. However, while these dimensions might be seen as optional, it must be judged in terms of its internal consistency: propositions in the theory should not be self-contradictory. It must also be judged in terms of its **external validity**: it should be able to predict phenomena or be able to interpret them. Most importantly, a theory should be falsifiable: it must be open to being proven wrong.

What we do in testing a theory is to try to prove it wrong. By showing where a theory is wrong, we show which bits need to be replaced and in most cases we also show what needs to be substituted. Research designed to test a theory will be organised so as to show whether a proposition deduced from that theory is wrong. If we fail to disprove the proposition, the theory survives to face another test. Research can never prove a theory, it can merely accumulate examples of where the theory has not been disproven. The reason a theory cannot be proven in absolute terms is that it must entail generalisation and the empirical research can only ever sample specific instances of that generality. Of course, a theory which survives many tests intact must be regarded as a good theory.

Nevertheless, not all theories which have survived are strictly falsifiable. Some theories become unfalsifiable because they rest upon a **tautology**. For instance, some critics of learning theory would argue that one of its fundamental assertions cannot be falsified because the concept of a reinforcer is defined in a tautological way. A reinforcer is defined as anything which acts to increase the frequency of a response. The theory then goes on to state that responses which are reinforced increase in frequency. The circularity in the argument is clear when the theory is reduced to its fundamentals in this way. Such a tautology means that the theory cannot be tested because a key concept cannot be operationally defined independently.

The Freudian theory ego-defence mechanisms cannot be falsified for a different reason. In this case, the theory attempts to explain how the conscious mind protects itself from material which must remain in the unconscious or preconscious minds. Freud explained that such material is handled by a series of ego-defence mechanisms (such as sublimation, displacement, regression, fixation, etc.). What makes this aspect of psychoanalytic theory untestable is the fact Freud offers such an array of defence mechanisms that it is impossible to formulate a test of the operation of one which would not be potentially abrogated by the operation of another. For instance, one might set out to test the notion of sublimation which would say that an unacceptable unconscious impulse driven by the id should be translated into one which is socially acceptable before it would gain access to the conscious mind. The first problem the empiricist would have is in knowing that the impulse existed at all. The second would be that the impulse need not be dealt with by sublimation, it could be treated through reaction formation. This would mean that even if you established when the impulse was occurring and monitored no evidence of sublimation, you would not have falsified the theory because the impulse had been dealt with by another equally valid defence mechanism. Freud basically produced what could be called an overdetermined model: a theory which allows multiple determiners of outcomes in such a way that no single determiner can be empirically proven to be irrelevant. Where a theory is unfalsifiable it becomes nothing more or less than an interesting interpretation of the phenomena. It is a story told about the phenomena. If it pleases you, you can tell it to others. It may be useful in making sense of what you observe. However, it remains a pre-scientific theory. Theories which are not open to falsification are not scientific theories.

If you build theories, you should make them genuinely testable and you should provide evidence that you have tested them at least minimally (that is, deduced propositions which you have failed to show were incorrect but which could have been shown to be incorrect!). If every psychologist who wanted to build theories did this, it would save every other psychologist a lot of time and effort.

## 2.2 Matching methodologies to theory

Different types of theory have to be tested using different types of research method. The nature of the theory limits the range of research methods which can be meaningfully used to test it. For example, a theory explaining variation in visual acuity is likely to need to measure acuity using some psychophysical technique. However, the extent of these limitations should not be overestimated. Most psychological theories can be tested using more than one method. In fact, it is advisable to try to test a theory using a variety of methods in order to prove that it is no artefact of the method which results in the theory being supported.

A piece of research can differ along a series of four independent dimensions:

1  Type of data elicited.
2  Technique of data elicitation.
3  Type of design for monitoring change.
4  Treatment of data as qualitative or qualitative.

### 2.2.1  Type of data elicited

In psychological research the type of data can vary in origin: it can be intrapersonal (for example, genotypic information, cognitions, emotions, etc.); or interindividual (for example, friendship networks, communication patterns, etc.); or societal (for example, institutional hierarchies, ideological systems, etc.).

### 2.2.2  Technique of data elicitation

Data can be elicited directly or indirectly from a target. Direct elicitation methods would include any stimulus to self-report (for example, interviewing, self-completion questionnaires, etc.) or self-revelation through behaviour (for example, role play, performance on tasks, etc.). Indirect elicitation methods would include techniques that rely upon the researcher observing behaviour (for example, participant observation) or using informants upon the target's behaviour, thought or feelings (for example, archival records, witnesses, etc.).

Data elicitation can vary in terms of the amount of control exerted by the researcher upon a target. This control can be manifest in restrictions imposed upon the freedom of the target to give information (for example, forced choice options rather than open-ended responses to questions). It can be evident in the extent to which the target is manipulated (for example, in experiments through the creation of artificial contexts or in surveys through the use of cover stories designed to mislead the target about the purpose of the study).

### 2.2.3   Type of design for monitoring change

The central task for psychological theories is to explain change. Researchers whose objective is to identify and explain change have a choice of three main classes of design for data collection: longitudinal, cross-sectional or sequential. A **longitudinal design** involves data being collected from the same sample of individuals on at least two occasions; the interval between data collections and the number of data collections varies greatly, it can be contained in a few days or spread over several decades. A longitudinal design allows researchers to establish changes in individuals over time as the sample ages or experiences some identifiable alteration in experience. In experimental parlance, a longitudinal design might be called a repeated-measures design. A **cross-sectional** design involves eliciting information from people in a number of different conditions expected to be significant to the change at a single time. Often this means studying people in different age cohorts because, particularly in theories of developmental psychology, age is deemed to be a major determinant of change. The term **age cohort** refers to the total population of individuals born at approximately the same time which is usually taken to mean in the same calendar year. The cross-sectional design permits age-related changes to be gauged.

A **sequential design** will choose samples from a particular condition (for example, a specific age cohort) but will study them at different times. The periodicity in sequential data gathering varies across studies. A simple sequential design might involve sampling the 21-year-old cohort of 1989, the 21-year-old cohort of 1979, and the 21-year-old cohort of 1969. This type of design would be targeted at revealing whether changes in a particular age group are affected by factors which are associated with their specific sociohistorical era.

When studying patterns of change that are age-related there are always three factors which could possibly explain observed relationships: development tied to the ageing of the individual; characteristics associated with the particular age cohorts studied; and impact of the specific time of measurement. '**Time of measurement**' is the term suggested by Schaie (1965) to refer to the set of pressures upon the individual generated by the socioenvironmental context at the point data are collected. The difficulty facing researchers interested in explaining age-related changes lies in establishing which of these three factors is the source of change. The strategy adopted by most researchers is to keep one of the factors constant. For instance, the longitudinal design keeps the cohort constant. The cross-sectional design keeps the time of measurement constant. The sequential design keeps the chronological age constant. Of course, this means that explanation of any observed age-related trend remains problematic since these designs always leave two of the three explanatory factors free to vary simultaneously. Irrespective of which of these three designs is adopted, two explanatory factors will be confounded. This represents the major methodological drawback in using such relatively simple designs. There is a secondary problem. By holding one factor constant, the design obviously rules out the possibility of exploring the effects of that factor in interaction with the others. Yet, in virtually all complex systems of change, one would expect interaction effects between developmental, cohort and time of measurement factors. The solution to this fundamental methodological problem has been to integrate the three design types in what is known as a **longitudinal cohort-sequential design**. This combines the longitudinal follow-up of a series of cohorts first sampled simultaneously as in a cross-sectional study with the sequential addition of new cohorts of the same ages to the study at each subsequent data collection point.

Even if a researcher believes the psychological construct under investigation is not influenced by the chronological maturation of the individual and not affected by the sociohistorical context of the data collection, the burden of proof rests upon that researcher to show that they are not important. It used to be thought that only a developmental psychologist really needed to consider whether to use a longitudinal cohort-sequential design. Now, particularly as lifespan development becomes an accepted stipulative adjunct to most theories of psychological functioning, all researchers need to understand the implications of these different types of design.

## 2.2.4 Treatment of data as qualitative or quantitative

Research methods can be differentiated according to whether data are submitted to a qualitative or quantitative treatment. A **qualitative treatment** describes what processes are occurring and details differences in the character of these processes over time. A **quantitative treatment** states what the processes are, how often they occur, and what differences in their magnitude can be measured over time.

It is important to reiterate that these four dimensions on which a piece of research can be described are independent of each other. Data type, elicitation technique, the design for monitoring change and the qualitative or quantitative treatment of the data can be put together in many varieties. For instance, it is possible to use a qualitative treatment of data acquired as part of an experiment conducted in a longitudinal study.

A researcher in structuring a study along these four dimensions will have to make hard decisions. The decisions will in part be determined by whether theory-building is at an inductive or deductive phase. A broader range of data types, elicitation techniques with lower control, cross-sectional designs and qualitative treatment of data may be most appropriate in the early inductive phase. The deductive phase leading to testable propositions is likely to be linked to the narrowing of data types, direct and controlled data elicitation, a mixture of change monitoring designs and the quantitative treatment of data. Sadly the decision is also too often influenced by preconceptions, prejudices and fears. Researchers get trapped into one methodological approach (that is, a package of one type of data, one elicitation technique, one design and one data treatment). Once a routine sets in this can be easier than getting to know (or even remembering) how to do the other things. Also, of course, often researchers acquire their reputation on the basis of using a specific sort of methodology. To relinquish it is tantamount to abandoning their claim to fame. The solution may lie in practising eclecticism of methodology from an early stage in a research career.

Such eclecticism is fostered by forcing yourself, when faced with the task of constructing any study to test a proposition deduced from your theory, to provide at least two realistic alternative methodologies. Then weigh the pros and cons of each. Work out the differences between what they will tell you. In most cases, even minor variations of methodology will substantially affect what you can conclude. Ultimately, researchers have to choose between alternative feasible methodologies in the full knowledge of what they might lose by passing over those which they reject. The chapters in this book make an attempt to help you to see what are the strengths and weaknesses of various techniques, designs and data treatments.

## 2.3 Integrating findings from different methodologies

If you understand different methodologies and use them in concert, there comes a point when you must ask yourself: 'How do I put the findings from one methodology together with those from another?' The easy answer focuses upon the theory. Assuming that each methodology is used to test one or more propositions derived from the theory, as long as the various methodologies yield conclusions which are compatible with the theory there is no problem. They are merely vehicles for theory-testing; they may travel by different routes but they get to the same destination ultimately.

The problems arise when different methodologies produce contradictory or inconsistent conclusions about the proposition tested. In the baldest terms, one may support the proposition, another may generate evidence which indicates that it is incorrect. The first step in this situation is to check that the methodologies were both executed properly. If they were, you should, if possible, collect further data using the same methodologies. If the inconsistent result is repeated, it is necessary to examine whether there is some identifiable attribute differentiating between the methodologies which could explain their inconsistent results. If such an attribute can be identified, it should be incorporated into another study in a controlled way so that its effect can be studied systematically. This may support the introduction of some caveat into the original theoretical proposition. If no such attribute can be identified, the proposition should be retested using a series of completely different methodologies. If these yield contradictory evidence, it is reasonably certain that the proposition will need to be reformulated. The combination of evidence from the various methodologies should show where its limitations lie and point to an appropriate revision.

Obviously, all this procedure of iterative data collection takes time and resources. The researcher will have to decide whether this aspect of the theory is sufficiently important to merit such effort. If the procedure is not followed, it is essential that the original finding which refuted the proposition is treated seriously. The temptation to dismiss the finding in such a situation must be resisted. There are many siren voices which will offer ways of discounting the finding in terms of the relative merits of the methodologies. Unless you clearly stated on an a priori basis that one methodology would be given priority in the event of inconsistencies in the findings, the methodologies must be treated retrospectively as having equivalent standing.

When it produces inconsistent results, an integrated approach to the use of several methodologies may be inconvenient but it also has great advantages. Every methodology has its limitations. The nature of these limitations differs. Using a series of methodologies allows you to compensate for the weaknesses of one methodology in a domain by supplementing or complementing it with another methodology which is stronger in that domain. The development of a coherent strategy for integrating methodologies, designed to test comprehensively clearly defined theoretical propositions, is the basic foundation for researching psychological processes.

## 2.4 Further reading

The following are good general discussions of approaches to researching psychological processes. Popper (1968) *The Logic of Scientific Discovery*; Kelly (1955) *The Psychology of Personal Constructs, vols 1 and 2*; Breakwell (1994) 'The echo of power: an integrative framework for social psychological theorising', which appeared in *The Psychologist*; and Schaie's (1965) 'A general model for the study of developmental problems', which appeared in the *Psychological Bulletin*.

# 3 Practical and Ethical Issues in Planning Research

*Martyn Barrett*

## Contents

# 3.1   Introduction

This chapter is concerned with the practical and ethical issues which need to be considered when planning psychological research systematically. There are many different issues which need to be taken into account if a piece of research is to achieve its intended goal, and each of these issues requires careful decisions to be made during the course of the planning process. Of necessity, this chapter will have to discuss these issues and decisions in a particular sequence. However, it is important to bear in mind that these decisions are not independent of one another, and that making one decision can have important implications for other decisions (for example, choosing to use a particular statistical procedure may have implications for the minimum size of sample which ought to be used, or an ethical decision concerning the invasion of privacy might lead one to choose interviewing rather than naturalistic observation for collecting data). This complex interdependence means that the process of planning psychological research does not consist of a simple linear sequence of decisions. Instead, as we seek operational definitions of the theoretical concepts that are contained in the hypotheses which we wish to test by means of our research, we are of necessity having to think simultaneously about possible ways of measuring these concepts in particular types of settings with various types of subjects, and thus also have to think about whether we have access to those subjects and whether it is feasible to collect such data on an appropriate timescale with the resources which are available to us in a way that can be analysed by the types of statistics which are pertinent to testing the hypotheses from which we started out. This complex interdependence of the various decisions which together comprise the planning process should be borne in mind throughout this chapter.

To a certain extent, many of the issues which will be discussed in this chapter might appear to be a matter of simple common sense. However, if this is the case, it is surprising how often such common sense fails researchers, particularly those early in their careers. There are all sorts of pitfalls which can bedevil psychological research and can prevent that research from achieving its intended goals. The hope is that this chapter will at least help to sensitise the beginning researcher to some of the more major pitfalls.

# 3.2   Formulating research questions

## 3.2.1   Selecting a topic to study

When planning a piece of psychological research, there is of course one particular step which needs to be taken first, and that is to identify and select a topic to study. There are all sorts of reasons why psychologists choose to study particular topics. They might do so because of a personal interest in the topic or because they make a value judgement about the importance of that topic. Or a topic may be chosen for a theoretical reason, perhaps because the researcher has spotted an assumption or a prediction made by a particular theory which has never been tested empirically. Alternatively, the researcher may have a concern with a particular social problem and want to contribute towards the resolution of that problem, or may wish to help improve the quality of life for a particular group of individuals. All of these reasons are equally valid. Essentially, they all boil down to an assessment that the topic which has been chosen is either interesting, important or useful.

However, from a practical point of view, it is crucial to also take into account a further criterion when selecting a particular topic to investigate: is it realistic and feasible to conduct research into this topic, given the practical and ethical restrictions on what the researcher is able to do? In order to derive an answer to this question, though, it is essential to move on from the general topic to the formulation of the specific questions which will be addressed by means of the research, so that the researcher can work out precisely what is required in practice in order to answer those questions, and can then work out whether or not these requirements can be met.

## 3.2.2   The need to formulate specific research questions

To take an example, the researcher might believe that aggression in children is an important topic to study. However, selecting this general topic for research is not sufficient to enable us to say whether the intended research is or is not feasible. First, it is necessary to state exactly what it is that the researcher wants to find out about this topic. For example, does the researcher want to discover how aggressive behaviour in children varies as a function of age, or the factors which cause children to be aggressive to others, or the responses which children's aggressive behaviour elicit from other people, or what? Notice that in all cases, if the researcher's goal is to discover something about the topic which has been selected, then it is always possible to state that research goal in the form of a question: How does children's aggressive behaviour vary as a function of age? What are the factors which cause children to be aggressive to others? What are the responses which children's aggressive behaviour elicit from other people? If the intended goal of the research cannot be formulated as an explicit question, or as a series of such questions, then that research does not have a coherent goal.

Let us pursue our hypothetical example a little further. Let us assume that the researcher decides that the question to be addressed by means of the research is the relatively mundane one of: How does children's aggressive behaviour vary as a function of age? Notice that it is clearly impossible for any researcher to study children's aggressive behaviour in all contexts at all ages. Consequently, in order to assess the feasibility of the research, the researcher now needs to qualify the research question further by stipulating the appropriate contexts which are of interest. For example: How does children's aggressive behaviour in the school playground/in the home/in the streets/etc. vary as a function of age? The feasibility of the study can now begin to be assessed against the criterion of whether the researcher can obtain access to children in the contexts which are of interest. The researcher also needs to specify the ages of the children who would be studied. Would the study cover children of all ages (is this feasible?) or just children of particular ages (if so, of what ages, and does the researcher have access to children of those ages?)? In addition, notice that the term 'aggressive behaviour' must also be defined in order to assess the feasibility of the research. For example, does 'aggressive behaviour' include inflicting psychological injury on others, as well as physical injury? If so, is it feasible to assess whether or not psychological injury has been inflicted? Also, must aggressive acts be intentional? If so, is it feasible to assess intentionality in children of the ages which would be studied?

Ethical considerations must also play a role in assessing the feasibility of studying this topic. For example, most people today would consider it unethical for a psychologist deliberately to elicit aggressive behaviour from children so that the characteristics of that behaviour can be studied. This would not be feasible on ethical rather than practical grounds. However, in the past, different ethical standards have applied. For example, Bandura's classic studies into aggressive behaviour in children, which were conducted in the late 1950s and early 1960s, entailed the provision of role models of aggressive behaviour for children to imitate (see Bandura and Walters, 1963). Thus, the ethical considerations which are used to evaluate the feasibility of a piece of research inevitably change over time and past practices should not be used as an automatic guide to what is ethically acceptable today. It should be clear from this example that, in order to decide whether or not a particular topic which has been selected for investigation passes the criterion of feasibility, it is essential to formulate not just research questions, but highly specific research questions.

However, there is also an additional reason why it is necessary to formulate specific research questions at the outset of the planning process. This is so that the researcher can ensure, during the course of planning, that the data which are collected will actually address the research questions which are of interest. There is very little point in jumping directly from the identification of a general topic to the collection of data and then trying to articulate specific questions about that general topic afterwards. Such a procedure is extremely unlikely to result in any of the data which are collected being appropriate for addressing the particular questions which the researcher will really want to ask about that topic. Instead, in order to ensure that the data which are collected are relevant to answering the specific questions which are of interest to the researcher, it is vital to use the specific research questions themselves to inform the design of the research from the outset, so that the researcher can be certain that the data which are collected will actually answer those questions.

### 3.2.3   Strategies to adopt when formulating specific research questions

When thinking about specific research questions, several strategies may be used to ensure that the questions which are formulated are suitable for the further planning purposes for which they are required. First, it is always helpful to formally articulate research questions in words. If you cannot articulate these questions in words, they are unlikely to lead to any productive research (see also Chapter 9). Second, the articulated questions should contain specifications of the particular situations or conditions in which the phenomena of interest would be studied, as well as specifications of the precise type of subjects who would be used in the research.

Third, it is important to articulate these questions in such a way that they can be addressed by means of a specified type of empirical evidence. This is achieved by providing **operational definitions** of the concepts which are included in the research question. An operational definition of a concept is a statement of the activities or operations which are needed to measure that concept in practice (or, in the case of an independent variable, a statement of the activities or operations which are needed to manipulate that variable in practice). For example, if the research question is 'How does children's aggressive behaviour vary as a function of age?', we obviously need an operational definition of the concept of 'aggressive behaviour', that is, a statement of how it would be measured in practice. For example, it might be defined operationally as 'any behaviour which two or more independent adult observers classify as having aggressive intent', or as 'any behaviour which, when a video-recording of it is played back to the child and the child is questioned about it, the child admits was intended to hurt another person'. Similarly, if a research question contains references to subjects' personalities or intelligence, the concepts of 'personality' and 'intelligence' could be operationally defined as the measures which are obtained by using a particular personality test (such as the EPQ) or intelligence test (such as the WISC-R), respectively.

A fourth point to bear in mind when formulating specific research questions is that all such questions must be empirically testable. For example, 'Do different people have the same subjective experience of the colour red?', 'Does the human foetus have a conscious mind?', and 'If a child believes in God, is that a true or a false belief?' are all empirically untestable questions. These questions are untestable because at least one of the concepts which each question contains cannot be given a satisfactory operational definition (the concepts 'subjective experience', 'conscious mind of a foetus' and 'God', respectively). Thus, the testability of research questions is very closely linked to whether or not it is possible to provide adequate operational definitions of their constituent concepts.

### 3.2.4   Choice of possible research methods

Having identified the specific research questions, and having established adequate operational definitions of the concepts, the researcher is then in a position to select possible research designs and methods of data collection which could be used to obtain the data to address these questions. For example, let us suppose that our hypothetical researcher has decided to investigate aggression in children by trying to answer the specific research question 'Do seven-year-old children produce more aggressive acts than five-year-old children in the school playground?', and has operationally defined 'aggressive acts' as 'any act which two or more independent adult observers classify as having aggressive intent'. In that case, the researcher is now in a position to choose either a cross-sectional or a longitudinal research design for studying the children at the two different ages, and is able to choose naturalistic observation as an appropriate method for collecting the data.

The specific considerations which should motivate the choice of any particular research design and any particular method of data collection at this point in the planning process are beyond the scope of the present chapter. The reader is therefore referred to the contents of the other chapters in this book in order to find out how particular research questions and particular operational definitions should feed into the decision to either use or not to use any particular research design or method. For present purposes, however, let us assume that the bridge has now been made between the specific research question to the possible research designs and possible methods of data collection.

### 3.2.5   The literature review

So far in this chapter, no mention has been made of the role which the literature review ought to play in planning a piece of psychological research. Obviously, though, a thorough review of the literature is an essential component of planning research into any topic. The literature contains accounts of all the existing psychological theories and concepts which can be used to generate or to structure research ideas; of the findings which have been obtained by previous researchers and which can therefore be either assumed and built upon, or questioned, when planning further research into that topic; of the arguments and lines of thinking which have proved profitable to previous researchers and which may therefore prove profitable to pursue further; and of the blind alleys down which previous researchers have gone and which therefore ought to be avoided.

Furthermore, the existing literature is an enormously rich repository which contains a massive amount of information about the topics which have been investigated in the past, about the specific research questions which have been asked by previous researchers, about the operational definitions which have been adopted in previous studies, and about the research designs and methods which have been used by previous researchers. Thus, the existing literature can be used as an invaluable source from which to mine all sorts of research topics, research questions, operational definitions, research designs and methods, all of which can be used to inform the process of planning research.

### 3.2.6   Accessing the relevant literature

There are two principal ways in which to access the literature relevant to any given topic. The first is to use a standard abstracting source. The most useful such source for the research psychologist is *Psychological Abstracts*. This contains the abstracts of the articles which appear in virtually all of the journals which publish psychological research. Nowadays, most psychologists access *Psychological Abstracts* in a computerised form which is called PsycLit. This contains the abstracts of psychology journal articles on a CD-ROM, which can be searched systematically by typing into the computer the keywords which define the topic in which you are interested. The system then displays the abstracts of the articles which have been located, and by reading these abstracts, it is usually possible to work out whether or not any given article is of sufficient relevance to merit reading in full (if your own library does not subscribe to the journal in which an article appeared, it may be possible for them to obtain it for you through their interlibrary loans system).

An alternative way of searching the literature is to begin from the reference lists of the central textbooks that have been written on the topic in which you are interested. It is often useful to begin by picking out from these reference lists the most recent major review articles which have been written on the topic in which you are interested, as well as any recent empirical articles which seem to be particularly important. The reference lists of both types of articles can then be used to locate other relevant empirical articles, and the reference lists of these empirical articles can be used to locate further empirical articles. If you use this method of accessing the literature, however, you should bear in mind that there is usually, at the very least, a two-year lag between articles being published in journals and those articles being picked up by and referred to in textbooks. Consequently, this method of searching the literature must always be accompanied by a systematic search through the most recent issues of all the major journals which publish articles on the topic in which you are interested, to ensure that you pick up on any article which has not yet filtered through to the textbooks.

Whichever method is used to locate the relevant literature, that literature should then be used to inform the entire planning process, from the selection of an appropriate topic, through the formulation of specific research questions and operational definitions, to the identification of the possible research designs and methods which could be used to address those research questions.

## 3.3   Assessing the practical feasibility of the research

Having reached this point, the research is now sufficiently well articulated to enable the researcher to assess the practical feasibility of conducting the research. This assessment may well lead the researcher to reject some possible designs or methods, or even to revise some of the operational definitions or research questions, if these now prove not to be feasible on purely practical grounds. It is therefore essential that, at this point, the researcher systematically thinks through all of the following issues.

### 3.3.1   Subjects required for the research

First, the researcher must think through the issue of subject availability. What type of subjects, with what particular characteristics, will the research require? Will these subjects need to be in any particular location, situation or context for the research to take place? How many subjects are needed? In answering this last question, account should be taken of the power of the statistical methods which are to be used to analyse the data, and power tables, which are sometimes included at the back of statistics textbooks, should be consulted in order to help determine appropriate sample sizes (see Chapter 23). Finally, are such subjects in this number available to the researcher?

If the answers to all of these initial questions are satisfactory, further questions then need to be asked. Are the subjects themselves willing to participate in the research? If payment is required in order to entice the subjects into participation, is the necessary budget available?

In thinking about this issue of subject availability, there are many factors which need to be borne in mind. For example, there are the problems of uncontrolled **subject attrition** (that is, subjects dropping out of the study while it is in progress) and **subject non-compliance** (that is, subjects not complying with the research procedure). Subject attrition and non-compliance are not always a consequence of subjects being bloody-minded. In large-scale longitudinal studies, for example, which take place over a period of many years, it is perhaps inevitable that at least some subjects in the study will move home, fall ill, or even die during the course of the study. Of course, if there are high levels of subject attrition or non-compliance, this leads to the sample of subjects becoming systematically biased, either for lack of mobility, for staying power, or for willingness to cooperate with the research procedure. Furthermore, it is always possible that such characteristics are related in a systematic manner to the psychological phenomena which are being studied. The problem of non-compliance can be particularly serious in research which involves question-naires about a sensitive topic being mailed to subjects for completion and return. Such questionnaires may only have a return rate somewhere in the region of 10–40 per cent. This rate of self-selection from a sample which was originally constructed on systematic principles represents a very serious biasing of the sample which will inevitably affect the generalis-ability of the findings which are obtained.

There are, however, some general precautions which can be taken by the researcher concerning subject attrition and non-compliance. First, the sample which is planned should always be large enough to allow for possible attrition and non-compliance. Second, when recruiting subjects, the researcher should always try to make participation in the study sound as interesting as possible; it is important to emphasise any parts of the study that might be especially interesting to subjects themselves. Avoid saying that participating in the study is a way of 'doing your bit for science'; this is not a formula which wins over hesitant subjects. Third, you should assure potential subjects of complete confidentiality and anonymity of their results where necessary. Fourth, you can offer to inform the subjects of the eventual outcome of the research; this may be done by producing a simple written summary of the research findings at the end of the study in jargon-free language, which can be sent to the subjects who participated in the research.

In some cases, the recruitment of subjects for the study can depend upon certain key individuals, or 'gatekeepers', who have to give their permission and cooperation in order for the subjects who are the target of the research to be used. Perhaps the two most common types of gatekeepers are the headteachers of schools, who control access to the children in their schools, and doctors, who can provide access to patients. Obviously, the feasibility of the research will then depend upon winning over the cooperation of these gatekeepers. Gatekeepers can have both disadvantages and advan-tages. For example, it may be difficult to win a headteacher over to the idea of a study of playground aggression if that headteacher maintains that no aggressive behaviour ever occurs in the playground of his or her school. However, once a headteacher has been won over, the researcher will then have open access to the very large numbers of children who attend that school (and will not have to recruit each and every subject individually).

Because the feasibility of such studies depends crucially upon the cooperation of the gatekeeper, it is always extremely important to ensure that gatekeepers are treated with courtesy. It is important that gatekeepers are only approached after the researcher has fully thought through all the precise details of what needs to be done in the study, so that the researcher is able to answer any questions concerning the study which may arise when discussing the research with the gatekeeper. This presents a professional image which helps to inspire the gatekeeper's confidence in the researcher. Again, during such discussions, the purpose of the study should be made to sound interesting, and the researcher can offer to send the gatekeeper a written summary of the findings of the research when the study has been completed.

One problem which can be unintentionally caused by gatekeepers is that they take it upon themselves to select which particular subjects are used in the research. For example, if the research requires schoolchildren to be tested individually outside their classroom, teachers may select only their brightest children to send to the researcher, hoping to impress the researcher with their abilities. However, such a process obviously results in a biased sample being used for the research. Thus, it is always sensible for the researcher to plan a systematic method for selecting which particular subjects should participate in the research (for example, picking every other child from the class register irrespective of their ability), and to agree this plan with the gatekeeper at the outset.

### 3.3.2   Equipment and materials required for the research

In assessing the practical feasibility of the research, the researcher must also consider very carefully all the equipment and materials which are needed for the study to take place. If any special materials or equipment are needed, does the researcher already have them. If not, and if they have to be specially purchased or constructed, are the necessary funds available for these purposes? If the funds are not available, could the materials or equipment be borrowed from or used at another institution or Department of Psychology? If materials have to be specially designed, or if equipment has to be specially constructed, can this be done on an appropriate timescale? Can such purpose-built equipment be properly tested to eliminate any possible teething and technical problems which it might have so that it will be fully functional by the time it is needed?

Finally, under this heading, the researcher should consider whether he or she needs time to learn how to use the relevant materials and/or equipment. For example, it can take a lot of time for a novice to learn how to customise computer software (for example, for presenting visual stimuli to subjects, or for recording subjects' reaction times) or to learn how to administer and score a standardised psychometric test. If time is required for mastering the materials or the equipment, it is important that the timetable for the research is drawn up in such a way that it allows an adequate amount of time for these purposes.

### 3.3.3   Consumable items required for the research

The researcher also needs to think through, at the planning stage, all the consumable items which will be needed for the research (that is, items which will be completely used up during the course of conducting the research). It is important that all consumables are properly costed to ensure that the funds which are required in order to conduct the research do not exceed the total budget available for the research. For example, the costs of any photocopying (of, for example, interview schedules or questionnaires), postage (for mailing out postal questionnaires), video or audio recording tapes, computer disks, computer printing, etc. should all be properly costed in order to ascertain whether the budget is sufficient for conducting the research.

### 3.3.4   Other costs which may be incurred by the research

There may be other costs involved in conducting the research. For example, will the researcher be able to conduct all the work on his or her own? If it is necessary for the researcher to have assistance from others in conducting the research, and if the people who provide this assistance need to be paid for their time, are the funds available to pay these people at the appropriate rate? For example, if the researcher needs help to collect the data (for example, to help interview subjects, to make independent observations of subjects, or to act as stooges in an experiment), or if assistance is needed in coding the data (for example, for running checks on the reliability of the coding), it may be necessary to pay the people who provide this help. If so, the total number of hours of assistance which will be needed must be properly costed in advance, in order to see whether the research can be conducted within the budget which is available.

Also, if the researcher and/or any person assisting needs to travel from the normal place of work to another location in order to test subjects (for example, to a school or to a hospital), this will require funds to cover the costs of the travel and of any subsistence which might be needed by the researchers (such as food or overnight accommodation). Once again, the costs which are involved need to be worked out in advance, taking into account the location of the subjects, the size of the sample, and the length of time that it will take to collect the data from each subject. Once again, the research will only be feasible if the total budget which is available to the researcher is able to cover these costs.

### 3.3.5   Pilot work

Let us assume that the researcher has run through all the preceding checks on subject availability and access, availability of materials and equipment, and the availability of the funds which are needed to cover consumable costs, research assistance costs, and travel and subsistence costs. If all of these considerations indicate that the research is feasible, it is often extremely useful to then conduct pilot work, in order to try out the methods, materials, equipment, etc. in advance of running the full-scale study itself.

Such pilot work should be conducted using a smaller group of subjects who have similar characteristics to those of the subjects who will be used in the main study itself. Pilot work can be used to test out the various operational definitions and research methods which are still under active consideration, and to see if some of these methods and definitions are more useful or are simpler to administer than others. Pilot work can also be used to establish whether subjects understand instructions, to ascertain how much time it takes to test each subject, to obtain practice in administering all the tasks and in making all the necessary measurements (ideally, the researcher should be trained to saturation before the main study commences, so that any training effects do not contaminate the main study itself), to find out whether tasks are sufficiently sensitive to discriminate among subjects, to examine whether the measures which are being made have stable measurement properties (that is, are reliable), etc.

It is often the case that, if a variety of different possible research methods and operational definitions have been under active consideration up to this point in the planning process, the pilot work helps to sort out the more useful and reliable methods and definitions, thereby facilitating the final selection by the researcher of those particular methods and definitions which will be used in the main study itself.

### 3.3.6 Identifying the statistical analyses needed and rechecking the sample size

Once the research design, operational definitions, and methods of data collection have been selected for use in the study, it is then essential for the researcher to identify in advance the types of data which will be collected, and the types of statistical analyses which will be performed on those data in order to answer appropriately the research questions which have been posed. The choice of statistical analyses will be determined by the research design, by the type of data which will be collected, and by the research questions which are being asked (see Chapters 23 and 24). Having selected appropriate methods of analysing the data, it is then necessary, at the planning stage, to check back to the sample size which is being planned, and to the availability of the subjects who are required for the study. It is vital to do this, in order to ensure that sufficient data will be collected from a large enough sample to enable the proposed statistical analyses to detect the relationships and effects of interest, assuming they are present in the data.

## 3.3.7  Formulating a timetable

Another aspect of planning research systematically is to formulate an explicit timetable for the research. This timetable needs to contain all the intermediate staging posts, and their deadlines, which will punctuate the research (for example, when the data collection will begin and end, when data coding will begin and end, when the statistical analyses will be conducted, when the writing up of the research will take place, etc.). In producing this timetable, it is essential to adopt a realistic stance, and to allow sufficient time for all the component activities which are involved, including any final piloting that may be required, the time that may be required for training additional researchers, the time needed for recruiting subjects, the time needed for testing all subjects or for collecting all data (does this involve testing all subjects simultaneously, or in sequence?; will you have to wait for subjects to make their returns of a mailed question-naire through the post?; is it necessary to build in time for the replacement of subjects who fail to attend for testing or fail to reply? etc.), the time which is needed for debriefing subjects, transcribing any data from audio or video recordings, coding the data, running reliability checks upon the data coding, entering the data into the computer, analysing the data, interpreting the results of the analyses, and writing the report.

Having produced this explicit timetable which contains a realistic estimate of the amounts of time needed for all the component activities, it is then necessary to go back yet again and recheck the availability of subjects, equipment and all other resources which will be used for the research. In particular, it is essential to check that subjects, equipment and resources will be available at the times which are required according to the timetable that has been worked out. After all, if the subjects are not available for testing when the timetable stipulates (for example, if schoolchildren are required for testing during a school's summer vacation), then, quite simply, it will not be feasible to conduct the research on that timetable. If there are any problems concerning either subject, equipment or resource availability, then it is necessary for the researcher to revise either the timetable or the content or structure of the study itself so that it fits into a feasible timetable.

## 3.3.8  Conclusion

Assessing the practical feasibility of a piece of research is clearly a complex activity. Not only are there many different aspects of the research that need very careful checking in order to ensure that the research is feasible in practice; in addition, if the research proves unfeasible on just one count, it may be necessary to revise the entire study. Nevertheless, having planned a piece of research through to this level of detail, if it turns out not to be feasible to run the study as planned, it is always worth considering the possible modifications which could be made to it before abandoning it entirely and starting from scratch once again (for example, other possible sources of subjects could be tried, extravagant but unnecessary costs could be cut back, the timetable for the study could be extended, etc.).

# 3.4   Assessing the ethical feasibility of the research

In the preceding section, we considered issues concerning the practical feasibility of a piece of research. The present section considers issues which are to do with the ethical feasibility of a piece of research. It is quite possible that a research study is feasible on practical grounds, but is unacceptable because it would be judged to be unethical to conduct that study. The criteria which ought to be used by psychologists in order to assess whether a particular study is or is not ethically acceptable have been formalised in statements issued by the British Psychological Society (BPS, 1993) and by the American Psychological Association (APA, 1992). Any person who is intending to conduct psychological research should obtain a copy of, and should study in full, one or other of these two statements (or an equivalent statement which has been issued by a corresponding professional body). The addresses from which the BPS and the APA statements may be obtained are given towards the end of this chapter. The following account draws heavily upon the principal criteria which are contained in the BPS statement.

## 3.4.1   The protection and welfare of participants

A fundamental principle which underpins all ethical codes relating to psychological research is that psychologists must always consider the welfare of the subjects who participate in their research, and must protect them from being either physically or mentally harmed by the research process. In practice, this means that the risk of harm to someone who participates in a psychological study should normally never be greater than the risks which that person would encounter during the course of their normal lifestyle. If there are any aspects of the study which might result in any harm or undesirable consequences for the subjects, the researcher has a responsibility to identify and remove or correct these consequences. If this is not possible, and if there is a risk that the participants in the research will suffer in some way, either physically or psychologically, as a result of the research, then that research would normally be considered to be ethically unacceptable.

Of course, there are certain types of psychological research where the risk of harm, unusual discomfort, or other negative consequences for the subject's future life might occur or might be greater than in everyday life (for example, in certain types of psychopharmacological studies, there may be unanticipated side-effects of the drugs which are administered to subjects). In such cases, the researcher must always obtain the disinterested approval of independent advisers before the research takes place (usually this advice is obtained from an independent ethics committee, either of the university or of the hospital in which the research is based). In addition, in such cases, the participants must be fully informed of the possible risks to them, and real informed consent must be given by each subject individually.

### 3.4.2   The principle of informed consent

More broadly, the BPS ethical principles stipulate that, wherever it is possible, researchers should inform participants in psychological research of all aspects of that research which might reasonably be expected to influence their willingness to participate in that research; in addition, researchers should normally always explain any aspect of the research about which a participant enquires. Thus, when a subject agrees to participate in a study, that person's consent should normally be informed by knowledge about the research. This is the principle of informed consent.

In some cases, of course, subjects may be unable to give informed consent. This is the case whenever the research involves either young children or adults with impairments in understanding and/or communication. In such cases, informed consent should instead be given either by parents or by those *in loco parentis*. In addition, it may be necessary in such cases (depending upon the potential risks to the participants) to also obtain advice and approval from an independent ethics committee. If such permission and/or such approval cannot be obtained, then the study would be considered to be ethically unacceptable and ought to be either revised or abandoned.

It is important to bear in mind, when considering the application of the principle of informed consent, that a researcher is often in a position of authority or influence over the participants. This position should never be used to pressurise the participants to take part in, or remain in, an investigation. Similarly, the payment which may be offered to subjects should not be used to induce them to accept risks which they would not normally accept in their everyday life without payment.

### 3.4.3   The use of deception

In the case of some psychological studies, however, it is simply not possible to tell the subjects everything which they could be told about the study because, if they had knowledge about the actual purpose of the investigation, they might alter those critical aspects of their behaviour which are of interest to the investigator, thereby undermining the purpose of the study. Alternatively, it is sometimes simply impossible to study a particular psychological process without deliberately misleading the subjects. According to the BPS ethical principles the basic guidelines which should be followed in all such situations are the following:

> The withholding of information or the misleading of participants is unacceptable if the participants are typically likely to object or show unease once debriefed. Where this is in any doubt, appropriate consultation must precede the investigation. Consultation is best carried out with individuals who share the social and cultural background of the participants in the research, but the advice of ethics committees or experienced and disinterested colleagues may be sufficient. (BPS, 1993: section 4.1)

However, the BPS principles also add that the intentional deception of subjects ought to be avoided wherever this is possible. Consequently, the researcher should always first consider whether there are alternative procedures available which do not require deception. If no such alternatives are available, and if it is judged that the intended deception is an ethically permissible procedure, then the subjects should be debriefed at the earliest opportunity.

## 3.4.4 The debriefing of subjects

In all studies where subjects are aware that they have taken part in an investigation, after the data have been collected, the subjects should be given any information which they might need or request concerning the nature of the study. The researcher should also discuss with the subjects their experience of the research process, so that if there are any unintended or unanticipated effects of the research, these can be monitored. Researchers also have a responsibility to ensure that, if any active intervention is required to negate the effects of an investigation upon a subject, such intervention should be provided before the subjects leave the research setting. Consequently, when drawing up the timetable for the research for the purposes of assessing whether or not the research will be feasible on practical grounds, sufficient time must be built into that timetable to allow for the debriefing of subjects after testing wherever this may be necessary.

## 3.4.5 Subjects' right to withdraw from an investigation

Researchers should also make it clear to subjects at the outset of the study that they have a right to withdraw from the research at any time, irrespective of whether or not payment or any other inducement has been offered. In the case of children, their avoidance of the testing situation ought to be taken as evidence of a failure to consent to the research procedure, and should be acknowledged.

Furthermore, the BPS ethical principles state that subjects should always have the right to withdraw any consent which they may have given previously to participate in the study, either in the light of their experience of the investigation, or as a result of their debriefing. In such cases, subjects also have a right to require that any data pertaining to themselves, including any recordings, be destroyed. Obviously, if a sufficient number of subjects exercise this right in any individual study, a sampling bias will be introduced to the study which could limit the generalisability of the results. However, this is a limitation which the researcher must accept, as the retention and use of the data which were provided by a subject who has subsequently withdrawn his or her consent is an ethically unacceptable practice.

### 3.4.6   The invasion of privacy in observational research

Research which is based upon the naturalistic observation of subjects in their everyday settings raises particular ethical concerns, because in such studies, informed consent may not be given by the subjects. Such studies must, therefore, respect the privacy and psychological well-being of the subjects who are studied. Furthermore, if consent is not obtained in advance, observational research is only acceptable in places and situations where those observed would expect to be observed by strangers. Particular account should be taken of local cultural values, and of the possibility that the subjects might consider it to be an invasion of their privacy to be observed while believing themselves to be unobserved, even though they are in a normally public place.

### 3.4.7   Confidentiality and the anonymity of data

The BPS ethical principles also stipulate that all information which is obtained about a subject during an investigation must be confidential unless it has been agreed otherwise in advance. All participants in psychological research have a right to expect that the information which they provide will be treated confidentially and, if published, will not be identifiable as theirs. If such confidentiality or anonymity cannot be guaranteed, then the participant must be warned of this before he or she agrees to participate in the study.

In addition, it should be noted that, in the United Kingdom, when data about an individual person are stored on a computer in such a form that the individual is identifiable, then the person storing those data must comply with the provisions of the Data Protection Act 1984. This involves registering with the Data Protection Registrar, for which registration forms are available from the Registrar's Office. For researchers who work within an institution, such as a university, there is often an institutional administrator handling these matters. The Data Protection Act is designed to ensure that those who record and use personal information on computers are open about that use and follow sound and proper practices.

### 3.4.8 Conclusion

From the preceding account, it should be clear that there are not only many practical considerations which need to be borne in mind while planning psychological research, but there are also many different ethical considerations which have to be accommodated if the planned research is to be ethically feasible. If the research which is being planned requires any of the preceding ethical principles to be violated in an unacceptable manner, then that research must be assessed as being ethically unfeasible. However, should a study be judged to be unacceptable on ethical grounds, having reached this point in the planning process, it is always worth reconsidering those specific aspects of the study which have been found to be problematic in order to see whether there are any alternative procedures which may be adopted which would be ethically acceptable. But if no such alternative procedures are available (and remember that any such alternative procedures would also have to be assessed as being feasible on practical as well as ethical grounds), then the researcher is obliged to abandon the research which has been planned.

## 3.5  Considering the possible outcomes of the research in advance

Finally, it can help to focus the mind while planning a piece of research to consider the possible outcomes of the research in advance. To this end, it is useful to break down possible outcomes into those things which will be delivered immediately upon the completion of the research, and the longer-term outcomes which might emerge eventually from the work.

Things which are immediately deliverable upon completion of the research would include: the answers to the specific research questions which the research was designed to provide; and the immediate research report (whether this is in the form of a final-year undergraduate research project report, an M.Sc. thesis, or an end-of-project report for a funding agency).

Longer-term products of the research could include: any further studies which might be required to clarify or to extend the results which will be obtained (focusing upon further studies which might be required for clarification purposes can be an extremely useful process for thinking through the limitations of the planned study); any applied policy recommendations which might be able to be made on the basis of the research to relevant authorities; and the publication of the findings of the research. Publication should, under normal circumstances, always be regarded as the proper endpoint of research. For it is only when research is published that it enters the public domain, becomes available to the scientific community and can be properly regarded as contributing to the general scientific understanding of the issues which it has been designed to study.

## 3.6　A final tip: the inexorable rule of Sod's Law

Sod's Law, expressed metaphorically, is: if you drop a piece of buttered toast, it will always land on the floor buttered side down. Expressed more directly, Sod's Law is: if anything can possibly go wrong, it will go wrong.

As any experienced researcher will be able to tell you, in scientific research, the rule of Sod's Law is inexorable. There is very little that can be done to thwart it, except to form an appropriate mental set at the very outset of the planning process, to think through every single aspect of the research in advance in minute detail, and then to double-check and triple-check everything before the research is ready to roll. While these activities in themselves may not necessarily thwart Sod's Law, they will at least enable you to congratulate yourself on those rare occasions that you manage to evade its worst consequences.

## 3.7　BPS and APA addresses

A copy of the British Psychological Society's *Code of Conduct, Ethical Principles and Guidelines* (1993) may be obtained from: The British Psychological Society, St Andrews House, 48 Princess Road East, Leicester LE1 7DR, UK.

A copy of the American Psychological Association's *Ethics Code* (1992) may be obtained from: APA Order Department, American Psychological Association, 750 First Street, N.E., Washington DC 20002–4242, USA.

## 3.8　Further reading

Detailed discussions of the various issues which are involved in selecting research topics, formulating specific research questions, and formulating operational definitions of concepts, are contained in Kerlinger (1973) *Foundations of Behavioural Research* and Selltiz, Wrightsman and Cook (1976) *Research Methods in Social Relations*. The book by Selltiz et al. also contains excellent discussions of the issues involved in assessing both the practical and the ethical feasibility of psychological research, while Shaughnessy and Zechmeister (1994) *Research Methods in Psychology* contains a very good discussion of the APA ethical guidelines.

# PART II

# 4   Levels of Measurement

*Chris Fife-Schaw*

## Contents

## 4.1   Introduction

While there are many aspects of the research process that do not involve measurement and, indeed, some fields of research where traditional measurement is purposively avoided, the great majority of research endeavours will involve some form of measurement. Whether or not a research hypothesis stands or falls may depend on how well the key concepts have been measured independently of whether or not it is a worthy hypothesis. What follows in this chapter is a discussion of measurement issues that have been central to the pursuit of 'positivist' psychological science. Key among the assumptions (see Cattell, 1981) is that before we can construct grand psychological theories and laws, we must first be able to measure and describe things with reasonable accuracy.

Some find this emphasis on the minutiae of classification and measurement systems somewhat removed from the goal of understanding human experience and behaviour (see Kline, 1988).

For this chapter, measurement is defined as the assigning of numbers to objects, events or observations according to some set of rules. Sometimes these numbers will be used merely to indicate that an observation belongs to a certain category, other times these numbers will indicate that the observation has more of some property than an observation that is assigned a lower number.

In much of psychology we have to measure psychological properties indirectly because we have no direct access to the mental constructs we want to measure. It is a straightforward matter to measure length and we can do this fairly directly by offering up our measuring instrument (rule or tape measure) to the object to be measured. In the case of IQ, for example, we can only infer levels of intelligence from tests that ask people to solve problems of varying difficulty. We assume that people who get more of the more difficult items correct are more intelligent, but we cannot observe intelligence in any more direct way than this. In many respects the existence of something called intelligence is itself a hypothesis and the debate about what IQ tests *actually* measure has often been a heated one in the past. While few people would argue about what a rule measures, the quantities measured by many psychological measurement instruments are more open to debate and much more obviously dependent on the theoretical perspective of the researcher than is the case in the physical sciences.

This is not to say that psychological measurements are of little value. A great deal of effort has been expended in establishing the reliability and validity of psychological measures over the last century. There are now libraries of well-validated tests for all sorts of psychological phenomena which can be used very effectively as long as the manuals are used appropriately. Chapter 13 outlines the principles involved in test construction and development commonly used in psychology.

While many established tests exist, researchers are often confronted by the need to create their own measures to deal with the specific problems they have. This may be because nobody has yet fully developed a test for the particular kinds of observations you are interested in. It may be that you are measuring something which has not been measured before or, perhaps, that the existing tests are too cumbersome for your purposes. Here, you will have to pay particular attention to the precise meaning and nature of your new measures.

It almost goes without saying that the goal should always be to measure things as well as possible. There are often trade-offs that have to be made, however. Measures that demand lots of time and effort from subjects may induce fatigue and boredom that may simply introduce unwanted 'noise' into your measurements. On the other hand, measures that are very simple and quick for the respondents to complete are frequently crude and inaccurate. Ultimately you will have to make the judgement as to whether your measures are 'good enough' for your purposes.

## 4.2   Classifying measurements

Whether you use a ready-made measure or create your own, you always need to know which class of measurement you have made. How you classify each type of measurement you make will have an impact on the kinds of numerical analyses you can perform on the data later on. Stevens (1946) proposed that all measurements can be classified as being of one of four types. This system has become dominant within psychology and no methods textbook would be complete without describing it. There are other systems of classification (see Minium et al., 1993) but Stevens's remains the best known.

### 4.2.1   Nominal/categorical measures

Nominal or categorical measurements (variables) reflect qualitative differences rather than quantitative ones. Common examples include categories like Yes/No, Pass/Fail, Male/Female or Conservative/Liberal/Labour. When setting up a categorical measurement system the only requirements are those of mutual exclusivity and exhaustiveness. **Mutual exclusivity** means that each observation (person, case, score) cannot fall into more than one category; one cannot, for example, both pass and fail a test at the same time. **Exhaustiveness** simply means that your category system should have enough categories for all the observations. For biological sex there should be no observations (in this case people) who are neither male nor female.

A key feature of categorical measurements is that there is no *necessary* sense in which one category has more or less of a particular quality, they are simply different. Males are different from females (at least at some biological level) and Northerners come from the North and Southerners do not. Sometimes, however, this will seem like an odd assumption. Surely 'passing', for example, is better than 'failing'? Well, yes, in certain cases this would be so, but this would depend on what your a priori theory about the measure was. If you believed that 'passing' was more valuable and reflected more positively on somebody (for example, that they were more intelligent, paid more attention, etc.) then that is a matter for you as a researcher, the use of a pass/fail category system does not inherently contain any notion of greater or lesser value.

For the purposes of using computers to help with our analyses, we commonly assign numbers to observations in each category. For instance we might assign (code) a value of 1 for males and 2 for females. The important point is that although females have a numerically larger number there is no suggestion that being female is somehow better or more worthy. Again, this can cause confusion especially as your computer deals only with numbers and not their meanings. You could, for instance, ask it to calculate the mean sex of the respondents and it would come up with a figure something like 1.54; clearly this is pretty meaningless.

Although the categories in a categorical variable do not necessarily have any value associated with them this does not mean that they *cannot* reflect some underlying dimension in some instances. As an example, you might classify people you are observing in the street as 'young' or 'old' because you are unable to approach them to ask their ages directly. While this is likely to be an extremely crude and inaccurate classification, this system implies an underlying continuous dimension of age even though we place people in only two categories.

The criteria for categorical measurement do not preclude the possibility of having a category of 'uncategorisable'. If you were to have such a category you would satisfy both the mutual exclusivity and exhaustiveness criteria but if there were a lot of 'uncategorisable' or 'other' observations then the value of your categorisation system may be brought into question. How useful is it to have a variable on which the majority of observations are 'uncategorisable'? This can only truly be answered with reference to your research question.

## 4.2.2   Ordinal level measures

This is the next level of measurement in terms of complexity. As before, the assumptions of mutual exclusivity and exhaustiveness apply and cases are still assigned to categories. The big difference is that now the categories themselves can be rank ordered with reference to some external criteria such that being in one category can be regarded as having more or less of some underlying quality than those in another category. A lecturer might be asked to rank order their students in terms of general ability at statistics. They could put each student into one of five categories: Excellent, Good, Average, Poor, Appallingly Bad. Clare might fall into the 'Excellent' category and Jane in the 'Good' category. Clare is better at statistics than Jane but what we do not know, however, is just how much better Clare is than Jane. The rankings reflect more or less of something but *not how much* more or less.

Most psychological test scores should strictly be regarded as ordinal measures. For instance, one of the subscales of the well-known Eysenck Personality Questionnaire (EPQ) (Eysenck and Eysenck, 1975) is designed to measure extroversion. As this measure and many like it infer levels of extroversion from responses to items about behavioural propensities, it does not measure extroversion in any direct sense. Years of validation studies have shown how high scorers will tend to behave in a more extroverted manner in the future, but all the test can do is rank order people in terms of extroversion. If two people differ by three points on the scale we cannot say *how much* more extroverted the higher scoring person is, just that they are more extroverted. Here the scale intervals do not map directly onto some psychological reality in the same way that the length of a stick can be measured in centimetres using a ruler.

Since many mental constructs within psychology cannot be observed directly most measures tend to be ordinal. Attitudes, intentions, opinions, personality characteristics, psychological well-being, depression, etc. are all constructs which are thought to vary in degree between individuals but tend only to allow indirect ordinal measurements.

This conclusion is a point of contention for many researchers since one of the implications of assuming these measures to be ordinal is that some parametric statistical tests should not be used with them. Indeed even the humble mean is not used appropriately with ordinal measures (the median is a more appropriate measure of central tendency). This sits uneasily with what you will see when you read academic journal articles where you will regularly see means and parametric statistics used with ordinal measures. We will deal with this issue later in this chapter (see also Chapter 23).

### 4.2.3   Interval level measures

Like an ordinal scale, the numbers associated with an interval measure reflect more or less of some underlying dimension. The key distinction is that with interval level measures numerically equal distances on the scale reflect equal differences in the underlying dimension. For example, the 2°C difference in temperature between 38°C and 40°C is the same as the 2°C difference between 5°C and 7°C.

As we will see later, many behavioural researchers are prepared to assume that scores on psychological tests can be treated as interval level measures so that they can carry out more sophisticated analyses on their data. A well-known example of this practice is the use of IQ tests. In order to treat scores as interval level measures, the assumption is made that the 5-point difference in IQ between someone who scores 75 and someone who gets 80 indicates the same difference in intelligence as the difference between someone who scores 155 and someone who scores 160.

### 4.2.4   Ratio scale measures

These differ from interval level measures only inasmuch as that they have a potential absolute zero value. Good examples of ratio scales are length, time, number of correct answers on a test. It is possible to have zero (no) length, for something to take no time or for someone to get no answers correct on a test. An important corollary of having an absolute zero is that, for example, someone who gets four questions right has got twice as many questions right as someone who only got two right. The ratio of scores to one another now carries some sensible meaning which was not the case for the interval scale.

The difference between interval and ratio scales is best explained with an example. Say we measure reaction times to dangers in a driving simulator. This could be measured in seconds and would be a ratio scale measurement as zero seconds is a possible (if a little unlikely) score and someone who takes two seconds is taking *twice* as long to react as someone who takes one second.

If, on average, people take 0.8 seconds to react we could just look at the *difference* between the observed reaction time (in milliseconds, say) and this average level of performance. In this case the level of measurement is only on an interval scale. Our first person scores + 1200 ms (that is, 2.0 seconds, 1200 ms longer than the average) and the second person scores + 200 ms more than the average. However, the first person did not take six times longer (1200 ms divided by 200 ms) than the second. They did take 1000 ms longer so the *interval* remains meaningful but the ratio element does not.

True psychological ratio scale measures are quite rare though there is often confusion about this when it comes to taking scores from scales made up of individual problem items. We might, for instance, measure the number of simple arithmetic problems that people can get right. We test people on 50 items and simply count the number correct. The number correct is a ratio scale measure since four right is twice as many as two right, and it is possible to get none right at all (absolute zero). As long as we consider our measure to be *only* an indication of the number correct there is no problem and we can treat them as ratio scale measures.

If, however, we were to treat the scores as reflecting ability at arithmetic then the measure would become an ordinal one. A score of zero might not reflect absolutely no ability at all as the problems may have been sufficiently difficult so that only those with a moderate degree of ability would be able to get any correct. We would also be foolish to assume that all the items were equally difficult. Twenty of the questions might be easy and these might be answered correctly by most people. Getting one of these right and adding one point to your score would be fairly easy. The remaining items may be much more difficult and earning another point by getting one of these right might require much more ability. In other words the assumption that equal intervals between scores reflect equal differences in ability is not met and we should strictly treat the scores as an ordinal measure *of ability*.

## 4.3   Discrete vs. continuous variables

Many types of measurement result in indices that consist of indivisible categories. If someone scores 13 on our 50 item arithmetic test, they might have scored 14 on better day but they could never have scored 13 and a half. Thirteen and a half was not a possible score as the individual questions can only be marked correct or incorrect. Measures like this are called **discrete variables** since they can only have discrete, whole number values. Some variables like height and time are referred to as **continuous variables** since they could be divided into ever smaller units of measure. We could measure height in metres then centimetres, then millimetres, then nanometres and so on until we got to the point where our measuring instrument could not make any finer discriminations. There are an infinite number of possible values that fall between any two observed values. Continuous variables can be divided up into an infinite number of fractional parts. Ultimately it is the accuracy of our measuring instrument that puts limits on the measurement of continuous variables. If our ruler can only measure accurately to the nearest millimetre we must settle for that degree of precision.

When measuring a continuous variable you end up recording a single figure but this really represents an interval on the measurement scale rather than a single value. It is therefore always an **approximate value**. If we time someone doing a task to the nearest second, say it takes them 20 seconds, we are really saying that the time taken lies somewhere in the interval between 19.5 s and 20.5 s. Had it actually taken them 19.4 s we would have rounded the time to 19 s, not 20. Similarly, an elapsed time of 20.6 s would have been rounded to 21 s (see figure below).

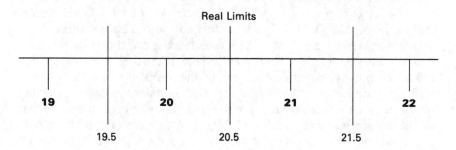

In this example we are deliberately only recording times to the nearest second but, in principle, the choice of any measurement tool carries with it a limit to the degree of accuracy that can be achieved and thus the rounding process will have to happen even if we are unaware of it. We will still be reporting a time that corresponds to an interval and not a discrete value. If our stopwatch could record times to the nearest 100th of a second, say, and we recorded a time of 20.12 s this would still mean that we were saying that the time taken lay somewhere in the interval between 20.115 and 20.125 s. These boundary values are referred to as **real limits**.

It is always appropriate to use the most accurate measure practicable. Any calculations you do using approximate values necessarily include that approximation in the final result. Use two or more approximate values in a calculation and the scope for misleading results increases dramatically. Hence it is always preferable to use approximate measures associated with the smallest intervals possible so as to minimise this problem. You should also note that, although our variables might be theoretically continuous, like time and length, the act of measurement always reduces the measure to a discrete one.

## 4.4 Measurement errors

The goal of all researchers should be to minimise measurement errors. Put formally, these are the discrepancies between the observed value of your measurement and the 'true' value. There is a simple formula to illustrate this:

$$\text{Observed score} = \text{True score} + \text{Error}$$

The 'Error' term may be positive or negative.

Obviously it would be nice to have the error term as small as possible. If you were measuring people's heights with a rule marked off in inches then you could probably only measure accurately to within half an inch. Having a rule marked off in millimetres would give rise to much more accurate measurement and finer distinctions between individuals could be made (see previous section). In a similar way, psychological measures should strive to make as fine a set of distinctions between people as possible. Assuming your measure is valid, it makes sense to have more points on your measurement scale rather than fewer.

This holds true only so long as you believe the individual points on the scale carry the same meaning for all subjects. When it comes to ratio scale and interval level measures such as time, this is not a problem. You could measure time to the nearest millionth of a second though you would probably find the necessary timing equipment a little too expensive! For most psychological research timing to the nearest millisecond is probably accurate enough. Things get much more difficult when you have ordinal measures, however. Problems arise when you try to label individual responses on your ordinal scale. Take the following as an example.

Let us assume you have an attitude statement about a political issue and you would like people to tell you how much they agreed or disagreed with it. You could provide a five-point scale as follows:

| 1 | 2 | 3 | 4 | 5 |
|---|---|---|---|---|
| **Strongly agree** | **Agree** | **Neither agree nor disagree** | **Disagree** | **Strongly disagree** |

Most respondents would know what they were required to do with such a response scale. While you could not be certain that all those who 'Agreed' had agreed to the same extent, you would probably feel reasonably happy that they did not intend to tell you they had very strong views on the topic. Similarly it is probably safe to assume that they are not entirely equivocal about the issue either.

If you gave this question to several hundred people in a survey, however, you might find that so many people had the same score on the item that it did not discriminate very much between people. In this situation you might want to increase the number response options available. A seven-point scale could be used and it would be reasonably easy to label the response options. You might even think a nine-point scale was appropriate though labelling all the points might prove more of a challenge. Indeed you could simply label the end and mid points leaving the rest unlabelled.

Why not opt for a 29-point scale instead? This would give even greater discrimination, surely? The answer is, regrettably, no. Respondents would now have trouble working out where they should indicate their response on the scale. Should it be the 18th or the 19th point or even the 20th? Such a response format increases the scope for confusion on the part of the respondent and thus will introduce, rather than reduce, measurement error. There is also the problem that we still do not know that all people responding at point 19 agree to the same extent. Such multi-point ordinal scales introduce an unfortunate illusion of precision.

## 4.5   Choices over levels of measurement

In the previous and very traditional section you will probably have noticed that I have implicitly suggested that ratio and interval level measurement are to be preferred over ordinal or categorical measures. The reason for this is that in most cases a good ratio scale measure will contain more information about the thing being measured than a good ordinal measure. You would probably rather have temperature reported in degrees Kelvin than on a scale of Very Cold/Cold/Neither Warm nor Cold/Warm/Hot/ Very Hot. You should always strive for greater accuracy of measurement where possible.

Naturally some kinds of variable are always going to be categorical (for example, sex) and some are always going to be ordinal (for example, most scaled measures; but see the section below). In such cases you should not regard your measures as somehow inferior. While it would be nice to think that ultimately we will have access to more direct measures of attitudes and personalities, for example, these are not likely for the foreseeable future.

There are, however, some common practices which should be discouraged. The most notorious of these is the collapsing of ordinal measures into categorial ones. It is quite common to see researchers take an attitude item with a seven-point Agree/Disagree response format and collapse the data into a simple three-point scale of Agree/Uncertain/Disagree. This practice degrades the measurement by removing the extremity information.

There are three kinds of motive for collapsing data in this way. One is the desire to use more simple statistical procedures, a second is to make graphs and tables clearer and the third is that you might not believe that your seven-point measure is very accurate or valid. With the ready availability of comprehensive statistics textbooks the first problem is easily overcome. While clarifying graphs and tables is an admirable aim it would be desirable to collapse the scores only for this purpose and conduct statistical analyses on the uncollapsed data. The third justification is also a justification for not using the measure. If you doubt the validity or accuracy of a measure then you should think twice about using it at all.

## 4.6   The relationship between level of measurement and statistics

Most good statistics texts present readers with 'decision trees' which help you select the correct statistical test to use providing you know the answers to a number of simple questions about your data and research design. These are very useful and simple versions are provided in Chapter 23 on bivariate analyses.

These decision trees ask about the level of measurement for your data as well as the nature of the distribution of scores on the measure that you expect in the population from which your sample scores were drawn. The topic of distributions of scores is dealt with in Chapter 23 but the level of measurement issue is pertinent here, particularly at the boundary between ordinal and interval level measures.

The attraction of **parametric tests**, ones that assume something about the distribution of scores in the population (for example, *t*-test, ANOVA), is that there are many more of them than **non-parametric tests**. They often allow you to ask interesting questions about your data that are not easily answered without using such parametric procedures. To say that your measure is only ordinal, rather than interval level, usually rules out these useful procedures. Chapter 24 outlines some of the many possibilities. Two views have developed over the appropriateness of treating ordinal measures as interval measures. Those interested in reading more on this debate should see Davison and Sharma (1990), Henkel (1975), Labovitz (1975), Stine (1989), Townsend and Ashby (1984), among many others.

One view states that, most of the time, providing you have a good quality ordinal measure, you will arrive at the same conclusions as you would have using more appropriate tests. It is sometimes argued (see Minium et al., 1993) that while most psychological measures are technically ordinal measures, some of the better measures lie in a region somewhere in between ordinal and interval level measurement.

Take a simple example of a seven-point response scale for an attitude item. At one level this allows you to rank order people relative to their agreement with the statement. It is also likely that a two-point difference in scores for two individuals reflects more of a difference than if they had only differed by one point. The possibility that you might be able to rank order the magnitude of *differences*, while not implying interval level measurement, suggests that the measure contains more than merely information on how to rank order respondents. The argument then runs that it would be rash to throw away this additional useful information and unnecessarily limit the possibility of revealing greater theoretical insights using more elaborate statistical procedures.

The more traditional and strict view (for example, Henkel, 1975; Stine, 1989) says that using sophisticated techniques designed for one level of measurement on data of a less sophisticated level simply results in nonsense. Computer outputs will provide you with sensible-looking figures but these will still be nonsense and should not be used to draw inferences about anything. This line of argument also rejects the claim that using parametric tests with ordinal data will lead to the same conclusion *most of the time* on the grounds that you will not know when you have stumbled across an exception to this 'rule'.

The debate on this issue continues. The safest solution, advocated by Blalock (1988), is to conduct analyses on ordinal measures using both parametric and non-parametric techniques where possible. Where both procedures lead you to the same substantive conclusion then, when reporting parametric test results you will at least know that you are not misleading anyone. You should be guided more by the non-parametric procedures if the conclusions are contradictory.

What would be unacceptable would be to select the statistical procedure that leads to results that support your hypothesis. You should attempt consistency in reporting findings so that you either decide that your data meet the assumptions for parametric procedures or that they do not.

Ultimately, whether this issue matters will depend on the seriousness of making a mistake and who your audience is likely to be. Research on a drug or an intervention that may change people's lives demands the most strict and conservative approach to your analysis. On the other hand, if your research topic is more esoteric and your audience is researchers in a field that has regularly used (abused?) parametric techniques on ordinal data, then you may find it difficult to get a hearing if you do not report findings in the accepted way.

## 4.7   Conclusion

This chapter has attempted to alert you to the main issues surrounding levels of measurement. As time marches on the research community may come to an alternative system of classifications (see the debate discussed above). However, the Stevens system described here remains the dominant one in psychology for the time being. Chapter 23 takes this a step further by looking at the principles of statistical inference in more detail. Be sure that you have understood this chapter before you read Chapter 23.

## 4.8 Further reading

All good statistics textbooks explain Stevens's classification system and the relationship levels of measurement and statistics though few books will go much beyond what has been presented here and in Chapter 23. Minium et al. (1993), *Statistical Reasoning in Psychology and Education*, has the virtue of spelling out many of the debates in a clear and accessible way. Many of the key papers on the debate about measurement and statistics have appeared in the *Psychological Bulletin* and are likely to continue to appear in this journal.

# 5 The Experimental Method in Psychology

*Alyson Davis*

## Contents

## 5.1 Introduction

One of the major tasks of psychology is to provide a description of human behaviour and its underlying psychological processes. Many different systematic research methods, including experiments, can provide sufficient evidence to describe human behaviour. However, the uniqueness and power of the experimental method is that it allows us to address the problem of *explanation*. It goes beyond the descriptive problem towards providing answers as to how and why that behaviour comes about. In other words, by using experiments it is possible to answer questions about the causes of behaviour. For this reason both undergraduate and postgraduate students receive substantial training in the principles of experimental design and carrying out experiments for themselves. Is this time well spent? The purpose of this chapter is to convince you that the answer is 'yes'. I shall outline the basic tenets of the experimental method and principles of designing experimental research in an attempt to justify the widespread use of experiments within psychology.

I have tried to concentrate on the *reasons* why the principles should be adhered to (most but not all of the time), for the sake of psychological theory and not just in the interests of 'good science'. In doing so I have used many examples from my own particular area of interest, namely, developmental psychology since this is where my own fascination with the power of experimental techniques has its roots. Furthermore, questions about development provide very clear examples as to why psychology cannot ignore questions about how and why psychological changes take place.

## 5.2   Experimentation and the scientific method

Historically, the widespread use of experiments in psychological research has arisen out of the early behaviourist schools of psychology, when Skinner (1953) proposed that psychology should concern itself only with observable behaviour rather than trying to infer mental processes which cannot be directly observed. Since that time the use of experiments in psychological research has become synonymous with psychology's accept-ance as a scientific discipline. This said, these early influences have also lead to experimental methodology being associated with a mechanistic approach to human thinking and behaviour. While there is a relationship between method and theory, most psychologists who adopt experimental methodology are testing theories far removed from Skinner's Learning Theory and are interested in precisely those unobservable mental pro-cesses which Skinnerians found so abhorrent. Nevertheless, there are some basic assumptions underlying experimentation in terms of its relationship with the scientific method which must be accepted by the researcher when adopting experimental methodology.

The method by which experiments seek out the causes of human behaviour (whether it be overt or mental), assumes acceptance of a deterministic and positivist framework, whereby behaviour is seen as being both objectively specifiable and caused by equally specifiable events. On these grounds alone some psychologists reject the experimental method out of hand as an unacceptable and inappropriate research methodology and propose a well-argued case for alternative methodologies (see Chapters 1 and 2). Therefore, from the outset it must be appreciated that in using experiments in research you are adopting a methodology which like any other method carries with it acceptance of certain philosophical principles.

## 5.3   What is an experiment?

In a recent rerun of the popular television series *The Good Life* one of the leading characters (Tom) is seen in the kitchen contemplating a row of three seed boxes. He declares to his wife his intention of carrying out an experiment into the effects of talking to his plants. All the boxes contain the same seeds. The seeds in Box A, he announces are to be spoken to for 10 minutes every morning in a calm, gentle manner. Those in Box B are to be shouted at for the same length of time, while Box C is to be ignored and not spoken to at all. Not perhaps, you may say, an example of cutting-edge science but it serves a purpose very well as providing an example which can be used to test against the formal definition of an experiment.

Is Tom carrying out an experiment? At the minimal level he is – not a perfect one, but one which meets the basic criteria. As mentioned briefly in the introduction an experiment is a test of cause–effect relationships by collecting evidence to demonstrate the effect of one variable on another. In its simplest form, two groups of subjects are treated in exactly the same way except for one (the **experimental** or **differential treatment**) and any observed difference between the groups is then attributed to the different treatment. Tom has these basic ingredients in his three seed boxes. He is testing the effect of speech (a variable) on another variable (growth rate of the seeds). He treats his groups of subjects (seed boxes) in exactly the same way except for one (whether they are spoken to kindly or shouted at). In fact, he goes one step further by introducing a different level of his variable by including a control condition whereby one box is not spoken to at all. There are, of course, many questions which would have to be answered in order to evaluate the appropriateness of Tom's experimental design – such as, are all the seeds of equivalent gestation and would they all be kept under the same conditions of lighting? However, the essential ingredients for an experiment are present. In later sections I shall unpack in some detail what these ingredients are but first we need to take a step back and ask how experiments come about.

Experiments do not design themselves simply by following a set of rules. They are designed as a means of answering questions, testing hypotheses and predictions about the psychological world. All of us carry theories about why people behave and think the way they do and below is a series of hypotheses or predictions which serve as illustrations:

- Watching aggressive television programmes makes people more aggressive.
- Men believe they are better car drivers than women.
- Children who are sensitive to rhyme in early childhood make better progress in learning to read than those who do not.
- Mothers who concentrate their babies' attention on objects are more likely to have children whose early vocabulary comprises nominals than mothers who do not.
- Remembering a list of items is easier if the list is read twice rather than once.

At one level these are all hypotheses, in that they predict some relationship between the different variables (for example, of television vs. aggressive behaviour, sex and driving ability, reading ability and academic progress, etc.). Hypotheses are formal statements of predictions derived from evidence from earlier research and theory or simply the result of a hunch. All these examples lie in the realm of psychological enquiry and yet not all lend themselves particularly well to the experimental method. Why is this? The crux of making decisions about appropriate methodology is the appropriateness of a particular method for addressing a particular type of research question. For example, in the case of men's belief about sex differences and driving skills, the example is formulated as a hypothesis but not one in which an experimental design would be most appropriate since the question is about belief rather than behaviour. This kind of attitudinal claim lends itself to questionnaire and survey methodology rather than experimentation (see Chapter 8). Similarly, the example about children's early vocabulary illustrates another way in which experimental methodology is not necessarily the most appropriate. By definition, natural language is not easily manipulated, and yet the hypothesis as stated is empirically testable, by means of systematic observation alone without experimental intervention (see Chapter 14). The final example is the most obvious case for experimental testing under classic experimental design since it would be relatively simple to compare groups of subjects who were given differential levels of repetition of an initial list to remember and compare their performance.

However, the relevance of the experimental method to these and any other hypotheses is that, whereas other methods would establish the existence of the relationship being claimed, one cannot address the question of causality without appeal to experimentation. For this reason we now turn to a more detailed look at causal relationships and how they can be established using experiments.

## 5.4 Causality and experimentation

Psychology students are reminded repeatedly of the dangers of inferring causality from a correlation. It is a lesson well worth learning since the pitfalls are not always obvious. The correlation may be spurious or caused by an intervening variable. An example should help illustrate this point. A recent radio news bulletin reported that in 1993 the truancy figures in secondary schools had increased and during the same period school examination scores had likewise increased. While it seems counter-intuitive that non-attendance at school causes improved exam performance we might have been tempted to accept it had the correlation been a negative one. Yet, the principle remains the same – causality needs to be established over and above the description of an existing relationship between two variables. How can this be achieved?

The most commonly used technique in psychological experiments is the canon put forward by the philosopher Mill (1874) – the **method of difference**. Using this method one tests two or more groups of subjects which differ in only one respect in their treatment and any observed differences in their performance can then be attributed to the different treatment. In principle, then, establishing causality is tantamount to providing an explanation which is the *only* explanation for the observed phenomenon. In practice, however, it is not possible to rule out all other explanations nor, according to Popper (1968), should we try to. Rather, the best structure that any theory or hypothesis can have is that it should be open to potential falsification. Most psychological researchers, along with physical sciences, typically accept that any current explanation is open to future disconfirmation. Moreover, 'good science', in order to flourish, relies on this principle.

## 5.5   Variables

Variables and the control and manipulation of variables are central to both defining what constitutes an experiment and for distinguishing a good experiment from a weak one. A variable is any characteristic that can vary across people or situations that can be of different levels or type. Thus, in the list of examples given above, aggressive behaviour, type of television, sex, driving ability, age, and reading ability are all types of variable. There are two basic kinds – independent variables and dependent variables. This distinction is central to experimental design and so I shall take each in turn.

### 5.5.1   Independent variables

The **independent variable** is that which the experimenter manipulates or controls and as such is the variable in whose effect the researcher is interested. The experimental hypothesis proposes that the independent variable will actually cause the change in the behaviour being measured (dependent variable). For example, from our selection of illustrations, the hypotheses suppose that the type of television viewed will determine the levels of aggression, likewise that phonological skill will determine reading ability. Note that in principle variables may be independent or dependent depending on the formulation of the research hypothesis – they can be causes *or* effects. In practice, however, some variables such as sex and age are fixed – that is, they are outside of the experimenter's control. **Fixed variables** are unlikely candidates as dependent variables since they cannot be influenced by even the most extreme of any conceivable independent variable!

One way of classifying independent variables is in terms of those which can be quantified in some way in that the experimenter can determine the amount or levels presented in the study, such as amount of drug administered or time allowed to perform a task. Such variables are termed **quantitative**. In contrast, other independent variables differ in kind and are termed **categorical**. Examples of qualitative, categorical independent variables include, race, sex, type of drug administered, and type of experimental instructions given. The conditions of an experiment refer to the levels of independent variable received by the subjects, or the levels of treatment. True experiments require at least two conditions in order that variable manipulation can occur but in principle there is no limit to the maximum number of conditions.

## 5.5.2 Dependent variables

Essentially, the **dependent variable** is the behavioural measurement made by the experimenter – it is the outcome which has been predicted to be dependent on the independent variable. Thus in our earlier examples, aggressive behaviour, reading ability, early vocabulary and driving ability are all examples of dependent variables. In the same way that independent variables must be carefully selected so that they can be easily and systematically controlled within the experiment so must the dependent variable be selected so that it can be sensibly and meaningfully measured. Given that the whole aim of the experiment is to determine the influence of the independent variable on the dependent variable, the dependent variable must be sensitive enough not only to detect some effect that stands up to statistical testing but also be sensitive to alterations in the level of the independent variable. Thus, in the example of our aggressive television experiment we have within our theoretical stance an assumption that the amount of aggressive programme exposure will impact on the amount of aggressive behaviour resulting from this. To test this we would need to plan very carefully how aggressive behaviour was to be measured in our experiment to pick up our predicted experimental effects.

The fundamental problem of deciding on an appropriate dependent variable stems from the very nature of psychological enquiry. Most psychological research is interested in outcome measures which are only indirectly related to the psychological process in which we are interested. Much present-day research is dealing with questions about mental processes which are not directly observable but where some behavioural measure is taken as being symptomatic of some underlying process. It is this inferential nature of psychological research which makes it so difficult. Learning, problem solving, developmental change and so on cannot be directly observed and so even the most clearly specifiable of problems needs great care in the selection of our outcome measure. The way of addressing this issue is by the use of an **operational definition** of the dependent variable, where one makes an explicit statement about the precise way in which observed behaviour is going to be scored or categorised as the dependent variable. In the case of our aggressive behaviour following violent television we would need to specify what constitutes aggression – whether it be acts of physical violence against others or against objects or verbal aggression.

The difficulties of precision in designing experiments cannot really be appreciated by reading textbooks or even scientific journal articles – direct personal experience however is very effective! Developmental psychologists are interested in the development of babies' ability to retrieve hidden objects since there are theoretical reasons for supposing that this provides some measure of the baby's general level of cognitive development (Piaget, 1952b). As such there is a relatively large literature reported in the scientific journals on the infant's reaction to hidden objects. Such experiments involve a dependent variable which measures whether or not the infant retrieves or searches for an object when it is hidden in various locations and means of concealment. It sounds simple enough, but the reality is far from simple.

What constitutes an effective attempt at search? The nine-month-old infant will move his or her hands around and in doing so displace the cover – is this searching behaviour? Likewise he or she may wait some time, cry, giggle, look around and then move towards an object, pick it up, drop it and even replace it. How can such behaviour be classified? It is tempting to suppose that these difficulties arise out of attempting experiments with subjects who are implicitly difficult to work with. The problem, I suspect, is much more fundamental to all forms of experimental research. Working with infants and young children simply makes explicit those problems of defining psychological measurement in general. Children, by way of their social naïvety, act as pertinent reminders of the difficulties in designing good experiments. In experiments, as in all systematic research, the stakes are very high. Claiming psychological causality on the basis of poorly designed studies renders experiments worthless at best and potentially damaging at worst. These difficulties can be formalised by appealing to the concepts of reliability and validity. **Reliability** refers to the consistency or stability of any experimental effect. The most common technique for establishing reliability is by replication. If the same experimental design leads to the same results on subsequent occasions and using different samples then the experiment is said to be reliable. Typically, however, experimenters do not replicate their own experiments on more than one occasion for pragmatic reasons and so reliability is commonly established by other researchers replicating a particular experimental paradigm within their own research.

Unfortunately, evidence suggesting that an experiment is reliable is no guarantee of its validity. **Validity** refers to whether or not an experiment explains what it claims to explain. In other words, the truth of the causality which is being inferred (see also Chapter 7 on internal and external validity). Validity can be dealt with to some extent by providing adequate operational definitions although these can sometimes be reduced to rather unhelpful truisms such as the frequently cited claim that 'intelligence is what intelligence tests measure'. The importance of validity in psychological experimentation cannot be overstressed, not only because of its status as a basic tenet of experimental method but also because of the very real human consequences which potentially arise when claims of causality arise from an invalid dependent measure. An emotive illustration can be taken from recent debates over allegations of child sexual abuse. In a series of recent cases in the United Kingdom charges of sexual abuse have been made on the basis of an anal dilation test made on the alleged victim. However, a debate has arisen as to the validity of anal dilation as evidence of sexual abuse in children. Clearly, this is an issue for empirical investigation – with sufficient research evidence the issue will be resolved but such examples bring home the importance of validity in all forms of testing.

Another example comes from the work of Milgram (1974) where, in a series of famous experiments on obedience, he asked subjects to administer electric shocks to other people when they failed to get simple learning problems correct (the 'victims' were confederates of the experimenter who were, in fact, not shocked). Usually over half of the subjects would end up administering apparently dangerous levels of electric shock to the 'victims' when told to do so. Milgram concluded that these studies had demonstrated high levels of obedience to authority in many apparently ordinary people. The validity problem here is that it is unclear that obedience, and obedience alone, was the cause of subjects' behaviour. Some may have 'seen through' the experiment and some may have felt that no serious academic could actually allow people to be hurt in an experiment. Milgram has also been criticised for creating an extremely stressing and distressing novel experimental environment that does not mirror 'real world' situations at all. The debate about the value and validity of Milgram's work continues even to this day.

A further issue related to the selection and measurement of the dependent variable is that of floor and ceiling effects. A **floor effect** occurs where a null result emerges because the majority of the subjects score at the very bottom end of the scale. To illustrate, suppose an experiment was investigating the effect of instructions on six-year-old children's ability to solve mathematical problems. If the problems involved multiplication and division then a floor effect may well emerge simply because the task is too difficult for all the children and thus insensitive to changes in the instruction type. This could be avoided by using a more simple dependent variable such as addition problems or by selecting older children to act as subjects.

**Ceiling effects** are the converse of floor effects and are found when subjects score too close to the top of the scale. Continuing with the example, had adults been presented with the same mathematical problems as the children, the task would probably be too easy and therefore result in a ceiling effect. Unfortunately, preventing floor and ceiling effects involves more than common sense and a good grasp of the relevant scientific literature. Instead, these effects are a prime example of the need to carry out pilot studies to check the appropriateness of your subject pool and variables before carrying out the experiment proper.

## 5.6   Experimental manipulation and control

The power of the experimental technique rests on its ability to assure that only the independent variable is permitted to vary systematically across the conditions of the experiment. Where one or more other variables unintentionally varies with the manipulated variable this results in **confounding**. Confounding of variables can render an experiment useless since it makes the results uninterpretable. An example should make this clear. Suppose you were investigating the effects of different techniques of teaching reading to children. To do this three teachers are trained in three different techniques and the children's reading ability is assessed before and after receiving one of the three methods. Any observed differences are then attributed to differences in teaching method. However, there are real difficulties in making such claims because the variable 'teacher' is confounded with the manipulated variable 'method'. In other words, one cannot distinguish whether any effects arise out of teacher differences or differences in teaching method. Even where it seems intuitively unlikely that a confounding matters, the danger is a very real one. In the above example the confounding would be serious since there is, in fact, good evidence to suggest that individual teachers can have differential effects on children's performance (Tizard et al., 1988).

Sometimes it is obvious where confounding has occurred, at other times it is far more subtle yet equally damaging to the strength of the experiment. Even in laboratory settings confounding can easily occur, such as testing subjects at different times of the day where the dependent variable is very sensitive to fatigue effects. As these examples demonstrate, the more closely related the confounded variable is to the independent variable the more serious the consequences. Recognising confounds after data have been collected is too late – the experiment is already ruined, therefore checking for possible confounding variables before running the experiment is essential. Discussing potential confounds in your design with other researchers is an effective way of preventing the problem, otherwise these are likely to be detected when a journal article is submitted and rejected on the grounds that the ambiguity of the results makes it unpublishable.

## 5.7 Basic experimental designs

There are two basic experimental designs which form the basis of all the more complex designs, and which differ according to the way they deal with the control of subject variation. The methods are **between-subject design** and **within-subject design**. These terms are synonymous with the labels independent (or separate) and related (or repeated) groups design. The most basic forms of these two designs are shown in Figures 5.1 and 5.2. If two or more totally separate groups each receive different levels of the independent variable then this constitutes a between-subject design. In contrast, if the same group of subjects receive all the various conditions or levels of the independent variable then this is an instance of within-subject design. Both these methods carry advantages and disadvantages and the selection of basic design must rest on the nature of the research hypothesis as well as pragmatic concerns.

### 5.7.1 Between-subject designs

Allocating subjects to different conditions within an experiment rather than presenting subjects with all the experimental conditions consecutively

Independent variable

| Experimental group | Control group |
|---|---|
| Subject 1 | Subject 21 |
| Subject 2 | Subject 22 |
| Subject 3 | Subject 23 |
| Subject 4 | Subject 24 |
| Subject 5 | Subject 25 |
| Subject 6 | Subject 26 |
| - - - - - - | - - - - - - |
| - - - - - - | - - - - - - |
| Subject 20 | Subject 40 |

Figure 5.1 *A between-subjects design: subjects are randomly assigned to treatment conditions*

Independent variable

| Experimental condition | Control condition |
|---|---|
| Subject 1 | Subject 1 |
| Subject 2 | Subject 2 |
| Subject 3 | Subject 3 |
| Subject 4 | Subject 4 |
| Subject 5 | Subject 5 |
| Subject 6 | Subject 6 |
| - - - - - - | - - - - - - |
| - - - - - - | - - - - - - |
| Subject *n* | Subject *n* |

Figure 5.2   *A within-subjects design: each subject receives both (or all) levels of the treatment condition*

is the most common design used in experimental psychology. Immediately, this method poses a threat to the power of the experiment because by definition there are different subjects in each group and these groups may share different characteristics at the outset of the experiment which will influence their performance. Let us take the example of the children in our earlier hypothetical experiment who are in three different classes each receiving a different method of being taught to read. In the discussion of confounding variables it was pointed out that there is a risk of teacher differences interfering with teaching method effects. In addition to this possibility there is also a chance that the three groups of children differed before the introduction of the different teaching problems. Perhaps the groups differ by chance – one class being significantly more able than the others, or they may differ by some predetermined factor such as the type of teaching method they received in an earlier class. So, how can this type of problem be overcome? The answer is by adhering to a fundamental principle of experimental design known as **randomisation**.

## 5.7.2   Randomisation

Randomisation is a technique to ensure that as few differences as possible exist between different subject groups, by giving every subject an equal chance of being allocated to each of the experimental conditions. Procedurally, randomisation is relatively straightforward to achieve. One assigns arbitrary numbers to each subject and literally pulls out these numbers from a hat. In a two-group design with ten subjects in each group the subjects corresponding to the first ten numbers selected would constitute one group and the second ten the other group. The mechanics of this procedure is simplified by the use of random number tables found in most statistics text books. Other methods of attaining random allocation to groups can be used such as tossing a coin, or in the case of our classes of schoolchildren alphabetical lists of children's names might be used. The precise method is irrelevant as long as the procedure ensures an equal chance of individuals appearing in each of the experimental groups.

It is important to note that this procedure does not eliminate or even reduce individual differences but simply distributes those differences randomly between the groups. So continuing our example, those children whose previous reading experience might facilitate their performance in the experiment appear in all the groups in roughly equal numbers. The ideal being aimed at is of totally equal distribution but because allocation is done on a random probabilistic basis this can never be guaranteed. However, because the chance of a very skewed distribution is very small indeed, randomisation of subjects is an important step in setting up even the smallest of experiments. As the number of subjects in an experiment increases, so does the likelihood of attaining an equal distribution of those subject variables which might interfere with the causal relationship being tested for. Despite the strength of randomisation as a technique and its relative ease of implementation, it is surprising how many experiments remain uninterpretable because of the researcher's failure to ensure random distribution of subjects across groups. See Chapter 7 for a discussion of quasi-experimental designs.

## 5.7.3  Matching

The sensitivity or power of an experiment refers to its ability to pick up any effect of the independent variable. Sometimes experimental effects may be very small and yet of great psychological significance. A classic example of such a situation is in sex differences. On most measures males and females do not respond differentially – the similarities far outweigh the differences. However, those psychological areas in which one sex outperforms the other are of great psychological interest but the actual size of the effects can be very slight indeed. Therefore, researchers interested in this area must ensure that the experiment is designed to be maximally sensitive.

Randomisation of subjects to experimental groups will guard against certain error but will not increase sensitivity. All is not lost, however, since there are steps which will achieve this, namely various means of matching subjects. If we take our example of a group of schoolchildren embarking on their different programmes of being taught to read, there are many instances of existing differences between those children which might interfere with our ability to assess the effectiveness of the different programmes. Prior reading training is one we have already mentioned, but other factors such as intelligence and age are also potentially significant. When running experiments with children, age is a difficult variable to deal with because development is so rapid in early childhood that even a six-month age difference between two subjects might exert a significant effect on the child's performance. Therefore, we would want to be sure that the children in each condition were of a similar age.

Randomisation of our class of children would help ensure that the average age of our groups was similar but we may need to do more than that. Where there is reason to believe that some variable which is not manipulated by the experiment may exert an effect, then it is necessary to make the additional step of actually matching subjects. In the case of age, we would make sure that for each subject in group A there was a child of the exact chronological age (in years and months) in groups B and C. Furthermore, if intelligence were a concern to us then we might take a further step of assessing IQ on some standardised test and then match children across groups according to IQ. When these kinds of precautions are taken then the probability of revealing a true causal relationship between our independent variable of teaching method and our dependent variable of reading performance is dramatically increased. The importance of matching when the experiment comprises very different subject groups becomes more salient. Suppose the experiment is comparing some kind of treatment intervention on groups of people with some disability such as autism, schizophrenia, dyslexia or Down's Syndrome. How can these subjects be matched? The answer to this lies very much in the realm of the experimental hypothesis. I shall use the example of dyslexia to highlight some of the traditional matching techniques and point out how these have recently been improved.

Some children, who have average or significantly above average IQ's have pronounced difficulties with learning to read and write. The term dyslexia is often applied to these children to describe this paradoxical gap between their intelligence and their literacy skills. The theoretical debate around the causes of dyslexia has assumed a specific cognitive or neuro-psychological deficit and not surprisingly has been the focus of many research studies and experiments. The typical experimental paradigm has been to take a group of children with reading difficulties and compare them with children of the same age and intelligence. Thus the groups were matched for mental age and the experiments then went on to probe the nature of the reading difficulty of the dyslexic group. More recently, however, research by Bryant and colleagues has criticised this approach on both methodological and theoretical grounds (Bryant and Bradley, 1985).

The traditional approach assumes that reading difficulties are caused by some deficit but the methodology used does not allow us to distinguish cause and effect. As Bryant points out reading difficulties not only have causes they also exert effects – a child with reading difficulties will be less able to deal with other aspects of the world because print is so endemic to everyday life. While experimental methods employing the mental age match design allow us to look at causal relationships, they do not allow us to decide which is the cause and which is the effect. A beautifully simple way around this problem is to introduce an additional matched group of children – those who are matched according to reading age, which is precisely what Bryant did in his series of experiments. This way, differences between the children at the same level of reading ability might truly reveal something about the nature of the 'deficit'.

One reason why I particularly like this example is that it shows that changes in methodology are not introduced purely in the interests of better scientific method. They have real and sometimes very dramatic theoretical consequences. It also illustrates how generations of scientists accept particular methods without noticing the flaws in current procedure.

## 5.7.4 Within-subject designs

Some types of experiment solve the problem of differences between subjects and the need for matching by using the same subjects in each of the experimental conditions. Within-subject designs, as they are called, have one very obvious advantage since each individual acts as his or her own control. When the same subject performs quite differently under each of the treatments then the effect of the independent variable is very clear indeed, but this method carries with it some disadvantages which in some cases make this method inappropriate whereas in others they can be dealt with by following certain precautions.

The first problem which within-subject designs pose arises because by definition the different levels or tasks in the experiment must be completed serially, one after another. The serial nature of testing can easily give rise to **order effects**, where doing one task first and another second influences the subject's performance. A clear example might be a task involving high levels of concentration, such as an auditory discrimination task in which two words are simultaneously presented, one in each ear, and the subject has to identify one on the basis of some given criterion which differs in each experimental condition. In such a situation, the subject is quite likely to show an incremental improvement from one condition to the next as they gain experience with the nature of the task such that performance in the first condition would always be inferior to performance in later conditions. Any experiment in which there is familiarity with the experimental set-up and procedure is at risk for showing order effects which will distort the interpretation of the results. Moreover, this type of order effect will arise regardless of the precise sequencing of conditions since it arises simply out of the fact that one condition must be first, second, third and so on.

A more specific kind of difficulty arising out of order of presentation is the potential for **carry-over effects**. These come into play when performance on one condition is dependent in part on the conditions which precede it and thus runs the risk of lowering the experiment's validity. Carry-over effects can be characterised in three ways. The first is where the subject gains experiment-relevant skills in one task which spill over into the next task presented. So in a two-condition (A and B) experiment let us suppose that while undertaking A the subject picks up skills which will enhance performance on B. When presented as A-B order, the subject's score on B will be artificially inflated compared with the same experiment run as a between-subject design.

A further scenario is where experience of one task actually creates a situation where the subject reinterprets the meaning of the experiment and the experimenter's intentions (either rightly or wrongly) and therefore changes his or her behaviour on all subsequent tasks. Examples of this latter type are particularly common when testing young children's cognitive understanding and indeed have been exploited in developmental psychology for their theoretical interest (for further discussion see Davis, 1991). One familiar example is in testing young children's understanding of number. Piaget (1952a) showed how children under the age of five or six often report that the number of objects in a row actually changes simply because an adult (acting as experimenter) spreads the row of objects out so that the row appears longer. This phenomenon is said to arise because the young child does not understand number invariance or number conservation. It is a very powerful and convincing effect to witness but even more striking if one then retests the child and instead of the adult spreading out the row, the adult picks up a teddy bear and the teddy is seen as spreading out the row of objects. Experiment after experiment has shown how children who fail to conserve when the transformation is undertaken by an adult, change to give conserving responses when a cuddly toy performs the action. Furthermore, these studies show significant carry-over effects. If children are tested in the teddy bear condition first then they are more likely to give correct conserving responses on the adult condition than children who are given the reverse order of presentation. Note the difference between order effect and carry-over effect here; it is not that children show an improvement from first to second task but that they show improvement only with a particular sequence of conditions.

So, I have been trying to suggest that carry-over effects can be of theoretical interest rather than simply viewing them as experimental pitfalls to be avoided at all costs. This said, they can only provide valuable insight if the experiment is designed so that they can be recognised. In the number conservation examples above the relevant experimental manoeuvre employed was that of **counterbalancing** – half the children were given the Piagetian version of the task first followed by the modified task involving the toy and the other half given the toy condition followed by the standard Piagetian condition. In a two-treatment design, this AB, BA counterbalancing is effective, efficient and easy to implement. Both order and carry-over effects can be readily recognised, but what of more complex designs involving many levels of the independent variable?

True counterbalancing becomes very unwieldy as the number of conditions increases – three conditions give six different orders and five generate 120! Consequently, researchers using more than three or four treatments will settle for **incomplete counterbalancing** as in **latin-square design**. A latin square ensures that each level or condition appears equally

Order

|  | | | | |
|---|---|---|---|---|
| Subject 1 | A | B | C | D |
| Subject 2 | B | C | D | A |
| Subject 3 | C | D | A | B |
| Subject 4 | D | A | B | C |
| Subject 5 | A | B | C | D |
| Subject 6 | B | C | D | A |
| Subject 7 | C | D | A | B |
| Subject 8 | D | A | B | C |
| Subject 9 | A | B | C | D |
| - - - - - - | - - | - - | - - | - - |
| Subject *n* | D | A | B | C |

Figure 5.3   *Counterbalancing by latin squares*

in each position. An example of a 4 × 4 table is shown in Figure 5.3 for four levels of treatment (A, B, C and D). Such an experiment would require at least 16 subjects (one in each cell) or multiples of four so that they are evenly distributed. It is worth noting that in a design as complex as this, any carry-over effects are being controlled for by being randomly distributed across the experiment and are not likely to be clearly apparent as in a two-condition design (AB, BA) unless very large numbers of subjects were being tested. I have organised this latter section along the dichotomy of between- vs. within-subject design. Like many of the other concepts that have been considered this is an oversimplification and to some extent a fairly arbitrary distinction made in the interest of ease of presentation and learning. In practice, many experiments involve the use of both within- and between-subject measures. These mixed designs are increasingly more common as access to complex statistical analysis becomes more available on personal computers. This said, it is not the case that complex design is on the increase for purely pragmatic reasons – there are good psychological grounds for this increase. Psychological processing is a multivariate activity – there is probably not one single phenomenon in psychology which can be described by appeal to a single variable.

## 5.8   Evaluating the experimental method

Throughout this chapter I have avoided having a section on advantages and disadvantages of the experimental method. However, the discussion which follows might well have fallen under such headings. Although the whole enterprise of experimental design rests on quantification, the decision about the type of methodology to be employed is not easily quantifiable. The decision rests on the nature of the research question, one's own experience and expertise and a host of other essentially qualitative factors. Some questions cry out for experimental investigation and it would be ill-advised in some instances to use other methodologies. But my own personal view of progression in psychology is not one where experimental methodology continues to be more and more sophisticated, thus squeezing out alternatives.

There are two issues at stake: one is whether or not the experimental method has a significant role to play in psychological research and the second is the subtlety of our ability to combine different methodologies. In the pursuit of causal explanations, experimental methods are identified as the only way of achieving such goals, but there is a certain arrogance attached to this claim because it tends to blur the unavoidable fact that there is little point in searching for causality unless we can be sure that a meaningful relationship exists which warrants our efforts to determine cause and effect in the first place. It is quite possible to follow the rules of experimental methodology to answer a ridiculous question in just the same way as a computer will calculate the average gender of subjects. The suggestion I am making is that the experimental method is dependent for its success on living alongside other methodologies for one very simple reason. The weaknesses of the key alternative to experimentation, namely correlational techniques, can be complemented by the strengths of the experimental method and vice versa (for a full discussion of this point see Bryant, 1990).

Experiments are frequently criticised (and rightly so) for the fact that they lack ecological validity. Findings generated in laboratory conditions where behaviour must be tightly controlled may not tell us anything interesting about life outside the laboratory. In other words they lack external validity. However, they are a good way, in fact the only way, of answering causal questions. Correlational studies, on the other hand, tell us very little about the causes of relationships between events, but they can be carried out in natural 'real life' settings and so tell us a good deal about people's normal behaviour. There are a few, but very powerful, instances where researchers have capitalised on the dovetailing characteristics of combined methodologies to great effect (see for example Bryant and Bradley, 1985).

## 5.9 Conclusion

I hope that in the course of this chapter I have highlighted not only the issues one needs to be aware of when designing effective psychological experiments but also gone some way in explaining why the experimental method has a real contribution to offer. Yet there is a sense in which one feels 'but life is not like that' when trying to define the ideal control condition or a readily measurable dependent variable. One of the over-riding difficulties of the experimental method is that the ideal often is humanly impossible as in the case where it would be too time consuming or where certain groups, conditions or variables simply do not exist. Some-times it is not possible to meet the criteria demanded by the formal experimental designs discussed here and we have to resort to quasi-experimental methods or adopt alternative methodologies entirely.

Furthermore, because scientific research is a human endeavour researchers themselves as much as their 'subjects' get involved in chains of unavoidable events which means that the most clearly defined of objective plans get waylaid. Even Skinner himself, as a disciple of objective methodology, laid down some less than scientific principles of the prag-matics of carrying out research, in a talk about his own experiences (for a discussion of these see Christensen, 1988).

Does the fact that our research will fall short of logical purity negate the whole exercise of striving for systematic objective study? The answer must be a definite 'no'. There is such a thing as good evidence and experimental methodology is currently one of the best research tools we have at our disposal to uncover it.

## 5.10  Project

Some well-established phenomena about the workings of human memory are relatively easy to replicate experimentally. For example, we know that people have good recall of familiar material. We also know that people are better able to recall grouped material than ungrouped material. The simple project outlined below presents an experimental design to test the effect of grouping material.

Is it the case that telephone numbers will be recalled more accurately if presented in the form of 254 - 6578 rather than 2546578? The most basic design would be to present subjects with a series of examples of grouped versus ungrouped seven-digit numbers as a within-subject design and score the number of examples correctly recalled from each of the two types. This design could be elaborated upon by including another independent variable – letters (vs. numbers) either as a within- or between-subject factor.

Issues to consider include:

- How would you control for practice effects?
- What are the advantages and disadvantages of using within- or between-subject design on the different variables?
- How would you select the numbers and letters to be used?
- What time delay would be used between presentation and recall?

## 5.11    Further reading

There is no shortage of good textbooks on experimental design issues but I have found the following to be very helpful and clear. Christensen (1988) *Experimental Methodology* is a good detailed guide to the principles of experimental design. Keppel and Saufley's (1980) *Introduction to Design and Analysis: A Student's Handbook* outlines the main types of experimental design alongside appropriate techniques for analysis.

# 6 Single Case Experimental Designs

*Sarah L. Wilson*

## Contents

## 6.1 Introduction: what are single case experiments?

Single case experiments are scientific investigations in which the effects of a series of experimental manipulations on a single subject are examined. An example of the application of single case experimental method would be the assessment of the effects of one or more treatments on one individual. Single case experimental research should not be confused with case studies – case studies are retrospectively written reports of observations on individuals, which may raise questions that initiate research; single case experiments are, of course, prospectively planned.

The origins of single case methodology are in clinically based research, stemming from the work of people such as Shapiro in the 1950s and Chassan in the 1960s. Today, there is still much clinical focus in the application of single case methodology. Examples of its use include the evaluation of behaviour modification and skill training programmes, assessment of drug effects and examining the effects of treatments in physical rehabilitation.

## 6.2    Problems with the group comparison approach

In applied research programmes such as these there can be objections, limitations and practical issues associated with the use of group comparison methodologies (see also Chapter 7).

### 6.2.1    Subject numbers

If the purpose of the study is to examine the effect of treatment on a particular disorder or syndrome, there may be difficulties in collecting sufficient numbers of subjects in order to match subject variables, which may interact with the treatment under investigation (for example, age, pathology, personality characteristics, IQ, social class), in order to make a control group feasible. In some of the rarer syndromes, such as vegetative state (Wilson and McMillan, 1993), collecting sufficient subjects for an experimental group can prove problematic, even when the research is based at centres which specialise in that particular type of patient; yet a shortage of subjects does not mean that the necessity for research is any less.

There are methods to overcome the subject shortage problem and enable group comparison approaches; either by carrying out the research over an extended period of time or using a multicentred study. Both approaches present practical problems, however. Using an extended period for the research can present funding problems and the research may also be vulnerable to changes within the institution within which it is set (for example, changes in care philosophy). The use of a multicentred approach can bring problems such as matching care environments, treatment philosophies, maintaining consistent style among the researchers and the practical difficulties in administering such a project.

## 6.2.2   Maintaining an uncontaminated control group

Circumstances may exist where, for the best possible reasons, relatives of subjects in the control group or care staff may attempt to use the experimental treatment on members of the control group. This may be a particular risk when relatives are participants in the treatment regime for the experimental group and may talk to other families. Such situations occur from a desire to help, even when the treatment is of unproven worth and are most likely in conditions where proven treatments are rare.

A strategy to cope with this problem in a group comparison study would be obtaining the control group from another centre, giving due consideration to the issues already discussed in relation to muliticentred studies. Even with this approach, however, there may be a risk of contamination.

## 6.2.3   Evaluation of individual treatment programmes

There are circumstances in which the use of any other approach than single case methodology is inappropriate. Specifically where a treatment regime has been designed with the problems of one individual in mind and there is a need to establish empirically the efficacy of the treatment or treatments in question with respect to that individual. Such circumstances can occur, for example, where behaviour modification programmes are being used.

## 6.2.4   Obscuring individual outcomes in group averages

In any group of experimental subjects, there may be homogeneity for particular variables (for example, diagnosis, age and duration of illness); however, the group could be entirely heterogeneous for other factors which could interact with the treatment (for example, history, attitudes, environment). This would lead to differences in treatment outcome within the group and the average response would not reflect any individual in the group.

## 6.2.5   Generalising findings to practice

In practice, the clinician may wish to apply the results of group research to assist in the treatment of individual cases; in their review of the limitations of group designs in applied research Bergin and Strupp (1972) noted two particular limitations in generalising results from group research to individual cases. One problem is that of inferring from the results for a relatively homogeneous group as representatives of a given population; the other generalising from the average response of a heterogeneous group to a particular individual.

The problem of homogeneity arises because, particularly when dealing with clinical or educational research, it is very difficult to achieve a proper random sample that will be truly representative of the whole population being investigated. The sample will be biased by the admission and treatment or management policies of the institution from which the sample is being drawn or the characteristics of the population in its catchment area. One of the major criticisms of Freud's work, for example, is that his studies are based on middle-class Viennese subjects. On the other hand if the sample is truly heterogeneous, the greater the difficulty in applying the results to one individual, and the specific effects of a given treatment on one individual with a particular set of problems becomes lost in the average (Barlow and Hersen, 1984:54). For example, a treatment for depression may alleviate severe agitation and sleep disturbance but have a deleterious effect on psychomotor retardation and depressive delusions. If the results from a heterogeneous population were to be considered as a whole, the adverse findings could be masked in the population mean with potentially dangerous consequences if the clinician in question was dealing with a patient with psychomotor retardation and depressive delusions.

Studies using heterogeneous populations and therefore having large intersubject variability may have results where some subjects produce marked improvements and others get worse; the resulting average improvement being statistically significant but weak in terms of its clinical significance.

## 6.2.6  Within-subject variability

Classically, group comparison studies require measurement pre-treatment and measurement post-treatment. The changes which occur within individuals during treatment may also yield valuable information; for example, the point at which treatment effects take place and whether they are sustained.

## 6.2.7  Ethical issues

One of the major sources of contention in research evaluating treatments is that of the ethics of withholding the treatment from the control group. The objections, which can arise from clinicians, relatives and, of course, the patients, are that those in the control group may not have the opportunity to benefit from the treatment in question or may actually suffer as the result of being included in the control group. The argument that the value of the treatment in question is unproven, hence the need for the study is an argument that may have little impact.

## 6.3 General issues in single case research

There are several issues to be considered when single case methodology is to be applied. First, there is the point which follows on from those concerning applying the results from group studies to individual cases in that there are equal problems in inferring from the results of single case studies to groups. One single case experimental study can be used to gain information about the subject and to produce hypotheses for further investigation with further single cases or with groups of subjects. If, however, the same experiment is repeated several times with similar subjects then a base for generalisation from single case studies can be created (Barlow and Hersen, 1984:56). In other words, single subjects can be grouped.

Single case methodology is not only suitable for studies where the effects of experimental manipulations are to be investigated. It can also be applied in studies where the aim is to gather a natural history. An example of this would be studying recovery from brain injury in a group of subjects who are heterogeneous in terms of variables which can influence the course of recovery such as nature and site of injury, time since injury, treatment regimes and demographic variables; who are sufficiently numerous to allow grouping for particular variables, and where individual recovery courses are also of intrinsic interest (Powell and Wilson, 1994).

## 6.4 Preparing a single case experiment

Having identified the topic of research, that is, what experimental manipulations are to be tried on which subject, the three preparatory tasks are as follows:

1  The selection of appropriate methods of serial measurement.
2  The selection of an experimental design.
3  Deciding on the criteria for determining the lengths of the phases of the experiment.

### 6.4.1  Selection of serial measures

The measurement selected must of course be appropriate for the aspect of behaviour which is to be experimentally manipulated. More than one method of measurement can be selected; all methods selected should meet the classical criteria of validity (that is, the assessment measures what it is purported to measure) and reliability. **Test-retest reliability** requires that repeated assessments will produce identical results if the subject is in an unchanged condition; that is, if there has been no change in the subject's state there will be no change in the results from the assessment. **Inter-rater** reliability requires that if two people are assessing the same subject at the same time but independently of each other then they will produce the same results. Inter-rater reliability is relevant when more than one person is to be carrying out the assessment; also in the situation when one person is responsible for carrying out the assessments over a long period, when drift from the agreed form can occur. Procedures such as having training sessions for the assessors can help achieve good inter-rater reliability and having clear, well-documented instructions for the assessment procedure is important for maintaining both forms of reliability. The assessment procedure should also be sufficiently sensitive to detect change when it occurs.

If the assessment selected has elements of skilled performance (Sunderland, 1990), then improvements may occur through practice. In order to minimise the effects of practice, the procedure of using a prolonged initial baseline phase in which the assessment may be applied a number of times, until the initial improvement in performance levels off, can be adopted or alternatively by providing some additional initial practice sessions to allow the subject to become familiar with the assessment procedure. Sunderland also recommends that the use of several attempts at the target task for each assessment and taking the best score should be considered to minimise the effects of any stray variations in performance; he also offers the caveat that in this case the serial assessment used should be brief in order to maintain motivation.

### 6.4.2   Selection of an experimental design

Whatever form of single case design is used it is of prime importance that only one variable should be changed at a time as when more than one variable is manipulated simultaneously, it is impossible to determine how much and in which way each variable contributes to any behaviour change.

### 6.4.3   A-B designs

The A-B design is the simplest experimental design in which the target behaviour is clearly specified and measurements are carried on throughout both A and B phases. A is the baseline phase during which the natural occurrence of the target behaviour or behaviours is monitored; in the B phase the treatment variable is introduced. A hypothetical example of an A-B design is illustrated in Figure 6.1.

There is, however, an important reservation concerning the clinical application of the A-B design; it may not be possible to tell whether any behaviour change that occurs following onset of the treatment results from the treatment per se or from spontaneous changes that are part of the recovery process. This issue is particularly germane when there is only

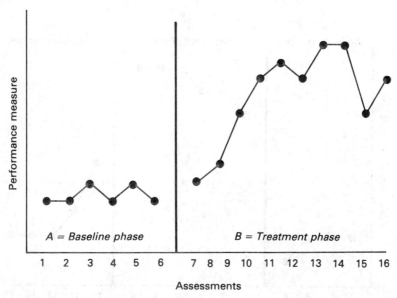

Figure 6.1 *Example of an A-B design*

weak evidence of an experimental effect such as when only a slight and gradual acceleration of the recovery curve is seen. One possible way of overcoming this problem is by the use of a **control variable**. A control variable would be another aspect of behaviour which would be as susceptible to the effects of recovery as the experimental variable, but not susceptible to the effects of the treatment. If the effects found following treatment were due to spontaneous recovery then the curves for the treatment and control variables should be parallel.

Another variation on the A-B design is the A-B withdrawal design or A-B-A design, where the treatment given in B is withdrawn for the second A phase. If, following the baseline phase A, behaviour changed during treatment phase B and then returned to baseline levels when it was withdrawn during the second A phase, then there is a high degree of certainty that the behaviour change was the result of the treatment given in phase B. A hypothetical example of an A-B-A design experiment is given in Figure 6.2. There are problems with the use of this design. One is the ethical dilemma in the clinical setting of withdrawing a treatment. Another problem is that if the subject has had a form of training (for example, spelling, doing up buttons) in the B phase, it may not be possible (or desirable) to undo that learning for the subsequent A phase.

The ethical dilemma of treatment withdrawal may be dealt with by using the A-B-A-B design; this design finishes with a treatment phase which can then be extended beyond the end of the study but a phase of withdrawal does allow the opportunity for the efficacy of the treatment given in the B phases to be evaluated. Specifically the phases are baseline (A), treatment (B), withdrawal of treatment (A), treatment (B). This design gives two

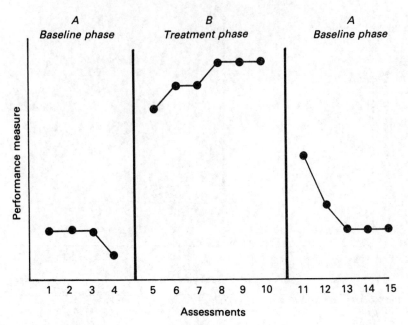

Figure 6.2   *Example of an A-B-A design*

opportunities for demonstrating the effects of the treatment over the target behaviour after the initial A to B comparison; specifically B to A and the A to B. A hypothetical example of an A-B-A-B design is given in Figure 6.3.

There are other variations on the A-B-A-B design; for example having many treatment and baseline phases (A-B-A-B-A-B-A-B-A-B) or by incorporating another treatment (A-B-A-C-A-B-A-C). In clinical settings, however, there may be circumstances in which it can appear unreasonable to other caregivers to withdraw an apparently successful treatment, even if it is going to be applied again when the treatment in question has had the apparent effect of eliminating an unpleasant behaviour. Yule (1987) describes the A-B-A-B design as probably not appropriate for demonstrating experimental control over the acquisition of new skills because of the difficulties in reversing behaviours that have become established; its greatest value is probably where the occurrence of an already existing skill is being manipulated.

## 6.4.4   Multiple baseline designs

There are clearly occasions when the use of withdrawal designs are impractical such as when treatments cannot be withdrawn or reversed due to practical or ethical reasons or problems in cooperation with other caregivers. In drug studies effects of active medication may persist into the placebo phase. Multiple baseline designs (Baer et al., 1968) can be used in situations where withdrawal or reversal of treatments are not feasible.

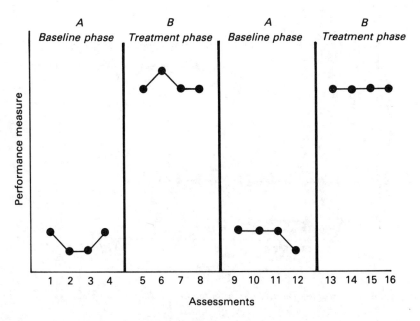

Figure 6.3 *Example of an A-B-A-B design*

In using a multiple baseline design, a number of different aspects of behaviour are identified and measured over a period of time to provide baselines against which changes can be measured. An example would be from a study of the effects of social skills training for mildly and moderately retarded adults (Bates, 1980); the aspects of behaviour being: introductions and small talk, asking for help, differing with others and handling criticism. Once the baselines are established, the experimenter then applies an experimental variable (treatment) to one of the behaviours. After an appropriate length of time, treatment is also applied to a second behaviour, leaving the remaining behaviours untreated and so on until all behaviours are being treated. Treatment is not applied to any behaviour until a stable baseline has been achieved for that behaviour. A hypothetical example of a multiple baseline design is given in Figure 6.4. The purpose of this design is to demonstrate the power of the experimental variable (treatment) in that each behaviour should maximally change only after the experimental variable is applied to it and those behaviours which are untreated should remain unchanged. If change only occurs in each behaviour after the experimental variable has been applied then efficacy can be assumed.

The multiple baseline design can be conceptualised as a series of separate A-B designs; for each behaviour the baseline being the A phase and the treatment being the B phase. As a consequence the limitations of the A-B design apply; without withdrawal of treatment the controlling effects on the target behaviours are not clearly demonstrated. The effects

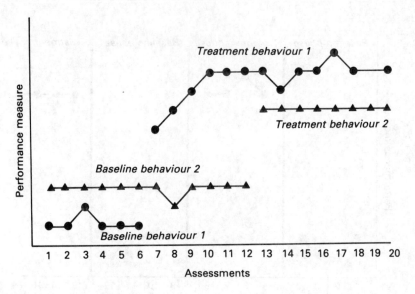

Figure 6.4   *Example of a multiple baseline design (across behaviours)*

of the treatment are inferred from the lack of change in the untreated behaviours and this assumption is based on the premise that the targeted behaviours are independent of one another. If the targeted behaviours covary then the treatment effects must be called into question. For a convincing demonstration of treatment effects Barlow and Hersen (1984:212) recommend a minimum of three to four baselines should be used if practical and experimental considerations permit.

There are three basic types of multiple baseline design. The one that has already been described as part of the general discussion is the multiple baseline across behaviours; this design is defined by Barlow and Hersen (1984) as the sequential application of a treatment variable to independent behaviours within the same subject. The two other types of design are multiple baseline across subjects and multiple baseline across settings.

In the **multiple baseline across subjects design**, a specified treatment is applied in sequence to a series of matched subjects who share the same environmental conditions (Barlow and Hersen, 1984). Each subject is assessed using the same measure(s) and as the treatment is applied to succeeding subjects, so the baseline for each subject increases in length. An example of the application of this design would be evaluating the effects of a behaviour management regime on children who have episodes of urinary incontinence. In this design only one behaviour is being investigated but this does not preclude gaining further information by monitoring other behaviours at the same time.

Barlow and Hersen (1984) define the **multiple baseline across settings design** as when a treatment variable is applied sequentially to the same behaviour across different and independent settings in the same subject. In

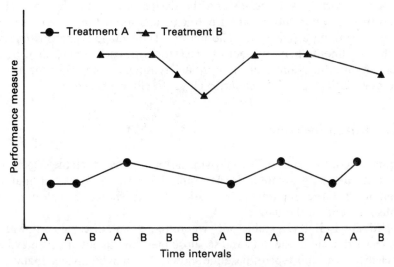

Figure 6.5 *Example of an alternating treatments design comparing treatments A and B*

this design, a single subject is used and a single behaviour is investigated; baseline measures are obtained for that behaviour in different environmental settings. The treatment variable is then applied in one environmental setting after the other. An example of the application of this design is provided by Kirchner et al. (1980) who examined the effects of the introduction of a police helicopter patrol on burglary rates in two high density residential areas. Kirchner et al. also incorporated an A-B-A withdrawal element into their design so the effects of withdrawing the helicopter patrol could be seen.

## 6.4.5 Alternating treatments design

This design has been proposed as a method of assessing the relative effectiveness of two (or more) treatments or conditions and is suggested as an alternative to the use of the between-groups comparison. This design is applied by the rapid alternation of two or more treatments or conditions within a single subject (Barlow and Hersen, 1984). Rapid, in this context, is not defined necessarily as rapid within a fixed period of time such as every hour; it could be that every time the patient is seen an alternate treatment is given. This design does not require a baseline period and the sequence of treatments should be decided on a random basis. Figure 6.5 illustrates a hypothetical study conducted using an alternating treatments design, showing that relative efficacy can be established by comparing data points from different treatments.

The alternating treatments design does have the advantages of not requiring withdrawal of treatment, produces utilisable data more rapidly than A-B-A withdrawal designs and the design is not sensitive to background trends in behaviour – the treatments are applied in the context of what is happening at the time. The major disadvantage is the possibility that the treatments may interact or interfere with each other; also, in a clinical situation it is unusual to alternate treatments, the other forms of single case designs provide scenarios closer to clinical practice.

### 6.4.6   Initial baseline

The function of the baseline is to provide a standard by which the effects of treatment can be evaluated. Barlow and Hersen (1973) stated that a minimum of three separate observation points should be plotted to establish a trend in the data.

The ideal baseline is a stable one, where there is no discernible upward or downward trend in the data and so subsequent treatment effects may be seen clearly. Another type of baseline shows a trend in behaviour that is in the opposite direction to the treatment effect. This sort of baseline is also acceptable since if there is a treatment effect it will be demonstrated quite clearly by reversing the trend in the data. One problematic type of baseline is where the trend in the data is in the same direction as the expected treatment effect and therefore it will be difficult to distinguish treatment effects from spontaneous change. Other problematic types include: alternating high and low trends, U-shaped, inverted U-shaped, and unstable which shows no particular pattern at all. One method of dealing with such problematic baselines is to continue them until a level trend has been achieved. This strategy may not be practicable however and it may be necessary to stipulate a maximum duration of the baseline period.

### 6.4.7   Subsequent phases

The same recommendation applies to experimental phases, that the phase should be of sufficient length to show a lack of trend and a constant range of variability. Carried to its natural conclusion this would mean that different phases could have markedly differing lengths; however, relative equivalence of phase lengths is desirable (Barlow and Hersen, 1984). It is recognised, as with baseline length, that ethical or practical considerations may place limitations on duration of phases.

## 6.5   Performing the experiment

Once the objective of the study has been established and a protocol decided upon, then the process of data collection can commence. The procedures used should, of course, be carefully recorded. It is important that any external events that occur during the course of the experiment which may influence the outcome are carefully noted, such as changes in state of health and major life events.

# 6.6    Data analyses

There are two ways in which to deal with data from single case experiments; one is visual inspection, the other is performance of statistical tests. It is sometimes useful to use both approaches, but sometimes visual inspection alone will suffice.

## 6.6.1    Visual inspection

The data should be presented as a graph. In the first instance a graph should be drawn including all the data points. It may prove useful subsequently, if there is high variability in the data, to produce graphs with smoothed curves by blocking the data; however, care should be taken to avoid distorting the results. Scales for the axes should also be selected with care. Too large a scale will flatten out any treatment effects and too small a scale might suggest that the data are more variable than is actually the case.

The use of visual inspection alone may be appropriate when what is required is to show whether there has been a treatment effect and that treatment effect is clearly discernible. There are other occasions, for example when the data are variable, when it is difficult to discern whether there is a treatment effect and then statistical analysis is called for. It must be remembered that in clinical applications, there can be a difference between statistical significance and clinical significance. Occasions have been noted when behaviour changes which were too small to be significant statistically did have clinical significance, also when behaviour changes which did reach statistical significance were not judged to have been clinically significant.

## 6.6.2    Serial dependency

Data collected in single case experiments *may* exhibit what is described as serial dependency; that is, successive observations may be related to one another so that preceding observations can be used to predict succeeding ones. Parametric tests such as $F$ and $t$ are based on the assumption that observations are independent of one another; the use of serially dependent data can significantly bias $F$ and $t$ tests leading to both Type I and Type II errors (see Chapter 23).

Serial dependency can be detected by the use of a statistical procedure known as **autocorrelation**. Autocorrelation refers to a correlation between data points separated by a particular interval. If an interval of one is used, the first observation is paired with the second, the second observation is paired with the third, the third with the fourth and so on. The correlation coefficient ($r$) is then calculated and examined for significance. Usually testing for autocorrelation with an interval (or lag) of one is sufficient to test for serial dependency, although a more sensitive analysis may be obtained by performing autocorrelations with different intervals. For example, using an interval of three, the first observation would be paired with the fourth, the second with the fifth and so on. It is recommended that autocorrelations should be calculated separately for data from the different phases of the experiment as treatment may affect dependency. Procedures have been suggested (Barlow and Hersen, 1984:294–5) to allow the use of $t$ and $F$ with data that have been found to be serially dependent; such as in an A-B-A-B design combining the data from the two A phases and comparing it with the data from the two B phases. The rationale for this is that the data from the first A phase would probably be more highly correlated with the data from the first phase than with the data from the second A phase, since autocorrelations tend to decrease with distance. However, not all statistical techniques that can be used to assess single case data are sensitive to serial dependency.

### 6.6.3  Statistical analyses

Having excluded the possibility of serial dependency in the data, then a $t$-test can be used to analyse the data from an A-B design. The usual application of $t$-tests is to data from groups studies; in related $t$-tests, repeated observations on the same subjects under two conditions are compared so that the effect of the conditions (or treatments) on the measure can be determined. Likewise, in independent $t$-tests, two groups of subjects are used and they are compared on a particular measure so that the effect of belonging to a particular subject group is evaluated.

In single case research, independent $t$-tests can be used to compare scores from a particular measure taken in the baseline phase with scores from that same measure taken during the treatment phase, so instead of comparing scores from groups of subjects we are comparing scores from groups of assessment sessions. Related $t$-tests can be applied when the design requires comparison of scores from two different conditions within session, for example comparison of pre-treatment and post-treatment scores. Instead of comparing two scores for each subject, we are comparing two scores for each assessment session. Where A-B-A-B or A-B-A-C type designs are used then analysis of variance can be applied to compare the data from the different phases.

There is a further consideration for the use of analyses such as these which test the differences in means if there are marked trends in the different phases. If the baseline and treatment phases both have a marked trend in the same direction, then the means are bound to be significantly different. For example, if there is a continuous upward trend, the data points from the B phase will all exceed the data from the A phase; the significance of the result will be a reflection of the trend. On the other hand, if a situation occurs such as a downward trend in the baseline phase and an upward trend in the treatment phase, there may not be a significant difference between the means, yet the treatment will clearly have had an effect. Trends in phases of the data can be examined quickly by use of the split-middle technique (White, 1972). The procedure is described in detail in Barlow and Hersen (1984).

Time series analysis can be used to examine trends in the data and also changes in level. This technique also provides a *t*-test that is appropriate when there is serial dependency in the data and is also not dependent on having stable baselines, but it is dependent on having a relatively large number of data points. This technique and the application of randomisation tests are also discussed in detail in Barlow and Hersen (1984). Sunderland's (1990) comment on the utility of statistical analyses in single case studies (even having excluded the possibility of serial dependency) is that

> the results should still be treated with a little caution as these statistical procedures are being used in a context for which they were not originally designed and other less important assumptions are still violated. It is therefore best to treat them as a way of describing the strength of any effects suggested by the graphical analysis, and no great reliance should be placed on the exact size of the probability values calculated. (1990:190–1)

## 6.7 Project

The first thing to remember is that because single case studies require serial measures then the practicalities of allocating the period of time have first to be considered. One type of experiment that could be carried out is to examine the effect of some change in lifestyle on an appropriate measure of performance. An A-B or A-B-A design could be used. An example of this would be whether the administration of caffeine (in the form of a strong cup of coffee for example) has an immediate facilitatory effect on information processing. A number of factors would have to be considered in designing this experiment; for example, size of dose, time between intake and test performance, and time of day effects. The baseline period would have to be caffeine free and would have to be of sufficient length so that it would not be biased by any features that might not be present when the treatment is introduced, such as having a cold. The possibility must be considered that if caffeine were consumed before the baseline period, some may remain. There is also the selection of the measure of information processing ability; a test such as the Paced Auditory Serial Addition Test (PASAT) (Gronwall and Wrightson, 1974; also described in detail in

Spreen and Strauss, 1991) would be suitable if a form were used where the test items were randomly generated by computer every time to avoid the possibility of the subject learning the test. The baseline period would also have to be sufficiently long for the effects of practice on performance to stabilise.

## 6.8  Further reading

Barlow and Hersen's (1984) *Single Case Experimental Designs* is, to my knowledge, the most comprehensive, extensive and well-known textbook on the subject. Yule's chapter on the evaluation of treatment programmes which appears in Yule and Carr's (1987) *Behaviour Modification for People with Mental Handicaps* is a readable introductory chapter, well illustrated with examples from published studies. Also worth a look is Sunderland's (1990) article, 'Single-case experiments in neurological rehabilitation' which is an accessible paper, written from a practical viewpoint, describing the stages of single case research.

# 7 Quasi-experimental Designs

*Chris Fife-Schaw*

## Contents

## 7.1 Introduction

In Chapter 5 the basics of classical experimental designs were discussed. Most textbooks and degree courses stress the desirability of doing experiments since they offer the most clear-cut route to testing hypothesised causal relationships between variables. The experimenter has control over the relevant variables and allocates subjects to conditions at random in an attempt to make sure that he or she knows exactly what is responsible for the changes observed.

This is to be contrasted with observational and correlational approaches (see Chapter 2) where we can observe that two variables appear related to one another. However, it is difficult to determine whether there is a causal relationship between the variables (one 'causes' the other) or some third variable is responsible for the observed relationship (see Chapter 23). Although this state of affairs may seem less than satisfactory, after all we usually want to be able to say what caused what, correlational studies are often the best we can hope for in many real world domains. Practical considerations limit the amount of control we can expect to have in such situations, so we have to be careful whenever we try to interpret relationships between variables.

In between correlational and experimental approaches lie two other kinds of approach; the **pre-experiment** and the **quasi-experiment**. Pre-experiments are not regarded as particularly useful but are informative in the sense that they highlight the positive virtues of quasi-experiments. Pre-experiments are best illustrated by an example.

## 7.2   Pre-experiments

I once attended a course on rapid reading in an attempt to increase the speed with which I could get through paperwork. The University was pleased to supply such training as it would help the staff perform better and this would, in turn, help the University to be more efficient. A consultant was hired to do the training. With the current political concern to evaluate everything, the consultant felt obliged to conduct an experiment to see if the training had actually worked. Before the training started we were given a report to read and we were asked to time our reading of it and answer some factual questions about the report's content. Having done this, the training went ahead and at the end of the day we were tested on our reading again. So that the times and test scores would be readily comparable we read the same text and answered the same questions. Needless to say reading speed had increased dramatically (four times quicker in my case) and accuracy remained high. The consultant, with obvious satisfaction, declared the day a success.

The problem here, of course, is that we do not really know if the training had any effect on reading speed at all. Whether we have been able to detect accurately the effect of the training is referred to as the **internal validity** of the experiment.

There are several problems with this procedure which challenge its internal validity even though at first sight it looks like a reasonable thing to have done. First, the test materials were the same on both occasions and since we had seen them only about seven hours previously there is a strong possibility that we would remember the content. Thus improvements may be reflecting memory for the material rather than increased reading speed. It is obviously easier to read something quickly if you already know what it is about. The same applies to the 'test' questions. Such threats to the experiment's internal validity are called **testing effects**. In all sorts of studies, repeatedly exposing subjects to the test materials is likely to make them familiar with them and less anxious about what they have to do. Such effects tend to inflate post-test scores.

In fairness, were the consultant to have used a different report and different test questions, it would have been even more difficult to know what any differences in reading speed could be attributed to. The second text might be easier to read or, possibly, more difficult.

A second problem concerns what are called **maturational effects**. Merely having the time to concentrate on reading speed even without experiencing the training may have led to improvements. As none of those tested had been allowed to spend the day thinking about rapid reading without being trained, we do not really know whether the training per se had an effect.

Another problem concerns **sample selection**. All those present felt that they had a reading speed problem and, at least at the start of the day, were motivated to improve. You had to volunteer for the course and there was no external pressure on people to attend. Having put a day aside to improve performance, not trying hard to improve would have been somewhat perverse. This factor, in conjunction with the potential maturational effects noted above may have served to increase scores on the retest. Again, we cannot really say how effective the training was, and even if effective here, it might be somewhat less useful when people are not so keen to be trained. This latter point refers to the **external validity** of the study – just how generalisable are the findings? If training works, does it only work for very committed people?

It should be noted that all of these problems are concerned with the experiment (as a pre-experiment) and do not say anything about the virtues of the course. It may have worked very well or it may not. Whichever is the case, this study shed very little light on the issue. This is obviously not an ideal way to demonstrate that the training package increased reading speed.

Other forms of pre-experiment are commonly found in news stories where some sort of intervention has to be evaluated. A crude example would be to see if peer teaching improved computing skills by comparing children's exam performances in schools that had adopted peer teaching with ones that had maintained traditional teacher-led methods. At one level this looks like a legitimate comparison between treatment groups – one that gets peer teaching and one that does not. Clearly a true controlled experiment is not possible as it would be ethically and politically unacceptable to allocate children randomly to schools and thus to the 'treatment' conditions.

Numerous problems follow in interpreting any differences that are observed between the groups. First, there is the question of whether the schools are comparable. Perhaps the schools that adopt peer teaching simply have more able or more socially advantaged children in them. Those children from higher socioeconomic backgrounds may be expected to have home computers and thus be more computer literate, for instance. There is also a possibility that some event, such as a cut-back in funds for computer maintenance may occur in one school and not another. Such a sudden change in one of the groups is known as a **history effect** and may lead to a difference between the groups which is not attributable to the treatment (peer teaching, here) but is due to something else.

# 7.3   Quasi-experiments

Many of the problems discussed in relation to pre-experiments reduce the degree of certainty you can have that the 'treatment' actually caused the observed differences in the dependent variable of interest (that is, the study's internal validity). Because of this, it is rare to see pre-experiments in high-status academic journals. However, many of the research questions that we would like answers to simply cannot be answered by resorting to true experiments. This is usually because we either cannot randomly allocate subjects to treatment conditions or it would be unethical to do so. Chapter 6 has already dealt with some of the more obvious medically related ethical problems of withholding a potentially beneficial treatment from patients. With less sensitive topics, even where withholding a treatment is not a problem, random allocation may simply be practically impossible. In the computer skills example above, for instance, we could not randomly allocate children to the schools.

Quasi-experiments should not be seen, however, as always inferior to true experiments. Sometimes quasi-experiments are the next logical step in a long research process where laboratory-based experimental findings need to be tested in practical situations so see if the findings are really useful. Laboratory-based experiments often reveal intriguing insights yet the practical importance, or substantive significance, of these can only be assessed quasi-experimentally. Laboratory studies may have shown that under certain, highly controlled conditions, peer teaching improves computer test scores but the 'real' issue is whether peer teaching is good for children in their schools. This is a question about the external validity of the laboratory-based studies.

Three classical quasi-experimental designs exist which attempt to over-come these threats to internal validity discussed above. What is presented below is a summary of the three prototypical designs; many variations of these are possible (see Cook and Campbell, 1979). Many of the principles involved are common to those discussed in Chapter 6 on single case designs and you should read that chapter as well if you are intending to design your own quasi-experimental study. It should be noted that quasi-experimental approaches, in common with true experiments, assume that there is a 'true' answer to the question of what causes the changes in the dependent variable.

# 7.4 Non-equivalent control group designs

As we saw in the example of the computer skills, the two groups (as defined by which school they attended) may not have been comparable. The intervention of peer teaching (the treatment) may have had an effect on test scores but we cannot be sure that the peer teaching group members were not already better at computing, prior to the inception of the new programme. The non-equivalent control group design (NECG) overcomes this by requiring a pretest of computing skill as well as a post-test. The pretest allows us to have some idea of how similar the control and treatment group were before the intervention.

Figure 7.1 shows some possible outcomes from a simple NECG design. In graph A the control group starts off scoring less than the treatment group, reflecting the non-equivalence of the two groups; finding a control group with exactly equivalent scores in a quasi-experimental design is difficult. Both groups improve after the intervention but the treatment group has clearly improved more than the control group. This is quite a realistic picture to find in studies of educational interventions like the computer skills study discussed earlier. We would expect the control group members to improve a bit as, after all, they are still being taught and are maturing. If the treatment has an effect then scores should have improved more than might have been expected if the intervention had not taken place. Graph B shows what might have happened if the treatment had no effect. Scores in both groups changed about the same amount.

The graphs in Figure 7.1 are prototypical and reflect improvements over time. It is, of course, possible for all sorts of patterns to be found. Non-equivalent controls may outscore the treatment group at the pretest; they may even be equal. Perhaps a treatment serves to allow the treatment group to 'catch up' with the controls. The treatment might *decrease* scores. There are many possibilities. In all cases you are looking for an interaction between treatment condition (treatment vs. control) and time of measurement (pre- vs. post-test). You would obviously test for such an interaction statistically (see Chapter 24) but by plotting graphs like these, you should observe lines of differing gradients; parallel lines usually indicate no treatment effect (but see below).

## 7.4.1 Problems with NECG designs

Almost by definition, NECG designs suffer from potential sample **selection biases**. In studies of 'alternative' therapeutic interventions in particular, there is often a problem that those who get a new treatment had actually sought it out, perhaps because traditional treatments had not worked for them. Such people may be highly motivated to see the new treatment succeed and might have ideological objections to existing treatments. There is also the possibility that those offering the therapy may select

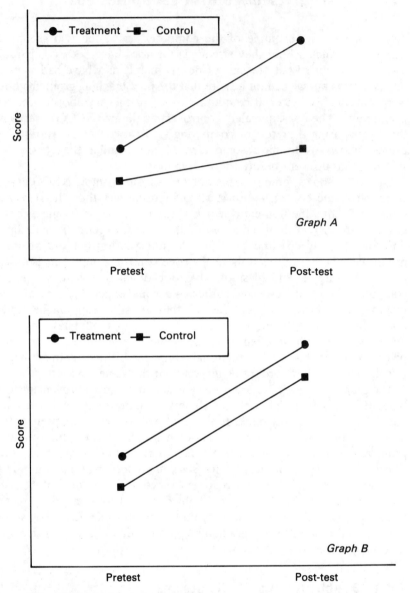

Figure 7.1 *Non-equivalent group designs*

people that they believe would benefit from it or who they think will comply with the regimen. Those who are thought likely to be 'difficult' cases, or for whom the disease may have progressed too far, might not be selected and may even end up appearing in the control group.

Clearly it would be unethical to refuse a new treatment to those who want it or to force those content with existing treatments to receive a new, and presumably still untested treatment. However, where possible, you should attempt to have control over, or at least full knowledge of, how the samples are selected. Be aware that those whose efforts are being evaluated may have a vested interest in the outcome of your study.

Even though we have pretest measures on which we can compare samples, this does not guarantee that the two groups were truly equivalent before the treatment started. If one group was more able or brighter, maturation may proceed at a faster rate in that group than the other. We might expect, for instance, that children's computer skills improve with age (maturation) and that more able children learn these skills more quickly and easily. Were the treatment group to contain proportionately more high ability children, group differences may arise out of these differential rates of maturation rather than exposure to the peer teaching method. This is referred to as a **selection/maturation interaction**. As the pretest is usually only used to compare groups on the dependent variable such a problem may remain undetected. One obvious solution would be to measure variables that might conceivably lead to differential maturation rates at the pretest (for example, IQ) though this naturally increases demands on subjects.

**Statistical regression towards the mean** is another phenomenon which may influence interpretation of the data. Regression towards the mean is reflected in very high pretest scorers scoring lower at post-test and very low pretest scorers scoring higher at post-test. If we are studying people who score at the extremes on the dependent variable we may mistake changes at post-test for this natural regression to the mean. Why this happens is a little difficult to grasp at first but depends on the fact that our test measures will naturally contain some errors (see Chapter 4). Cook and Campbell (1979) use an everyday example which is fairly easy to understand; what appears here is merely an embellished version of their example.

If we have an ability test, say an exam, we might do worse than our 'true' ability might merit because we were distracted by other students, we were extremely badly hungover (worse than usual) and had revised the topics most of which did not come up on the paper. We know that if we took an exam for the same subject again we might expect to do better next time, more accurately reflecting our ability. This is because we would expect these sources of error (failures to record our true ability) to be less likely to *all* co-occur next time around. Similarly, if we were very lucky, the exam might only contain questions on the topics we had revised for and we might be fortunate enough to sit the exam on the only day of the year when we were not hungover and everybody behaved themselves in the exam hall. This time we might get a mark that somewhat overstated our true ability in the subject. However, we probably would not expect to be so lucky if we took the exam again without further revision.

Across a sample of people, those with mid range scores are likely to be about equally influenced by these errors (inflating and reducing scores) so they would cancel out on average leading to no systematic bias in our experiment. People at the extremes, however, are *less likely* to score more extremely on being retested as some of those who had extreme scores at pretest will have done so because their scores had already been inflated (or reduced) by large errors. Since extremely large errors are relatively less likely than moderate size errors, two consecutive large errors in the same direction are very unlikely. This means that post-test scores will tend towards the population's mean score.

For experiments, this is a particular problem when the treatment group has been selected *because* of people's low scores on the dependent variable (for example, selecting people with poor computing skills for the peer teaching method). The simplest way to guard against this (though easier said than done) is to ensure that your control group is also drawn from the pool of extreme scorers. The ethics of denying an intervention to children who are particularly bad at computing are clearly an issue here. The problem is also more likely to influence results if your dependent measure has low test-retest reliability. The less reliable the measure (that is, the more error-prone it is) the more there is likely to be regression to the mean.

Finally, for now, history effects can effect the validity of NECG studies. If some event in addition to the treatment intervention occurs between pretest and post-test in one group only, then it is not clear what any group differences at post-test should be attributed to. For example, an evaluation of a persuasive campaign to promote commuting to work by urban railways in different cities may be invalidated if the 'treatment' city suffers from road travel chaos caused by unanticipated roadworks on the main commuter routes during the period of the study. People may flock to the trains but only because driving to work (their preferred method) was nearly impossible.

You should be aware that history, selection and maturation effects can work both to enhance groups differences *or* obscure them.

## 7.5   Time series designs

Time series designs involve having only one sample but taking measurements of the dependent variable on several (more than three) occasions. Such designs are sometimes referred to as **interrupted time series** designs as the treatment intervention 'interrupts' an otherwise seamless time series of observations. Figure 7.2 gives an illustration of some hypothetical time series data. As you can see the main feature that you are looking for when collecting time series data is that the only substantial change in scores coincides with the intervention. The virtue of such a design is that it is relatively less likely that short-term historical events (that is, history effects) will either co-occur with the treatment and/or that they will have a lasting effect over time. It is also unlikely that small differences pre- and

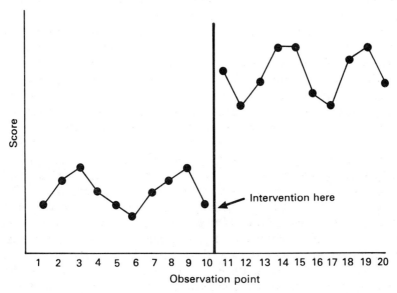

Figure 7.2 *Example time series data*

post-intervention will be maintained if the treatment really has no effect. Any maturation effects should be reflected in gradual trends in time series data and not radical changes coincident with the treatment intervention.

For time series studies to work well, multiple data collection/observation points are required. It is difficult to detect trends of any kind with just three observation points so, where possible, opt for as many observation points as is realistic but pay due regard to subject fatigue/boredom/irritation.

## 7.5.1   Problems with time series designs

Time series studies potentially suffer from the threat of **testing effects** to their validity. As these studies, by definition, require repeated administration of the same dependent measures, there is a tendency for people gradually to do better as time goes on. This is a separate phenomenon from **maturation effects** as testing effects arise out of familiarity with the measurement procedures. When presented with a novel test, for instance, we usually do not know what is required and may be anxious about our performance. Repeated exposure to the test material should reduce these anxieties and allow us to perform better. It is also possible that respondents might come to know what they are being asked about and develop more efficient answering strategies allowing them to respond more quickly. This is especially a problem where measurements are timed. The net impact of testing effects is that, if the *magnitude* of the treatment effect itself is small, it may get swamped by the testing effects. If the size of the treatment effect is relatively large there will be little problem in determining that the treatment actually had an effect.

Another potential problem concerns **instrumentation effects**. These refer to changes in accuracy of measurements over time. One good example would be the reporting of crimes. Over time the likelihood of reporting (and the police recording) crimes changes as a function of changes in the social representation of the crimes rather than their frequency per se. What may have been regarded as common assault in the past may come to be seen as a racially motivated attack in more enlightened times. Similarly, women are now encouraged to report sexual attacks and the social opprobrium that used to follow a claim of rape is now somewhat reduced, though still present. What this is really about is a change in the way the measures are taken and their relative accuracy. Studies that involve measures taken by observers are particularly at risk from instrumentation effects as observers learn how to use the coding schedule more efficiently or, more likely (and worse), become fatigued by the schedule and attempt their own reinterpretation of it.

**Subject mortality** refers to the loss of subjects from your study over time. Time series studies, especially those that cover long periods, are prone to subject mortality problems which are usually outside of the experimenter's control. Some subjects may, indeed, die during the study but it is more normal that some will drop out through boredom, or a lack of interest or perhaps because they move house. If you do not have a large sample to start with you run the risk that you will have too few people left at the end of the study to enable you to draw any reliable conclusions at all.

Subject mortality would not be such a great problem were it a truly random event. However, reasons for leaving that are related to the nature of the study (for example, a lack of interest in the research topic or the intrusive nature of the measures) can lead to a situation where the surviving sample becomes progressively more biased in favour of showing that the treatment works. Say you were trying to evaluate the effect of a locally based waste recycling advertising campaign and had instigated regular assessments of how much waste people had recycled. Even if you started with a fairly representative sample of the population, you might well find that by the time you had started the adverts and were collecting post-intervention observations, only environmentally committed people were still ready and willing to help you with the project. In all likelihood, your estimates of average post-intervention waste recycling behaviour would be considerably higher than the pre-intervention averages but this would be mainly due to sample mortality rather than the adverts.

Careful mapping of sample survivors' pre- and post-intervention behaviour would overcome this problem but this is naturally a rather unsatisfactory solution since such a campaign was presumably intended to change the behaviour of the less environmentally committed people who were lost to the study. Needless to say, strenuous efforts need to be made to maintain the sample.

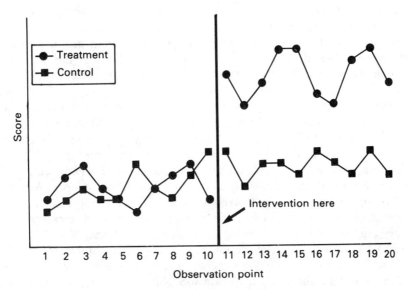

Figure 7.3 *Time series with non-equivalent control group*

## 7.6 Time series with non-equivalent control group designs

Many of the problems associated with time series and NECG designs are neatly overcome by the combination of the two approaches in the time series with non-equivalent control group (TSNECG) design, sometimes also called the **multiple time series** design. An extended series of data collection points are used with both the treatment group and the non-equivalent control. Figure 7.3 illustrates what we would hope to find if there really was a strong treatment effect. While it is clear from Figure 7.3 that there is variability in scores over time and that there appears to be a gradual improvement in scores in the control group, potentially through testing, instrumentation or maturation effects, the post-intervention scores for the treatment group are considerably higher than for the controls.

### 7.6.1 Problems with TSNECG designs

The price to be paid for minimising so many threats to validity is all-round increased cost and the need to study many more subjects. This is not a problem when conducting research on existing archival data (see Chapter 21) but may be a serious problem if you intend to collect fresh data.

Differential sample mortality in the two groups can be a problem. If people who are somewhat apathetic to the study are differentially more likely to be lost from one group than the other, then group differences may be artificially enhanced or constrained. It is also possible with studies that last for some period of time that the control group will become exposed to, or aware of, the treatment. People in the two groups may mix and discuss the intervention and control group members may either seek the treatment for themselves or withdraw from the study through becoming aware that they may never be exposed to the treatment/intervention.

Sometimes, merely being aware of the existence of a 'problem' that needs treating may change behaviours of control group members. If control group members come to feel that they are being deliberately disadvantaged in some way they may choose to perform less well when measurements are taken. This may be a serious problem when researchers are heavy-handed and insensitive in the way they handle people. Alternatively, control group members may compensate for not receiving the treatment by trying harder to perform well. This is called **compensatory rivalry** and would serve to obscure true treatment effects.

TSNECG designs are not immune to the other threats to validity discussed earlier especially if the magnitude of the treatment effect is weak and the variability between scores on successive observations is relatively high. In common with the single case designs discussed in Chapter 6, detecting a treatment effect is easiest when it is possible to establish a fairly clear-cut stable baseline in both the control group and the treatment group prior to the intervention. As with true experiments, it may be necessary to increase sample sizes substantially in order to provide the necessary statistical power to detect these weak effects.

## 7.7   Modifications to the basic designs

The basic designs described here are really the tip of the iceberg in terms of possibilities. With NECG designs there is no necessity that there are only two treatment conditions (treatment and control). It is perfectly possible to have different levels of the treatment or combinations of treatments in one design. For example, we might extend the computer skills example to include a control (traditional teaching) group, a group that had two periods a week of peer teaching and one that had three per week. In fairness to traditional methods of teaching, we might also divide the control group into one that had two periods per week and one that had three periods. Clearly, this new design is much more useful to curriculum developers since it not only tells us whether peer teaching is better than traditional methods but also whether spending more time on computing yields worthwhile increases in skill level. Assuming we had enough schools prepared to help, we could even add a group that gets both traditional and peer teaching for a total of three periods.

Sometimes concerns about **testing effects** may lead us to believe that post-test measures will be unduly influenced by people having completed the pretest. An example might be of a knowledge test with a short period between pre- and post-test. In such a situation we might expect people to remember the items, thus inflating the apparent power of any intervention. It is also often the case that merely asking people about some aspect of their lives changes their behaviour in that domain. For instance, merely asking about your waste recycling activities might make you think that you ought to recycle more waste. Somebody showing interest in your behaviour may change it. This is called the **Hawthorne effect** after the electricity plant in Illinois where the phenomenon was first formally described in studies on attempts to enhance worker performance (Roethlisberger and Dickson, 1939). It is possible to get over both sorts of problem by using separate pre- and post-test samples so that different individuals take the pre- and post-tests. This approach is only sensible if you have a large pool of people from which to draw your samples and you can draw them by some fairly random procedure.

For time series designs and TSNECG designs it is possible to adopt some of the treatment withdrawal designs described in Chapter 6. These involve intervening with the treatment and then, at a later point, withdrawing it and observing a simultaneous fall in scores on the dependent measure. This approach works best when the treatment is not expected to have a lasting effect on the dependent variable and has to be 'maintained' in some sense, for the effect to be shown. An example might be to evaluate the effectiveness of camera-based speed checks on stretches of road. Speeds could be monitored surreptitiously for some period before erecting the camera systems then, after a period with the cameras in place, they could be removed to see if speeds gradually increased in their absence. Like the single case A-B-A-B design (Chapter 6) the cameras could be re-erected later to see if speeds fell again.

## 7.8   Conclusion

Having read through this chapter and followed all the potential problems associated with each quasi-experimental design, you might be forgiven for concluding that such an approach is too fraught with difficulties to make it worthwhile. The difficulties, however, are inevitable whenever you forego experimental control in order to do research outside of the laboratory. What I hope to have shown you is that there are some rigorous methods available and, while they will not necessarily lead you to unambiguous answers to your research question, they do at least highlight the likely threats to validity. If you know where potential interpretative problems lie then you can address them and make some estimate of the likely impact these could have had on the results of your study. Quasi-experiments, providing they are conducted with due care, can be the most powerful available means by which to test important hypotheses.

# 7.9   Project

Taking the rapid reading course as an example of an intervention that needs evaluating, design a better quasi-experimental study to test the virtues of the training and write out a mock proposal to a university to ask for funds to formally evaluate such training programmes. Make sure that the proposal explains how each aspect of the design overcomes the threats to validity discussed above. You must also bear in mind the practical problems associated with conducting the study. For instance, it should not be so complicated or long-winded that it bores trainees or costs more than the training itself! If you have to make compromises in the design, explain how these might affect the interpretation of the findings and how substantively significant these problems might be.

# 7.10   Further reading

The classic text in this area is Campbell and Stanley's (1966) *Experimental and Quasi-Experimental Designs for Research*. This is a very short book of only 70 pages which had first appeared as a chapter in Gage (1963) *Handbook of Research on Teaching*. It is the place where quasi-experimental designs were first comprehensively explained. Cook and Campbell (1979) produced a more detailed text entitled *Quasi-Experimentation: Design and Analysis Issues for Field Settings*. This contains discussions of the major designs and a few more, as well as information about the appropriate statistical models to be used with each design.

# 8 Surveys and Sampling Issues

*Chris Fife-Schaw*

## Contents

## 8.1 Introduction

This chapter will cover two issues: sampling issues and the use of survey techniques. These two topics are dealt with in some depth in sociology and political science and, though psychologists regularly conduct surveys, it is fair to say that psychologists' surveys might benefit from the methodological sophistication found elsewhere in the social sciences.

Conceptually, surveys and sampling techniques are not tied to any particular philosophical viewpoint. Those adopting a hypothetico-deductive approach will be concerned to sample appropriately as will those taking a more constructivist perspective. Whenever the goal is to make statements about a group of people then, unless you approach all the members of that group, how you draw your sample of that group will have an impact on how much confidence you can have in the generalisability of your findings.

Similarly, surveys are not tied to any particular data gathering technique. While questionnaire and structured interview surveys are most common, it is perfectly possible to collect qualitative data within a survey. Even experimental investigations can be done using survey techniques though these are still quite rare (but see Gaskell et al., 1993). Physiological and other, more invasive, measures can also be collected in certain types of survey providing the resources to get respondents to a suitable testing site are available.

## 8.2  Basic survey designs

Chapters 1 and 2 have already outlined many of the 'meta-design' issues involved in designing studies but these are especially relevant in survey design and well worth considering in more detail. Within limits, researchers are free to design their surveys in any way they wish though there are a number of well-understood designs that you should consider before embarking on a new design.

### 8.2.1  Cross-sectional surveys

This is the simplest survey design as it involves approaching a sample of respondents once only. Since the sample is regarded as a cross-section of the population(s) under study it is possible to make comparisons between subgroups (for example, males vs. females, older vs. younger people, etc.) and look for relationships between variables (see Chapter 23).

*Advantages*: By far the greatest advantage is the relatively low cost associated with gathering the data. All other things being equal, response rates are generally quite high. You can devise your study and get the results in a fairly short period. Conclusions can be drawn and published quickly in time for other agencies to make use of your data for policy change purposes, etc.

*Disadvantages*: The data are unduly susceptible to **time of measurement** effects. These are influences on responses that are due to immediate historical events. For example, attitudes towards using public transport might be changed dramatically by a major rail crash on the morning that your survey takes place. In a more subtle manner, media attention on the topic of your study may influence responses to some of your items. Often only a part of your sample (for example, television viewers) will be exposed to this and you may not know which part has been so exposed. Sometimes this may seem like a good thing since you may be interested in media influences on attitudes but, since this is a hypothesis about *change*, then the cross-sectional design is not really appropriate.

## 8.2.2   Time series surveys

These are best thought of as a series of cross-sectional surveys on the same topic using the same (or very similar) survey instruments. Having selected a suitable period for separating the surveys, you draw a *new* sample for each wave of questioning. Opinion polls such as the regular polls reported in national newspapers are usually part of time series surveys. Monthly assessments of support for the political parties can be plotted to see if levels of support have changed systematically in response to political/historical events that occurred between waves of questioning.

*Advantages*: The principle aim is to assess the impact of time of measurement effects. In the poll example, the research questions are usually about whether historical events changed responses. Did that train crash have a lasting impact on willingness to travel by train?

*Disadvantages*: Studies are expensive to mount since you need multiple samples of around the same size as a single cross-sectional survey if you want accurate measures of key variables. **Cohort effects** can become confounded with time of measurement effects. Although each sample is assumed to be equally representative of the relevant population they may well differ from one another as a result of simply being a different cohort of people. Problems arise when trying to attribute differences to historical events and these events alone. The observed differences may just reflect the fact that you are asking a different cohort of people for their responses.

## 8.2.3   Longitudinal designs

Longitudinal designs involve drawing a single sample and measuring their responses on more than one occasion. Any number of recontacts are possible in theory and these designs are especially useful for tracking developmental changes and the psychological impact of life events, etc.

*Advantages*: The main advantage is the ability to follow individuals and to monitor the impact of events on responses. They permit the study of **age-related development**. Since changes can be monitored within individuals, the problems of cohort effects are removed. An increase in score on a variable can be compared with the *same individual's* score at an earlier time.

*Disadvantages*: Time of measurement effects can be confused with age-related development. If historical events serve to increase values of some variable you are interested in, observed increases that are in line with the increased age of respondents may be misinterpreted as developmental trends rather than the historical effects they really are. Apart from the obvious increased cost over cross-sectional studies, these designs suffer from **sample attrition**. At each subsequent wave of questioning some people will drop out of your study leaving a reduced sample of people to provide usable data at all points in the study. The people who stay with the survey may be a biased sample. While you may start with a fairly representative sample, those who stay with you may be systematically different from those who leave. They may be more interested in the topic of the research, they may be more compliant, they may be the kinds of people who do not move house often, etc.

Attracting people to the study in the first place may be more difficult if they are forewarned about future contacts. Some people may be happy to fill in one questionnaire but unwilling to commit themselves to filling in four. As you will have to have some way of identifying respondents' questionnaires/interviews so that you can recontact them, anonymity of responses cannot be claimed. A significant number of people will be put off by this especially if the topic of study is in anyway sensitive.

Another difficulty concerns **sample conditioning**. People who are studied on several occasions soon come to know what is required of them and the types of questions that will be asked. Because of this they may no longer be 'naïve' respondents and some may intentionally attempt to find out more about the research topic.

Really long-term longitudinal studies (for example, the National Child Development Study) require long-term commitment of resources from funding agencies. Such far-sighted generosity in the face of the possibility that the study may fail to reveal anything of interest makes this approach comparatively rare.

## 8.2.4   Longitudinal cohort sequential designs

In the above discussion three sources of influence on the responses have been mentioned: age-related change, time of measurement effects and cohort effects. Cross-sectional designs keep time of measurement constant, time series designs usually keep age-related changes constant by using similarly aged samples and longitudinal designs keep the cohort constant.

| 1989 | 1990 | 1991 |
|------|------|------|
|  |  | $F_{16}$ |
|  | $E_{16}$ | $E_{17}$ |
| $D_{16}$ | $D_{17}$ | $D_{18}$ |
| $C_{17}$ | $C_{18}$ | $C_{19}$ |
| $B_{18}$ | $B_{19}$ | $B_{20}$ |
| $A_{19}$ | $A_{20}$ | $A_{21}$ |

*Notes:*
A–F represent age cohorts
Subscript represents age at data collection

Figure 8.1   *An example longitudinal cohort-sequential design (LCSD)*

This means that interpreting data from any of these designs always leaves two of these three possible influences free to have 'caused' the observed responses and often we cannot tell exactly which is most influential.

The longitudinal cohort-sequential design (LCSD) attempts to overcome this by combining elements of all three designs into one much larger design. Some cohorts of respondents are studied longitudinally while other new cohorts are added at a later date for comparative purposes. Figure 8.1 gives an example of such a design from the Social and Psychological Consequences of HIV/AIDS for 16–21-year-olds study (Breakwell and Fife-Schaw, 1992). In this diagram you can see that age-related effects can be assessed by comparing longitudinal changes in different cohorts. For instance, is a change observed between $D_{16}$ and $D_{17}$ also present when $E_{16}$ is compared with $E_{17}$? Cohort effects are indicated if, at all stages in the study, the rank ordering of cohorts on a particular measure remains the same. Time of measurement effects can be estimated by comparing responses in cohorts across time. If some event has a broad impact on responses, changes between, for instance, $D_{16}$ and $D_{17}$ should also be observed between $A_{19}$ and $A_{20}$ and likewise in cohorts B and C. While there are more pure and complicated versions of this design (see Breakwell and Fife-Schaw, 1994) this basic model allows, in principle, the possibility of investigating interactions between these effects.

*Advantages*: The potential to investigate main effects and possible inter-actions between age-related, time of measurement and cohort effects are the LCSD design's main advantages.

*Disadvantages*: As with the standard longitudinal design, sample attrition remains a problem. This is even more apparent when you want to compare a new cohort, which has yet to suffer attrition through repeated contact, with an older one which has been depleted. Comparisons between such cohorts need to be conducted with considerable caution.

Although the LCSD is a very powerful design, interpreting analyses may be somewhat less easy than implied above. Often real effects are weak or interactions between effects complex. While there would be no scope for detecting them with some of the other survey designs, considerable analytical sophistication is required to make sense of data generated by such a design.


## 8.3   Sampling issues

Before commencing *any* study you should ask yourself whether the nature of your sample will matter for any conclusions you might want to draw from it. If you are studying a perceptual or neurophysiological phenomenon, you may think that all humans are likely to be similar and that any collection of people willing to do your experiment will be all right. For many such phenomena this may be a safe assumption, but there will always be the odd exception and the problem is that you may not know when you have found that exception. If you assume that any subject will be as appropriate as any other, then you should at least be aware that you are making this assumption. For most other psychological phenomena, *who* you study does matter.

As well as mattering from a substantive theoretical viewpoint, good sampling is required if inferential statistics are to be used. Many commonly used statistical tests *assume* you have drawn random samples and use **sampling theory** to estimate the 'significance' of any effects you find. Poor sampling introduces unknown sources of error into these calculations so that statistical results may prove difficult to interpret.


### 8.3.1   Standard errors

In most common applications of survey techniques the aim is to estimate the size of something in the population. A crude example might be to estimate the average adult female height and the amount of variation there is around this average. As it would not be possible to ask everyone, you would need to draw a representative sample of females and measure their heights. In your sample you would be able to find the mean height and the standard deviation quite easily. Let us say they came out at 64 inches and 10 inches respectively.

These two figures, the mean height and the standard deviation, are called **sample statistics** since they refer to your sample. Normally you do not really want to know about the mean and standard deviation in your particular sample, you want to estimate the mean in the population. To do this you treat your sample mean and standard deviation as *estimates* of the true population mean and standard deviation. These 'true' quantities are referred to as **population parameters**. While your mean score is acceptable as an estimate of the population mean, the formula for estimating the population standard deviation is as follows:

$$\text{Estimated standard deviation} = \sqrt{\frac{\sum X^2 - (\sum X)^2/n}{n - 1}}$$

The X terms in this equation are the raw observations (heights) and *n* refers to the size of your sample. You should note that the $n - 1$ term in this equation corrects for the fact that the variability of scores in your sample is likely to be smaller than it really is in the population. As sample size increases, so the impact of subtracting one from the sample size has less effect on the estimate.

Unless you have the opportunity to draw a new sample, this estimate is the best you have of the true population mean and standard deviation. In reality the true population mean might be 65 inches and the standard deviation 11 inches. Your sample, because it is a sample, is always likely to yield a less than perfectly accurate estimate of the population parameter.

It is important to recognise that *any* summary statistics, including statistics such as correlations, variances and regression weights, are best thought of as **parameter estimates**. The accuracy of these estimates, as with our mean height example, will depend on how well the relevant constructs were measured, how well the sampling was done and how large the sample is.

## 8.3.2 Sample size – the bigger the better?

When attempting to make parameter estimates, it is usually the case that the bigger the sample (assuming it to have been drawn appropriately) the better the estimates. As sample sizes increase the standard error associated with any parameter estimate gets smaller.

Standard errors of parameter estimates are very important for the confidence you can have in the estimates themselves. If you took lots of *random* samples and calculated the means within each you would end up with a distribution of sample means. In most cases this distribution would be a normal distribution. The standard deviation of this distribution (not the distribution of raw scores in the sample) can be calculated from information you have gained from just one sample using the following formula. The standard deviation $\sigma$ of the distribution of sample means is called the **standard error** (SE) of the mean ($\bar{x}$).

$$\textit{Est. SE of } \overline{X} = \text{Est. } \sigma_{\overline{X}} = \frac{\text{Est.}\sigma}{\sqrt{N}}$$

Again, this is an estimate of a population **parameter**. We did not collect all possible samples so we are estimating the standard error. As with standard deviation of raw scores we can use the standard error to indicate how likely it is that the population mean lies between particular values. For instance if the mean female height in a *sample* of 25 women was 64 inches and the estimated population standard deviation was 10 inches then the standard error of the mean would be:

$$\frac{10}{\sqrt{25}} = 2$$

We know from the theory of normal distributions that 95 per cent of the scores in a normal distribution lie between the mean and 1.96 standard deviations from the mean. In our example this indicates there is a 0.95 probability that population mean lies somewhere between 67.92 $(64 + (1.96 \times 2))$ and 60.08 $(64 - (1.96 \times 2))$. This gives us some **confidence limits** so that if we are asked what the population mean height was we can say we are fairly (95 per cent) certain that it lies somewhere between 60.08 and 67.92.

The standard error of the mean decreases with increased sample size. If we had sampled 100 women yet still achieved a mean of 64 inches and an estimated population standard deviation of 10 inches the new standard error of the mean would be:

$$\frac{10}{\sqrt{100}} = 1$$

Now we are 95 per cent certain that the population mean lies somewhere between 62.04 and 65.96, somewhat less of a range than before (3.92 vs. 7.84 inches). Note that we have had to collect four times as many data to halve the size of the 95 per cent confidence interval. In reality you will have limited resources, and drawing very large samples will be out of the question. However, it would be unwise to rush ahead with a study using a small sample if it was likely to lead to parameter estimates that carried unhelpfully large standard errors.

This example has used mean height as the population parameter of interest. Obviously this is not a psychological variable but the principles illustrated here would apply equally to any psychological variable. Any parameter estimated from sample data (for example, a mean score, a correlation, a variance, a ratio, etc.) will have an associated standard error (calculated with differing formulae) which you should always seek to make as small as is practical. The standard error is an estimate of how much **sampling error** you have.

# 8.4   Sampling strategies

How do you select the sample? This decision will depend on the type of measurements you want to make, the nature of the population being studied, the complexity of your survey design and the resources available.

The first stage in any survey is to define the population from which you want to draw your sample. This is a decision that should be based on theoretical considerations. For example you might be interested in the effects of youth unemployment on psychological well-being and thus need to study samples of employed and unemployed youth. Or, you might have a developmental hypothesis that some cognitive abilities changed around the seventh or eighth year so you might sample children of ages 5, 7, 9 and 11, etc.

For most sampling strategies you will need a **sampling frame** which is a list of all the members of the population from which you can then draw your sample. This might sound easy at first but practical restrictions often curb your initial ambitions.

A truly representative survey of employed and unemployed young people in the United Kingdom is likely to prove very expensive and even more so if you intend to interview respondents. Assuming you really meant to get a representative sample of young people, then you would need to be prepared to travel to the Scottish Islands as well as the Scilly Isles. You would also need access to prisons and psychiatric hospitals and then there is the question of whether people temporarily staying abroad should be included. What will you do about those who are seriously ill, or too disabled to respond or homeless, or, perhaps, cannot speak English sufficiently well to understand your questions?

Similarly in the developmental example, your theory is probably not restricted in its applicability to UK children. Developmental theories often attempt to be universally applicable and you are unlikely to intend to draw a representative sample of the world population of children. If you resort to surveying children in local schools can you be sure that they really do represent all children? Perhaps the local schools draw on predominantly middle-class or socially advantaged areas. Perhaps they do not contain many children from ethnic minority groups.

In both cases you would probably have to limit the scope of your study and restrict yourself to populations that you can reasonably get access to. Be aware that this puts restrictions on the degree to which you make generalisations based on your data.

# 8.5   Classical sampling strategies

## 8.5.1   Simple random samples

As the name suggests, the aim of simple random samples (SRS) is to achieve a sample where each person in the sampling frame has an equal chance of being selected for the survey. There are many ways to obtain a simple random sample (also sometimes called a **probability sample**). The first is to put all the names into a hat or tombola and simply draw out as many names as you need for the sample. This is reasonable when you have a small sample but, if you had a list with 10,000 names on it you would have to write them all onto bits of paper first and this could be very time consuming. You could number all the names in your population listing and use a random number generator but you must ensure that once a name is selected it cannot then be selected again. This is called **sampling without replacement** and is normal practice.

An alternative approach involves defining a **sampling interval** that you use to select potential respondents from the sampling frame. Let us say you have a sampling frame that contains 1600 names and you want a random sample of 200 to receive your questionnaire. The sampling interval here would be 1600/200 = 8. The next step is to use random number tables to select a number between one and eight to give the **seed** number to start with. Say you get a five. You would select the fifth person on the list, then the 13th (5 + 8), then the 21st (13 + 8) and so on. Strictly speaking, this procedure is not truly random sampling since once the fifth person has been selected the fourth and sixth cases cannot be selected as the order of the list determines who is now selected. However, for most purposes these procedures produce samples that are as good as those using tombola-type procedures.

*Advantages*: The SRS permits the full use of conventional statistical techniques. In many respects the SRS is to be regarded as the 'ideal' sampling strategy when parameter estimates are being made.

*Disadvantages*: SRS approaches are somewhat cumbersome when you wish, say, to sample from the whole of the United Kingdom. Interviewers would need to be sent to all corners of the country possibly to conduct only one or two interviews. While, generally speaking, an SRS will be representative of the population as a whole any particular sample may not contain people with certain key characteristics. For instance, by chance you may fail to survey anyone from very high income groups and this might be important if your survey concerned attitudes towards charity donations.

## 8.5.2   Stratified random sampling

The stratified random sampling procedure addresses one of the disadvantages of the SRS approach by initially dividing the sample into **strata** or separate subpopulations. In the above example we might use Census information to divide the sampling frame up into people who live in high, medium and low income areas (what counted as 'high', 'medium' and 'low' would need to be carefully defined first). Once done, simple random samples are drawn from within these three strata. The three strata do not contribute an equal number of people for the sample but a number in proportion to the expected, or known, sizes of these strata in the population. There are proportionately fewer high earning people than low earners and your eventual sample must reflect these proportions as accurately as possible.

*Advantages*: The procedure increases the likelihood that key groups end up being in your sample while still maintaining much of the random element that is desirable for parameter estimation. Stratification also lowers the standard error of estimates by removing the effect of between-strata variation (for a more technical discussion of this design see Moser and Kalton, 1971).

*Disadvantages*: In many cases you will not have the necessary information with which to create the strata. It would be unwise, for instance, to use foreign-sounding names as the basis for dividing population lists up in terms of ethnicity. Information on ethnicity is usually unavailable in population listings. This may well apply to the key variables of interest in your study.

### 8.5.3 Cluster sampling procedures

This approach gets over the difficulties of travelling distance and cost associated with the SRS approach by first selecting a smaller number of clustering units and then drawing the sample from within these smaller units. You might wish to sample schoolchildren's attitudes towards exams but it would be impractical to use an SRS design to achieve this. Instead you could select schools as clustering units. These would be selected at random and then all pupils within these schools would be sampled. For the purposes of increasing the accuracy of any estimates you wish to make it is usually better to have a larger number of small clustering units than to have a small number of larger clustering units. In this example it would be better to have schools as the clustering unit and select a larger number of them than to cluster on the basis of education authorities, say, and have to select only a few of them.

*Advantages*: Geographically large areas can be studied without excessive travel and subsistence costs being involved. These are especially useful designs in cases where sampling frames for all individuals are not readily available. A listing of all pupils in the country does not exist, yet lists within schools are readily available or can be created easily. It is possible to create multi-stage designs by selecting clusters and then conducting random sampling (or some form of stratified sampling) within the cluster.

*Disadvantages*: As people within a cluster tend to be more like one another than individuals in different cluster units, the standard errors associated with parameter estimates tend to be higher than with SRS designs. It is also possible accidentally to select clusters that contain no, or very few, people belonging to a certain stratum of the population. By chance, for instance, you might select schools from areas with few members of ethnic minorities in them thus under-representing that group.

### 8.5.4 Quota sampling

Quota sampling attempts to create a representative sample by specifying quotas, or targets, of particular types of people that need to be included to represent the population. As an example, let us assume we know that 50 per cent of the population in a particular age group are female and that 16 per cent of males and 14 per cent of females are left-handed pen users. We want a sample that is representative of both sexes and handedness, we decide on a sample size, say 100, and then set quotas. We need 50 males and 50 females. We also need to balance the handedness of respondents appropriately within the sexes so we set four quotas as follows: 8 left-handed males (16 per cent of 50), 42 right-handed males, 7 left-handed females (14 per cent of 50) and 43 right-handed females.

Once defined the researcher approaches people in the relevant age group, confirms their sex and asks them about handedness when using a pen. People become sample members as long as the quotas have not been filled. Once we have our seven left-handed females we reject any subsequent left-handed females that come along.

*Advantages*: The great advantage of quota sampling is that a sample that looks something like the population in terms of key characteristics can be obtained very quickly and cheaply. No population listing is required, only information about the population characteristics with which to define quotas is needed.

*Disadvantages*: All sorts of selection biases may serve to render the sample unrepresentative of the target population. People who are not physically or temporally near the sampling point could never enter the sample. The researcher might only approach people who look like they would be polite and cooperative. People who are not easily classified as male or female just by observation may be excluded by not being approached. If you have multiple levels of controls on the quotas (for example, male left-handers, aged over 60 with ginger hair) filling some quotas may prove very difficult.

Most common statistical tests in psychology calculate standard errors assuming the sample is a simple random one. They are not strictly appropriate for quota sample derived data. Moser and Kalton (1971) discuss ways of assessing the representativeness of quota samples and statistical procedures that are appropriate for use with them.

## 8.5.5  Theoretical sampling

Where the aim is not to estimate population parameters but to develop theory it may be appropriate to sample groups of people who are most likely to provide theoretical insights. A study on the impact of unwanted pregnancies using large-scale SRS surveying procedures would be rather cumbersome. Approaching pregnant women in local clinics and self-help groups would seem a more efficient way of gaining useful insights into the problems of unwanted pregnancy. This approach is common in qualitative research (Glaser and Strauss, 1967) and where statistical inference is not required.

*Advantages*: You talk to the people who are likely to give you the greatest insight into the research question. Travel and labour costs are minimised.

*Disadvantages*: You may not end up talking to people who would provide information that contradicts your theory. Other researchers may choose to dismiss your work because their theoretical sample supported a different theoretical position.

### 8.5.6 Other sampling strategies

**Random Digit Dialling (RDD)** survey techniques are rapidly gaining acceptability within the social sciences. This is really a cross between a sampling strategy and a data collection technique. Put very simply, a computer randomly generates telephone numbers and the researcher conducts a simple screening procedure to see if anyone at the end of the telephone is a member of the population of interest to the study. If so, a telephone interview is carried out. Attempts are usually made to make such procedures as random as possible and traditional objections to the technique on the grounds that not everyone has a telephone, while still relevant, are now regarded as less serious than in the past (Groves, 1989; Marcus and Crane, 1986).

**Snowball** techniques are particularly useful for difficult-to-get-to populations for which population listings will not be available (for example, drug users, cult members). In these cases, a small number of known members of the target population are asked to introduce you to other members who, in turn, are invited to nominate other members to help you. By this means you hope your initial small sample will 'snowball' into a larger one. This procedure may often be the best available to you though it has obvious built-in biases. You will only ever get to contact people who are in the social network you tap into. People in another network or in no network at all will not be sampled.

## 8.6 Where to get population listings

For large-scale surveys of the general population of adults the *Electoral Register* and the *Postcode Address File* are the most commonly used sampling frames. The *Electoral Register* is available in libraries and main Post Offices and lists people eligible to vote. Before using this list you should read one of the many sociological guides to its use (for example, Arber, 1993; Butcher and Dodd, 1983) as it contains some known biases which may have significance for your research problem.

The *Postcode Address File* lists addresses to which mail can be sent. This is available in computerised form which makes it convenient and it has better coverage than the *Electoral Register* (Dodd, 1987). As this is not a list of individuals you will have to conduct an initial screening survey to see if anyone in your target population lives at the address. Obviously some addresses will not be domestic residences so you might want to use the 'Small User File' which lists addresses that receive a small amount of mail.

Studies with young people may involve school registers/records to obtain population listings. While such lists are not necessarily accurate, these are one of the few sources that also provide the respondents' ages. Access is best achieved by an initial approach to headteachers though for a large study an approach to the Education Authority for 'in principle' agreement to release names would be advisable. Headteachers are under no obligation to provide these lists and they may reasonably ask that parental agreement is sought before any child's name is released to you. There is a degree of clerical work involved in collating such lists and permissions, so it would be appropriate to offer clerical assistance and/or money to pay for the clerical work. Most headteachers would like some feedback on the results of the study.

Access to samples based on hospital or GP records may be appropriate for studies dealing with health-related topics. An approach to the Family Practitioner Committee or the local Hospital Ethical Committee will be necessary. They will need to be assured that the study has some value both to the research community and, in principle, to the eventual sample members. Ethical committees may well demand design changes to your study before they agree to let your research go ahead. One of the most common requirements is that respondents give **informed consent** before taking part in the study (see Chapter 3). While this is ethically desirable for all surveys, research on medical issues usually requires greater explanation than is the norm in other survey topics.

If you intend to keep any information on computers about people you should register as a holder of such information to comply with the Data Protection Act. Most universities and health authorities have an officer who deals with registering users. Respondents have a number of rights under this act which they can exercise regardless of whether you register under the act or not. Registering will make it easier for you to know what respondents can expect from you in terms of confidentiality and access to the data.

## 8.7  Response rates

When reporting any study involving sampling, the response rate should be given. As you have no control over whether those approached actually help you with your work, the representativeness of your results depends on how many people finally took part. In general you should always seek to maximise response rates either by repeated recontacts or the provision of face-to-face interviewers to help people complete questionnaires they are having difficulties with. Sending reminders, repeat questionnaires or offering to return at a more convenient time will work up to a point but, depending on the research topic, additional contacts may serve to alienate people. In a sexual behaviour survey, endless repeated copies of an explicit questionnaire being put through people's doors may cause offence, for example.

It is good practice to report response rates in some detail by giving a breakdown in terms of types of non-response. Inevitably, some people will not be found at the address you have, they may have died or moved or the address may be wrong or the building derelict. It is reasonable to adjust the base against which response rates are calculated by removing these cases and reporting responses against an **achievable base**. These potential respondents were never really in a position to refuse to help you and reflect inaccuracies in the sample listings. Providing these inaccuracies are not systematically related to some characteristic of those incorrectly placed on the lists, this practice is acceptable. However, some others will be willing to help but unable to actually help (for example, being ill or unable to read). Of course some will simply refuse to help you because they do not want to for some reason. Record these different types of non-response systematically.

You must be careful not to obscure **non-response biases** when reporting response rates. Non-response biases occur when your data collection procedure systematically excludes certain kinds of people. An example would be travelling salespeople or those who work on oil-rigs who are less likely to be at their home addresses when you call to interview them. Be aware of such potential biases and acknowledge them when reporting your findings.

Technically, it is not appropriate to calculate simple response rates for quota samples. It is good practice to give an indication of how many people approached refused to help you, however. As you took the first people you came across who represented each quota and you may have unconsciously approached people who looked like they would help, then it is difficult to calculate a meaningful response rate.

There is much discussion about what constitutes a 'good' return rate yet there is really no absolute answer to this since so much depends on the topic of the survey, the design and the nature of the sample. Postal surveys of the general public can achieve rates as high as 80 per cent for some relatively innocuous topics yet they drop dramatically to below 40 per cent if the topic is especially sensitive (for example, sexual behaviour). There is a general tendency for females to be more cooperative than males and for younger people to be more cooperative than older people. Interviewer-based surveys tend to get better responses (by around 10–15 per cent) since it is easier to throw a questionnaire in the bin than refuse a nice polite person who calls at your door. Long questionnaires, those that take hours to complete, yield lower rates than those that take 20 minutes. There are always occasional exceptions to these generalisations which make attempting to define 'good' rates a very tricky business.

Too much emphasis on response rates can be misplaced particularly when it comes to the kinds of surveys conducted in psychology. Surveys of groups who are under some compulsion to comply (for example, children surveyed in school) might produce very high rates yet this reflects the quasi-compulsory nature of the data collection method rather than the quality of the data per se. The same applies to surveys of students. These high rates do not mean that the resulting data are necessarily more valid or somehow 'better' than data gathered through a more voluntary strategy. Similarly, studies can achieve high response rates yet produce questionnaires that contain vast amounts of missing data.

While not advocating an 'anything goes' approach to evaluating response rates, lower rates do not necessarily mean the data are worthless. It is possible, for example, to report **lower bound prevalence estimates** using information about the response rate to create alternative kinds of confidence limits to be associated with parameter estimates (see Breakwell and Fife-Schaw, 1992). It is also appropriate to describe the achieved sample as accurately as possible and compare it against known characteristics of the population (for example, by using Census data) to assess just how representative the sample is. Yet another strategy is to compare parameter estimates gained with your data against those achieved by other studies which have possibly used a range of alternative sampling strategies (cf. Fife-Schaw and Breakwell, 1992).

## 8.8   Conclusion

This brief review of sampling and surveying should give you some idea of the important pitfalls of the various kinds of design. The last decade has seen a growth in the number of psychologists involved in large-scale survey investigations and this trend looks likely to continue. Surveys offer the potential to answer a range of research questions that have until now remained in the realm of speculation. Surveys are now more cost effective than ever before and funding agencies are progressively more willing to invest in big surveys than at any time in the past. However, the value of such surveys will continue to depend crucially on good design and attention to the kinds of issues discussed here.

## 8.9   Project

Put together a research proposal for two surveys to estimate the acceptability of various different levels of increase in rent for campus accommodation. Assume your population is students at your nearest university. Work out the relative costs and practicalities of using a simple random sample postal survey vs. an interviewer-based quota sample survey. Find out the best way to contact students for the SRS procedure; you might want to contact them in their departments or perhaps at their homes. For the purposes of this exercise, assume that you would have to pay a student interviewer £5 per hour to do the interviewing. Work out all the details of when, where, how and how much for the two surveys. Try to aim for a sample of 10 per cent of the student body. Having worked out the relative costs for the two methods, think about which one should be advocated and why. Is the greater cost of one method likely to be offset by greater accuracy? How would you present this to the university authorities if you wanted them to commission you to do the survey?

## 8.10 Further reading

Most texts on survey and sampling issues tend to be orientated towards sociologists and other social scientists rather than specifically to psychologists. This should not prevent you reading them since the issues related to sociological data apply equally to psychological data. Moser and Kalton's (1971) text – *Survey Methods in Social Investigation* – is widely admired as one of the most detailed yet accessible works on survey design and sampling.

# 9 Facet Theory: Defining Research Domains

*Ian Donald*

## Contents

## 9.1 Introduction

Facet theory is a metatheoretical approach to scientific research that was initially proposed and developed by Louis Guttman in the 1950s and onwards. Since its inception the explicit aim of the facet approach has been theory construction and the discovery of laws in the behavioural sciences. It has attempted to achieve this by integrating three components of research. These can all be found in Guttman's (Gratch, 1973) definition of a theory as 'an hypothesis of a correspondence between a definitional system for a universe of observations and an aspect of the empirical structure of those observations, together with a rationale for such an hypothesis.'

Guttman's statement clearly emphasises the importance of the formal definition of the area being studied, and the integration of hypothesis and data analysis. It is the definitional stage that is often in need of a technique for making it more systematic and precise. It is to this that facet theory makes one of its most significant and important contributions.

The definition of theory provided by Guttman clearly points to the need for empirical investigation and the need for statistics of one form or another. However, the heavy emphasis on statistics, in most research methods texts and courses, together with the tendency to ignore content definition, needs to be put into perspective. Louis Guttman forcefully makes the point that:

> Those who firmly believe that rigorous science must consist largely of mathematics and statistics have something to unlearn. Such a belief implies the emasculation of the basic substantive nature of science. Mathematics is contentless, and hence not – in itself – empirical science. . . . rigorous treatment of content or subject matter is needed before some mathematics can be thought of as a possibly useful (but limited) partner for empirical science. (1991:42)

Central to scientific activity, then, is understanding and defining exactly what it is that is being studied. Despite the impression many students are given as undergraduates, being a statistician is not what will make them a good psychologist, although it may impress their friends and teachers. It is knowledge and a substantive understanding of their discipline that will help them formulate the precise definition of the universe they research, and it is this precise definition, rather than statistics, that is most likely to lead them to contribute to cumulative science and the development of laws of human behaviour.

The emphasis placed on the development of definitions and hypotheses *prior* to data collection and analysis is, of course, not unique to facet theory. For instance, the point was also made by Thurstone (1951), a major figure in the development of factor analysis, who noted that it was the design of experiments, which called for psychological insight, rather than computing, statistics or algebra, what he called the 'servants in the investigation of psychological ideas', that occupied most of his time.

Despite some major figures in the development of research procedures and analysis pointing to its importance, few attempts have been made to develop a method to guide theory and theory construction. For instance, factor analysis, which is also concerned about the content of domains, has little to say about what should be included in a domain or how it should be specified and structured. What is required, as others have noted, is a **multiproperty input logic** (McGrath, 1967).

Increasingly, psychological research investigates phenomena that are multivariate. To help with this, an array of sophisticated statistical procedures has been developed. But, the multivariate problems also require a way of defining them. Unfortunately this has received considerably less attention than statistics. Yet, as Guttman (1991) has pointed out, 'grand theories about relationships are rather useless from a scientific point of view if they do not include an a priori definitional system for observations'. What this involves is defining the boundaries of an area of research, and providing a way of expressing that definition in a precise form. Facet theory is the only approach that has so far attempted to provide a means of doing this (Coombs, 1983; Dancer, 1990).

It has been suggested that the basic activity of facet theory is common to good research in general (McGrath, 1967). However, what facet theory provides is a systematic means of both formally presenting definitions and guiding a researcher's intuition and intellectual effort. In the next sections the concepts and components used in facet theory to achieve this will be explained.

## 9.2   Components of domain definition

### 9.2.1   Facets

The starting point of good research is to specify exactly what the researcher's area of concern comprises. Usually this is done by researchers thinking of the issues that they want to cover when researching an area, and is usually an implicit and rather informal affair. For instance, in discussing questionnaire development, Newell suggests that

> it is important to explore the previous work carried out on the subject. This will
> not only provide a framework for developing questions . . . but will also ensure
> that the project can build upon previous studies. . . . A first draft of a
> questionnaire will be based largely on questions derived from previous studies
> and on *brain-storming*, that is, writing down all questions that may be useful for
> the study. (1993:98; emphasis in original)

So, the first thing that is done is to look at other studies and questionnaires and to borrow those questions that seem useful to present concerns; to these are added further questions that the researcher can think of at the time. This is quite a good description of the way in which questionnaires are developed in practice. It is, however, clearly not very systematic, and does not ensue from a clear a priori definition of the area of concern.

In facet theory the content of a questionnaire, the **content universe**, is achieved by specifying the major conceptual components of that domain as **facets**. These facets will precisely prescribe the boundaries of the research, define the content universe and are directly used to generate questions or observations. The process for generating the facets *may* be similar to that described by Newell (1993), but the result will be a little different and more formal.

Technically, a facet has been defined as 'a set playing the role of a component set of a Cartesian set' (Shye, 1978:412). This definition emphasises the roots of facet theory in set theory. A less technical definition is provided by Brown who describes a facet as 'a conceptual categorization underlying a group of observations' (1985:22). While both definitions are correct, it is likely to be more helpful to understanding exactly what a facet is if a more concrete example is developed.

Consider, as an example, that an organisation has just spent millions of pounds on building a new office block. It realises that it is important that the new environment meets the needs of its employees, but does not know if the new building is achieving this. Consequently, they commission research to evaluate the office building. Using the approach described by Newell (1993) the first step would be to plunder the many office evaluation studies carried out previously. This would provide several questions. The researcher would then think of some more that should be added to address other concerns not covered by those questions. In contrast, using the facet approach, the first step would be to discover the main components (facets) of office evaluation. This also might be done by looking at previous studies, and considering the theoretical issues and questionnaires others have described. Here, however, the intent is not to find specific questions that can be included in the new evaluation questionnaire, but to identify the main components of office evaluation. This process can be shown using the following hypothetical questions:

1  Do you have space in your office?
2  Are the lighting levels at your desk adequate for you to work?
3  From where you are located, are you easily able to communicate with your colleagues?
4  Do you have enough storage space around your desk for storing documents?
5  Does the building make you feel alienated?
6  Is the heating in your office comfortable?

The first task in facet theory is to identify what the components of these questions are. Looking at them it can be seen that some questions are about people's desks, others are about their office, and another is about the building. That is, questions ask about different **environmental scales**. Environmental scale might, then, be one component, or facet. A closer inspection of the questions reveals that some are asking about the amount of space there is, others ask about locations, while yet others are concerned with such factors as heating and lighting. Thus, not only do the questions refer to different environmental scales, they also ask about different aspects of the environment. This second component can be called the **environmental referent**. A further examination of the questions suggests another possible component, although this is not as clear as those already identified. Question two asks about the environment in relation to carrying out work, this also applies to question four. However, questions five and six are different. Rather than being about work, they are about subjective feelings. A third possible component that focuses on the outcomes or goals a person has in the office may consequently be suggested. This component may be termed the **focus** of the environmental interactions.

By examining these six questions, three components of office evaluation have been identified. Potentially, these are facets. Although in this example existing questions have been examined to show how facets can be derived, the same process could have been followed by examining some issues raised in the relevant literature, or by interviewing people in offices, and then content analysing their responses. At this stage a prospective user of facet theory might be wondering why they should bother with this exercise, rather than simply borrowing the questions and using them as they are? The answer to this should become apparent as the discussion proceeds.

To recap, basically, then, a facet is a distinct conceptual category describing a discrete component of a particular object or area of research. From the example discussed, three facets were identified – environmental level, environmental referent, and focus of environmental interactions. In other studies there would be different facets, for instance age, sex, ethnicity, or area of well-being may all be facets.

## 9.2.2   Types of facet

There are three basic types of facet – background facets, domain facets (sometimes called content facets) and range facets.

**Background facets** describe what may be considered the context of the study or its population parameters. For example, age and sex would usually be considered background facets as they are likely to be used to describe or characterise the participants in a study. In carrying out the office evaluation, for example, it may be that there is interest in a comparison between different designs of offices occupied, or differences in evaluations by people doing a variety of jobs. Both of these may be background facets.

**Domain facets** describe what may be considered as the 'body' of the area of interest. For example, the facets describing the content universe of office evaluation are the domain facets. In this case they will describe what it is that is being evaluated, for instance, the environmental level, the referent and the focus.

The two types of facet, background and domain, represent different foci for the research. In studying domain facets concern is generally with the internal structure of a domain; that is, what it consists of. Background facets are usually considered to discover individual or situational differences in relation to that domain.

**Range facets** describe the possible responses to the stimuli provided by the domain facets. That is, for example, the response of the population (described by the background facets) to the domain (described by the domain facets). When the range of each item is ordered, and ordered in the same sense (that is, has the same underlying meaning), it is considered a **common range** (Borg, 1977). As the common range defines the possible responses to the domain, it is an important facet in defining the nature and definition of the study area.

The importance of the range may, at least in part, be illustrated by looking at office evaluations. It is possible to propose at least two possible common ranges. If the study is about the extent to which a person finds their office satisfactory, the common range will, perhaps, be from 'very satisfactory' to 'very unsatisfactory'. However, if the study is alternatively about the extent to which people feel that their environment helps them achieve their goals, the common range could be 'helps a great deal' to 'hinders a great deal' in the fulfilment of their goals. These represent two different, although potentially related, studies. For instance, an aspect of the office design may be satisfactory while simultaneously not being helpful in aiding a person's achievement of their goals. This could be because the goal is not important and so easily satisfied. Thus, the two evaluations would be somewhat different, and that difference is reflected by the different common ranges.

Questionnaires using Likert-type rating scales are often used in facet theory. It is important, therefore, to draw a distinction between the common range and the rating scales used in questionnaires. While the common range may be represented by the response scale in a questionnaire, it is *not* simply a rating scale. For example, the rating scale of a questionnaire may be in terms of agreement with particular statements such as 'very strongly agree' to 'very strongly disagree'. Here the questionnaire item would be phrased as a statement such as 'The position of my workspace helps me to meet informally with my colleagues'. The participant would indicate the extent to which he or she agrees or disagrees with the statement. Even with such a response scale, the common range might still be 'helps' to 'hinders'. In these circumstances, the common range is embedded in the item itself. Clearly, when statements such as these are used as items, there needs to be careful thought about their wording to ensure that they share the same range. There are examples where questionnaires have been designed using such a rating scale as this as a way of avoiding the necessary care required to map each item into a common range. The consequence is usually a poorly designed questionnaire and difficulties with data analysis.

### 9.2.3 Elements of facets

Each facet, no matter what its type, consists of a number of **elements**. The elements of a facet have been defined as 'the different values or the points that logically and completely describe all the variation of the [facet]' (White and Mitchell, 1976:60). Basically, an element is a discrete component of a facet. For instance, male and female would be the elements of the facet of sex. Elements may also be numerical, such as intelligence scores. Usually, elements are not as obvious or so easy to define as those given in these examples. This is because facets themselves may be, initially, more ambiguous, the possible number of elements may be unclear, and whether an element belongs to a facet or not may not be at all clear in the early stages.

To return to the example of office evaluation, a number of hypothetical facets have been suggested. It is possible to develop these by trying to specify what the elements of each facet are. Starting with the background facets, people's jobs within the organisation, and the different types of office they occupy, have both been proposed as of interest. The elements of these now need to be identified. This may be done by obtaining a list of the types of job carried out by people in an organization, by reviewing the existing literature, or any other of the usual means. For the present purposes it can be taken that there are three job types: secretary, typist and administrator. Looking at the second facet, there are two types of design identified: cellular and open plan offices. These are the elements of the facets.

Three domain facets of office evaluation have been identified: environmental scale, referent and focus. Taking the first of these, following a review of the literature, existing questionnaires, interviews, and so forth it might be discovered that there are three levels: desk or workspace, office and the building as a whole. For the next facet, the various referents need to be identified. Again this can be achieved by reviewing the literature and existing questionnaires. In the example worked through previously, there were two basic elements: those concerned with the environmental **services** such as heating and lighting, and others that were essentially about **spatial** features of the environment such as storage space and locations. It probably comes as no surprise that this example is drawn from existing research. So, taking one prepared earlier, a third element, **social** (different people in the office) can be added. This element was not included in the hypothetical questions simply to keep the example down to a reasonable size. The final facet identified was the **focus**. Broadly, people's goals at work showed a distinction between those to do with work, and those that are less formal, almost emotional. Therefore, two elements, **instrumental** work goals, and **affective** goals can be proposed.

The final facet is the common range. Again there would be a rationale for the nature of the range that would be derived from a review of theory and previous studies. For the present the range previously specified, 'helps a great deal' to 'hinders a great deal', will be used. The facets and their elements are summarised below.

Background facets:
  Job: secretary, typist, clerk
  Office type: cellular, open plan

Domain facets:
  Scale: workspace, office, building
  Referent: services, spatial, social
  Goals: instrumental, affective

Range facets:
  Helps a great deal
  Helps a little
  Neither helps nor hinders
  Hinders a little
  Hinders a great deal

Of course, the number of elements of the range may be greater if a finer discrimination in people's evaluations were required. For those interested in the technical details and terminology, this collection of facets represents a Cartesian set.

## 9.2.4 Properties of facets and elements

The facets and their elements have so far been specified without mentioning the rules that govern what can and cannot be included. In this section these rules are outlined.

Each facet and its elements should be **mutually exclusive** in relation to the other facets and their elements. That is, the classification of an object as belonging to one facet should be independent of it belonging to another facet. For example, a facet of sex, with the elements of male and female would not be included along with a facet consisting of gay and lesbian, as if someone is a lesbian, they are by definition also female. This example will be returned to later to show how ignoring this rule would lead to definitions and items that would be inappropriate. The elements within a facet should also be mutually exclusive.

Each facet should consist of a **collectively exhaustive set of elements**. That is, the elements should fully cover all possible categories of which the underlying concept of the facets consists. Of course, it is likely that some facets will consist, potentially, of a vast number of elements. Consequently, the researcher may decide to exclude some elements.

The facets should **collectively exhaust the domain** of interest. This means that every component comprised by a particular area or phenomenon should be included. In the social sciences it is unlikely that the facets developed by a researcher will fully exhaust the aspects of the domain of interest. Initially this requirement is an ideal. However, as psychology progresses, more facets will be identified and so the ideal will increasingly be met. It is an ultimate, long-term goal.

The next two requirements are not specifically concerned with the properties of the facets per se. They are requirements placed on the researcher when he or she is proposing a facet study. First, the logical relations among the elements of a facet should be specified. Second, the logical relations among the facets should be specified. These two points relate to the second component of Guttman's definition of a theory. The researcher should a priori specify the expected relations between the facets and elements. Basically, this is a substantively based prediction of, and rationale for, the structural relationships within the data derived from instruments developed from the facets. As this chapter does not go into issues of data analysis these two requirements will not be considered further.

## 9.3   Mapping sentences

Once the background, domain, and range facets have been identified, they are linked together in a **mapping sentence**. Shye describes a mapping sentence as 'A verbal statement of the domain and of the range of a mapping including connectives between facets as in ordinary language' (1978:413). A mapping sentence is a concise way of specifying a content universe – the components of a research domain and the relationships between them. It should be noted that a mapping sentence represents a definitional system and it does not represent a hypothesis. However, to the extent that the definitional system is open to empirical verification it may comprise many interrelated hypotheses. As Shye notes

> Various hypotheses may be stated in terms of the constituents of a mapping sentence and its features: its facets, the relationships among facets, the orderings of elements within a given facet, the relative degree of association between items that are formed in certain ways from facet elements, and so on. All these can enter into the formulation of hypotheses. (1978:180)

As an example, the facets identified for the domain of office evaluation have been arranged in the mapping sentence shown in Figure 9.1. The background facets are included here at the end of the mapping sentence. However, they can be included at the start, or as is often the case, background facets might not be included in a mapping sentence. However, in any formal research statement or definition the population parameters should be specified.

This mapping sentence provides a precise and clear definition of the content universe of office evaluation, it defines and sets the boundaries of what office evaluation comprises, and what the boundaries of the research are.

Now the question of why a researcher would bother going to the trouble of establishing the components of a domain can begin to be addressed. Describing some of the advantages of a mapping sentence goes some way to providing the answer.

```
The extent to which person (x) evaluates the {REFERENT=R}
                                             {1.Service }
                                             {2.Spatial }
                                             {3.Social  }


conditions of the    {SCALE=S  } as helping/hindering the
                     {1.Desk    }
                     {2.Office  }
                     {3.Building}

                                                    Helps a great
                                                    deal

achievement of their {GOALS=G         } is----->       to
                     {1.Instrumental}
                     {2.Affective   }              Hinders a great
                                                   deal


where person (x) is a {JOB=J           } in an {OFFICE=O   }
                      {1.Secretary     }        {1.Private  }
                      {2.Typist        }        {2.Open plan}.
                      {3.Administrator}
```

Figure 9.1   *Mapping sentence for office evaluation*

## 9.3.1   Advantages and uses of a mapping sentence

There are many uses and advantages which accrue from developing a
mapping sentence. Even if a researcher does not go on to carry out data
analysis, the advantages none the less apply. Levy (1976), Guttman and
Guttman (1976), Brown (1985) and others have outlined what they
consider to be the principal uses of a mapping sentence. Essentially a
mapping sentence provides the following:

1   A precise definition of the universe of content or observation, and a
    succinct statement of the research design that is readily communicable.
2   Specific instructions on how to make observations; a template from
    which questionnaire and other observational items may be constructed.
3   An aid to the perception of systematic relationships.
4   A way of modifying aspects of facets or their interrelationships that
    facilitates the extension and reduction of the content of a domain by
    allowing the addition and collapse of facets.
5   A detailed definitional framework for the observations such that theory
    construction is validated.
6   An aid to the development of comparable and cumulative research.

All of these advantages can be illustrated and clarified by reference to
existing studies. The examples given below each illustrate several of the
advantages of developing a mapping sentence.

## 9.3.2   Extension and modification of domains

The first example is concerned with the extension and modification of
research domains. It also demonstrates how the use of facet theory can aid
cumulative science. The example will be drawn from work in office and
place evaluation. Only a brief account can be given here, but more detail
can be found in Donald (1985).

One of the problems that had been identified within environmental
evaluation research was the lack of cumulative theoretical development,
with each study or evaluation being made almost as if none had previously
been conducted (Donald, 1987). Following several evaluation studies using
facet theory, Canter (1983a) proposed a general mapping sentence for
place evaluation. That mapping sentence is shown in Figure 9.2. This is
called a **general mapping sentence** (GMS) for place evaluation because it
can *generally* be used for defining a content universe for the evaluation of
places, and is not specific to any one type of place. Consequently, the facet
elements have been specified in a relatively abstract form. The rationale
for each facet is rather detailed and so cannot be discussed here. However,
such an exposition is not necessary to appreciate the point to be made. A
full account of the substantive background can be found in Canter (1983a)
and Donald (1985).

Clearly there are similarities between the GMS and the office evaluation
mapping sentence shown in Figure 9.1. Essentially, the same facets are
present, all that has been changed, to varying degrees, is the content of the
facets; namely, the elements. In terms of developing a mapping sentence
for office evaluation, rather than starting from square one, it is possible to

```
Person (x) evaluates the extent to which being in place (p)

facilitates {FOCUS=F               } of his/her {REFERENT=R}
            {1.the overall essence }            {1.service }
            {2.the general qualities}           {2.spatial }
            {3.specific aspects     }            {3.social  }


objectives at the {LEVEL=L        } levels of interaction by
                  {1.local        }
                  {2.intermediate }
                  {3.greater      }

                  greatly facilitates

stating that it ······>          to            with his/her

                  greatly hinders

objectives where (p) is a place of which person (x) has direct
experience.
```

Figure 9.2   *General mapping sentence for place evaluation*

use the general mapping sentence to suggest facets that might be relevant for offices. Then all that is required is that the elements are specified in a form relevant to the particular place. For the referent facet this is relatively easy as the elements are the same both for the general and particular case. The level facet is a little more difficult, but still relatively straightforward. It will be noticed that in the GMS the facet is labelled 'level', and for the office mapping sentence it is called 'scale'. For present purposes these can be treated as the same. It does raise the point, however, that the same facets that at first sight seem different can be generated in two unrelated studies, yet examination of their content shows them to be conceptually the same. The focus facet is more difficult, and indeed there are some differences between the general and office mapping sentences. But, without going into lengthy discussion, it remains the case that a focus exists for both.

In addition to a general mapping sentence helping in the generation of specific mapping sentences, findings in relation to the particular mapping sentence for office evaluation, can be fed back into the general mapping sentence, and so on to other studies in perhaps different types of environment. This is clearly part of a process of cumulative development.

This continuous, cumulative development can be illustrated by showing how the original mapping sentence for office evaluation (Figure 9.1) has developed, following further studies, with the addition of a fourth facet. The new mapping sentence is shown in Figure 9.3. It can be seen that a **unit** facet has been added. Research based on the previous mapping showed that the original three facets were important aspects of the definition and so should be kept. However, a new research project required the consideration of group as well as individual goals. The existing mapping sentence contained the basic framework for evaluations. To address the new issues, all that was required was the addition of a single facet, rather than returning to square one. It was therefore possible to 'slot in' a further facet to elaborate the domain. Beyond the specific context in which the mapping sentence shown in Figure 9.3 was developed, the unit facet could be added to the general mapping sentence as, perhaps, a **social unit** facet with the elements of **self/individual, group, society**.

The place evaluation example shows how if there is already a mapping sentence in the area of interest it can be used directly to define the domain of another study. However, it is also possible to take facets from several different domains. For example, if a study of political attitudes was required, it would be possible to exploit studies in other areas as a means of developing a mapping sentence. To demonstrate how readily this can be achieved within facet theory, a mapping sentence for political attitudes will be developed here. There have been several attitude studies carried out using facet theory. A consistent facet, which is also supported in the general attitude literature, is **mode of attitude expression**. There are generally considered to be three different modes of expressing attitudes:

```
The extent to which person (x) evaluates the {REFERENT=R}
                                             {1.Service }
                                             {2.Spatial }
                                             {3.Social  }


conditions of the    {SCALE=S  } as helping/hindering the
                     {1.Desk    }
                     {2.Office  }
                     {3.Building}


achievement of the {GOALS=G       } of the {UNIT=U         }
                   {1.Instrumental}        {1.individual   }
                   {2.Affective   }        {2.department   }
                                           {3.organization }


          Helps a great deal
is ----->          to
          Hinders a great deal


Where person (x) is a {JOB=J         } in an {OFFICE=O   }
                      {1.Secretary    }      {1.Private  }
                      {2.Typist       }      {2.Open plan}
                      {3.Administrator}
```

Figure 9.3   *Revised mapping sentence for evaluation*

instrumental (action), cognitive (thinking and believing) and affective (feelings). These provide the first facet of the mapping sentence.

Attitudes have to be expressed towards something, the attitude object. Thinking about what it is that is done by political parties helps to define that object. Essentially one critical and perhaps defining aspect of the nature of a political party boils down to its policies. The important factor here is likely to be what the policy area is. Again, it is possible to see whether there are any facets used in other studies that may be helpful. The answer may be policy towards various aspects of people's lives that are part of their social values system. There have been a number of studies in the area of social values that include a facet of 'life area'. Levy (1990) provides an example of facet research in this area. The facet and elements proposed by Levy can, with some small modification, be added to the mode facet already identified.

The final question may be whose policy is it that attitudes towards are being assessed? As there are no mapping sentences for this some thought may be required. If the interest is in the main political parties in the United Kingdom, the final facet could be 'party' with the elements of Labour, Liberal Democrat, Conservative. The three facets are combined into the mapping sentence for political attitudes in the United Kingdom shown in Figure 9.4.

```
Person (x's) attitude expressed in an

{Mode=M          } towards the policies of the {Party=P
{1.instrumental}                               {1.Labour        }
{2.cognitive   }                               {2.Liberal       }
{3.affective                                   {  Democrat      }
                                               {3.Conservative}


                                            Very Positive

in the {Policy Area=L        }   is------>        to
       {1.financial economy}
       {2.public order       }              Very Negative
       {3.employment         }
       {4.community          }
       {5.education          }
       {6.family             }
       {7.health             }
```

Figure 9.4  *Mapping sentence for political attitudes in the United Kingdom*

The mapping sentence provides a possible definition of the domain and content universe of political attitude. It should be apparent how the existence of facets from other studies and domains could be readily identified and combined to form the basis of a new study. It is worth noting that this definition was developed literally in the time it took to type it, and with no experience of carrying out research in the area. Of course, those more experienced in studying political attitude could develop more useful facets and definitions of the domain. However, it still represents a reasonable definition for a couple of minutes' work. It also means that this study has facets in common with other studies, such as values, which would allow comparison between the two areas to be made. Exactly how this would be done, and how it would contribute to the development of psychology and the areas involved is, unfortunately, beyond the scope of this chapter. Also, further facets and elements could be added to this basic mapping sentence if they were identified or if the interest of the study changed. Having seen how research can evolve in this way, it would be helpful to move on to see how a mapping sentence can help with the development of research instruments.

### 9.3.3  Structuples and multiple classification

Mapping sentences provide a powerful framework for content analysis and for generating questionnaire items, and other observational data collection tools. The basic concept relevant to this is a **structuple**. A structuple is technically defined as 'an element of a Cartesian set; it is a profile composed by selecting an element from each facet' (Shye, 1978:9–10).

Each structuple represents one possible item or observation in relation to the domain. A structuple is constructed by drawing one, and only one, element of each, and all, domain facets in the mapping sentence. If, for example, a mapping sentence consists of two facets, A and B, and each facet has two elements – $A_1$ and $A_2$, and $B_1$ and $B_2$ – there are four ($2 \times 2$) unique structuples: $A_1B_1$, $A_1B_2$, $A_2B_1$, and $A_2B_2$. By generating all possible structuples, a complete multiple classification of the domain and the observations to be made is obtained. The full set of items, all possible structuples, provides the content universe of a domain. It is preferable when carrying out research that observations are made for every structuple. However, as Shye notes, 'there is nothing in the logic of theory construction that suggests that this must be so' (1978:10).

The office mapping sentence shown in Figure 9.1 can be used to provide a more concrete example of the process of developing items. From this mapping sentence it is possible to generate eighteen ($3 \times 3 \times 2$) structuples that can be used to form the basis for an office evaluation questionnaire. For example, the structuple $R_2S_2G_1$ can be expressed as 'The extent to which person (x) evaluates the space ($R_2$) in their office ($S_2$) as helping them achieve their instrumental ($G_1$) goals is ("helps a great deal" to "hinders a great deal").' Of course, this question needs to be expressed in appropriate everyday language. Thus it becomes something like 'To what extent is there sufficient space in your office to store the papers you need for your work?' Another example may be $R_2S_1G_1$, which could form the basis of a questionnaire item such as 'To what degree is there sufficient privacy ($R_2$) at your desk ($S_1$) to allow you to carry out confidential work ($G_1$)?' Naturally, while the structuples provide the framework for questions, attention still has to be paid to the wording of items to ensure that they conform to the usual criteria of good questions (discussed in Chapter 12). For example, they should not be leading or ambiguous questions.

It is useful at this point to return to the rules governing what can and cannot be included in and as a facet. It will be remembered that the facets and their elements should be mutually exclusive. To illustrate this, the example was given that sex (male and female) and sexuality (gay and lesbian) should not both be included as domain facets in the same study. There are theoretical rationales for this. However, to keep matters quite simple one basic reason can be shown by looking at what this would imply in terms of item generation.

The two facets could be included in a hypothetical mapping sentence for attitudes towards sexuality. The mapping sentence is shown in Figure 9.5. If structuples are generated from this mapping sentence it soon becomes apparent that there is a problem. For instance, a question asking about person x's attitude towards lesbian men ($S_1G_1$) would be ridiculous. In this example either the facet of sex or sexuality is redundant. It is worth noting

```
Person (x's) attitude expressed in an


{Mode=M         }  towards {SEXUALITY=S} {SEX=G  }
{1.instrumental}           {1.lesbian  } {1.men  }
{2.cognitive   }           {2.gay      } {2.women}
{3.affective

           Very Positive

is-----〉          to

           Very Negative
```

Figure 9.5   *Mapping sentence A for attitudes towards sexuality*

```
Person (x's) attitude expressed in an


{Mode=M         }  towards {SEXUALITY=S  } {SEX=G  }
{1.instrumental}           {1.homosexual } {1.men  }
{2.cognitive   }           {2.heterosexual} {2.women}
{3.affective

           Very Positive
is-----〉          to
           Very Negative
```

Figure 9.6   *Mapping sentence B for attitudes towards sexuality*

before going further that if sex were a background facet describing person x, there would not be a problem as it is not a facet that is describing the domain.

A much more useful mapping sentence for attitudes towards sexuality, that also follows the rules for the specification of facets and elements, is shown in Figure 9.6. Clearly this mapping sentence would generate more sensible questions. If the researcher's interests also included bisexuality a third element could easily be added to facet S. Note also that facet M has been drawn from previous research.

## 9.3.4   Advantages of using structuples in item generation

Using structuples to form questions in this way has many practical and theoretical advantages. It is readily apparent exactly how each question is different from or similar to each other question. For instance, the two example questions for office evaluation above differ in terms of one element of one facet, the scale facet. The first item has the structuple $R_2S_2G_1$, and the second $R_2S_1G_1$. This means that any differences in the responses to the two questions are likely to be a consequence of that facet.

With questionnaires designed without the use of facet theory, it is assumed, often implicitly, that the researcher knows what the difference between any two questions is. However, unless they know *exactly* what the components of all their questions are, this assumption may not be valid.

The use of a mapping sentence and structuples also ensures that all the basic questions that can be asked about a domain are apparent as the basic framework for each is systematically produced. Naturally this may be achieved without a mapping sentence simply by thinking of a list of questions. However, it is more likely that all possibilities will be covered using a systematic tool such as a mapping sentence.

Related to the other points, using a mapping sentence ensures that all the questions are exactly comparable. This is an important aspect of item generation that is often overlooked. Reconsidering the original hypothetical office evaluation questions presented above helps to illustrate this. To recap there were six questions:

1  Do you have space in your office?
2  Are the lighting levels at your desk adequate for you to work?
3  From where you are located, are you easily able to communicate with your colleagues?
4  Do you have enough storage space around your desk for storing documents?
5  Does the building make you feel alienated?
6  Is the heating in your office comfortable?

An examination of each question's content reveals that some are incomplete, and therefore poor questions in terms of the domain as defined. For instance, question one does not include the focus facet. Therefore, it is not possible to know whether people's answers to the question are given in terms of space for carrying out work-related tasks, or for some more affective goal. The same applies to question three. In this case the communication referred to may be related to work or be about general social conversations. Question five is about the building and the affective outcome of people's experience of that building; however, it does not include a referent element. Consequently, if a person does find the building alienating, it is not known if that is because of spatial factors, for instance its size, service factors, such as the lighting, or social characteristics including, for instance, the people in the building. Thus the mapping sentence helps to show that some of these questions are incomplete, thus ambiguous, and it also shows what each question lacks.

Knowing how questions differ can also be important when it comes to comparing results from different studies. This has been shown in studies carried out in the area of office evaluation. Donald (1985, 1994) for instance found that people's evaluations of their workspace were independent of their evaluations of their office as a whole. In another study of offices, Marans and Spreckelmeyer (1986) found that, on the contrary, evaluations of the environment at one level were influenced by evaluations of another level. How are these differences to be explained? The answer is that it is not possible to do so, because it is unclear what the components of Marans and Spreckelmeyer's questions are, and so it is unclear whether the questions from the two studies are comparable at a fundamental level. It is apparent that some of Marans and Spreckelmeyer's questions ask about the office and others about people's workspace. However, it is not clear whether there are any other systematic differences between them. For instance, it may be that the questions Marans and Spreckelmeyer developed that concerned the workspace also addressed only affective goals, and those asking about the office were essentially concerned with instrumental goals. That is, the questions may all have had two facets on which they differed, rather than the assumed one. Using a mapping sentence as the basis of the questions would avoid this problem.

Facet theory and the use of a mapping sentence to generate questions can also aid cross-cultural research, as well as studies comparing different contexts. In cross-cultural research a major problem involves the translation of questions from one language to another. The focus of the research tends to be on making comparisons between the two and more cultures in relation to their answers to specific questions. However, it is possible to make comparisons at the more fundamental level of structuples.

The argument here is that questions are a sample of many possible items thought to measure a particular domain. This being so, the individual, specific questions are not what is important. The critical factor is that they represent some aspect of the domain. It is the structuple on which a specific question is based that is therefore important. Consequently, comparisons may be made at the level of structuples. This in turn means that provided the structuples are known for each question, the exact translation of those questions becomes a secondary matter. At its extremes it could be suggested that there is no need to have the same questions in two different studies if the same structuples are present. Therefore the important task is to ensure that the items cover the basic structuples. Translating structuples, and mapping sentences, is easier and likely to be more precise than translating detailed questions. Of course, there will be some variance in responses due to the detail of the question, and so where possible, the questions should be as similar as the context allows. However, variance in the response to two questions sharing the same structuple should be less than the variance between two questions that have different structuples. Therefore, at a theoretical level, it is still the structuples rather than the individual questions that are of primary importance.

The generation of structuples can also point to areas of research and conceptualisations of the domain that may require revision and close attention. Shye made this point, writing that 'experience with applying facet analysis to research contents hints that it is useful to examine carefully all structuples that can be formed; often we would find that these complement the defined concept in an appealing way, inviting us to consider shaping the original concept accordingly' (1978:10). Essentially, this draws attention to the fact that the process of developing a mapping sentence, and then generating structuples from it, can lead to an awareness of weaknesses in the original conceptualisation of the research domain. For instance, a researcher may have an important question in mind that they wish to ask, but which does not fit within the framework provided by any of the structuples. This would suggest that there is an inadequacy in the original mapping sentence. Further, the mapping sentence may generate structuples that lead to questions that do not make sense. If there are a number of such structuples, it again suggests that there is a need to revise the mapping sentence. This was shown in the previous example of sexuality. Given that the mapping sentence defines the domain of study, this also means that the original conceptualisation of the domain requires revision. In effect, this process allows the *logical* test of the validity of one's conceptualisation of the domain before data collection. Of course, empirical validation is sought once the concept has been logically refined to an acceptable degree. However, a logical test before data have been collected can lead to a considerable saving in resources.

Beyond the systematic multiple classification of objects facilitating a clearer understanding of a domain, and facilitating conceptual precision, it can also prove to be more appropriate and fruitful than other methods of classification. McGrath argues, for example, that 'many theoretical efforts based on "Type A" vs. "Type B" typologies have failed to gain general usefulness because cases with the attributes of *neither* A nor B or of *both* A and B readily arise' (1967:194, original emphasis).

This may be particularly relevant in studies using one or other form of content analysis. Rather than an activity being classified according to one category or another, they can be assigned to structuples. This allows more complex classifications, while preserving the rigour and clarity necessary for content analysis.

Before moving on to the conclusion of the chapter an important comment should be made about the examples that have been used. Throughout the discussion of facet theory the examples have primarily been concerned with questionnaires. This is simply because this form of data gathering instrument allows issues to be demonstrated most clearly. Facet theory, however, can be used to generate almost any kind of data collection method, and is not confined to questionnaire design.

# 9.4 Mapping sentences and definitions revisited

This chapter began by discussing the need for precise definitions of domains and content universes. Now that facet theory has been described, and mapping sentences explained, it is a good time to conclude by returning to the issue of definition, and to be more explicit about how a mapping sentence provides a definition.

Dancer makes the point that 'introductory psychometric textbooks routinely state that the content of items comprising a measure should be viewed as providing a *definition* of the construct being measured' (1990:366, original emphasis). This issue was hinted at earlier when discussing cross-cultural research. It should now be clear that a mapping sentence specifies the definitional framework for the content universe and hence observations. Therefore, the mapping sentence for a domain provides the definition of that domain or construct. The construct comprises all the possible structuples generated by the mapping sentence. In terms of set theory, these structuples, and content universe, represent a Cartesian set.

The definition provided by structuples rather than the usual collection of items has advantages. For example, as a 'consequence of [mapping sentences] being *analytical* – and not merely technical or ordinary speech – definitional systems' (Guttman, 1991:48, original emphasis), they can point to missing ideas. Also relevant is the formality in communication that is essential to the development of science. Guttman (1991) has noted that in science there are three levels of language in which concepts can be described and defined. From least to most formal, these are ordinary speech, technical terminology and formulae. For science to be objective and cumulative, and to coordinate observations with theoretical ideas, it is necessary to use formal language. Through the use of mapping sentences, definition and the expression of the observational designs can be achieved with a high degree of formality.

Typically, when questions are generated to measure a particular concept, and so define that concept, they are usually framed in everyday language. At best they reach the level of technical terminology. A mapping sentence, as Guttman (1991) notes, is a formula, but written with the minimum of abstract notation. Facet theory therefore represents a scientifically more appropriate language in the social sciences for expressing definitions than the language of everyday speech than is the norm. To date, facet theory provides the only means that exists in the social sciences of expressing concepts and theories in a formal language.

One of the characteristics of facet definitions that helps them to be formal and analytical is the notation that may be used. At the most basic level, it is clear that this chapter began by discussing content in the form of actual questions written in everyday language. However, by the end of the chapter questions were being specified in the more precise form of structuples such as $R_2S_1G_1$. The power and importance of this should not be underestimated. There are other aspects of the notation of facet theory that are important, but they would take this chapter into issues that are not really appropriate for an introductory text.

Before concluding, a final issue about definition and theory needs to be dealt with. In facet theory the definitions of a concept or domain tend, at present, to be in the form of describing or specifying what that domain comprises. In that sense the definitions are descriptive. This can be contrasted with definitions that are concerned with process. The importance of a descriptive stage in definition and research has received growing recognition among social scientists (Donald, 1985). More broadly, the physical sciences usually have description of content as a central aspect to their theories before any discussion of process. In chemistry, for instance, establishing the molecular structure of elements, as expressed in the periodic table, which is descriptive, was necessary before understanding the processes by which such elements bond and combine. It is also worth pointing out that it was also by examining what may be considered to be the structuples of chemical elements that missing elements could be hypothesised and identified. If the social sciences have something to learn from the physical sciences it is the importance of sound descriptive definitions of domain and content prior to discussion and research of process. Facet theory is making a major contribution to description, and is now beginning to work on issues of process.

This chapter has concentrated almost exclusively on definition. However, once a definition has been proposed in the form of a mapping sentence, the next stage is to establish whether there is empirical support for that definition. To achieve this the interrelationships between items (structuples) is examined by analysing the data gathered using the various research instruments. The analyses that are most appropriate are those that reveal the structure of research domains. In facet theory the non-metric multidimensional scaling (MDS) procedure of Smallest Space Analysis (SSA), also termed Similarity Structure Analysis, is most often used to examine structure. The use of SSA in partnership with mapping sentences itself would require a further chapter. However, there is some discussion of MDS in Chapter 24. There are also publications, included in the further reading section below, which more directly discuss the use of SSA in facet theory. These also include an exposition of laws established in the social sciences using facet theory.

## 9.5   Project

To carry out a full project in facet theory would require data collection and analysis using techniques and covering issues that have not formed part of the discussion here. However, the task of developing a mapping sentence itself provides many intellectual challenges that may not have been apparent in this exposition of facet theory. It is by being forced to face some of these that it is possible to appreciate some of the rigour of the approach.

The proposed project is apparently straightforward, and is to select a study in any area of interest, and develop a mapping sentence for that domain.

There are many areas that can be chosen, for this exercise. One that seems to have some potential is personality another is the massive area of attitude studies. Once the area has been decided, choose a study to examine and improve. A good place to start is with the research instruments themselves. Find a published questionnaire or measure and look at the content of each item and try to identify what the components of that item are. You need to ask questions such as, do they have identifiable facets? Does each item contain all the facets? What are the different facet elements? Once the mapping sentence is developed, the items can be reviewed to see if they are all complete. Those that are not can be developed so that the full set of structuples is specified. If this procedure is followed, it is likely that the mapping sentence, definition and research instruments will be an improvement on the original.

## 9.6 Further reading

Canter (1985) – *Facet Theory: Approaches to Social Research* – provides one of the most widely read volumes on facet theory which has good introductions to various aspects of the approach. A special issue of *Applied Psychology: An International Review*, 39(4): 363–512, 1990, is also well worth reading. Canter (1983b) is a useful article.

There are a number of more technical texts on facet theory and its associated data analysis techniques. Borg (1981) *Multidimensional Data Representations: When and Why*, Shye (1978) *Theory Construction and Data Analysis in the Behavioral Sciences*, and Lingoes et al. (1977) *Geometric Representations of Relational Data*, focus either entirely on facet theory, or contain numerous papers on the approach. Levy (1994) – *Louis Guttman on Theory and Methodology* – has edited a collection of key papers by Guttman which provide essential reading for facet researchers.

# PART III

# 10 Psychophysical Methods

*David Rose*

## Contents

## 10.1 Introduction

Psychophysical methods are primarily techniques for measuring the parameters of the sensory and perceptual systems, and of mental information processing in general. However, they have also found application in the assessment of anxiety, stress, memory, criminal behaviour, social attitudes, advertising effectiveness, and so on. Additionally, these methods are increasingly used in personnel selection, for jobs where fine sensory aptitudes are predictive of success (for example, flying, military target recognition, detecting tumours in X-ray clinics).

Perhaps the commonest use of these methods is for finding the minimum intensity of a stimulus that can be detected, that is, the **detection threshold** or **absolute threshold**. Hence for most of this chapter the independent variable under discussion is stimulus 'intensity'. However, the principles can be applied to many other types of variable, both sensory (for example, line length, colour) and general (such as word frequency, facial attractiveness, salience, and so on).

This chapter first summarises theoretical understanding of what limits sensory detection, and then reviews the techniques available to investigate those limits. Later, procedures for measuring the strengths of percepts above threshold are considered. Finally, some general issues of experimental practicality are discussed.

## 10.2 Principles of absolute thresholds

I have often been amused by the reactions of novice students to near-threshold stimuli. For example, in a practical in which they were required to read words presented very briefly in a tachistoscope, some students complained that the apparatus was not working properly, because sometimes they could read a word clearly but on other occasions, repeating exactly the same presentation, the word was unrecognisable.

Of course, the apparatus was functioning perfectly; it was the students who were varying from trial to trial. People are not robots (especially not students); they do not function like clockwork. Their reactions to a stimulus are not exactly the same on every occasion. Instead, they fluctuate in their sensitivity. In the terminology of information theory, people are full of **noise**: random, apparently spontaneous factors, internal to the subject, affect human performance. Biologically based theorists ascribe this noise to the spontaneous firing of action potentials that occur along sensory nerves; but noise can also be regarded more generally as informational garbage (or information loss) at any level in the system. Some stimuli are so weak they are drowned out by this noise, and hence are not detected at all. Stronger stimuli may be detected, but appear more or less intense, depending on the amount of noise around at the instant when the stimulus occurred.

So consider first a subject's reaction to a simple stimulus presented briefly, say a spot of light shone briefly onto a screen, or an auditory tone, a touch to the skin, or whatever. The magnitude of the sensation felt by the subject will not be constant every time we repeat the stimulus. Sometimes it will be larger, sometimes smaller. If the stimulus is extremely weak, then on some presentations the subject may not notice it at all. Stimulus detection then becomes a probabilistic affair. The weaker the stimulus, the lower the probability of it being detected.

The probability of detecting any given stimulus can be measured by presenting that stimulus repeatedly and counting the number of times the subject perceives it. We then convert that number to a percentage of the number of stimulus presentations or **trials**.

By choosing a series of stimuli that differ in strength, we can estimate the amount of noise in the sensory system. Plotting the probabilities for each stimulus strength gives us a graph called the **psychometric function**. A typical example is shown in Figure 10.1. Probability of detection varies

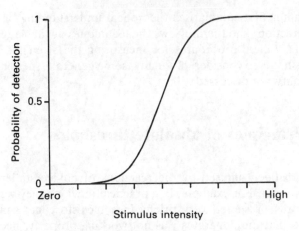

Figure 10.1   *The psychometric function*

from practically zero for very weak stimuli, to 100 per cent for strong
stimuli.

The notion of absolute threshold as an all-or-none detection level is thus
somewhat obsolete. Basically, it assumed that weak stimuli are not
detected because they do not activate the sensory system sufficiently; only
sensory events that exceed a minimum, threshold amount are able to pass
on to higher levels of perception and awareness. The word 'threshold' is
nevertheless still often used as a shorthand for the dividing line between
correct and incorrect performance. In Figure 10.1, the stimulus intensity
that would give us 50 per cent detection is conventionally defined as the
absolute threshold.

The slope of the psychometric function is proportional to the amount of
noise in the system. Steep slopes indicate low noise (a robot with no noise
would give a step function, changing sharply from no response below
threshold to 100 per cent responses above threshold), while shallow slopes
reveal the presence of much noise, that is, subject variability over time
(Treisman and Watts, 1966).

A problem with the above experiment is that, if the subject knows a
stimulus is actually presented on every trial, the subject will maximise the
number of trials he or she gets correct by saying 'yes, I detected it' every
time (or at least, 'yes, a stimulus was there'). Subjects are notoriously
obstreperous in this fashion: they will regard the experiment as a test, and
try to score as highly as possible, regardless of what you want them to do.
So the only thing to do is to introduce some blank, 'catch' trials, on which
you present a stimulus of zero intensity, and make it clear that responding
'yes' to a blank trial will incur horrific penalties, or at least a withering
glare.

Nevertheless, subjects still do sometimes respond positively to blank
trials, even when they are not trying to out-guess you but are genuinely
trying to respond appropriately. Why does this happen? It is because the
noise in their sensory system has momentarily risen to such a large extent it

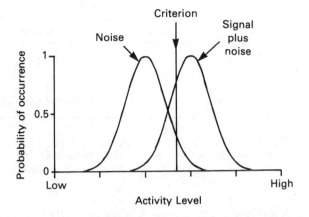

Figure 10.2   *The activity levels in the nervous system with and without the presence of a stimulus, expressed as probabilities*

is mistaken for the level of activity normally evoked only by a real (but weak) stimulus.

The situation that pertains in a sensory system during such experiments is illustrated in Figure 10.2. The noise in the system fluctuates from moment to moment, so the probability of there being a given level of activity at any instant in time is described by the distribution labelled 'noise' in Figure 10.2. A Gaussian curve is usually an accurate description of the noise distribution (Green and Swets, 1966). The sensory system normally lives with this noise within it, and learns to ignore it. When however a stimulus occurs, the level of activity within the system is elevated, by an amount proportional to the stimulus's strength. Over many, repeated instances of the same stimulus, the probability distribution is shifted to the right. This is now called the 'signal-plus-noise' distribution. It has the same shape as the noise distribution if (as often, but not always, occurs) the stimulus simply adds a constant amount to the level of activity in the system.

If the stimulus is strong, the signal-plus-noise distribution is easily distinguished from the noise-alone distribution, because it constitutes much higher levels of activity. When the stimulus is weak, however, there may be considerable overlap between the two distributions. What can the sensory system do to maximise its performance? If it ignores all levels of activity that are normally present between trials, due to the internal noise, it will miss many stimuli, that is, the ones that occur when there is so little noise that the signal-plus-noise activity is still less than sometimes occurs due to noise alone. If, however, it wants to detect every stimulus, it must accept lower levels of activity as indicative of stimulus occurrence; but then it will mistakenly respond on some catch trials, namely, those when the level of internal noise is high. According to **signal detection theory**, the sensory system accepts all levels of activity above a certain **criterion** as

Response

|  |  | Present | Absent |
|---|---|---|---|
| Stimulus | Present | hit | miss |
|  | Absent | false alarm | correct rejection |

Figure 10.3 *The four possible logical outcomes of experimental trials on which there either may or may not be a stimulus presented, and on which the subject must either respond that a stimulus was detected or one was not*

indicating that a stimulus has occurred, while all levels below the criterion are rejected as due to internal noise. The criterion is normally set to an intermediate, compromise level, above the point at which all stimuli are detected, and below the point at which mistakes are made on catch trials (Green and Swets, 1966).

Four outcomes from each trial are thus possible (see Figure 10.3). On catch trials, the subject may deny the occurrence of the stimulus: this is known as a 'correct rejection'. If the subject mistakenly says a stimulus did occur, this is a 'false alarm'. On trials with a stimulus present, denial of the occurrence of the stimulus is known as a 'miss', while a claim to have detected the stimulus is called a 'hit'. The probabilities of each of these four possibilities are equal to the areas under the probability distributions in Figure 10.2, above and below the criterion.

The stronger the stimulus, the greater the distance between the means of the two distributions in Figure 10.2. The symbol used to represent this distance is $d'$, while the criterion level of activity is known as $\beta$. As stimulus strength increases, the proportion of hits will increase, while the number of false alarms will be unaffected, if $\beta$ stays the same. However, one of the important postulates of signal detection theory is that $\beta$ can vary, depending on the circumstances of the experiment (see further, below). So when stimulus strength increases, it is possible for $\beta$ to increase proportionately, such that the probability of scoring a hit remains constant despite the now higher intensity of the stimulus. In that case, however, the proportion of false alarms will be seen to decrease. So it is always possible to disentangle the effects of the stimulus, in creating a higher mean level of activity in the system, and the effects of changes in criterion. The two variables, $d'$ and $\beta$, can vary independently, but they are related to the proportions of hits and false alarms. The values of $d'$ and $\beta$ can be calculated from the proportions of hits and false alarms, either by looking them up in published tables (for example, Freeman, 1973), or by computing the integrals under the probability distributions in Figure 10.2 directly (Rose, 1988). (These assume the noise and signal-plus-noise distributions have equal variance.)

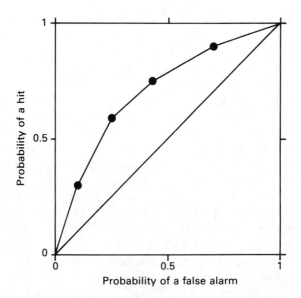

Figure 10.4   *A receiver operating characteristic for a constant stimulus intensity. The four points were obtained by varying* β. *If stimulus intensity were zero, the points would fall on the diagonal; higher intensities, and hence higher d' values, cause the points to move towards the top left corner of the graph*

A common way of plotting the results of such experiments is in the form of a **receiver operating characteristic**, or **ROC curve** (see Figure 10.4). This shows the proportions of hits and false alarms in the experiment. Changes in $d'$ or β alter the ratio between the two variables, but in a manner predictable from the theory depicted in Figure 10.2.

Changes in $d'$ and β can be deliberately induced by the experimenter to plot a series of ROC curves. Manipulating stimulus intensity will affect $d'$. Changes in pay-off are the commonest way of altering β; if the reward for scoring a hit is high and the punishment for giving a false alarm is low, subjects will lower their criterion, which has the effect of increasing the proportions of both hits and false alarms, at the expense of correct rejections and misses. Severely punishing any false alarm has the opposite effect. (In practical terms, if you are a radar operator watching for incoming nuclear missiles, you need to set a low criterion to avoid missing any. On the other hand, if you are out in a hunting party you need a high criterion for target identification, to be sure you do not shoot your companions by mistake.) β can also be altered by making the probability of stimulus occurrence (that is, the percentage of catch trials) higher or lower. A neat way of generating an ROC curve is to get your subject to rate the confidence with which his or her judgement is made (Green and Swets, 1966). This is equivalent to asking the subject to generate and maintain several different criterion levels simultaneously.

## 10.3    Forced-choice techniques

On every trial there has to be a method by which the subject can tell when the stimulus may occur; on a catch trial, for example, you cannot leave your subject sitting there indefinitely waiting for something to happen. So the trial has to be demarcated in time, with the stimulus presented (if at all) during that time. One way is to allow your subject to 'self-pace', that is, to start each trial by pressing a button, and the stimulus then occurs immediately or very soon after. (Self-pacing has the advantage of enabling subjects to rest, scratch themselves, sneeze, or whatever, whenever they like.) More common, however, is to signal the trial **interval** with another stimulus. For example in vision experiments it is usual to sound a (clearly audible) tone when the stimulus might appear. For auditory experiments the signal might be a light coming on. The subject thus knows when to attend and when to make a response.

A common variation on these techniques is to present two such demarcation indicators. These may follow one another in time, or may be located at different positions in space. The stimulus to be detected is presented on every trial, together with one of the indicators, and the other indicator accompanies a blank or catch stimulus. The subject knows that every trial contains a stimulus, but has to say with which demarcation indicator it is associated. This is know as a **forced-choice**.

So in temporal forced-choice experiments there are two indicators, separated by a pause, and the subject has to say whether the stimulus occurred in the first or the second interval. In spatial forced-choice, the indicators might be placed, say, to the left and right of each other, and the subject has to say in which location the stimulus was presented.

In fact, the number of demarcation indicators need not be only two (**2-alternative forced choice**, or 2AFC); there can be several, but there is always only one stimulus and hence one correct answer.

The psychometric functions derived from forced-choice tasks are similar to the one in Figure 10.1, except that the 'floor' is no longer 0 per cent detection. In a 2AFC task there is a 50 per cent chance of guessing correctly even when the stimulus is very weak, so the function increases from 50 per cent to 100 per cent performance as stimulus intensity rises, and the curve is compressed to fit between those limits.

## 10.4    Methods for measuring absolute thresholds

The experimental technique described above and illustrated in Figure 10.1 is known as the **method of constant stimuli**. It is the most comprehensive way of monitoring a subject's reactions to a stimulus, giving data on both threshold and noise (the slope of the psychometric function). Its main disadvantage is that many trials are required (plus some pilot trials to find which stimulus intensities to use). The probability estimates for each stimulus intensity should be based on at least 50 trials. At least four stimulus intensities need to be presented – excluding any on which the subject happens to score 0 per cent or 100 per cent, since firstly, it is then impossible to know where the function intersects with the floor or ceiling, and secondly, the data are usually fitted with a cumulative Gaussian curve, and this goes to infinity at 0 per cent and 100 per cent. In total 300 trials should be regarded as an absolute minimum for reliable estimates of threshold (and even more trials for estimates of noise). At (typically) 5 seconds per trial, this means 25 minutes of intense concentration by the subject. Even with frequent rests, subjects are unable to maintain a constant state of alertness for such long periods: fatigue, boredom and other extraneous variables will alter their operating characteristics during the experiment. In many practical circumstances, these factors are exacerbated: testing young children, busy executives or patients in hospital, for example. For this reason, other techniques abound that measure threshold more quickly. They do so by abandoning any attempt to estimate noise accurately, concentrating instead on collecting data near threshold.

First consider how one should collect data to give the quickest, most efficient estimation of threshold. In Figure 10.1, the threshold or 50 per cent performance level is the point where the slope (of a cumulative Gaussian) is maximal. In general, it makes sense to collect data near the point of maximal slope, because at that point small changes in the stimulus give the biggest changes in the subject's behaviour. Stimuli that the subject gets 98 per cent or 99 per cent right do not tell us so much about the threshold as stimuli the subject gets 49 per cent or 51 per cent right.

So, many techniques attempt to present the stimuli only at those medium intensities. The subject's responses during the experiment are often used to help the experimenter adjust, from trial to trial, the intensities chosen for presentation. These are generally known as **adaptive techniques**. Sometimes, these are used in preliminary investigations to pilot the choice of stimuli to be presented later in a full-blown method of constant stimuli experiment, but nowadays they are used very often in their own right.

At one extreme, the subject may be given absolute control over stimulus intensity, and the experimenter does nothing. Thus in the **method of adjustment**, the subject alters the stimulus, by turning a knob, or pressing at will two buttons that respectively increase or decrease intensity. The instructions are to adjust the stimulus to the point of detectability (or loss of detectability). This adjustment may be repeated many times, beginning alternately from above or below threshold, and the results averaged. Alternatively, the subject may be asked to track the threshold, perhaps oscillating the setting continuously by a small amount around the threshold. This can be a useful technique in situations where the threshold may be changing, for example in the period immediately after exposure to an intense stimulus. The method of adjustment is quick and easy to do. However, one can never be certain what criterion level the subject is using. Some, particularly naïve subjects, will refuse to admit they detect the stimulus unless it is clearly present, and will adjust intensity accordingly. Other subjects may move the setting to the point just below the level where the stimulus has disappeared. There is no way of finding out from the data alone what kind of strategy the subject is using. Also, the setting from an individual can be quite variable, perhaps due to the subject changing criterion during the experiment.

In the **method of limits**, the experimenter adjusts the stimulus in a more formal simulation of the method of adjustment. The stimulus is initially set well above threshold and is reduced in **steps** from trial to trial until the subject fails to detect it. The stimulus level at that point is recorded. The stimulus is then set well below threshold and its intensity is increased from trial to trial until the subject succeeds in detecting it. The point at which the subject's response changes is recorded. These descending and ascending series are repeated until enough data have been collected, and the end-points of all the series are averaged. It is normal to find some overshoot in this system, that is, the ascending series give higher estimates of threshold than the descending series. Also, subjects can anticipate what kind of response is expected in the next trial, since it is easy for them to work out the rules that determine stimulus intensity from trial to trial.

Another disadvantage of the method of limits is that many trials present stimuli clearly above or below threshold, and thus elicit largely predictable responses from the subject. In **staircase methods**, however, the stimuli are focused more closely around the threshold level. As before, the stimulus is initially presented above threshold and then lowered in steps until the subject fails to detect it. The next step is then an increase in intensity, but starting from the point of failure, not from well below threshold as in the method of limits. The stimulus level continues to be raised from trial to trial until a successful detection is made, and then the stimulus is stepped progressively down until the subject fails to detect it again. This sequence of ascending and descending runs continues, with the stimulus level thus oscillating closely around the threshold (Cornsweet, 1962). Figure 10.5 shows the typical course of an experiment. A block of trials may continue until, say, 10 reversals of the direction of stimulus change have occurred, which would take typically 40 to 70 trials (depending how large the step size is, relative to the subject's noise level). The reversal points are noted, and are averaged at the end of the experiment to give an estimate of threshold.

Staircase techniques are very common and there are many variations. The first is designed to cope with the possibility that the subject may anticipate the next stimulus; knowing that clear detections will lead to a reduction in stimulus contrast on the next trial, and failures to detect will lead to an increase, the subject may realise what kind of response would be expected on the next trial and respond appropriately. This problem is

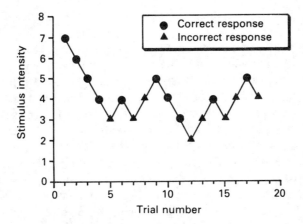

Figure 10.5 *Changes in stimulus level during a staircase experiment*

removed by interleaving two or more staircases (Cornsweet, 1962). In its simplest form, the first trial begins staircase one, the second begins staircase two, the third trial is the second on staircase one, the fourth trial is the second on staircase two, and so on. The subject soon loses track of which staircase is which. Better still is to pick the staircase randomly on each trial, rather than presenting them in strict alternation. With more than two staircases interleaved, the situation is even better. Moreover, these staircases need not be identical in terms of the stimulus tested. For example, if you wish to know whether red, green or blue lights are seen equally well you can present three staircases, randomly interleaved, one staircase for each colour. (Although the subject may know from the colour which staircase has just been tested, as long as he or she cannot anticipate which colour will be tested on the next trial, the results will be valid.) What is also beneficial is that the three thresholds will be assessed simultaneously, thus avoiding the possibility of subject practice, fatigue or boredom biasing the result, as they might if you tested each colour sequentially.

A popular variation is to alter the rules, so the stimulus intensity is not lowered every time the subject gets one right, but only after two (or three, or more) correct responses from the subject. (The subject still only has to get one wrong, however, to cause an increase in stimulus intensity on the next trial.) The effect of this is to converge the staircase onto a higher point on the psychometric function: for example 71 per cent for the two-down-one-up rule, instead of 50 per cent for the normal one-down-one-up rule (Wetherill and Levitt, 1965). This makes the staircase slightly longer to run, but has a number of advantages.

First, subjects are in general much happier if they know the stimulus they are looking out for. Presenting the occasional clearly-detectable stimulus helps, since it literally reminds the subject of the target. If the staircase presents stimuli that on average are detected 71 per cent of the time, this problem is reduced, relative to those with near 50 per cent detectability levels.

Second, some workers collect all the data from a staircase experiment and instead of simply averaging the reversal points and ignoring the trials in between each reversal, they use all the data to build a psychometric function (see Figure 10.1, for example; Hall, 1981). Thus many stimulus levels may be presented during a staircase, most of them several times over. This enables the probability of response to be calculated for each stimulus level. A collection of these probabilities can be used to form a psychometric function. By presenting several staircases with different rules, perhaps interleaved, for example staircases that converge on the 50 per cent level, the 71 per cent level, and so on, the data can be deliberately spread out to give a good coverage of the full range of the psychometric function (Jaskowski, 1993). (Using the method of constant stimuli you need to find out before the experiment what that range is; with staircases, the stimulus levels adjust themselves automatically to fill the range.) From psychometric functions, it will be remembered, an estimate of the noise can be obtained as well as the threshold level.

Third, with forced-choice staircases, the threshold measure obtained is often an underestimate of the true threshold (Rose et al., 1970). This is called **bias**, and occurs because of the nature of guessing when the stimulus level is low. Consider a very weak stimulus that evokes activity below $\beta$. The subject is then forced to guess which demarcation indicator is correct, and will do so approximately 50 per cent of the time. A correct guess has the effect of lowering the stimulus on the next trial, so the subject will likely have to guess again. The net effect is that the stimulus level drifts down well below threshold. (It is a fact that random guesses may carry on being right in an unbroken sequence more often than most people think; it takes longer than you would expect to even out right and wrong guesses.) So in the end some of the reversal points in the staircase will be much too low. The converse problem does not occur: correct guesses elevate stimulus intensity, so the subject soon detects the stimulus correctly without guessing. The problem of bias can be reduced by keeping the stimulus level up, for example near 71 per cent detection level rather than 50 per cent. (However, there is an even better way of avoiding this problem, which is to increase the number of alternatives in the forced-choice task to three or four, so the subject does not guess correctly so often.)

Further variations on the staircase technique are designed to converge progressively onto the threshold, by starting with fairly large step changes in the stimulus between one trial and the next, and reducing the step size as the experiment progresses. Thus the early trials direct the stimulus quickly to the approximate region of threshold, and subsequent trials fine-tune the stimulus closer and closer to the threshold level (Pentland, 1980; Taylor and Creelman, 1967; Tyrrell and Owens, 1988).

Staircases can, like the method of adjustment, be used to track a changing threshold, provided the rate of change is slow. If the changes are rapid, the only alternative is the **method of a thousand staircases**. For example, adaptation to an intense stimulus exposed for a minute or two usually leads to an after-effect that lasts at most a few minutes; tracking these changes cannot be done with a conventional staircase. Instead, the experiment has to be repeated many times, with sufficient time between experiments for complete recovery. In each experiment a number of trials (notionally, '1000') are presented, each at strictly the same time relative to the period of adaptation (for example the first trial might be 5 seconds after adaptation, the next 10 seconds, and so on). The outcome of the first trial in the first experiment is used to determine the stimulus level that will be presented in the first trial of the second experiment. The response to the first trial in the second experiment determines the stimulus in the first trial of the third experiment. Meanwhile, the second trial in the first experiment determines the second trial in the second experiment. And so on. Each staircase consists of a series of trials, one trial in each experiment. The length of the staircase equals the total number of experiments done. Each staircase converges on the threshold at the particular instant in time its trials were all presented, relative to the time of exposure to the adapting stimulus (Cornsweet and Teller, 1965).

The most modern **adaptive techniques** use far more complicated calculations between each trial to decide which stimulus level to present next. They depend upon theoretical assumptions about efficiency and the shape of the underlying psychometric function. The computer programs are, however, not necessarily long; for example, the best-known, Quest, contains only about 40 commands in Basic (Watson and Pelli, 1983). I cannot go into numerical detail here, but merely mention that the methods generally concentrate upon placing the next stimulus at a level that will give most information about the location of the threshold (see, for example, Harvey, 1986; King-Smith et al., 1994). This level is not always at the threshold, because (a) the point of maximum slope of the psychometric function is not always at the threshold (the underlying curve is not always a cumulative Gaussian), and (b) binomial sampling error is maximal at 50 per cent response levels, which makes response probabilities near 50 per cent less reliable than those at higher or lower values. The errors become progressively smaller above and below the 50% level. In two-alternative forced-choice experiments, a 50 per cent response level is expected for very weak stimuli, and in this case the optimal stimulus to present is somewhat above the threshold intensity. The optimal level in any given experiment thus depends on the number of forced-choice alternatives, and on the slope of the psychometric function. The number of trials needed to obtain a measure of threshold can be as few as 20–40 depending on how accurate you want your answer to be; the more trials, the more precise your estimate will be.

## 10.5   Difference thresholds

The field of psychophysics is not, thankfully, limited to studying absolute thresholds. We can also investigate what happens when clearly detectable stimuli are presented. The first question we can ask is, however, still one about thresholds – namely, what is the minimum detectable difference between two stimuli that can be noticed? This is known as the **difference threshold**, or **just noticeable difference (j.n.d.)**. The basic methods available to us include all those listed above: constant stimuli, adjustment, limits and staircases, with or without forced choice. For example the subject might be shown two spots of light and asked to adjust the intensity of one until it is just noticeably brighter than the other. The variable stimulus may be called the **test** or **probe stimulus** while the other, that is kept constant, is the **standard** or **comparison stimulus**.

The first parameter we can vary in experiments on difference thresholds is the intensity of the standard stimulus. In other words, we can test whether a weak, but clearly detectable stimulus, has to be incremented by a lesser or greater amount than a strong stimulus must be incremented, to enable a subject to detect the difference. This is the basic paradigm that led to Weber's Law, which states that the increment threshold is a constant fraction of the standard stimulus. So if a dim spot of light has to be increased in intensity by 2 per cent before the subject can see the difference, an intense spot must also be incremented by 2 per cent of its luminance before the subject will notice. Weber's Law applies to a large number of sensory situations, although the value of the 'Weber fraction' varies enormously (for example, 2 per cent for light intensity, 3.3 per cent for weight, 33 per cent for sound intensity, 0.3 per cent for sound frequency, 20 per cent for taste intensity). The Weber fraction rises above its normal value at very low intensities, where noise becomes significant (so a standard of zero intensity does not have a difference threshold of zero, but of the absolute threshold). The fraction also tends to deviate for very intense stimuli.

A second issue in difference threshold experiments is whether the standard stimulus is presented with the same time-course as the test stimulus. There are two common paradigms here. First, the standard may consist of a continuously presented background while the test is a brief probe presentation superimposed on the background. Second, the background may be set to zero intensity, while the standard and test are both (equally) brief; the subject has to discriminate between the two types of brief stimulus. (A third situation is possible but rarer: stimuli may be given for the same long period and the subject has as long as desired to inspect the stimuli before responding.) The first paradigm bears on many real-world tasks, but has some disadvantages: for stable performance, the subject first has to adapt to the background, and this often takes longer than is generally thought (this problem applies to the second paradigm too); and brief, 'transient' test stimuli might be detected by different mechanisms to those that detect continuously presented 'sustained' background stimuli. The second paradigm can also resemble some real-world tasks, but may run into problems about what the subject is actually doing. Thus it is possible for the subject to build up in memory, over the course of many trials, a representation of an 'average' stimulus. The subject may then judge which of the two brief stimulus presentations was most clearly the greater relative to that memory trace rather than to each other. In fact, some experimenters deliberately leave out the standard stimulus and merely ask the subjects to judge whether the test stimuli are above or below average – the **method of single stimuli**. This can give quite good results, showing that memory for the stimulus can act as a stable reference (Woodworth and Schlosberg, 1954).

The third point to note is that difference thresholds can be measured for decrements as well as increments away from the standard. These two thresholds are not always identical. For example luminance decrements are easier to detect than increments of equal physical magnitude.

An alternative approach is to present a series of test stimuli that range both above and below the standard in the same experiment. The subject is forced to choose whether the test appears greater or less than the standard. A single curve (usually, a cumulative Gaussian) is fitted to all the data. The stimulus level where both responses are equally (50 per cent) probable is identified and is labelled the **point of subjective equality (p.s.e.)**. The standard deviation of the Gaussian is taken as a measure of the difference threshold. This method is, however, used principally where the p.s.e. is the main parameter of interest. The use of a single cumulative Gaussian rather than two such ogives, one for the increment threshold and one for the decrement threshold, shows that the theoretical underpinnings of the p.s.e. approach are somewhat different from that used for assessing j.n.d.s directly.

## 10.6   Sensational measurements

A major concern of the early psychophysicists was to measure the strength of sensation. The commonest technique for doing this is **magnitude estimation**. Individuals are first shown a standard stimulus and asked to associate that stimulus with a particular number, for example 100. They are then shown a test stimulus and asked to rate the strength of that stimulus relative to the standard. So if, for example, they thought the test stimulus to be half the strength of the standard, they would give the test a rating of 50. If they thought it twice as strong, the rating would be 200. And so on. A series of test stimuli of various strengths can be used to build a picture of how apparent magnitude ($\Psi$) varies with physical magnitude ($\phi$). Generally, it is found that the relationship is a power function, $\Psi = \phi^i$, where

$i$ = 0.67 for sound intensity, 0.3 for brightness, 3.5 for electric shock, and various other values for the other sensory dimensions. Magnitude estimation is a simple technique which requires little training of the subject and yet elicits reliable data from an individual. However there can be wide variability between subjects, so many have to be studied if normative statistics are required.

A variation on the response technique is **matching**. People are asked to adjust the strength of a comparison stimulus to 'match' the intensity of a test stimulus that differs in some way. The setting can be made by the method of adjustment, or by any other technique. In **cross-modal matching** the stimuli are in completely different sense modalities, for example a spot of light might be adjusted to match the perceived intensity of a touch to the skin. However, it is also common to see **intra-modal matching**, for example, adjusting the intensity of a red light to match the intensity of a white light.

There are in fact two ways this procedure can be used. First, a range of different test stimuli can be adjusted to match the intensity of a standard. For example different coloured lights can be matched in apparent intensity to a standard white light. Plotting the data as a function of the wavelength of the test stimulus then gives an **iso-intensity contour**. A family of such contours can be plotted for standard stimuli of different intensities. For example if the white light is just at absolute threshold, then lights of all the other colours will be adjusted to their respective thresholds. The lowest possible contour in the family will thus be the threshold for light detection as a function of wavelength. For a comparison (for example, white light) stimulus above threshold, lights on its iso-intensity curve will all appear equally strong. In many cases (for example, sound intensity, black–white contrast), these curves tend to flatten out at high intensities, so perceived intensity becomes independent of the physical parameter under consideration.

Alternatively, the adjustable stimulus may remain the same, in all but intensity, throughout (in our example, it remains a white light), while the test stimuli are of different qualities (for example, colours) but constant physical intensity. This gives measures of the apparent intensities of the test stimuli that are more akin to those obtained by magnitude estimation; in effect, the subject is adjusting the intensity of the (white) light to match the apparent intensity of the test stimulus.

Another technique for scaling the apparent intensity dimension is **fractionation**, in which subjects are presented with two stimuli that are identical in all but intensity, for example, white lights. They are asked to adjust one of the stimuli so it appears half the intensity of the other. Subjects can be asked to quarter, or to double, the apparent intensity, but it is easier to stick to halving and build up a scale of apparent intensity by varying the intensity of the comparison stimulus. For some stimulus dimensions, **bisection** can be used. A stimulus has to be adjusted so it lies exactly half-way between two other stimuli. (This is more common for dimensions other than intensity, an obvious example being spatial distance judgements.) In effect, the subject has to decide whether the two intervals between the three stimuli are identical.

Magnitude and scaling techniques do not depend upon there being a linear relationship between perception and response. Any monotonic relationship will do. Another response that can be used under some circumstances is **reaction time** (RT). In general, reaction times decrease as stimulus intensity rises. This effect is clearest at low intensities; RT tends to stabilise at higher intensities. Measures of RT are therefore sometimes used to assess stimulus strength. The procedure is relatively simple: subjects merely have to press a button as quickly as they can when the stimulus occurs. A warning signal is usually given first, and then a waiting period of random duration before the stimulus is presented (to prevent the subject anticipating when it might occur). A lot of trials are needed for each RT measurement (of the order of 100 repetitions at minimum), and a lot of practice trials have to be given before performance stabilises. Moreover, it is problematic how to average the data, since the RT distribution is almost always positively skewed (that is, there are more very long RTs than there are very short). Some workers transform the data non-linearly, averaging the logarithm or arcsine of the RT; others use the median, or average only the central 90 per cent or 95 per cent of the distribution. Finally, the procedure requires stimuli with sudden onset, so sensory mechanisms detecting sustained stimuli cannot be assessed in this fashion.

In some cases, perceptual effects can be monitored by **nulling** them with another stimulus. This method can be used in situations where the perceptual effect is illusory, or a distortion of the real stimulus. Such distortions include those induced by surrounding stimuli (simultaneous contrast; for example, when a small stationary visual stimulus is viewed against a moving background, the stimulus appears to drift in the opposite direction). Alternatively, the distortions might be after-effects of adapting to an intense stimulus (successive contrast; for example, the motion after-effect). There must be a clear null point along the stimulus dimension, for example stationariness in the case of movement, white in the case of apparent colour, constant intensity in the case of stimuli that appear to be increasing or decreasing in intensity, and so on. The idea is that the illusory or distorted percept will be cancelled by the perceptual effect of the real, on-going input, yielding a percept that is at the neutral or null point. So apparent movement, for example, may be nulled by moving the test stimulus in the opposite direction and asking the subject to judge whether the stimulus appears stationary (Blake and Hiris, 1993). The dependent variable is the amount of real movement that exactly cancels the apparent movement. This technique is quite sensitive and is relatively easy for the subject to do. However, issues of interpretation arise, in that the test stimulus is not neutral, but is entering the sensory system and affecting it during the test period. There may be quite complex or unknown interactions between the system's response to the test stimulus and the processes within the system that are generating the effect you are trying to measure.

## 10.7   Some general tips on running experiments

Performance on novel tasks is not necessarily stationary over time. Practice makes subjects better, while fatigue and boredom may have the opposite effect. The number of practice trials that should be given before the data collection proper starts is an empirical matter: one should always check that performance has levelled off (or at least that change is minimal compared with the variability intrinsic to performance). The usual procedures of randomisation or counterbalancing of conditions should be followed to reduce the effects of residual non-stationariness on the interpretation of the results (see Chapter 4). Most psychophysical tasks are, in fact, extremely boring to do, involving intense concentration on a stimulus array that hardly ever varies. Motivation is therefore very important, as are frequent recreational breaks from the laboratory. Uninterrupted sequences of trials (blocks) should not exceed about 100 trials in length, or last more than 10 minutes. Successive trials may follow one another closely in time to speed things up, but subjects will be happier, and less likely to make errors, if they can pause at any time during a block for a rest. In many experiments data will need to be combined from different blocks; this involves theoretical assumptions about stationariness, but is usually unavoidable.

Other refinements allow for human fallibility. Subjects can make errors not just because of sensory limitations but also for mechanical or for other extraneous reasons. First, their fingers may slip or become misaligned when pressing the response keys, so they activate the wrong one by accident. Second, their attention may wander during a trial, or they may sneeze or be distracted. So in vision experiments they may blink, or allow their eyes to deviate from the fixation point; in auditory experiments the telephone in the next room may ring or their stomachs may gurgle; in olfactory experiments they may fart (well, the experimenter never does); and so on. There are two ways of coping with this. One is to allow for it in the data analysis, for example by assuming that the psychometric function (Figure 10.1) will never reach 100 per cent even for very strong stimuli, because of these errors (Hall, 1981). The curve can then be compressed so it asymptotes at, say, 99 per cent instead of 100 per cent (that is, assuming 1 error in 100 trials; other figures are of course possible if your subject is more reliable – it is a matter of judgement). The second method is to give your subject a 'cancel-the-previous-trial' key, so if a problem arises that the subject is aware of, he or she can press the emergency button and the computer will reset the values of all its variables as though that trial had never occurred. The latter method can, of course, only be used if the stimulus presentation order contains some randomness, so the subject cannot cheat by simply pressing the button over and over to obtain multiple presentations of the same stimulus before making a decision.

In detection tasks, an important consideration, as mentioned previously, is the subject's knowledge or memory of the target. Knowing how the stimulus appears aids performance and lowers threshold; uncertainty has the opposite effect. There are two ways uncertainty may arise. One is memory loss. This may be reduced by allowing the subject to see the stimulus consciously and clearly, either occasionally during the experiment (for example, by presenting a range of stimulus intensities that includes some well above detection threshold) or deliberately at the beginning of each block of trials. Some workers present a supra-threshold stimulus before every trial in the experiment; however this is dangerous, because that stimulus could easily mask the near-threshold test stimulus that follows it, or it may cause adaptation, or it may have unknown effects on memory (is it a sensory buffer, working memory or long-term memory that needs to be activated? Will it cause retinal after-images in visual experiments?).

The second common source of uncertainty is the random mixing of different stimuli within the same block of trials. Thresholds are higher when the subject knows that the stimulus on any given trial may take one of two (or more) forms, such as different colours of lights, rather than all the stimuli being the same (apart, of course, from intensity). In fact the more uncertain the subject, the worse performance gets for each stimulus individually.

Knowledge of results, or feedback, is also important. Subjects perform better and more stably when they receive feedback. This is usually given in the form of a brief indicator as to whether they were right or wrong on the previous trial. For example, in an experiment on vision, a tone may sound only after correct trials (a tone that is clearly different from the tone that demarcated the observation interval), or there may be two different tones, for correct and incorrect trials.

## 10.8  Project: visual acuity

What is the finest detail that the human eye can resolve? The question is asked every day, by opticians up and down the country, when they use letter charts to test visual acuity. In scientific practice, however, it is commoner to use a simpler stimulus than a letter chart; one example is a grating stimulus made of parallel light and dark lines. Figure 10.6 shows a grating, together with a fine checkerboard. When viewed from only a short distance, the checkerboard will blur into a uniform grey colour, while the

Figure 10.6 *A grating (test) stimulus and a comparison patch. Note that the comparison is printed here as a fine checkerboard so that when copied, the average luminance of the two patches will be the same. If we had printed a uniform grey comparison patch, your copying device might not reproduce it at the correct luminance, so from a distance the two patches would be distinguishable by their apparent brightness, instead of by the visibility or invisibility of the individual bars of the grating*

bars of the grating are still visible. Seen from a much greater distance, the individual bars of the grating will cease to be resolvable, and the grating will also look like a uniform grey rectangle, identical to the grey patch formed from the checkerboard. The task is to find the point at which the two stimuli become identical in appearance, where the bars of the grating are too fine to resolve.

Copy the stimuli in Figure 10.6, and use them to find the limit of visual resolution by using one of the absolute threshold techniques described above. The easiest way to do this is to alter the viewing distance, by moving (either the subject or the stimulus) forwards and backwards. At each distance the subject must make a forced-choice decision as to which patch is the grating (this is a 2AFC task). The experimenter should rotate the stimuli by 180° randomly from trial to trial so the subject cannot tell which patch is which except by perceiving the bars. (The two stimuli may be presented one above the other as shown here, or rotated 90° so the correct answer becomes 'left' or 'right'.) Alter the viewing distance according to the psychophysical method chosen, and thus find the resolution limit, that is, the maximal visual acuity.

The answer should be expressed as the number of cycles of grating per degree of visual angle subtended at the eye. One 'cycle' equals the width of one black plus one white bar: the grating patch shown here contains 19.5 such cycles. The visual angle subtended at the eye is the angle whose tangent equals the width of the whole grating in centimetres divided by the threshold viewing distance in centimetres. Divide 19.5 by that angle (in degrees). The answer should be in the range 40 to 60 cycles per degree, for normal vision.

The above method is slightly loose in that the overall dimensions of the stimuli vary with viewing distance. A better method would be to make several copies of the stimuli, each at a different magnification; this can be done easily on some modern photocopiers, or by a photographic enlargement technique. The stimuli should then be cut down so they are all the same overall size. They can then all be viewed from just one distance. (The calculation of visual acuity must then take account of the fact that there are fewer bar cycles in the stimuli.)

## 10.9   Further reading

Gescheider (1985) *Psychophysics* is a detailed but clear exposition, especially of signal detection theory and magnitude estimation. Kling and Riggs (1972) *Experimental Psychology* contains two good chapters on psychophysical methods by T. Engen. Matlin and Foley (1992) *Sensation and Perception* is an introductory textbook with a clear opening chapter on psychophysical methods. Sekuler and Blake (1994) *Perception* is an excellent textbook with a useful appendix introducing psychophysical methods.

# 11   Psychophysiological Methods

*Paul Barrett*

## Contents

## 11.1   What is psychophysiology?

Specifically, the field of psychophysiology is concerned with the manipulation of psychological variables and their corresponding observed effects on physiological processes. Basically, psychophysiology is concerned with observing the interactions between physiological and psychological phenomena. More generally, psychophysiology can be said to encompass both the study of behavioural consequences of physiological properties of the body at a biochemical and anatomical level, and the effects of behaviour on these same physiological properties.

This chapter aims to provide the reader with an understanding of the breadth of possibilities in psychophysiological work. The tone of this chapter is less discursive and more didactic than many of the other chapters in this book. It is intended to serve as an appetite whetter for those readers who may wish to pursue this kind of research.

Much of psychophysiological investigation is concerned with examining the concepts of emotion, behavioural states, stress, cognitive task performance, personality, and intelligence. In each case, the relationships between psychological factors, stimulus perception and recognition, situational indices, and physiological response, are used in an attempt to shed light on the initiation, execution, maintenance and termination of behavioural events. Ultimately, the field can be partitioned into six major areas of endeavour.

### 11.1.1  Social psychophysiology

Social psychophysiology is the study of the interactions between physiology and behaviour when those behaviours are involved in social processes. For example, the investigation of non-verbal communication and group dynamics by observing the interplay between various behaviours and each individual's dynamic physiological changes such as pupil size, muscle tone and skin electrical resistance (see for example, Birnbaumer and Ohman, 1993; Blascovich and Kelsey, 1990; Wagner and Manstead, 1989).

### 11.1.2  Developmental psychophysiology

This is the study of the ageing process, looking specifically at how changing properties of physiological systems and anatomical structures affect behaviour. In addition, the changing nature of the interaction between the psychological and physiological factors is also examined. For example, a developmental study may examine the ability of infants to behaviourally show preferences for certain objects, examining also the 'orienting' response as measured by various non-invasive nervous system parameters (see for example, Gibson and Peterson, 1991).

### 11.1.3  Cognitive psychophysiology

This concerns the relationship between information processing and physiology (see Jennings and Coles, 1991). That is, examining the relationships between cognitive task performance and physiological events. For example, looking at how the level of attentional focus of an individual may be associated with particular features of brain electrical activity.

### 11.1.4   Clinical psychophysiology

This is the study of psychological disorders and their relationship with physiological functioning and malfunctioning (see for example, Halliday et al., 1987). In addition, this area is also concerned with the examination of the effectiveness of treatment regimes and drug effects on the psychological behaviour and affect of the individual. For example, in looking at chronic depression, it is sometimes useful to look at the benefits of any treatment applied both in terms of the behavioural outcomes and in the changed nature of physiological parameters such as brain activity, sympathetic nervous system responsivity, and biochemical substance assays (Carlson et al., 1993).

### 11.1.5   Applied psychophysiology

This area is involved with the application of psychophysiological techniques and findings to occupational, recreational, clinical and other areas of interest. For example, the monitoring of certain physiological activity within an individual and providing instant and appropriate feedback of this activity is known as biofeedback. This technique is used as an aid for relaxation therapy, stuttering, respiration control and a variety of other practical problems whose treatment may be amenable to self-control therapeutic techniques (Forgays et al., 1992).

### 11.1.6   Individual differences

This is a relatively new area that looks specifically at the relation of physiological processes and anatomical structures to measures of personality and intelligence (generally defined by psychometric measures, for example, Gale and Eysenck, 1993). These measures may be of typically dynamic psychophysiological form, such as the relationship between the overall amplitude of brain-evoked potentials to varying levels of stimulation, and introversion–extroversion (the augmenting–reducing phenomenon), or may quantify aspects of anatomical physiology and relate these to the psychometric or psychological indices, for example, from histological surveys of human cadavers, the number of dendrites and their length correlate positively with the level of education attainment within individuals.

## 11.2   The principal areas of physiological data acquisition

This section is a brief résumé of important facts and information surrounding the quantification of parameters describing the function of particular physiological structures and systems. It is not intended to be a comprehensive overview but rather a snapshot of the diversity and richness of the measurement process in psychophysiology.

## 11.2.1 Muscle activity

*Abbreviation*: Electromyographic (EMG) activity

*What is measured*: The electrical potentials that are associated with contractions of muscle fibres. These potentials are brief impulses lasting between 1 and 5 milliseconds (ms).

*Transducers*: These vary from invasive needle electrodes inserted into muscle tissue and recording individual fibre potentials, to non-invasive surface electrodes that are glued to the skin above the particular muscle of interest, recording the mass action of muscle fibre groups.

*Signal properties*: The amplitude of recorded signals can vary between about 1 and 1000 microvolts ($\mu$v), although recordings of less than 20 $\mu$v are difficult to obtain. The frequency of the electrical impulses can be anywhere between 20 and 1000 Hz.

*Quantitative measures*: These vary depending upon the focus of investigation. For example, when looking at the behaviour of a single nerve fibre or homogeneous group of fibres, the single or compound (many fibres) action potential may be measured in response to a precise, targeted stimulus such as a small electric shock. Measures extracted from this potential include those of impulse amplitude and nerve conduction velocity. Alternatively, when looking at long-term activity of muscle fibres, integrated amplitude, frequency of nerve firing (impulses) and gradients of frequency responses may be examined.

## 11.2.2 Sweat gland activity

*Abbreviations*: Electrodermal activity (EDA) or galvanic skin response (GSR)

*What is measured*: The electrical properties of the skin that are associated with eccrine sweat gland activity. This activity is responsive to changes in emotionality and cognitive activity in general. Electrical activity can be recorded by measuring the voltage potential between an electrode over an 'active' site and a reference electrode on an inert site. These are called **skin potentials**. Alternatively, by imposing a constant voltage across the electrodes, across the surface of the skin, the current between these electrodes can be measured. This current is indexing the conductivity of the skin between the two electrodes. Alternatively, a constant current may be maintained between the two electrodes by constantly adjusting the voltage, this voltage adjustment indexing skin resistivity. Both momentary fluctuations (phasic) and relatively stable measures (tonic) can be recorded.

*Transducers*: Two non-invasive, metallic, surface electrodes generally placed on either the palm or fingers of one hand.

*Signal properties*: If measuring skin potentials, the voltage amplitude between the two electrodes may be recorded. Normally this ranges between about 1 to 6 millivolts (mv). If measuring **skin resistance**, then given a baseline level of resistance around 100 k$\Omega$, values ranging around this baseline level between 0.1 to 50 kohm (k$\Omega$) may be observed. That is, given a relatively stable level of resistance of about 100 k$\Omega$ to the passage of electric current through the surface of the skin, variability of resistance around this baseline value can reach up to 50 k$\Omega$ or more in magnitude (ranging between 50 and 110 k$\Omega$). **Skin conductance** is generally measured in microSiemens ($\mu$S = $\Omega^{-1}$). Given a baseline level of conductivity of 10 $\mu$S, conductivity can be seen to vary generally between about 8 $\mu$S and 20 $\mu$S. A typical response duration would be between about 1 and 3 seconds. Of course, these example values will be heavily dependent on the type of experimental conditions used to elicit changes in potential, resistivity, and conductivity.

*Quantitative measures*: Basically, these are measures of response waveform amplitude and latency, rise/fall times, and frequency of responses. In addition, gradients over time of these measures can be analysed, as in the case of habituation of response amplitude to repetitive stimuli.

### 11.2.3 Eye movements – pupillary response

*Abbreviations*: Pupillary response (PR) and electro-oculography (EOG).

*What is measured*: Pupillography or pupillometry is the measurement of pupil diameter using low-level infrared light reflected from the surface of the eye. EOG is the term that describes the measurement of eye movements, indexed by the change in voltage potential between the positive cornea and negative retinal segment of the eye. In addition to PR and EOG, eyeblink rate and duration can also be measured.

*Transducers*: For PR, an individual's eyes are illuminated by low-level infrared light. A low light level video-camera is used to record pupil size, with digital signal processing of the video images to provide a continuous measurement of pupil diameter. EOG uses non-invasive pairs of electrodes placed around the eye. Electrodes placed at the side of the eye record horizontal movement, those placed above and below the eye record vertical movement.

*Signal properties*: In PR, pupil diameter changes can be measured over a 0.5 mm to 10 mm range. Spontaneous, continuous pupil size changes vary around 1 mm or so. EOG amplitude varies between about 0.4 to 1 mv. Currently, EOG signals can record movement up to 70° from a central position with a resolution of 1.5°. Eyeblink duration is generally seen to fall between 100 and 400 ms, with rates heavily dependent upon specific situational factors.

*Quantitative measures*: For PR, measures encompass pupil diameter and rate of change in diameter in response to either a specific stimulus or longer-term emotional state. EOG measures encompass eye movement speed, direction, type (smooth pursuit as in tracking tasks or fast saccades as in reading or examining a static stimulus), eyeblink rate and duration.

## 11.2.4   Cardiac response and blood pressure

*Abbreviations*: Electrocardiography (ECG) and blood pressure (BP)

*What is measured*: ECG is the recording of the electrical potentials generated by the heart muscles over the period of one heartbeat. The **PQRST complex** is the labelling applied to the electrical waveform produced by the sequence of contractile responses in a heartbeat. The P-wave is the small change in potential caused by the initial excitation of the atrial (upper heart chambers) muscles just prior to their contraction. The QRS complex represents the contraction of the left and right ventricular (lower chambers of the heart) muscles that pump blood from the ventricular chambers to the lungs and rest of the body. The R-wave is the point of maximum ventricular excitation. The T-wave indicates repolarisation of ventricular muscle. The term **systole** is used to describe the atrial and ventricular contraction phases (P-S) and **diastole** to describe the relaxation phase (T-P) of the passive filling of the atria and ventricles. Blood pressure measurement is based upon the measurement of the systolic and diastolic phase wavefronts in the blood moving through the arteries. Blood volume measurement assesses the amounts of blood that are present in various areas of the body during particular activities.

*Transducers*: For ECG, surface electrodes can be placed on the wrist, ankle, neck or chest. For the measurement of blood pressure, a **sphygmo-manometer** (pressure cuff) and stethoscope is used to detect the systolic and diastolic pressures. For blood volume measurements, conventionally a photoplethysmograph is used to detect the amount of blood passing in tissue directly below the sensor (using the principle of light absorption characteristics of blood). This device is normally placed on a fingertip or an earlobe.

*Signal properties*: For the ECG, the cardiac cycle lasts about 830 ms (based upon a heartbeat rate of 72 beats per minute (bpm)). For a cycle of about 800 ms, the heart is in ventricular systole for 200–250 ms and in diastole for 550–600 ms. The R peak wave is as high as 2 mv in amplitude. The average heartbeat rate is about 75 bpm. Systolic blood pressure (measured in millimetres of mercury displacement (mmHg)) ranges from 95 to 140 mmHg with a figure of 120 mmHg as the average pressure. Diastolic blood pressure ranges from 60 to 90 mmHg with about 80 mmHg as the average pressure. Blood volume measures are always relative to some baseline within an individual. The signal is generally an amplified analogue voltage that indexes light absorption by the photoelectric sensor.

*Quantitative measures*: Within ECG, measures of heart rate (counting the number of R-waves over a minute), and heart period (the duration between R-waves), are the most popular descriptors of cardiac activity. However, with a multicomponent waveform as the PQRST complex, and the physiological processes that underlie the waveform, meaningful measures can be generated from many combinations of latencies or amplitudes between and within the PQRST complex. The measurement of blood pressure yields simple pressure indices, however, the ratio between the systolic and diastolic pressure values is of significance as is the absolute value of each pressure parameter.

## 11.2.5  Respiration

*Abbreviation*: None

*What is measured*: The breathing and gas-exchange process. More specifically, oximetry examines the arterial blood oxygen ($O_2$) levels and infrared capnometry examines the lung carbon dioxide ($CO_2$) levels. Abdominal and thoracic respiration rate and depth may also be measured.

*Transducers*: For oximetry, a specially calibrated photoplethysmograph is used, with output calibrated as percentage of saturated haemoglobin. For capnometry, a nasal catheter is inserted about a quarter of an inch into a nostril and held in place with some tape on the upper lip. $CO_2$ expiration pressure ($PCO_2$) and end-tidal $CO_2$ (the concentration of $CO_2$ in expired air) pressure ($PCO_2$) or percentage volume of expired air ($PETCO_2$) can be measured. For abdominal and thoracic breathing measurement, pneumography and strain gauges are most often used.

*Signal and quantitative measures*: Generally these are analogue voltages, digital values, or direct pressure manometer readings that index the gases or strains being measured. There are up to 50 measures that can be extracted from an examination of the output from oximetry, capnography and pneumography. These vary from measures of volume displacement, frequency and pressure, to proportionate fractionation of gases in expired air and oxygenation of the blood. The analysis of respiration has inexplicably been neglected in psychophysiology. However, the recent book by Fried and Grimaldi (1993) is a remarkable testament to the richness of relationships between respiration and psychological factors, and to the theoretical importance of respiration to conventional models of arousal and physiological functioning.

## 11.2.6 Electrical potentials of the brain

*Abbreviations*: Electroencephalography (EEG), averaged evoked potential (AEP), magnetoencephalography (MEEG).

*What is measured*: The electrical activity of the mass action of neurons within the cortex and midbrain structures. In addition, since electrical currents generate magnetic fields, these can also be measured (MEEG).

*Transducers*: For EEG, these can vary from invasive needle electrodes, placed directly into the exposed cortex or deeper structures, to non-invasive electrodes placed upon the surface of the scalp. These electrodes are used to record voltage differences between one or more cortical sites and a *relatively* electrically inactive area (such as an earlobe). For MEEG recording, superconducting quantum interfering devices (SQUIDS) are used to detect the minute magnetic fields within the brain. These are basically extremely sensitive superconducting electrodes that can detect the dynamic fluctuations of minute magnetic fields underneath their surface. Unlike EEG electrodes, SQUIDS do not have to be in contact with the scalp or cortical tissue as there is no reliance on electrical conductivity of electrons through body tissues.

*Signal properties*: The electrical signals emanating from the brain are of the order of microvolts. Spontaneous EEG is the term used to describe the continuous stream of activity that is always present within the brain. This activity can be characterised as patterns of oscillatory waveforms that have conventionally been subdivided in terms of their frequency as follows:

**delta** – low frequency – from 0.5 to 4 Hz, amplitude from 20 to 200 μv
**theta** – low frequency – from 4 to 7 Hz, amplitude from 20 to100 μv
**alpha** – dominant frequency – from 8 to 13 Hz, amplitude from 20 to 60 μv
**beta** – high frequency – from 13 to 40 Hz, amplitude from 2 to 20 μv

If, instead of recording the spontaneous activity of the brain, a brain response is evoked by a quantifiable stimulus, then it is possible to examine the change in electrical activity in direct response to a known stimulus. This technique is known as **evoked potential EEG**. Some of these evoked potentials can last less than 10 ms (such as the brain-stem auditory evoked potential generated by subcortical brain tissues) or up to a second or longer as in the case of the *Bereitschaftspotential* or readiness potential (a slow shift in voltage that is observed as preceding voluntary or spontaneous movement within an individual). Generally, because of the low level of brain response over and above the normal background EEG activity, many evoked responses are collected and then summed to produce an average evoked response (AER), also known as an AEP. The basis for this summation is that activity in the waveform that is not generated in response to the stimulus will be almost random and hence sum to near zero over occasions, while activity that is related to the stimulus will be enhanced by adding these stimulus-generated signals together.

*Quantitative measures*: Within spontaneous EEG data, the most popular method of analysis is based around Fourier decomposition of the waveform into cosine and sinewave components (that is, the number and type of oscillatory components of a particular frequency and magnitude that can account for the complex waveform). From these components, the power spectrum (the amount of electrical energy accounted for by each particular frequency that could possibly make up the complex waveform) provides direct, quantitative measures that index signal power at certain frequencies. More recent methods of analysis have re-expressed multi-electrode output as a spatial contour map – the topographical EEG map. This is a method of interpolating activity between electrodes in order to produce a set of smoothed gradients that can be 'mapped' over the surface of the scalp, encompassing all electrode positions and the intervening spaces between electrodes. In addition, chaos theory (non-linear dynamic analysis – fractal dimensionality analysis) has very recently been applied to the background EEG as a method for determining the 'complexity' of the EEG. This methodology basically computes the number of differential equations that are required to generate a segment of EEG. If few equations are required, then the EEG is said to be low-dimensional (note that a totally random waveform would require an infinite number of such equations and would thus have infinite dimensionality). For AEP research, measures invariably focus on peaks and troughs in the waveform, characterising these components by their amplitude and latency from the point of stimulation. Some work has also focused on the spectral composition of the AEP but, because of the brief duration of the waveform, such analyses tend to be error-prone. (A new method of displaying instantaneous power at frequencies within short impulse functions is now available in the engineering world – the wavelet transform. However, as yet, very little work with this transform has taken place in the area of human biosignal research.)

Finally, nuclear imaging, endocrinology and neuroimmunology have been ignored in the above résumé. This is not because they lack importance. Far from it, some of the most exciting results in the study of the biological bases of behaviour are now emanating from these three areas of research. However, the facilities (and finance!) required by these methodologies are such that only a few centres in the United Kingdom and worldwide can offer a postgraduate student access to these technologies. Some references for further reading in these areas are provided in section 11.5 below.

# 11.3 Quantifying biosignal data

## 11.3.1 The level of measurement

As can be seen from the information presented in the section above, the measures made from psychophysiological data are at true ratio level measurement (see Chapter 22). That is, there is a constant unit of measurement used that enables differences between any two sets of parameter values to be considered equal, if their differences are also equal. Additionally, unlike most psychological data/parameters, there is a true zero in nearly all biosignal data. Zero voltage means exactly that, no voltage at all.

## 11.3.2 Hardware, signal processing and data volume

Therefore, having established that the scale of measurement is superior to nearly all psychological data, it is apparent that many issues in the quantification of parameters that bedevil psychology fade into insignificance in this area. However, the cost of this philosophical simplicity is the price of computational and methodological complexity. The measures made are invariably electrically based, exact to a predetermined level of accuracy defined by the properties of the sensors and any amplification used, and prone to levels of noise that can utterly distort any parameter or signal. So, in order to attempt to measure any physiological parameter from any part of the human body, fairly detailed knowledge is required of the underlying physiology to be assessed, physical properties of the sensors/transducers to be applied, knowledge of the properties of the signals thus generated (electrical engineering and digital signal processing techniques), and an appreciation of the plethora of possible methods of analysis (both bivariate and multivariate methods of waveform analysis, periodicity analysis, event detection, pattern recognition, and clustering techniques).

A simple measure such as heart rate (counted in bpm) seems a trivial parameter to acquire, until you ask yourself how are you going to measure the heart rate (HR). Having found out that two electrodes placed say on each wrist will enable the acquisition of the information, your next problem is to work out how you are going to extract the HR parameter itself. That is, how do you record the electrical signals? Assume next you are provided with an amplifier, chart recorder, and a device which outputs a number every 10 seconds or so which indicates beats per minute. Looking at the number, you see the HR is alternating between 50 and 70 beats per minute. Is this acceptable? The individual being assessed is sitting quietly. Your local expert happens by and notices that the 50 Hz hardware notch filter is off. In addition, checking the earth electrode shows that very poor electrical contact is being made between this and the individual. By improving this contact and switching the notch filter in-line, the HR stabilises around 70 bpm. To understand what has happened requires knowledge of the expected HR, the properties of metallic electrodes, earthing problems, the operation of a notch filter and the appreciation of how an HR monitor works. This is all before you begin to manipulate a single psychological variable. Note also that here you were dealing with a relatively large biological signal. Imagine attempting to measure high frequency EEG of maybe 5 μv in amplitude with amplifiers that have background, self-generated electronic noise of about 1 μv, and where mains noise can be of the magnitude of 10–20 μv. The knowledge required to ensure that the signal you are seeing is actually biologically generated and not some property of the hardware in use, or of bad measurement technique, is quite considerable.

Unlike much purely psychological research, it is possible to generate quantitative physiological data that are literally pure error. This is a problem in some topographical EEG systems that provide maps of brain electrical activity computed from many electrodes placed upon the scalp. Most systems have automated filtering such that only frequencies between 0 and 40 Hz are displayed. However, if an electrode becomes detached from the scalp or its connecting wire breaks (inside the insulating plastic), this electrode will pick up large amounts of background mains noise (and any other stray frequencies present in the environment). Depending upon the efficiency of the filters, this electrode position will either be seen as producing very low amplitude signals across the signal spectrum or high frequency beta of moderate amplitude (where beta activity was defined as being from 20 Hz upwards). In this latter case, the filter did not remove *all* 50 Hz activity and, due to spectral smearing (given a low sampling speed and short segment of EEG) this gets mapped as high frequency activity in your EEG records. Experienced EEG technicians and researchers can invariably detect this. For a novice researcher, it poses a serious problem. Once again, only knowledge of the measurement process and the characteristics of the hardware can guard against this incorrect interpretative process.

## 11.3.3   Designing the experiment and choosing parameters to measure

If you set up an experiment protocol, and have acquired some electrophysiological data, your next problem is deciding what parameters to extract from these data. This stage of the measurement process *must* be decided on the basis of a priori measurement/psychological hypotheses. Data dredging (extracting every conceivable parameter and attempting to relate them to the psychological parameters) in the hope of finding something is virtually impossible to implement in this area. So many parameters can be computed such that attempting to sift through your data in this manner is a recipe for disaster. You will run out of time, computing facilities and energy! The best modern laboratories keep all physiological data on some form of archive medium (whether magnetic or CD-ROM). However, only certain hypothesis-specific parameters are extracted from this archive for use in the examination of psychological relationships. Should other hypotheses evolve over time, the archive data can then be reanalysed (where relevant) in order to permit the extraction of the new parameters.

One major problem you may face is that the system you are using to acquire psychophysiological data may only permit certain forms of analysis or, more rarely, provide no parameters at all. That is, you may have access to a skin conductance meter, amplifier and computer which will acquire and store the continuous conductance levels. However, if you do not have a program that analyses this output in terms of response latency and amplitude, then the data are practically useless. Your only options are to write all the incoming data to a chart recorder and carry out all such measures by hand, or obtain or write a computer program yourself that implements the procedures necessary to extract these parameters. This highlights another global feature of psychophysiological data acquisition, the collection of data can take a few minutes, however the volume of data generated can easily swamp the computer system, and the analysis of one subject's data by hand can take days! For example, digitally acquiring data from 16 EEG electrodes, sampling and acquiring the voltage value at each electrode 1000 times a second for a duration of 1 second, yields 16,000 numbers per second, invariably stored as two computer bytes (words) per number which thus generates 32,000 computer bytes per second. If, say, you are recording the 1-second segments 30 times (in response to 30 discrete stimuli prior to averaging), you will have generated 960,000 bytes (almost 1 Mb) of data to be stored per subject tested. Test 50 subjects and you can see immediately the problem of archiving, duration of analysis, and computing equipment requirements for EEG research!

Of course, returning to the HR example above, it may be that only five such measures are made throughout an experiment, where say the only focus of interest is the effect of difficulty of task problem on HR. The drawback to such simple experiments is that the explanatory power of any results is limited by the paucity of variables analysed! As Fried and Grimaldi (1993) also point out in their discussion of pulmonary (respiration) research, using observable movements of the chest or abdomen (pneumography) alone as indicators of respiration activity is not to be recommended, as $PETCO_2$ activity demonstrates that such movement can be quite unrelated to actual airflow into and out of the lungs. Thus to use respiration rate or depth as an indicator of increasing or decreasing airflow is liable to be prone to error. In the same way, the use of HR alone is not of much practical use except as a simple descriptor of one particular feature of cardiac activity.

# 11.4　Project

A relatively simple project that requires little hardware is the examination of the changes in individuals' HR to neutral vs. emotionally laden pictures. Examples of neutral stimuli can be pictures of say a car, a tree, a house, a brick, a pair of scissors. Examples of emotionally laden pictures may be a scenic view of mountain peaks, a war-injured child, the aftermath of a road accident, a partially clothed man or woman, a group of people laughing. Of course, although these stereotypical stimuli may be considered by myself and you to be neutral or emotionally laden, it is not until you examine the physiological changes and judgements of others that the stimuli can be categorised in this way with some degree of objectivity.

For this project you will need 10 subjects, 10 neutral and 10 assumed emotionally laden pictures. You will require an HR monitor that outputs heartbeats per minute on a display screen. You will need two surface electrodes that can be self-adhesive, taped, or glued with collodion to the subject's wrists and an extra one to act as the earthing electrode.

The subject will be seated in a room, in a comfortable chair at a table. You will sit opposite the subject, with the HR monitor display facing you but unable to be seen by the subject. You will place the HR electrodes on the subject, one on the inside of each wrist, ensuring that the electrode impedance is less than 5 k$\Omega$. The left wrist lead should be plugged into the positive input of the HR monitor so as to ensure an upward deflection of the R segment of the ECG. The third electrode (earthing electrode) can be placed on the back of one of the subject's hands and plugged into the HR monitor. *Ensure that all electrodes have low impedance.* You should now be able to observe an HR count on the monitor. Set the count update frequency to a 10-second interval, using a trigger button to initiate the start of a 10-second period. Nearly all HR monitors will have this facility.

Inform the subject that you are going to show him/her some pictures, one at a time. The subject will have about 10 seconds in which to view the picture. After this time has elapsed, the picture will be removed, and after a brief interval, another picture will be presented by you. Prior to each subject taking part in the experiment, randomise the order of the pictures to be presented, and create a picture sequence–HR response coding frame for that subject. Allow the subject to sit quietly for one minute, taking an initial baseline HR reading at the end of this period. Then begin the picture display sequence. When you initially display a picture to the subject, press the HR trigger button to initiate sampling. After 10 seconds, the HR in bpm will be displayed on the monitor. Write this down on your coding frame against the picture displayed, remove the picture from the view of the subject, and wait for about 20 seconds before presenting the next picture. After all pictures have been displayed in this manner, thank your subject for their cooperation, remove their electrodes, and inform them of the nature of the investigation.

Having tested all individuals in this manner, you will now be in possession of 10 HR records across 20 pictures. In order to normalise the data across subjects (equating for the difference in baseline HR across subjects), express each individual's picture-related HR measure as a deviation from their baseline HR, for example, HR minus baseline HR. A simple analysis might then be to average these deviation HR measures across each picture (10 subject HR measures per picture). The picture with the highest average HR deviation might be said to be the most 'arousing' picture. To further aid in this interpretation, it might have been useful to ask the subject (after the presentation of each picture) to indicate the degree to which they felt the picture was significant to them personally. This could be done using a five-point scale ranging from neutral to highly significant. These ratings could then be correlated with the average deviation HR across the pictures in order to demonstrate a possible relationship between psychological and physiological processes.

## 11.5   Further reading

Andreassi's (1989) *Psychophysiology: Human Behaviour and Physiological Response* (2nd edn) is an excellent introductory text. It is probably the best general textbook for students who are completely new to the area. This book is mandatory for any student wishing to study psychophysiology at a basic level. Cacioppo and Tassinary's (1990) *Principles of Psychophysiology: Physical, Social and Inferential Elements* should be the second book to be read after Andreassi's text. This is a remarkably comprehensive book that would serve as a reference source for both undergraduate and postgraduate students. This book is mandatory for any student seriously interested in psychophysiology.

Dempster's (1993) *Computer Analysis of Electrophysiological Signals* is a good introductory text on the analysis of psychophysiological data – excellent for students who already have some knowledge of basic statistical methods. Since electroencephalography is one of the largest research areas in psychophysiology, it is useful to take a look at Fisch's (1991) *Spehlmann's EEG Primer* (2nd edn). It is written at an introductory level suitable for students who have no prior knowledge of psychophysiology. For students who wish to undertake projects involving EEG, this is an essential handbook that provides much practical as well as some theoretical information. Finally, Fried and Grimaldi's (1993) *The Psychology and Physiology of Breathing* is an absolutely brilliant book. It contains an excellent introductory section on psychophysiological measurement and provides a masterful description of respiratory functions and processes. In addition, the provocative and challenging hypotheses in the book make this probably one the best 'specialist' books in this area. If you are to study psychophysiology at any level, you must read this book.

# 12　Questionnaire Design

*Chris Fife-Schaw*

## Contents

## 12.1　Introduction

The humble questionnaire is probably the single most common research tool in the social sciences. The principle advantages of the questionnaire are its apparent simplicity, its versatility and its low cost as method of data gathering. For many research topics, questionnaires provide data which are of a good enough quality to both test hypotheses and to make real-world policy suggestions. Where people wish to make population parameter estimates, the cost advantage of questionnaires over interviews means that many more people can be sampled for a given budget than might otherwise be possible. Questionnaires are a relatively well-understood technology and there are numerous guides to designing good questionnaires (for example, Oppenheim, 1992; Sudman and Bradburn, 1982).

Designing the perfect questionnaire is probably impossible, however. Experience shows that you can rarely design one that all your respondents, let alone your academic peers, are happy with. Similarly it is unlikely that you will complete a questionnaire study without asking yourself the 'why didn't I ask about that?' question. This should not be seen as a failing of questionnaire methods themselves so much as an inevitable part of the research process. This is not to say that careful questionnaire design can be ignored. There have been too many questionnaires produced over the years that contain simple errors that have seriously undermined the value of the data collected. You should always strive to minimise the number of these errors and hopefully what follows will alert you to the more obvious problems.

The focus of this chapter is on self-completion questionnaires though the section on item wording contains some ideas that apply equally to interview schedules. You should read this chapter in conjunction with Chapter 8 on surveys and sampling.

## 12.2 What information do you want?

The very versatility of the questionnaire as a data gathering technique means that it is difficult to generalise about its appropriate uses. It is, however, useful to try to classify common aims since the temptation is often to milk questionnaire data to meet a number of these aims simultaneously while fulfilling none of the aims particularly well. An awareness of these general purposes should help focus the questionnaire design process.

### 12.2.1 Hypothesis generating

In this mode, questionnaires are useful for asking a large number of people 'what if', exploratory types of question. The intention is to get a feel for how people respond to certain issues. When attempting to elicit interesting insights in this way, it is often desirable to allow people to make open-ended responses, unconstrained by your prior expectations of what classes of response are useful to you. While this kind of information can also be obtained by unstructured interviews and group discussions, a questionnaire study can give you a feel for the range of likely responses and a rough idea of how common certain responses are.

Sometimes the goal is to see if there is any underlying dimension, or putative cause, that influences responses to a set of items. In such cases, exploratory data analytic procedures, such as exploratory factor analysis and cluster analysis are commonly used (see Chapter 24). As there is often no established theory generating hypotheses about the items, only some raw hunch or intuition, such analytic procedures are best thought of as generating hypotheses about the nature of certain items for testing in future studies.

## 12.2.2   Test development and validation

A common application of questionnaires is in the realm of test development. This can take many forms. A set of items (questions on the form) may be being tested as a potential scale to measure a psychological trait. The aim is to collect responses to the items so that various psychometric procedures can be used to assess the scale's reliability and validity. A set of items supposedly measuring some psychological construct may be administered to groups with known characteristics so as to attempt to assess the validity of the measure. Chapter 13 outlines many of the standard procedures associated with this use of the questionnaire.

## 12.2.3   Population parameter estimation

Once a range of measures exists, either as published tests or as the result of procedures outlined in section 12.2.2 above, questionnaires can be used to assess population scores on such tests. For instance, you might be interested to estimate the levels of psychological well-being among police officers. After appropriate sampling, you could administer a questionnaire containing the General Health Questionnaire (GHQ; Goldberg, 1972) and treat the resulting scores as an estimate of the 'true' level of psychological well-being among police officers. These estimates can then be compared with norms, the responses of other groups who have taken the GHQ in the past. Parameter estimates can be made for almost any type of question you could ask.

## 12.2.4   Hypothesis and model testing

If measures of key constructs already exist then questionnaires can be useful for hypothesis testing purposes. Common examples would include testing causal models (for example, the Theory of Planned Behaviour) or confirming the factor structure underlying responses to a set of pre-existing items. Hypothesised differences between identifiable groups on specified measures is another common application as is the evaluation of an intervention (for example, a teaching programme).

Ideally, you should keep the above aims separate and conduct different studies to deal with each aim in turn. In reality, limited resources are likely to mean that you will combine some of these aims within one questionnaire study. For instance, it is common practice to specify a new measure (for example, a set of scaled items) and then attempt hypothesis testing within the same data set. This practice tends to mean that the validity of the measure is not established and, while inter-item reliability can be assessed, the interpretation of the data necessarily requires greater caution than would be the case had established measures been used.

There is an important distinction to be made here between dishing out lots of questionnaires and fishing through the data to find statistically significant relationships and a more theoretically driven exercise. With the advent of easy-to-use computer programs such as SPSS, there is a growing temptation to confuse exploratory, hypothesis generating uses of questionnaires with hypothesis testing. This should be avoided where possible.

## 12.3   Open vs. closed response formats

Before looking at individual types of question it is worth saying something about possible response formats.

A major distinction lies between open-ended and closed-ended response formats. With **open-ended** formats the respondent is asked to write down the response to a question in any terms that he or she sees fit. When asking about occupations it would be prohibitive to list all possible occupations, so you would normally allow respondents to make an open-ended response and simply write down their occupation. As another example, you might ask people to give their reasons for recycling glass bottles and allow them to list as many reasons as they felt they had for recycling. **Closed-ended** formats require the researcher to have a reasonable idea of the likely responses to the items in advance. In the recycling example, they would need to provide a list of likely reasons for recycling and ask respondents to indicate which of the reasons applied to them.

The advantages of closed-ended formats are that they clarify the response alternatives for the respondent and they reduce the number of vague or ambiguous answers that might be given. Open-ended questions often prompt people into providing multiple responses even if these responses are substantively the same. Also, from a clerical point of view they reduce the number of **coding errors** in the data set. Coding errors occur when an open-ended response is misinterpreted by the researcher at the stage of turning verbal responses into numbers that can be used for statistical analysis. Respondents can usually answer closed-format items quickly, making responding to you at all more attractive.

The disadvantages of closed-ended formats are of many sorts but perhaps the most important is that they can create artificial forced choices and rule out unexpected responses. Your list of reasons for recycling may not include one that is very important for some people. Making up the response categories is often difficult as they must cover the full range of likely responses.

Another problem concerns the shared meanings attached to the words used in the questionnaires. For instance, the term 'tea' is used differently by people from different social strata and different geographical locations. Most people would recognise 'tea' as a drink but for some people it is also a light snack in the afternoon and for others a larger meal in the early evening. This is rather a quaint example, but closed-ended response formats assume that people share the same understanding of the items and response categories as does the researcher. There are many other biasing effects that occur when using closed-ended formats which will be discussed in more detail later in this chapter.

While it might seem that the problems with closed-ended response formats are legion, the main reason for their continued popularity lies in the difficulties of analysing open-ended responses. Open-ended responses simply do not lend themselves to numerical analysis in the same way that closed response formats do. It is possible to turn such responses into numbers and, of course, it is possible to analyse data without recourse to numbers and statistics, but most questionnaire designers tend towards maximising the number of closed-ended items wherever possible.

To get over the problems with closed-ended items, it is essential that the items you choose to use and the response options you give are ones that potential respondents would use and understand. This means that you must go out and talk to likely respondents to find out what *they* think the key questions are and what their responses would be. Running a series of focus groups (see Chapter 18) is often very useful for this purpose. Taped interviews or focus groups, once transcribed, give useful insights that ought to be drawn upon when designing your questionnaire. Having done this it is still important that careful pilot work is done to see if respondents understand your questions and respond appropriately.

## 12.4 Common response formats

Figure 12.1 shows examples of **categorical** response formats. Note that with categorical response formats it is possible to have items where respondents can circle more than one response as is the case with question 4 in Figure 12.1. Such items are referred to as **multiple-response items**. Care is needed when coding the responses to such items into the computer

| 1 Have you ever attended school in the UK? | YES<br>NO |
|---|---|
| 2 Are you male or female? | MALE<br>FEMALE |
| 3 If there were a General Election tomorrow which political party would you vote for? | CONSERVATIVE<br>LIBERAL<br>LABOUR<br>OTHER PARTY<br>WOULDN'T VOTE<br>DO NOT KNOW |
| 4 Which of the following items have you purchased in the last week? (*You may circle more than one item*) | APPLES<br>PEARS<br>ORANGES |

Figure 12.1    *Examples of categorical response formats*

since, for example, question 4 contains effectively three separate responses; one for whether apples were purchased, one for pears and one for oranges.

Examples of common **rating scale** response formats are shown in Figure 12.2. Here the respondent is asked to circle one of the five possible responses. It is perfectly possible to present the response options as shown in Figure 12.3. Having numbered each option the respondent can be asked to write in the number that corresponds to his or her chosen option in a box next to the question statement.

An example of a **ranking** response format is shown in Figure 12.4.

## 12.5    Common wording problems

In this section I have grouped together a range of common wording problems that you should be aware of. Oppenheim (1992) and Sudman and Bradburn (1982) among other texts provide more examples of these types of wording problem.

If you use **vague/ambiguous terminology** in the phrasing of your questions you cannot be sure what responses to the items mean. An example would be in the wording of frequency response options for behavioural report items (see Figure 12.5). Just what does 'frequently' mean here? Every hour? Twice a fortnight? Respondents will try to guess what you mean by 'frequently' but they may not all make the same guess, leading to hidden ambiguity in the data.

Another problem in this category concerns ill-defined terms. In sexual behaviour research, for instance, researchers were initially keen to ask

Please say how much you agree or disagree with
the following statement: (*Please circle one
response only*)

Government policy on public transport will be
good for the environment in the long term

STRONGLY AGREE
AGREE
UNCERTAIN
DISAGREE
STRONGLY DISAGREE

*or*

How important is rail privatisation to you,
personally?

EXTREMELY
  IMPORTANT
VERY IMPORTANT
MODERATELY
  IMPORTANT
NOT VERY IMPORTANT
NOT IMPORTANT AT
  ALL

Figure 12.2  *Common rating scale response formats*

| 1 | 2 | 3 | 4 | 5 |
|---|---|---|---|---|
| Strongly agree | Agree | Neither agree nor disagree | Disagree | Strongly disagree |

Figure 12.3  *An alternative layout for rating scale responses*

Which of the following do you feel are the most important factors to consider
when choosing a new car?
*Please **rank** the following in order of importance. Number them so that
1 = most important, 2 = next most important, through to 6 = least
important.*

Fuel consumption          _____
Maximum speed             _____
Quick acceleration        _____
Having a safety cage/cell _____
Servicing costs           _____
Status/prestige           _____

Figure 12.4  *An example of a ranking response format*

| How often do you clean your teeth? | FREQUENTLY |
|---|---|
| | OFTEN |
| | INFREQUENTLY |
| | NEVER |

Figure 12.5   *Example of a vague response format wording*

people if they felt they were promiscuous or not. Unfortunately, research has shown (Spencer et al., 1988) that the public are unsure what 'promiscuous' means in terms of absolute numbers of sexual partners. Indeed, some people believe promiscuity is a term that applies to anyone who has had more partners than they have. Therefore, beware inherently ambiguous terms.

It might seem a good idea to use **technically correct terminology** to get over problems of the ambiguity of day-to-day language. In some research topics this may be appropriate but you should pilot your form carefully to be sure that respondents will understand the terms. If appropriate, you can give both a technical and a lay explanation for problematic terms in the introduction to the questionnaire. However, you should always seek to use plain English wherever possible.

In many research areas you are interested to ask people 'What would you do if. . . . ?' types of question, that is, **hypothetical questions**. Such questions about hypothetical future situations must appear reasonable to respondents if their answers are to be meaningful. If you were to ask, say, 'If it appeared that the Labour Party could win the next election would you vote for them?' the meaning of the response would depend on the respondent accepting that the Labour Party being in a position to win the election was a realistic premiss. You might think it was, and some respondents might agree with you, but others might not. Responses from these two groups may not be comparable and there is little you could do about this unless you also asked whether this premiss was acceptable first.

**Leading questions** such as 'Would you agree that the Government's policies on health are unfair?' will suggest to some people that you would like them to agree with you. Similarly, 'Do you agree that Brand Z washes whiter?' might be harder to disagree with than a more neutrally worded item. In such cases you may be indicating something about what would be regarded by some as a 'right' response. Therefore, avoid leading questions.

Item wordings should not contain implicit **value judgements**. In a similar way to leading questions, you should not express your own views, or those of the research sponsor, in questions items.

**Context effects** are somewhat more subtle effects on responses that are dependent on the nature of the rest of the questions on the form. Take the following question as an example: 'How many pints of beer did you drink last week?'. In the context of a survey into young people's lifestyles and leisure activities this seems like a reasonable question and young males in particular might give relatively high figures in response. If you had asked the same question in the context of a questionnaire on health behaviours and heart disease, responses might well be lower. You should be aware of the potential impact of surrounding questions on your target item.

Items that involve multiple premisses, also known as **double-barrelled questions**, are to be avoided as the meanings of responses are unclear. For instance, 'Do you believe the training programme was a good one and effective in teaching you new skills?'. If someone disagreed with this item it could be because they thought the programme was generally good but ineffective for them personally, or bad and ineffective or even effective for them despite being of poor quality. Here it is not clear exactly which premiss is being disagreed (or agreed) with.

Items should not contain **hidden assumptions**. The classic example of this sort of problem is contained in the item: 'When did you stop beating your wife?'. This assumes you used to beat your wife and, indeed, that you had a wife to beat.

While it might seem a source of irritation to the questionnaire researcher, people like to present themselves in a positive light when answering questionnaires – this is termed **social desirability** or, sometimes, '*faking good*'. If you were asked if you ever gave to charity, for instance, then saying 'no' (assuming this to be the correct answer) says something about you that you may not want to convey to the researcher. Many apparently innocuous questions have response options which, if selected, might indicate something negative about the respondent. This leads to potential biases in response patterns which you would usually wish to avoid. However, on some occasions it can be useful to use items with certain socially desirable responses since this can sometimes be of some theoretical or analytical use to you. The Crowne-Marlowe Social Desirability Scale (1964) is sometimes used for this purpose.

You should be wary of assuming that all your respondents find your questions as acceptable as you do. When you are engaged in research on **sensitive issues** (for example, death, sex, religion) you should be aware that your items may cause offence to certain groups. It is general good practice to ask about sensitive issues as directly, yet with as much sympathy for your respondents, as is possible. Do not try to get at sensitive information indirectly by attempting to deceive respondents. If you cannot ask something fairly directly then you should think about approaching the issue by using an alternative method to the questionnaire.

# 12.6   Types of information gleaned from questionnaires

Questionnaires can be used to gather a variety of types of information. You can ask about people's background and other factual, demographic information. You can ask about their behaviours or their attitudes or beliefs, knowledge or their intentions and aspirations. Each sort of information is associated with particular difficulties which are discussed below.

## 12.6.1 Background and demographic data

Most questionnaires will ask for some information about the respondent's background. Numerous texts deal with how to ask for this **demographic** information (for example, Sudman and Bradburn, 1982) and it is well worth the time consulting such books if in doubt about how to phrase certain items. Although these types of information are readily accessible to the respondent themselves, it is surprising how often people resist giving this information. You should consider some of the following issues.

Do you need to know a person's **age** exactly? Some respondents may not want to declare their ages exactly, so it may be appropriate to ask people to indicate their approximate age in a series of age bands (for example, 18–25, 26–35, 36–50, etc.). How many bands you need will depend on how crucial it is to distinguish between respondents on the basis of age. If you need to know ages more accurately, then you should ask directly making it clear how accurate you want the answer to be. You can ask for ages in years, or in years and months. It is possible to ask for dates of birth as an alternative. Requesting greater precision runs the risk of some respondents failing to answer at all.

It is good idea to make **biological sex** a forced choice, Male/Female item. If you leave the response category open-ended someone will put something inappropriate in.

**Ethnicity and nationality** are two bits of information about respondents that you may need to ask about despite the fact that the very act of asking for this information is heavily laden with political baggage. Many people confuse nationality with ethnicity and, as a researcher, you should be absolutely clear what information you need *and why*. Remember that being 'British' is a statement about nationality not ethnicity. Respondents may reasonably want to know why their ethnicity or nationality is relevant to your study and what use you will make of this information. Research that may reveal important differences between ethnic groups may be regarded as politically suspect by whichever group is likely to come out worst in the survey. If you must ask about nationality and/or ethnicity you should be sure that such information cannot be used to systematically disadvantage any group. Indeed this applies to all demographic data. If you wish to ask about this, the items shown in Figure 12.6 may help reduce confusion.

Social stratification (**Social class/socioeconomic status**) is a topic on which so much has been written it is difficult to provide simple guidance on good practice. There are several systems of classification of which the

What is your *Nationality* (e.g. British, French)?          _____

What is your ethnic origin (e.g. Caucasian, Afro-
Caribbean, Asian)?                                          _____

Figure 12.6   *Example questions to assess nationality and ethnicity*

What is your job called?                          _____
What job do you do?                               _____
Where do you work?                                _____
What does the employer make or do?                _____

Is the work full-, or part-time? (*Please ring one answer*)

                              FULL-TIME
                              PART-TIME (less than 30 hrs a week)

Figure 12.7   *Example occupation questions*

Registrar General's Classification of Occupations is the best known. Most
systems involve defining class on the basis of the nature of the person's
occupation. This means obtaining enough information about someone's
job to permit accurate classification. A common problem is that if someone
says they are an 'engineer' this could mean anything from someone who
repairs televisions through to someone who designs nuclear power stations.
You need more information such as provided by the items shown in Figure
12.7 (adapted from the ESRC 16–19 Initiative, Banks et al., 1992).

When studying women it is difficult to know *whose* social class/status
should be assessed. There is a debate (see for example, Dale et al., 1985)
about how women's social class should be measured particularly as
women's jobs tend to carry a lower occupational status than men's jobs in
some classification systems. Basing a woman's class/status on her husband's
occupation is common practice but is probably unsound and ignores those
who are not married.

Difficulties also occur when trying to classify young people's occupations. Occupations common among people at the beginning of their careers
tend to have low status yet they may still lead to high-status careers in later
life. Using parental class/status is one possible solution but it is unclear at
what age a person's occupation should be regarded as a good indication of
class/status. Classifying students and the unemployed also remains problematic.

When asking about social class/status you should be clear in your mind
what it is you really want to know about the respondent. In many cases it

might be more appropriate to simply ask about factors such as income and education since it may be these variables you are really interested in.

A person's **income** is perhaps one of the most sensitive issues you can ask about in social research. Requests for exact amounts are often regarded with suspicion and common practice in market research is to provide income bands (for example, £0–£5000 per annum, £5001–£10,000 per annum, etc.) and ask respondents to select one band only. Respondents need to be assured that their responses will not be handed over to the Inland Revenue or other government agency.

With many factual types of responses it can be useful to ask respondents to tick a box if they do not wish to provide certain bits of information. This helps you distinguish between data that are missing because people did not want to provide some information from the missing data of those who simply neglected to fill in the form completely. Providing an option not to respond like this may help to make people feel more relaxed about providing other sorts of information. Making people feel they have to answer absolutely everything may make some feel they would rather not respond at all. Obviously, you should not do this with items that are crucial to your study's design.

## 12.6.2  Behavioural reports

By their very nature questions asking about past behaviours assume accurate memory for events as well as a willingness to report these to a researcher. Both assumptions need to be considered afresh for each new item you generate.

It should come as no surprise that sensitive and socially undesirable behaviours are often misreported if reported at all. Enquiries about sexual activities are thought to produce over-reporting in some groups and under-reporting in others (see Boulton, 1994). Reports of involvement (or not) in illegal practices are also likely to be prone to error.

It would be a mistake to assume that biases apply just to the reporting of private and/or undesirable acts. Sudman and Bradburn (1982) report studies that suggest over-reporting biases apply to socially desirable behaviours too (for example, charity donations, library use). Given these problems, the best solution in the absence of corroborative data, is to introduce additional items elsewhere in the questionnaire to test for consistency in reporting. If respondents are going to misrepresent their behaviour to you, then if their reports are logically inconsistent at least you can have clear grounds to exclude their responses from your analyses.

In some circumstances it may be possible to make respondents believe that you will have an alternative way to find out about their behaviour. In a questionnaire study on children's smoking behaviour, Evans et al. (1978) took saliva samples at the time of questioning and led respondents to believe that the saliva would be used to confirm their behavioural reports on the questionnaire. In fact, the cost of saliva testing was too high to permit all samples to be tested but, compared with a control group, the group who thought their behaviours could be monitored reported higher levels of smoking. Where appropriate, this strategy seems likely to improve the quality of behavioural report data though you should be wary of deliberate attempts to deceive respondents especially if you will be unable to fully debrief them.

Assessment of the frequency with which behaviours have been done in the past is an area where there is much current research activity on how to best do this (see Gaskell et al., 1993). What is clear is that you should avoid vague response categories (such as 'regularly') as discussed above. When asking about very regular, mundane events people may find it easier to estimate how often they have done the act in a given time period since they are unlikely to remember every time they did the act. When asking about more memorable, major life-events, more specific recall can be requested.

### 12.6.3   Attitudes and opinions

People's attitudes and opinions are often of great interest but there is little consensus on how measuring them is best done. The most common procedure is to present a statement and ask people to rate, on a scale (usually five or seven points) how much they agree or disagree with the statement (see Figure 12.8). It is possible to use more than five or seven points. You can provide a line with the ends labelled 'Strongly agree' and 'Strongly disagree' and ask respondents simply to mark their preferred position on this agreement dimension with a cross. This procedure requires the researcher to lay a ruler on each response to retrieve a usable score for computational purposes.

I would be happy to have a nuclear waste plant in my back garden.
(*please circle one answer*)

| 1 | 2 | 3 | 4 | 5 |
|---|---|---|---|---|
| **Strongly agree** | **Agree** | **Neither agree nor disagree** | **Disagree** | **Strongly disagree** |

Figure 12.8   *Example attitude statement and response scale*

An alternative to the rating scale is the forced choice design where two opposing statements are presented and the respondent must choose to endorse one or the other. This procedure is less common as it does not give information about the extremity of agreement/disagreement. However, five- or seven- point rating scales can suffer from people's over-reliance on the neutral response ('Neither agree nor disagree') rather than committing themselves to expressing an opinion.

All pen-and-paper attitude measurement makes a number of assumptions. First is that people actually have attitudes towards the issues and then, that they have ready access to them. Second, they assume that these can be adequately reflected in simple ratings or forced choice judgements. Sometimes you will see the type of rating scale presented in Figure 12.8 referred to as a Likert scale. This is only technically true if the item has been developed so that it generates normally distributed data – this may not always be the case.

### 12.6.4 Knowledge

Quite often it would be useful to assess factual knowledge in a questionnaire survey. Such 'tests' can be carried out but the validity of responses and thus knowledge scores has to be considered to be in some doubt. Unless you can be present at the time of testing you cannot be certain who answered the test. This could apply to the whole questionnaire, of course, but people may simply ask someone else for help with the difficult questions so that they do not appear ignorant. Tests of this sort can be used reasonably successfully in non-survey settings on populations such as school pupils and employees where you can exert some control over the testing conditions.

### 12.6.5 Intentions, expectations and aspirations

Many social psychological theories are concerned with accounting for intentions, expectations and aspirations which are fairly easily assessed with questionnaires. You should be careful to specify an appropriate timeframe for such items as vague specifications can lead to vague responses. For instance, if you were to ask 'Do you expect to travel abroad in the future?', respondents could quite reasonably say 'who knows'. A much better form would be to ask 'As far as you can tell, do you expect to travel abroad in the next year?'.

## 12.7 Existing scales and measures

When using established measures it is often tempting to alter the wording of some items to make them sound better or to clarify them a little. It is quite surprising how many established measures contain wording errors like those outlined in the earlier sections of this chapter. It is also the case that scales developed in other countries can contain culturally specific phrases or assume some familiarity with cultural norms that would be somewhat inappropriate for your sample. Should you change items, wordings or leave them as they are?

It is not possible to answer this with a categorical 'yes' or 'no'. One side of the argument says that any tampering with item wordings will change the nature of the scale so that it is no longer equivalent to the original. Hence, comparability of scores between your study and existing research using the scale is no longer appropriate. You might be tempted to make minor changes in the hope that scale scores will still be comparable but, in the absence of supporting validity data, this cannot be assumed.

The other side of the argument says that it is poor research practice to administer questionnaires that contain phrases or assumptions that your respondents are unlikely to be familiar with. It may alienate them or make them think the items are silly or not serious. As an example, early versions of the Wilson-Patterson Conservatism Scale (Wilson and Patterson, 1968) contained items asking people to endorse (or not) chaperones, pyjama parties and beatniks among other potential indicators of conservative attitudes. At the time (the 1960s) chaperones, pyjama parties and beatniks were topical and made sense in such a questionnaire but today these items would raise eyebrows.

The point about the latter example is that the scale would presumably no longer be particularly valid (indeed Wilson subsequently revised the scale). Even though you might wish to compare current levels of conservatism with those found in the 1960s and 1970s by using an equivalent measure, it is doubtful that such a comparative study would be very informative. You should always consider this potential lack of validity when thinking about using an existing measure that was not validated on the type of sample that you are going to study. You may need to consider attempting to establish validity yourself (for example, by using a criterion groups approach – see Chapter 13).

## 12.8   Questionnaire layout

This section deals with issues to do with the presentation of your questionnaire. There is always a trade-off between better presentation, and thus better quality data and higher response rate, and increased cost. This is important even if you are going to be present when the questionnaires are administered. At the end of this section there is an example of a questionnaire page layout that illustrates many of the points discussed in this chapter. This is intended to be illustrative only; there are many alternative layouts that could have been used and this is not intended as *the* way to lay out your questionnaire.

Unless you will be present at the administration, explanatory notes should always be provided in order to foster **respondent motivation**. These should spell out the broad aims of the study and why the individual's compliance is important. The individual must be encouraged to feel that his or her responses are valued by you and that you will treat the responses with respect. Wherever possible, you should ensure anonymity for respondents. If the research design is such that you need to be able to identify individual respondents, acknowledge this and ensure confidentiality (and, of course, mean it). If you intend to keep computerised records of responses that could identify respondents, you should seek to be registered under the Data Protection Act as a holder of such information. Tell respondents that you have done this.

If you intend to provide feedback to respondents (which is good practice), explain how this is to be achieved. Compliance is likely to be higher if respondents can find out what happened to the research and what benefits may have come from it.

You should always thank respondents for their help in the introductory notes *and* at the end of the form.

It is good housekeeping practice to use **case identifiers** in order to be able to identify individual questionnaires (though not necessarily individual respondents, note) so that should you find problems with the data later on you can use the computer to tell you which questionnaire the problem is associated with. If you fail to do this with a large survey it will be very difficult to make valid corrections to the data.

There are no rules to guide you to the optimum **length** for a questionnaire since this depends so much on the topic of the study, the method of distribution (for example, postal, face-to-face) and the anticipated enthusiasm of your respondents. There are some rough guidelines that can be given, however.

The problem facing most researchers is how to ask all the questions they want to ask without tiring or boring their respondents. How long it takes to answer a questionnaire can only really be assessed by using pilot work and efforts should be made to pilot the form on people who are likely, on a priori grounds, to have difficulty with it. Experience would suggest that forms that take more than 45 minutes to complete are only appropriate where the respondent can be assumed to be very highly motivated to help you.

Very short questionnaires (one to two pages) have the virtue of not taxing respondents unduly though they may not be taken very seriously either. It would be rare to have a substantive research issue that could be dealt with in such a small questionnaire and some respondents may think the exercise can only be superficial and thus adopt a less than serious attitude towards answering.

Concerning the issue of **question order** there seems to be a growing convention in social research to collect information about respondent demographics (age, sex, etc.) at the end of a questionnaire. This is information that people have ready access to and, if asked appropriately, they will have little difficulty in providing it. As respondents tire of your questionnaire they get asked the less taxing questions.

It is also rare to place extremely sensitive questions right at the beginning of a form. People need time to get accustomed to the types of

| | |
|---|---|
| 1 Are you currently unemployed? | YES |
| | NO |

**If you answered 'YES' to question 1, ignore question 2 and carry on with question 3**

2 How many hours did you work last week? _____ hours

**Everyone should answer question 3**

| | |
|---|---|
| 3 Are you male or female? | MALE |
| | FEMALE |

Figure 12.9 *An example of a filter question*

issues you are interested in and starting off with your equivalent of 'When did you stop beating your wife?' will not make the respondent feel at ease.

**Question density** is another important issue. You may be tempted to cram in lots of questions into a small number of pages so that the questionnaire booklet does not appear too large and daunting. This is generally counterproductive as squashing lots of items into a small space makes the form look complex and raises the possibility that respondents will get confused and put their responses in the wrong places. Clear, self-evident layout will enhance the possibility of getting valid information from your sample.

Questions that do not apply to everybody often results from being forced to use a single form to ask questions. For instance, you may not wish to ask unemployed respondents about how many hours they work. If you cannot provide a separate questionnaire for the unemployed, you will need to use **filter questions**, examples of which are shown in Figure 12.9.

**Typeface and size** are important because some people will find reading small, densely packed text difficult to read. Therefore, pick a clear font (typeface) and make it reasonably large. Use a different font for instructions and bold lettering for filter questions if you have such a facility.

Assuming you are interested in computer analysis of responses, it saves some time to have some of the information about how the data is to be coded for computer input printed on the questionnaire (**coding column information**) in a column that is 'For Office Use Only'. This is unnecessary if you are going to use an optical mark reader to scan in the data (for example, FORMIC) but for those without such facilities coding columns can save labour later in the process.

Most computer packages (such as SPSS, SAS, BMDP) need to know which column of the raw data file contains the response to which item. By printing this on the questionnaire you can see at a glance which column the response should appear in. This saves constantly referring to a separate

7. Have you got any children of your own? *(Tick one)*

Yes ☐ 1    No ☐ 2

If yes, how many? *(Please write in)* _____

8. Are you or your partner expecting a baby? *(Tick one)*

Yes ☐ 1    No ☐ 2

9. Please tell us about your parents or step-parents. Read the options below and tick one box for 'mother' and one box for 'father' to tell us what they are doing.

| ARE THEY NOW | Mother (Stepmother) | Father (Stepfather) |
|---|---|---|
| In full-time paid employment | 1 | 1 |
| In part-time paid employment | 2 | 2 |
| Full-time looking after the home | 3 | 3 |
| Unemployed | 4 | 4 |
| Doing something else | 5 | 5 |

10. How old were your mother and father when they left school? *(Tick one box for each parent)*

| | Mother (Stepmother) | Father (Stepfather) |
|---|---|---|
| 15 years or less | 1 | 1 |
| 16 years old | 2 | 2 |
| 17 years or more | 3 | 3 |
| Don't know | 4 | 4 |

11. 1. Have you ever left your parents' home (or the home of the people who brought you up) for six months or more? *(Tick one)*

Yes, in the past ☐ 1    Yes, still away from home ☐ 2    No ☐ 3

2. If yes, how many times? *(Please write in)* _____

3. If yes, why did you leave home? *(Please write in)*

12. Below is a set of opinions. Please indicate how strongly you agree or disagree with each opinion.

*(Tick one box for each opinion)*

| HOW DO YOU FEEL ABOUT LEAVING HOME? | Strongly agree | Agree | Uncertain | Disagree | Strongly disagree |
|---|---|---|---|---|---|
| 1. It's better to get a place of your own if you've got the money | 1 | 2 | 3 | 4 | 5 |
| 2. People are better off living with their parents | 1 | 2 | 3 | 4 | 5 |
| 3. I feel my parents treat me like a child when I'm at home | 1 | 2 | 3 | 4 | 5 |
| 4. Having a place of your own is too much worry | 1 | 2 | 3 | 4 | 5 |

Figure 12.10   *An example of a questionnaire layout from the ESRC 16–19 initiative*

code book and can allow you to type in the data straight from the questionnaire with minimal errors.

Figure 12.10 gives an example of a page from a questionnaire used in the 16–19 Initiative study of the social and political socialisation of young people (Banks et al., 1992). This page occurred at the end of the questionnaire and deals with some demographic information and some attitudes. The column on the right contains information for the coders to use so that they type in the correct codes in the computer data file. In the 'For Office Use Only' column the 'BEGIN CARD 6' means that this is the sixth line of data for the respondent. The answer to question 7 will go into column 7 of this sixth card line and will be a '1' if they say 'Yes', they have children and '2' if they say 'No'. If their mother was in part-time paid employment a '2' would be placed in column 9. Question 11.3 is an open-ended question about reasons for leaving home. A pre-existing set of two-digit codes was generated from previous pilot work so that the reasons could be quickly coded and placed in columns 14–15. Question 12 contains a series of fairly standard attitude items. Note that column numbers are not the same as question numbers.

## 12.9   Conclusion

This chapter has attempted to alert you to many common problems in questionnaire design. The solutions proposed here are intended as guides to good practice but you should not feel that these are the only possible solutions to these difficulties. A lot more inventive use could be made of questionnaires than is currently the case. Guides such as this necessarily deal with common problems but you should not limit yourself to asking about the broad general topics covered here. Breakwell and Canter (1993), for example, illustrate a number of possibilities for alternative question-naire approaches to the social psychological topic of social representation; such experimentation should be encouraged in other research domains too.

## 12.10   Project

Following up on the project described in Chapter 8, design a questionnaire for use in the postal survey of students' attitudes towards potential increases in accommodation rents. Think of some psychological factors that might be relevant in predicting whether or not such increases would be acceptable. For instance, you might look at political conservatism as a possible factor. Are the politically conservative more accepting of increases than the politically left-wing who might wish to maintain subsidies for students. How would you tap into such a factor on a questionnaire?

## 12.11   Further reading

Oppenheim's (1992) *Questionnaire Design, Interviewing and Attitude Measurement* is a good and clear introduction to questionnaire design as is the older Sudman and Bradburn (1982) *Asking Questions: A Practical Guide to Questionnaire Design*. Schuman and Presser's (1981) *Questions and Answers in Attitude Surveys: Experiments on Question Form, Writing and Context* reports an intriguing series of experimental studies with survey data which highlight the sensitivity of respondents to quite minor wording changes in questionnaire items. Those wishing a more contemporary angle on some of these effects should take a look at Gaskell et al.'s (1993) article in *The Psychologist*.

# 13 Using Psychometric Tests

*Sean Hammond*

## Contents

## 13.1 Background

One of the most widely used methods of data collection in psychological research is psychometric testing. However, it must be said that there are a plethora of sub-optimal studies in the psychological research literature whose major failing is the ill-advised use of psychometric methodology. In this chapter I intend to address some of the main issues in psychometric testing in the hope that the reader should be able to make informed decisions when selecting a test for use in a research project.

There appear to be two main reasons for the popularity of psychometric tests in psychological research. First, psychometric tests have been developed to measure an extremely broad range of mental characteristics including aptitudes, competencies, personality traits, mood states, psycho-pathology, psychosomatic symptomatology, attitudes, motives and self-concept. These developments have provided the researcher with a wide variety of measurement tools which make a large number of psychological variables accessible for research. A second reason for the popularity of psychometric methods is the relative ease with which it is possible to collect large amounts of data. A great many psychometric tests, though by no means all, allow the researcher to gather data at one sitting from large numbers of respondents.

However, one reason why so many studies based on psychometric test data remain unconvincing is because the interest in using psychometric tests is not attended by an equal interest in the technicalities and sophistication of the psychometric principles that underlie their proper use. This lack of interest in psychometrics itself, coupled with an uninformed use of psychometric methods, has burdened the psychological research literature with poorly operationalised studies with little or no potential for replication.

Psychometrics means literally 'measurement of the mind' and psycho-metric tests are designed to measure the intrinsic mental characteristics of a person. One of the main problems confronting the researcher in psy-chology is how this measurement can be effected. Almost by definition, the variables under consideration will be those characteristics of the individual that do not lend themselves to simple physical measurement. For example the degree of extroversion that an individual has or his or her level of numerical reasoning are characteristics that are not accessible to such measuring devices as rules or weighing scales. Nevertheless, accurate measurement is a necessary prerequisite for any scientific exploration.

Due to this lack of direct access to the mental characteristics under scrutiny, the discipline of psychometrics has developed a detailed set of procedures and models for statistical estimation. Essentially, these pro-cedures rely on the presence of a large number of indicators which allow us to 'focus in' on the characteristic being measured. In most psychometric tests these indicators may be viewed as the individual items or questions of which they are composed.

## 13.2 Types of psychometric tests

There are many different types of psychometric test, each using a different strategy for data elicitation. The type of test is dictated by the theoretical orientation of the researcher as well as the kinds of questions being asked. For our purposes we will broadly describe the various types under four headings: projective tests, self-report inventories, objective tests and idiographic measures. Each of these types of test has a place in psychologi-cal measurement although each has its own application, advantages and limitations. It is always depressing to read an account of a researcher who believes that his or her preferred technique should be used in preference to all others. The choice of test must depend entirely on the nature of the research and the theoretical framework being applied. However, the underlying psychometric issues are similar irrespective of the test form. These are that the test should be reliable, valid and appropriate for the particular study it is being used for.

## 13.2.1　Projective tests

Projective tests are designed to be indirect measures of an individual's mental state. The common element in all these tests is that the testee is asked to proffer an unstructured response to some form of stimuli or task. Projective tests are typically widely used in identifying personality characteristics related to abnormal psychological functioning. One primary use of such tests is to examine aspects of the person that are considered to be unconscious. The basic idea is that issues a person would not normally be able to articulate directly may be accessed by the process of projective testing.

The most widely known projective test is the Rorschach ink-blot test in which the respondent is presented with a series of ambiguous stimuli in the form of ink-blots and is required to say what each brings to mind (Erdberg and Exner, 1984; Rorschach, 1921). The tester then interprets the responses according to a scoring protocol derived from some a priori theory (often psychoanalytic). He or she is then able to derive a score for the respondent often leading to placing the respondent within a diagnostic category.

There is a wide variety of projective tests available (Klopfer and Taulbee, 1976; Ziller, 1973). One popular form involves presenting respondents with pictures and asking them to compose a story around the image. Themes within these stories are then identified by the tester, again using an a priori theoretical framework, which enables a categorical judgement to be made of the respondent's mental state. Examples of these tests are the Blackie Test (psychoanalytic framework) (Blum, 1949) and the Thematic Apperception Tests (Murray's Needs framework) (Atkinson, 1958).

One of the weaknesses of projective tests is that they often operate at the nominal level of measurement, that is, simply provide a categorical description of the respondent. Procedures for more elaborate quantification of individual's responses do exist for some of the most well-used projective tests although they are nearly always complicated to learn (Atkinson, 1958; Exner, 1986). This is because of the almost infinite variety of possible responses which need to be coded and categorised.

Projective tests are frequently criticised due to the fact that they appear to lack objectivity. The tester's interpretation of open-ended information is

Figure 13.1 *An example of a Rorschach ink-blot*

often said to be subjective and arbitrary. While this is certainly a major issue in projective testing it is one that can be addressed with care and the rigorous application of objective scoring criteria. Of course, the basis of these criteria is the a priori theoretical model upon which the test is built. This means that projective tests are not normally appropriate in an eclectic research context. For this reason they are not widely used in research and tend to be more widely used in therapeutic contexts.

## 13.2.2   Self-report questionnaires

The use of self-report questionnaires as a means of measuring psychological characteristics grows out of the simple assumption that the best way of finding out about an individual is to ask direct questions. A large number of well-used self-report questionnaires exist and most of them are designed to measure personality traits or attitudes. The reason for this abundance is their comparative ease in administration and the almost limitless range of psychological characteristics that can be addressed.

One of the first self-report questionnaires to be developed was the Woodworth Personal Profile which was used during the First World War as a means of screening conscripts into the army and examples of some of the questions are provided in Figure 13.2. Woodworth's questionnaire is bizarre by today's standards but it is a useful reminder of how test items will reflect the prevailing attitudes and values that existed at the time they were developed.

Do you daydream frequently?
Do you usually feel well and strong?
Do you think you have hurt yourself by going too much with women?

Figure 13.2   *Example items from Woodworth's Personal Data Sheet*

It is important, therefore, that the questions, or items, in a self-report questionnaire are relevant to the characteristic being examined. Clearly, the accuracy of the measurement depends to a great extent upon this relevance. Thus, if we were developing a questionnaire to measure extroversion we may include questions on social activities and impulsivity while a question on a person's fondness for bicycles would have no bearing on the domain in question. This is an issue of content validity and we return to it later.

Questionnaires are often criticised as research tools due to the problem of response bias. This describes the situation in which respondents systematically fail to answer the questions accurately. There may be many reasons for response bias. It may be due to a deliberate attempt to present an image of themselves which is not true, a situation known as 'faking good'. In addition, respondents may possess an in-built tendency to answer 'yes' or 'no' to our questions producing a response bias termed 'response set'. Alternatively, the respondents may simply not know the answer to the question either through lack of self-knowledge or because the question is posed in an ambiguous manner. Thus, an important assumption in using self-report questionnaires is the accuracy of individuals' responses.

### 13.2.3   Objective tests

The development of the discipline of psychometrics grew out of early attempts to measure human abilities. The Social Darwinist approach of Sir Francis Galton in his desire to estimate intellectual potential from physical characteristics soon gave way to the more pragmatic approach of Alfred Binet. Binet devised a series of tasks, performance on which served to indicate the intellectual level of young children. Some examples of Binet's tasks are presented in Figure 13.3. Nearly all ability tests developed since have been based on Binet's basic strategy. Thus, tests of numerical reasoning present the respondent with a series of numerical tasks (for example, addition, division, etc.) while tests of verbal reasoning present the respondent with verbal tasks (such as synonyms and comprehension).

A distinction is often drawn between tests of **knowledge** and tests of **performance**. So the former type of test simply prompts the respondent to provide information, as in a history test with the item, 'Which year was the battle of Hastings?'. Alternatively, the test may ask the respondent to

Point to various parts of face (Age level 3)
Repeat 5 digits (Age level 7)
Recite days of the week (Age level 9)
Repeat seven digits (Age level 12)

Figure 13.3 *Examples of Binet's tasks*

carry out a task, as in the numerical reasoning test with the item, 'What is 16 multiplied by 7?'.

A further distinction may be made between **power tests** and **speed tests**. A power test asks respondents to respond to each item in their own time placing no time constraints upon them, while a speeded test asks respondents to respond to as many items as they can within a specific timeframe. Obviously, the speeded test is more practical to administer but it does carry the assumption that speed is associated with ability.

For the test to be useful it must be able to discriminate between respondents. Therefore, it is important that the tests are appropriate for the particular group of respondents on whom they are used. If the test is too easy a large number of the respondents may get every question correct and this will mean that the resulting measurement will not enable the tester to discriminate between respondents. In other words our research would be compromised by the existence of a **ceiling** (or floor) **effect**.

### 13.2.4 Normative, criterion referenced and idiographic tests

When we have obtained a test score, the problem remains how to interpret it. Simply having a 'Neuroticism' score of 12 tells us nothing about the respondent unless we can refer the score to some kind of standard. Most psychometric tests in use today are normative or norm referenced which means that data exist which tell us what range of scores is expected from the population under consideration. This requires that the means and standard deviations of a large representative sample are available to the tester so that he or she can interpret the meaning of an individual's score. These descriptive statistics are termed the 'norms'.

For example, most intelligence tests will be constructed so as to produce scores with a mean of 100 and a standard deviation of 15. A respondent with an IQ score of 130, therefore, is deemed to have a high IQ while a respondent with a score of 100 is deemed to be of 'average' intelligence. This means that the interpretation of the test score requires that there exists some normative information in the form of means and standard deviations relevant to the population from which a particular respondent is drawn. A vast majority of psychometric tests are developed as normative tests in which the test norms serve as a standard against which individuals are measured.

Of course, this assumes that the test score occupies a point along a continuum and that the population scores will conform to a normal distribution. Without a normal distribution the mean is not a useful measure of central tendency and so the standard deviation is meaningless as an index of variation. All norm referenced psychometric tests make this assumption of normality by definition.

It is possible to use criteria other than test norms for interpreting test scores as long as they are clearly specified in advance. This strategy is employed by a class of tests known as **criterion referenced** (Glaser, 1963). In this case an external performance criterion becomes the standard against which a respondent is judged. Typically, criterion referenced tests are used in the assessment of competencies particularly in an educational assessment context (Nitko, 1988).

For example, a set of reading problems may be given to a child. The criteria for entering a particular class is that the child will correctly solve each problem. If the child does not answer each question correctly they fail to reach the criterion and are not accepted into the class. The main point in criterion referenced tests is that the respondent either reaches a pre-specified criterion or does not. Obviously, this means that the criteria have to be established very accurately and precisely justified before the test is made available for use. Criterion referenced tests may also be interpreted normatively since the resulting score is usually a continuous, number correct, value. The test norms may be used for interpretation as well as the criterion pass mark as long as normative information exists.

The tests described so far rely for their interpretation upon a comparison, either with normative or external a priori criteria, so that an individual respondent can be placed in some relative position. However, there are situations in psychological research where focus is upon the individual respondent and placing him or her on a relative scale is irrelevant. An example of such a study might be one where a researcher wishes to follow a patient over a course of psychotherapy and attempt to measure the change in psychological state. In this case, the respondent may be asked to complete some form of questionnaire on a number of occasions and the changes over time serve as the focus of interest.

This approach is known as **idiographic** since it focuses on the individual respondent in isolation. This means that the questions that are asked of the respondent may be unique to him or her and indeed one of the most popular strategies for idiographic measurement is the use of a repertory grid in which the respondent generates the constructs that are of most personal relevance. This means that the assessment device is idiosyncratic and there is no commonality between respondents in the constructs being measured.

The idiographic approach has the drawback that comparisons between respondents are difficult if not impossible and the aggregation of idiographic data is meaningless. However, the approach may be of great value when the focus of interest is upon the dynamic processes within individuals.

## 13.3  The problem of reliability

As we have seen above, psychometric measurement depends upon estimation rather than direct measurement. As a result psychologists cannot expect to achieve perfectly accurate measurement. The role of the test developer is to produce tests which have the greatest accuracy possible and to provide for the test user details of the degree of accuracy that may be expected when using the test in question.

The earliest psychometric measurement theory stems from the work of Charles Spearman and is called variously, Classical Test Theory, True-Score Theory or Reliability Theory and it remains today the most widely applied basis for psychometric measurement. A number of other psychometric models have grown out of the classical approach, notably Generalisability Theory and Item Response Theory. Unfortunately discussion of these theories is beyond the scope of this brief chapter and the interested reader is referred to the introductory texts by Hambleton et al. (1991), Shavelson and Webb (1991) and Suen (1991). More detailed accounts may be found in Lord and Novick (1968), Cronbach et al. (1972) and Mislevy (1993).

The true-score model serves as the basis for classical test theory. In this model it is assumed that the test score is influenced by two factors. First, and most obviously, the true extent of the characteristic being measured will influence the tests score. The second influence is random error. This may be represented formally as:

$$\text{Observed} = \text{True} + \text{Error} \qquad (13.1)$$

Thus the test score, or observed score, is a function of the 'true' score and the error. The error may be positive or negative so that when we obtain a score from a test it may be an overestimate of the true score, or an underestimate. It is the job of the test developer to produce reliable psychometric tests in which the error is minimised. A reliable test is one where the 'true' score is close to the 'observed' score.

The error associated with a test score may be systematic or unsystematic. **Systematic error** refers to aspects of error that are built into the test itself and biases the resulting score consistently in one direction. Such error may be due to the use of ambiguous items or the situation where the test is influenced by another variable which is not being assessed. **Unsystematic error** refers to error which is external to the test itself and is assumed to be random such that it might equally result in inflated or attenuated scores. Classical test theory is built upon the assumption that the test has been constructed with sufficient care that systematic error is negligible and only unsystematic error exists.

Classical test theory also makes a number of assumptions about the nature of this unsystematic error variance:

1   Error variance is random.
2   Error variance is normally distributed with a mean of zero.
3   Error variance is completely independent of 'true' variance.
4   The error variance of different tests is not correlated.

The implications of these assumptions are that, if we tested an individual on a large number of tests for a single characteristic, the mean of these 'observed' scores will equal the mean 'true' score for that individual. This is because the error variance is partialled out by the operation of adding all the test scores together. This is shown in Figure 13.4. Thus, the argument that summing the responses to each item gives a reasonable estimate of the 'true' score only holds true if we can accept the assumptions of classical test theory.

The reliability of a test is an indication of whether it measures anything at all. As we have already said, the reliability of a test is an indication of the similarity between the 'true' and 'observed' scores. One way of conceiving reliability, therefore, is to think of the correlation between the 'true' score and the 'observed' score. Similarly, it may be possible to conceive of reliability as the ratio of 'true' variance to the total test variance:

$$\text{Reliability } (r_{tt}) = \frac{\sigma^2_{\text{true}}}{\sigma^2_{\text{observed}}} \tag{13.2}$$

In this way reliability can also be seen as the proportion of variance in test scores that is due to the variability of true scores. This is equivalent to the squared correlation between 'true' and 'observed' scores. The simple correlation between true and observed is known as the reliability index while the squared correlation between true and observed is termed the reliability coefficient.

|  | Partialling Error | | |
|---|---|---|---|
|  | Observed Score | True Score | Error |
| Time 1 | 22 | 21 | 1 |
| Time 2 | 24 | 21 | 3 |
| Time 3 | 18 | 21 | −3 |
| Time 4 | 19 | 21 | −2 |
| Time 5 | 22 | 21 | 1 |
| Mean | 21 | 21 | 0 |

Figure 13.4   *Simple example of classical test theory*

The greater the reliability a test has the less the error and the less the error the greater the accuracy. Therefore, reliability is associated with the accuracy of the test. If we are looking at the score of one person on a test of known reliability ($r_{tt}$) it is possible to estimate the accuracy of that person's score by calculating what is called the standard error of measurement (SEM).

$$\text{SEM} = \sigma_{\text{observed}} \sqrt{1 - r_{tt}} \tag{13.3}$$

The SEM allows us to generate confidence intervals for a single respondent's score. The SEM can be used to estimate the accuracy of a person's test score for two tests with differing reliability coefficients.

So far we have talked about reliability theoretically and have shown that it may be conceptualised as the correlation between true and observed. However, in practice we do not know the value of true and so the estimation of reliability is not quite as simple as this account might suggest. In order to estimate the reliability of a test psychologists have adopted the notion of consistency. The idea being that randomness is inconsistent, therefore, if we can identify consistency in our test we have the confidence of knowing that it is not simply a function of random error. There are a number of kinds of consistency that we can explore in our test but there are essentially four that are traditionally used.

### 13.3.1  Consistency between parallel tests

The idea of large numbers of parallel, similar, tests forms the basis of the development of classical test theory. The argument follows that if a perfectly parallel pair of tests exists then differences in scores must be due to measurement error since the true score will be the same for both tests. Where no error exists, the scores between the two tests will be perfectly consistent with each other. If enough parallel tests are used the average score of all the tests will equal the true score given that error variance is random. Of course, we must assume, as with classical test theory, that the tests have equal variance and the error variance of the tests are uncorrelated. Having made this assumption we can then estimate our correlation coefficient in the case of two parallel tests by calculating the correlation between them. The correlation between the two parallel forms is equivalent to the squared correlation between the 'observed' and 'true' scores.

Despite the fact that consistency between parallel forms is theoretically directly linked to the concept of reliability (Gulliksen, 1950) there are a number of glaring practical problems with this approach to reliability estimation. Most obviously, the procedure requires that we develop not one but two tests for the characteristic in question. Having done this we then have to ensure equivalence between the two forms. As we will see, test development is not a trivial procedure and requires a great deal of

investment of time and resources. In addition the time of test administration is doubled because both tests must be taken by the respondents.

### 13.3.2   Consistency across time (test-retest reliability)

Another approach to reliability estimation involves assessing the consistency of a test over time. To assess reliability a test is given to a sample of
respondents at time 1 and then is administered to the same respondents
later at time 2. The interval between the two administrations may vary
from a few days to a few years. The consistency of the scores between the
two administrations of the test is a measure of the reliability. In this case
reliability is viewed as an index of stability in which the test is thought of as
parallel with itself. The assumption is that any differences across time will
be due to measurement errors. The same basic assumptions can be made as
with parallel tests. Therefore, the correlation of the two administrations is
an estimate of the reliability coefficient.

One of the problems with estimating reliability by test-retest is deciding
on the appropriate interval between administrations. If the interval is too
short respondents may remember their responses to the first administration
and this may distort their responses at time 2. Usually, test-retest reliability
estimation requires an interval of one month or more. A second problem is
that this type of reliability assessment assumes that the characteristic being
measured is stable over time. It would make little sense to assess test-retest
reliability for a test of mood state since we would fully expect changes in
the characteristic to occur over time. Certain personality traits such as
extroversion are generally held to be stable over time as is intelligence.
However, the test user should be clear that this form of reliability
estimation makes assumptions, not only about measurement error, but
also about the thing being measured.

### 13.3.3   Internal consistency

A more practical method for estimating the reliability of a test is to
examine its internal consistency. This is based on the principle that each
part of the test should be consistent with all other parts. An early approach
based on this principle was suggested by Spearman (1907) and came to be
called the split half approach. In this procedure the test is administered to a
large sample and is then divided into half. This may be done by taking
even-numbered items as one half and odd-numbered items as the other
half. A score is obtained for each half of the test and a correlation between
the two halves ($r$) is calculated. The split half reliability coefficient is then
calculated by the following formula:

$$r_{tt} = \frac{2_r}{1 + r}$$
(13.4)

However, although the principle of split half reliability is reasonably straightforward there is one fundamental drawback and this is that different ways of splitting the test can produce quite different reliability coefficients. What was needed was a procedure that gave the average of all the possible combinations of split halves. This was precisely what Kuder and Richardson (1937) provided in a formula that came to be called the KR20 (Kuder and Richardson's 20th formula):

$$\mathrm{KR}_{20} = \frac{N}{N - 1} \cdot \frac{\sigma^2_{\text{observed}} - \Sigma pq}{\sigma^2_{\text{observed}}} \qquad (13.5)$$

The KR20 was developed for use with dichotomous items but it is very simply generalised for use with items measured on continua or rating scales. This generalisation was due to Cronbach (1951) and came to be called Cronbach's alpha. Alpha ($\alpha$) can be estimated in a number of ways but two methods are shown in formulae (13.6a) and (13.6b):

$$\alpha = \frac{N}{N - 1} \cdot \frac{\sigma^2_{\text{observed}} - \Sigma \sigma^2_i}{\sigma^2_{\text{observed}}} \qquad (13.6a)$$

$$\alpha = \frac{N}{N - 1} \cdot 1 - \frac{N}{N + 2\Sigma r_{ij}} \qquad (13.6b)$$

where $N$ is the number of items, $\sigma^2_i$ is the variance of item $i$ and $r_{ij}$ is the correlation between item $i$ and item $j$. The second formula (13.6b) shows the relationship that alpha has to the inter-item correlations. As we would expect with a procedure designed to estimate internal consistency, alpha is related to the average of all the inter-item correlations. The higher the correlations between the items the greater the internal consistency. This makes sense if we assume that all the items are indicators of a common characteristic. Thus each item must have variance in common with all the other variables. In other words, the reliability of a test is related to the homogeneity of the items with each other.

### 13.3.4 Inter-rater consistency

So far we have assumed that the test score is measured on a continuum and this is usually the case. However, we mentioned earlier that some psychometric tests produce measurement at the nominal level. Clearly, the procedures for estimating reliability detailed above, relying as they do on the correlation coefficient, are not appropriate for such data. In this case it is usual to estimate reliability by examining inter-rater consistency. For this procedure, two test scorers are used to generate the categorical score for a number of respondents. A contingency table is then drawn up to tabulate the degree of agreement between the two raters. The percentage agreement gives a rough estimate of reliability although a better estimate is obtained by calculating an index of agreement. This is usually Cohen's Kappa ($\kappa$) which ranges between 0 and 1 and represents the proportion of agreement corrected for chance (Cohen, 1960):

$$\kappa = \frac{Pa - Pc}{1 - Pc} \tag{13.7}$$

where *Pa* is the proportion of times the raters agree and *Pc* is the proportion of agreement we would expect by chance. In fact, it is possible to extend kappa to take into account more than one test scorer and so achieve an even more accurate estimate of reliability. Details of these extensions are beyond the scope of this chapter but the interested reader is referred to the basic papers of Fleiss (1971) and Light (1971).

## 13.3.5  General considerations

Unlike the kinds of statistical coefficients psychologists commonly deal with such as *t*, *F* and *r*, reliability coefficients apply only to the sample studied. This means that, strictly speaking we should not generalise from one sample to another. However, for the sake of simplicity they are usually treated as sample statistics and this does mean that they should be estimated on very representative samples. If the test reliability was estimated on a sample that differs from the sample upon which the test is to be used there is no guarantee that it will have a similar reliability in the new sample. For example, giving an IQ test developed for the general population to a sample of university students may produce reliability coefficients markedly lower than expected because the students would produce smaller test score variance. For this reason care must be taken when choosing a ready-made psychometric test for a research project.

It is also worth noting that the estimates of reliability described above are lower bound estimates. Thus, Cronbach's alpha coefficient gives us a low estimate of the reliability. The actual reliability may be slightly higher. While the type of test dictates the type of reliability estimate that is appropriate, it is generally assumed that KR20 and Cronbach's alpha are the most accurate estimates of reliability available within the classical test approach.

We should now turn to the tricky question of what is a 'good' reliability coefficient. Received wisdom (Nunnally, 1978) suggests that reliability coefficients should be greater than 0.7 before we can assume sufficient reliability for a research tool. However, if a psychometric test is being used for diagnostic of job selection purposes, it should have a reliability of at least 0.90.

The basic principle in deciding on whether a test is reliable is to remember that the reliability coefficient is a measure of the proportion of overlapping of 'true' and 'observed' variance. Thus, a test with a reliability of 0.7 means that 30 per cent of its variance is residual and irrelevant, a reliability of 0.6 suggests a test in which 40 per cent of its variance is made up of error.

The reliability of a test is dependent on the number of items in the test. Providing the items are of sufficient quality, the more the items the greater the reliability. This is entirely to be expected given that items are indicators of an underlying characteristic. Obviously, the more the indicators the more accurate our estimate of the 'true' score. This has often been used as an argument to excuse poor tests. A test with, for example, five items may be found to have a reliability of 0.5, and test developers have been known to argue that the reason for the low reliability is that the test only has five items and that it is a good test nevertheless. In fact, the test is not a good test on two counts. First, it is inadequate because it does not have enough items to describe the underlying characteristic, and second, it is highly unreliable. A small number of items does not excuse poor reliability estimates.

## 13.4 The problem of validity

In estimating the reliability of a test we are examining its viability as a measurement device. If we find that the reliability is low we have to assume that the test does not measure anything with any degree of credibility. The reliability of a test is not specific to the characteristic being measured. In other words, we may have a highly reliable test but discover that it does not measure the thing we think it does. This leads us to the problem of validity which may be posed as the question, 'How well does the test measure what it purports to measure?'.

As reliability asks whether a test measures anything at all it should be apparent that reliability logically precedes validity. We may have a reliable test that is not valid but we cannot have a valid test that is not reliable. Without reliability we cannot have validity.

An example of how we may have a reliable test without validity came to the author's attention a few years ago while conducting an undergraduate research methods class. The task was to construct a personality measure of a Freudian construct and the topic chosen was penis envy. The students dutifully set to work to write a set of questions that tapped this particular domain. Eventually a 50-item questionnaire was constructed which was then distributed to about 200 young women (the theory suggests that males do not manifest penis envy). Upon analysing the responses we were pleased to note that our internal consistency coefficient exceeded 0.8 suggesting that we had constructed a reasonable measurement device. However, a small but enterprising group of students had also collected data on a group of males, the expectation being that since the domain was not relevant to this population the responses to the questions would be random and produce very low reliability. As it happened the reliability was higher for males and, disconcertingly, males appeared to manifest higher scores on penis envy than did females. The problem was one of validity. We had constructed a reliable test but it was not a test of penis envy as was supposed. In fact it was probably better described as a test of salaciousness.

Assessing the validity of a test, therefore, requires a precise knowledge of the psychological domain under consideration together with a clear operational definition of each characteristic being measured. There are essentially three approaches to test validation. These are termed 'content validation', 'criterion validation' and 'construct validation'. Cronbach (1971) sees them as three different methods of inquiry.

## 13.4.1 Content validation

Content validation simply asks the question, 'Is the content of the test relevant to the characteristic being measured?' We may check the **face validity** of a test which is simply the subjective evaluation of the relevance of the test items. This particular form of validity check does have a place although it is often not given much credence because it lacks objectivity. Let us suppose that we have a particular characteristic we wish to measure (for example, degree of psychosis). We would first search through the literature until we come across a number of tests that purport to measure psychoticism. We would then need to examine the content of the test items to assure ourselves that the test does coincide with our own operational definition of the construct to be measured. In other words, is our operational definition the same as that of the test which is manifested in the content of its items? Thus, Eysenck and Eysenck's (1976) test of psychoticism measures what most people might term 'psychopathy' while the Minnesota Multiphasic Personality Inventory (MMPI) scale for 'schizophrenia' is more closely associated with the traditional use of the term 'psychotic'.

Having a test with clear face validity may also be useful in obtaining compliance from respondents since, if the items appear irrelevant, testees may become irritated. Nevertheless, in some cases face validity may be a liability since the respondent may identify the purpose of the questions and then proceed to answer them in a biased manner. Clearly, it is up to the researcher to determine whether a high degree of face validity is important for the study.

Content validation procedures are important when developing a test as it is necessary to construct items that sample the psychological domain in question. One strategy is to ask 'expert' judges to evaluate the relevance of the items to the characteristic being measured. If the judges agree that an item is not measuring the characteristic or they disagree on its relevance, the item may be considered equivocal and its content validity is questionable.

| 1 | $2 + 6 + 4 - 6 = ?$ |
|---|---|

2 *Bill has 2 apples, Jane gives him six bananas. Sam, who is trying to impress Jane with his generosity, gives Bill 4 more apples. Maggie then steals six apples from Bill. How many pieces of fruit does Bill have left?*

Figure 13.5 *Two items reflecting content validity*

In content validation, an important consideration is the complexity of the test item. A highly complex item may diffuse the focus of the question and result in contamination from some other characteristics that are not being measured. For example, the two questions in Figure 13.5 require the respondent to perform a simple arithmetic operation. However, question 2 is far more complex than question 1 and requires that the respondent has a reasonable reading ability. As a result, if question 2 were found in a test of children's arithmetic reasoning, we would have to question its content validity, since it is contaminated by the irrelevant variable 'reading ability'.

Content validation, then, is largely a qualitative process and it depends upon the tester having a clearly defined idea of what it is he or she wishes to measure.

## 13.4.2   Criterion validation

Criterion validation involves testing the hypothesised relationship of the test with external criteria. This is a more quantitative process than content validation but it requires that the tester is able to generate a reasonable set of hypotheses as to how the test should relate to the criteria variables. Criterion validation may be carried out under a number of headings including predictive validation and concurrent validation.

**Predictive validation** asks the question, does the test predict later behaviour? For example, a child's IQ score may be expected to predict scholastic success and a person's score from a test of the type A behaviour pattern should predict the later development of heart disease.

Predictive validation is vital when developing tests for aptitude or job selection since these tests are designed specifically to measure the potential of a person. It is necessary that a test being used to assess a respondent's potential should have a convincing body of empirical evidence demonstrating its relevance to the characteristics under consideration. Certainly, 'off-the-shelf' tests of personality appear to be poor predictors of job performance (Johnson et al., 1988).

Obviously predictive validity is a very important feature of a psychometric test since our choice of a psychometric test in research is commonly informed by assumptions of its predictive quality. However, when constructing a psychometric test the practicality of predictive validation is quite difficult due to the time involved. Many test constructors will adopt the more short-term strategy of postdictive validation in which test scores of individuals who already own the characteristic being predicted are compared with those without it. Thus, if our test purports to predict performance in a particular job, high-fliers in the job will be compared with those who are less adept. This is not strictly predictive validation because we cannot be sure that the variables being measured by the test have not been modified by an interaction between the person and the job. If high-fliers and inept employees had been screened before they started work we might have found no difference in test scores but the experience of the job might have differentially modified the characteristics being tested.

**Concurrent validation** involves observing the relationship between the test and other criteria that are measured at the same time. More often than not this involves a correlation between the test in question and one or more other measures for which a hypothesised relationship is posited. Thus, for example, scores on a self-report test of extroversion may be correlated with peer ratings of sociability. Usually multiple criteria are used and the pattern of correlations between the test in question and its validating criteria are examined to assess the concurrent validity of the test. It is always a good idea to include among the validating variables, a number of variables which are not expected to correlate with the test. In this way we can also check the specificity of the test.

### 13.4.3 Construct validation

It is important for multiple item tests that the internal structure of the test is examined. This often involves fitting the observed responses to some kind of measurement model. We have already seen that one way of assessing reliability is to examine internal consistency of the test items. The resulting coefficient (usually Cronbach's alpha) is based upon the homogeneity of the items, a high alpha occurring when the items correlate well together. In this way reliability evaluation may be viewed as a kind of construct validation. In this case the internal structure of the items is assumed to reveal inter-item homogeneity.

Another commonly hypothesised structure is that the items form a unidimensional scale. In this case the items are expected to have a particular pattern of correlations which reflects their order along a single latent trait. Some authors have confused unidimensionality with internal consistency and it is important to realise that alpha coefficients tell us nothing about the pattern of the inter-item correlations. The way to assess the unidimensionality of a scale is to use multivariate data analytic methods which allow you to examine the underlying structure of the test items (see Chapter 24). **Item response theory** is built upon the assumption of unidimensionality and it has a number of sophisticated techniques for confirming or disconfirming this structure.

It is also common for the test developer to suggest that there may be multiple dimensions underlying the test items. In this case, a number of distinct scales are expected to be found within the item pool. A good example of this is the 90-item Eysenck Personality Questionnaire which measures four traits – extroversion, neuroticism, psychoticism and response bias. The structure of the inter-item correlations is such that all the items designed to measure extroversion correlate well together but correlate less well with items from the other scales. This is expected to be true for each of the remaining traits. The procedure that is commonly used when assessing this multidimensional measurement model is known as factor analysis and it is described in Chapter 24.

Construct validation, then, involves testing hypotheses about the structure of the test. This often involves the use of quite sophisticated data analytic methods.

### 13.4.4   General issues of validation

Up to this point the reader would be excused for thinking that validity is an intrinsic feature of the test in question. In fact, one of the most widespread problems of validity in the use of psychometric tests in research relates not so much to invalid tests but rather to the invalid use of tests. When scholars are casting around for a standard test to use in their research they need to be particularly careful that the test they choose is appropriate for their use.

For example, British researchers often make use of tests developed on American samples. It is important that the test user justifies his or her use of such tests on British samples. Equally, a great many tests in common use are very old and there is no particular guarantee that items constructed even 10 years ago have the same meaning as they do today. The onus is on the researcher to provide a full and informed justification of his or her choice of psychometric test.

There are essentially four points about validity that should be born in mind.

1   There are numerous methods of validation which may be seen as different modes of enquiry (Cronbach, 1971). Their relative importance depends upon the test in question, its proposed usage and the conceptualisation of the construct it purports to measure.
2   Validity cannot be estimated by a single coefficient but is inferred from an accumulation of empirical and conceptual evidence.
3   Validation is cumulative. The validation of a test is an ongoing process which should last for as long as the test is used.
4   Validity is as much a function of the appropriate use of a test as of the test itself.

## 13.5 Conclusion

In this chapter we have discussed the two main issues in the use of psychometric tests – reliability and validity. The development of a psychometric test is a long and detailed process and a full account is beyond the scope of this chapter. However, the issues that we have raised while discussing the problems of reliability estimation and validation are central to test construction. Nevertheless, the psychological literature is peppered with poorly constructed tests where even these basic principles have not been adhered to. The continuing use of such weak tests does nothing for the science of psychology and simply serves to generate more random numbers to distract us from our true purpose as researchers, which is the identification of replicable and stable laws that govern behaviour. It is the role of researchers who wish to use psychometric tests to maintain high standards in the selection of the tests they use. This requires that researchers using psychometric tests should be aware of the major issues in psychometric methodology. This chapter has attempted to provide a basis for this awareness but its necessary brevity means that it cannot hope to provide a full account. It is hoped that researchers planning on using psychometric tests will consult further texts such as Kline (1993), Suen (1991) or Murphy and Davidshofer (1991).

## 13.6 Further reading

Paul Kline has written a number of introductory books in the area of psychometrics. His *Handbook of Psychological Testing* (1993) is a good comprehensive introduction which should be accessible to both under-graduate and postgraduate researchers. An equally comprehensive book is Cronbach's (1990) *Essentials of Psychological Testing* (5th edn). This book goes into slightly more technical detail than Kline's tome and it serves as an authoritative reference. Another very readable account of psychometric testing issues is Anastasi's (1990) *Psychological Testing* which stands as one of the seminal works in its comprehensive treatment of the issues involved. For the complete beginner, Rust and Golombok's (1989) accessible treatment, *Modern Psychometrics*, offers a practical introduction.

Finally, any researcher who is seriously considering psychometric research should consult a text on test theory. An excellent starting point is Suen's (1991) *Principles of Test Theories*. This introduces the principles underlying classical test theory as well as Item Response Theory and Generalisability Theory.

# 14   Direct Observation

*Jill Wilkinson*

## Contents

## 14.1   Introduction

Observation is a fundamental aspect of any science and has played an essential part in the development of psychology as a scientific discipline. The major strength of direct observation is precisely that it is direct. There is virtually no time delay between the occurrence of the responses in question and their recording, by either the observer or some recording device. Observations are also more direct than interviews or questionnaires in that they do not require the subjects to respond in word representations to stimuli presented in word representations.

Observation was the most important method of data collection in the early years when psychology was involved in establishing itself on a par with the natural sciences and keen to dissociate itself from its earlier 'unscientific' origins in introspection and philosophy. Psychology accordingly came into the laboratory. Here the subject is in a controlled environment in which conditions can be held constant and the individual components of the situation manipulated. In this way the effect of each variable can be examined in turn. One of the main problems with this approach was it took us farther and farther away from what people actually did in their lives and how, in reality, they behaved in the situations they encountered. In its haste to progress, psychology seems to have rather rushed through what, in the natural sciences, is the basis of scientific research: the systematic and rigorous observation and description of phenomena in their natural state, before attempting to exert any form of manipulative control.

As the discipline progressed, the emphasis shifted from the observation of overt events, to an interest in the covert, cognitive aspects of human functioning and the subsequent decline in the role of observation in experimental psychology. This has coincided with, and to some extent been compensated for by the emergence of interest in very different approaches to observation, noticeably **ethology**, which tends to focus on behaviour in natural settings and which aims to exert little or minimum experimental control over the subjects under observation.

Regardless of the ebb and flow of interest in the various approaches to the use of observation, it remains one of psychology's most important research tools. It is of particular value to those studying the behaviour of populations who cannot give accounts of themselves. For example, Wilson et al. (1991) used observation in their study of the effects of sensory stimulation with patients in prolonged coma and Dunn (1988) carried out a number of systematic studies of children's understanding of the feelings and behaviour of others in their family world. Dunn was particularly interested in observing the children 'within the drama and excitement of family life' (1988: i) and used a combination of observational procedures including detailed pre-coded categories of behaviour, narrative notes and audiotaped recordings to examine behaviour such as teasing, witnessing disputes between mother and a sibling, making justifications and excuses for disputes and enlisting adult help during sibling conflicts, or those with profound learning difficulties. There are also some behaviours or situations on which subjects would be unable to report with any degree of accuracy, such as non-verbal behaviour which often takes place outside our conscious awareness (for example, Beattie, 1983) or domestic situations where there is a high level of emotion. Observation is also useful in situations where there may be some investment in impression management or a 'correct' way of responding. For example junior doctors may know theoretically how they should break bad news to a patient and this may influence any self-report of their responses in such situations.

These are just some of the of areas of investigation in which direct observation might be the preferred method or one of several methods of collecting data for a particular study. Clearly what is observed will depend on the goals and purpose of the study in question, but the examples do highlight the wide range and variation of possible target behaviours from a discrete non-verbal response to a highly complex social interaction. This chapter will outline the main approaches to observation and then discuss some of the practical and theoretical issues and the various stages in planning and implementing observational research.

## 14.2 Observational approaches to the study of behaviour

A knowledge of the various approaches to direct observation is particularly important when considering using observation as a means of collecting data. The two possibly most influential trends come from very different theoretical perspectives: experimental psychology and ethology. Other important influences include ecological psychology and ethnography. The kind of data each approach yields is quite different and will be discussed in section 14.8.

**Systematic observation** was developed in the context of experimental psychology and has traditionally been the mainstay of behavioural theory and research. Here the methods of observation are systematic and standard procedures for obtaining data and can be considered as extensions of measurement theory and methods. In order to conduct this type of systematic observation, the researcher needs to define the categories and units of behaviour to be observed and to work out ways of measuring them. This usually involves timing, counting or rating them. This may necessitate a period of informal observation of the behaviour in its natural state, but this will involve nothing like the detailed recording characteristic of the ethogram described below.

**Ethology** is a very different approach to observation. It is an interdisciplinary science combining zoology, biology and psychology to the study originally of animal, but more recently, of human behaviour usually in the natural rather than the laboratory environment. The ethological approach is characterised by a particular method of direct observation which aims to record the behaviour completely impartially in all its detail, correlating it with the stimuli which evoke it. No evaluations are made, nor attempts made to infer motivations, intentions or emotions of the subjects under observation. The resulting account is called an **ethogram**. Only when the ethogram is complete will ethologists consider formulating hypotheses which can form the basis of experiment and analysis and only when the ethologist knows what behaviour there is to modify, will any attempt be made to modify it. On the whole though, ethologists prefer to leave their subjects alone.

Another area that has developed and employs its own observational procedures is **ecological psychology**. This approach has similar aims to that of ethology, that is, to describe and analyse the life-systems of individuals in their natural environments and detailed commentaries are made of all activities and stimuli with which the person comes into contact. There are, however, some fundamental differences between the two approaches, the most crucial being that whereas ethological reports must be purely descriptive, ecologists are concerned with making inferences about the attitudes, motives and intentions of their subjects.

**Ethnography** is an approach to research which employs observation as one of a range of methods of collecting and analysing data. This is dealt with in Chapter 20.

## 14.3   Types of observation

**Casual observation** often takes place at the planning stage of research. Observing a situation with relatively open eyes, ears and mind can provide valuable insights and yield information indispensable for subsequent meaningful data collection. Casual observation is helpful for making decisions about the best location in which to make the observations and for developing the categories to be used in systematic observation. It is essential to make notes of casual observations as first impressions are usually the most vivid and are most useful when written down immediately.

**Formal observation** is the planned and systematic application of a system of procedures for conducting the observations or gathering the data usually from one or a combination of the theoretical approaches discussed above. It usually involves an unintrusive observer who makes field notes and/or times, counts or rates behaviours or events. Sometimes a video-camera will replace the observer in the field or laboratory and the tape will be subsequently analysed. The rest of this chapter is concerned mainly with these kinds of formal observations.

**Participant observation**, as the name implies, differs from casual and formal observation in that the observer is part of the events being studied. There are a number of advantages to this approach. It enables access to possibly more private events which subjects would not allow an outsider to observe; it can give access not only to behaviours but the attitudes, opinions and feelings and it overcomes the problem of observer effects (see section 14.9). The main criticisms are that it is impossible for the participant observer to be objective, that the observations will be subjected to fluctuations in the attention of the observer, the ethical and procedural problems of becoming an observer if the person has a role in the setting and the not inconsiderable personal demands made on the researcher by the dual role and the possibility of role conflict.

## 14.4   What to observe

It would clearly be impossible to observe everything. Which situations, events, behaviours or actions are selected for observation will depend on factors such as the nature of the research problem/question, the hypothesis to be tested, the specific relationships being examined and the underlying theoretical framework. Data must ultimately be reduced to a form where they can be analysed and this is usually achieved by classifying, rating and/ or measuring the duration and frequency of behaviours or events. This can be done either at the time of the original observations and the data recorded in a pre-coded form (the standard behavioural approach), from written objective non-evaluative narrative accounts (the ethological approach) or classification may start in the field and be developed and refined 'back home' (ecological and ethnographic approaches). Responses can also be recorded on audiotape or videotape and subsequently analysed in the laboratory.

Usually the first stage in deciding what to observe is to conduct some informal observations and to identify the broad categories of behaviours to be studied. Examples of categories might be 'assertive behaviour', 'pupil initiative', 'temper tantrums'.

Decisions also need to be made not only about what to observe but *who* to observe, and this may have a bearing on the choice of categories. For example, in examining the conversational behaviour of someone suffering from a psychiatric disorder is he or she the only person targeted for observation or would you be interested in the effect that person's behaviour might have on others involved in the interaction?

Another very important consideration at this stage relates to the breadth of information sought within the broad categories, usually referred to as **units of behaviour**. Small segments of behaviour such as short phrases, expressive gestures, looking at and face touching are known as **molecular** units and are relatively easy to define and measure reliably. However, molecular units of behaviour taken out of context may have little meaning in the real world and thus validity is reduced. There are some notable exceptions where individual behaviours are pertinent to the research problem, for example, in social skills research (for example, Bellack et al., 1983) and studies of non-verbal behaviour (for example, Beattie, 1983).

The **molar** approach takes larger behavioural wholes as units of behaviour. The size of the molar units can vary considerably depending on the subject of the research and the theoretical orientation of the researcher. Ecological molar units can be quite long sequences of behaviour lasting several minutes and include events such as going to school or walking with a friend. Other examples of molar units might be 'buys sweets at the newsagents', 'does homework'. These type of molar units are usually defined as occurring within the conscious awareness of the individual. That is, the person knows what he or she is doing.

Molar units can also be qualitative and might include categories of behaviour such as 'cooperativeness', 'friendliness', 'discomfort' or 'openness'. Molar categories of this type tend to be more psychologically meaningful (and therefore more valid) than discrete molecular units of behaviour. They are, however, likely to require a fair degree of inference on the part of the observer and data are often in the form of ratings, which are, of course, subjective. This may therefore reduce the reliability and validity of this sort of data. Attempts have been made to define operationally molar constructs like 'friendliness' by trying to identify and list the behavioural components. This can achieve a high degree of precision and reliability. The problem is that in doing this, often the whole flavour of what is being observed is also reduced.

Clearly, there is no 'ideal' solution to the problem. Both molecular and molar units have their advantages and disadvantages in terms of reliability and validity. The size and type of the unit of observation chosen will depend on the type of study undertaken. The most important thing is to choose the size of unit which makes sense in terms of the aims of the research, to be aware of the limitations associated with the size of unit and to be as rigorous as possible in overcoming them.

## 14.5  Defining behaviours

Examples were given above of the kind of units of behaviour which are often the subject of observation in psychological research. But what is meant by, for example, 'looking at (the other person in the interaction)'? Is looking at the person's kneecaps counted as 'looking at him'? Clearly the answer from a common-sense view is 'no'. But what about looking at his neck or chin? This is not so clear-cut. Similarly we all know a smile when we see one. Or do we? When does a smile become a grimace? What about 'nervous' smiles? It gets worse when we get on to the qualitative molar behaviours in the example. We use constructs like openness in our everyday communications and people seem to know what we mean. But do they always agree with you? If not is this because you have different perspectives on the person in question, possibly see them in different contexts, or is it because your idea of openness is not quite the same as the other person's? This is all right in everyday life. People can argue about and hopefully resolve their differences. This is one of the fundamental ways in which everyday and scientific observations differ. The behavioural scientist needs to be able to measure behaviour reliably, and in order to do this, the measurement of the constructs needs to be valid. There is no point in having a list of seemingly quite specific behaviours unless people can agree on precisely what is meant by the various labels employed to describe them.

Where responses are being classified and possibly measured at the time of the observation, definitions of the behaviours need to be constructed and evaluated in advance of the period of observation. Where the data are recorded on videotape or by detailed narrative, decisions about units of behaviour and their definitions can be made with reference to these taped or written records. The observer using narrative would nevertheless need to have some idea of the size of unit in order to record the observations at a level of detail required for subsequent analysis.

Definitions of the units of behaviour should be clear, complete, unambiguous and couched in terms of observable characteristics. Dunn and Kendrick (1982), for example, in a study of siblings, define the unit of behaviour 'child gives' as 'child gives, shows or points out object to mother' and 'child sits' as 'child sits without playing, eating, drinking, or talking or any activity other than sucking thumb or handling comfort object'.

It is usually more straightforward when the unit is expressed in behavioural terms, as in the preceding example. When the unit involves a quality of behaviour, such as 'friendly', 'aggressive' or 'open' behaviour it is rather more complex but attempts should be made at an operational definition in order to tell others what *you* mean by the term. For example, 'By "openness" I mean readily gives information about self when asked. The information should include more than that demanded by the question and should be at a level of self-disclosure similar or only slightly deeper than the preceding content.' It can be seen that this still involves the observer having to make inferences from the subject's behaviour and using judgements about self-disclosure, although some guidelines are given to the observer in this respect. While this may not be acceptable to a behavioural 'purist' it may, in the interest of collecting some data, be permissible. Ideally, a complete definition should be constructed to include the descriptive name, the definition and elaboration (rather like in a dictionary) and typical examples, borderline examples and examples of what would not be included. These definitions should then be tested out on a pilot study and modified accordingly.

The above procedure is very time-consuming and unless the scope of the observations is fairly narrow would probably be out of range for most postgraduate students working on their own. What often happens in practice is that researchers often use and modify categories, behavioural units and definitions developed by other researchers working in the same or related area. You cannot assume, however, that because the work has been published you can accept uncritically other people's definitions. They are not always as rigorous as they should be and may need further refinement. Because this level of information is usually not published in research papers, you will probably need to write to the researchers requesting the information and explaining your reason for doing so.

## 14.6 Sampling

Having decided on the broad categories and possibly on the more specific units of behaviour and their definitions you need to think about how you are going to sample the situations, events or behavioural units in question. There are a number of methods of sampling behaviour, the most relevant being event sampling, time sampling and the use of simulated situations.

**Event sampling** is used when studying a particular type of event, such as temper tantrums, fights, playground games and marital rows. It is extremely important to have very clear definitions of the class of event in order to be sure that what is being observed is what you call a 'temper tantrum' and also that you do not miss the event while trying to decide if it is one! One of the main strengths of event sampling is that there is an inherent validity in studying a 'complete' phenomenon from beginning to end rather than the more 'piecemeal' behavioural acts which are often the focus of time sampling. Event sampling also enables the observation of events that are relatively rare and would probably not be picked up by time sampling. Clearly, though, with event sampling the researcher needs to know when the event is likely to occur or to be prepared to wait until it does occur.

**Time sampling** is the selection of periods of observation at different points in time. Observation units can be chosen in a systematic way, say, two five-minute observation periods at specified times during each of the three nursing shifts on a ward, or randomly, four five-minute observation periods selected at random from a universe of five-minute periods. There are many ways in which time samples can be set up and selected but how many periods and for how long and whether they are systematic or random will be influenced by the research problem. With time sampling the researcher is assured of obtaining representative samples of behaviour, but only behaviour that occurs relatively frequently. The main drawback to time sampling is that it lacks continuity and the quality of completeness found in event sampling.

Event sampling and time sampling assume that the behaviour in question is going on 'out there' somewhere; but what happens if you want to sample responses which take place only rarely or not at all in the subjects' natural environment, such as conversational skills of schizophrenics living fairly isolated lives in the community, or people's behaviour when confronted by the threat of fire. Sometimes behaviour can only be, or is best, sampled by constructing **simulated situations** in which the subjects knowingly or unknowingly take part. A particular type of simulated situation called a role-play is often used in clinical research and studies evaluating the effects of various types of training programmes and procedures. Role-plays offer highly standardised situations which allow for comparisons to be made between subjects or groups and usually take place in laboratory settings. An example of a role-play set up for the purpose of observing conversation with strangers in a semi-social setting might involve constructing a situation with a stooge who would have been instructed to respond in various pre-arranged ways, such as asking particular questions or responding to the subject in a friendly or cool way. The subject would be informed of the context of the interaction and instructed to behave in particular ways, such as to start a conversation with the stooge, or to try to make the stooge feel 'at home'. One of the main problems with using this sort of simulated situation concerns the ecological validity of such procedures; that is, the degree to which the behaviour of the subjects in the laboratory corresponds to their behaviour in the natural environment. Results of studies of generalisability of behaviour in role-played interactions is equivocal, but it has been found that longer played interactions have greater ecological validity than role-played scenes which require only brief responses. Ecological validity, however, is not always an issue. You might be interested not in what subjects actually *do* in their natural environments but what they *can* do. It is important to remember that subjects cannot produce behaviours in the laboratory that are not in their repertoires. Conversely, because they do not exhibit a behaviour in a simulated situation, does not necessarily mean it is not present in other situations.

One way to increase ecological validity of simulated situations is not to let on to the subject that they are taking part in the experiment. There are many examples of people being invited to a laboratory to be the subject of one experiment unaware of the fact that they are taking part in another one. For example, conversational skills of subjects have been observed in a waiting area while waiting to take part in the 'real' experiment (Gutride et al., 1973) and subjects' responses to (simulated) epileptic seizures while ostensibly involved in a project about student problems (Latane and Darley, 1970). This sort of deception clearly has ethical implications and these must be fully explored before undertaking any research employing such procedures.

## 14.7 The environmental setting

There is a vast range of possible environmental settings that could be used for conducting research involving direct observation. In practice, however, most observational data are collected in clinics or hospitals, in people's own homes, in schools and in laboratories. Whether the observations take place in the laboratory setting or in the field will depend on considerations such as sampling (discussed above), the theoretical approach adopted and the degree of environmental control desired.

As ethology is primarily concerned with the precise observation of organisms in their natural habitat and ecological psychology with the interaction of the environment with the behaviours of the organisms in it, observations from these perspectives take place almost exclusively in the field. Behavioural research, on the other hand, is frequently conducted in the laboratory where it is possible to have a higher degree of environmental control often considered desirable in experimental psychology. It would be necessary, however, to make the observations in the natural environment when the target behaviours only occur in the presence of other events which cannot be duplicated in an analogue setting, such as playground fights, behaviour at football matches and marital arguments (although there are undoubtedly some couples who could produce the behaviour in question at any time, in any place, including the laboratory).

Although there is considerable ecological validity in observing behaviour in its natural setting there are some drawbacks other than those discussed in relation to sampling. You will probably require the consent and cooperation of others in the environment, your schedule for observing could be disrupted by factors beyond your control, naturalistic observation is time-consuming and you may encounter ethical, legal or practical problems if you want to use video- or audiotape. For a discussion of the ethical problems of observing private behaviour see Middlemist et al. (1976) on personal space invasion in the lavatory and also Koocher (1977) on bathroom behaviour and human dignity.

## 14.8    Methods of collecting and recording observational data

Observations can be recorded in a narrative form or on video- or audiotape and subsequently transformed into data by classifying, or measuring the various elements of behaviour. Alternatively, data can be collected at the time of observation by a similar process of classifying and measuring. If data are being collected directly from the observations as they occur, then the categories and measurement strategies, as discussed above, will have been predetermined and no permanent record is kept of the sequence or details of the actual responses other than can be inferred from the data.

**Narrative data** comprise a form of 'raw' data which only take on any meaning when translated into categories or numerical form. Typically narrative accounts aim to reproduce behavioural events in a written form in much the same way, and in the same sequence, as they originally occur, often aiming for little or no interpretative content. In reality, observers are selective in their observations (see section 14.9) so not everything that happens can be recorded and many researchers find that without some inference, interpretation of narrative data is difficult.

Usually, narrative is used to describe particular episodes, or anecdotes, where there is a beginning, a middle and an end. You will already have made decisions about what constitutes the class of episode in question (see section 14.5) and the size of the units of behaviour, whether molar or molecular or a combination (see section 14.4). You need also to decide on the level of inference you are going to allow in your written account. There is no 'correct' way or set pattern to writing up anecdotal reports but they should always be as complete as possible. It is better to include too much at this stage than too little. Material can always be discarded in the analysis.

There is usually a main person under observation in the episode and reports should include the basic actions and statements (using direct quotations wherever possible) of this person and the responses and reactions of the others involved. Enough details of the setting should also be included and should indicate when and where the behaviour occurred and under what conditions.

Reports should also be as objective and accurate as possible. It is better to say 'she left the room, fists and jaw clenched, slamming the door noisily behind her' than 'she left the room angrily'. Notice how it is description at a molecular level that gives clues about the emotional tone. Sometimes it is more difficult to communicate meaning without evaluative labels. 'She handed her the letter in an offhand way' could be described in objective behavioural terms, but some of the flavour of the action would undoubtedly be lost. It should be noted, however, that this is one person's *interpretation* of what happened and where interpretations are included or inferences made, they should be differentiated from the main description by the use of inverted commas or some other marking device.

It is important to write up the report as soon as possible after the period of observation, during which notes can be made of key words or essential features of the incident. Writing and observing at the same time is quite a skill in itself and audiotape recorders are often used to supplement the observations. When undertaken with due rigour, anecdotal descriptions can be valuable research tools as well as fascinating to construct. They are useful for recording behaviour in a variety of contexts such as classrooms, hospital wards and the home environment.

**Field notes** are a type of narrative data often used in ethnographic studies and by other participant observers. Like anecdotal reports, they aim to present the sequence of action and interaction but they are less concerned with describing behaviours and events and more with interpreting aspects of the situation which are of particular interest to the researcher. The transformation of the observations into data therefore starts in the field and is an ongoing process which, in turn, influences the subjects of subsequent observations.

**Videotaped data** could also be described as narrative data, but similarly, only becomes 'real' data when converted into a form which can be subsequently analysed. With the development of the now ubiquitous video camera many researchers and students alike envisaged a transformation in observational procedures and the possibilities seemed endless. Video-recordings offer a relatively cheap and semi-permanent record (that is, unless you accidentally record over it) which can be played back repeatedly allowing for analysis at a level of detail and reliability not previously possible from observations made directly in the laboratory or field.

There are a number of factors to be taken into account when thinking of using video-recordings. Subjects are often moving targets unless instructed to remain seated, or in a situation, like a meeting, where you can anticipate that they will remain seated. In the natural environment other people can get between the camera and the subject resulting in the loss of possibly quite important information. Therefore, what you are hoping to record and how you are going to follow the actions of your subjects needs careful consideration. Where the scene involves people other than the main subject, you will need to decide in advance who to include in the recording. If you decide that the responses of others are important and should be included, this will reduce the amount of data available to you from the actual subject. You might not, for example, have the face in sufficient close-up to observe the subtleties of facial expression, or the direction of eye gaze. If you try to overcome this when filming by using the zoom, it should only be used at fixed, predetermined times during the filming, otherwise you will be adding you own interpretation to the 'raw' data, thereby threatening its validity.

These days most people are well used to being filmed: by security cameras, by their relatives, by film crews on location and by anthropologists! Nevertheless, using a camera in a public place or even in an institution can cause quite a stir. This can interfere both with the process of collecting the data and also the behaviour of the subjects (reactivity of subjects to being observed is discussed in section 14.9). Filming in public places also has ethical and legal implications particularly if the people you are filming are unaware that they are the subjects of your research or if you are filming in a potentially 'sensitive' area, such as where drugs are sold. These complications are less likely to arise if you are filming in an institution, where issues of access will probably be the responsibility of the organisation, but this is something you need to check out carefully. Getting permission to film in an institution might also involve negotiating with a large number of people and this could be extremely time-consuming and frustrating (see Chapter 3).

Filming in the laboratory is usually much easier. Because you can have a great deal more environmental control in the laboratory than in the natural setting, you can position cameras and instruct subjects in order to optimise your chances of recording the behaviours in question. In the laboratory cameras may be placed unobtrusively or positioned in such a way to provide recording from several angles, or of different people in an interaction, if you have access to split-screen facilities.

Many cameras have in-built facilities for recording the time, date or other numbers or letters. It is usually a good idea to use these and also the coded number of the subject so that the recordings are readily identifiable. Some systems also have timing devices which will display the running time on the screen and which can be zeroed at the start of each recording. This can be very useful for timing or pinpointing particular behaviours or sequences when transforming the recordings into data.

Considerable care needs to be taken at the filming stage as the data into which the tapes are transformed will only be as valid as the recordings themselves. As with any form of narrative data the recordings should be as complete as possible. Redundant material can always be discarded at a later stage.

**Checklists** are used for classifying and measuring the frequency and/or the duration of behaviours during the observation period itself and can also be used for converting video-recorded material into data. Checklists usually consist of a number of behavioural units or categories with clear descriptions of each unit (see sections 14.4 and 14.5). Then, depending on the characteristics of the units of behaviour and what the researcher wants to know, the observer can note the existence or non-existence of the behaviours on the checklist, can count the number of occurrences of the behaviour (the frequency) or can take various measures of duration in relation to the behaviours in question. Where the units of behaviour are molar, frequency and duration measures can be made directly from observations. With molecular units, such as glances or posture shifts it is easier if the observations are recorded on videotape. This also has the advantage of making it possible to code any number of behaviours, rather than the limited number it is possible to observe in the field.

**Frequency data** are obtained by counting the number of times a behaviour occurs during an observation period. This can then be expressed as a rate per minute, per hour or per day to allow for comparisons to be made between observation periods of different lengths. Frequency measures can be recorded on a simple mechanical counter and are relatively easy to obtain providing you can actually see them, that you have clear, unambiguous definitions and descriptions of the behaviours you are attempting to count and that the behaviours have a clearly discernible onset. If you cannot identify when a behaviour starts, then you cannot code it reliably. Frequency measures, however, cannot give any information on duration, intensity or the quality of behaviour.

There may be particular reasons why you might want to collect frequency data which are to do with the subject of the research. It is also the case that some behaviours lend themselves to counting, others to timing and some to both. Where the behaviour is relatively brief and clearly defined, such as a head-nod, a major posture shift or asking for information, then frequencies are probably the most appropriate measures. When there are longer sequences of behaviour, such as responses to questions or 'nervous' self-touching behaviour then it may be better to use **duration** measures. As with frequencies, you need to be able to tell when the behaviour starts and also when it ends. Response duration measures can be transformed into frequency data, percentage of total time and average response duration. In addition to measuring the duration of the response itself, you might be interested in measuring the time between a specific stimulus and the response or 'latency', for example, the time between the end of a question and the beginning of the response, or the inter-response time. Stop watches or the running clocks on videotaped material are the simplest way of recording duration times. Event recorders can also be used if available. These usually consist of a number of buttons, corresponding to behavioural categories, on a control board which are electrically connected to pens. The observer depresses the appropriate button when the behaviour begins and holds it down until the behaviour terminates. Pens mark on continuous paper and provide a permanent record over time.

Frequency and duration measures in themselves do not give information about when the events occurred unless you record the time which elapses during and between the responses. One way of doing this is to record your observations using some type of **interval-recording** system. With interval recording, the observation period is divided into usually quite brief intervals of time, say 10 seconds, which are indicated by some sort of cueing device such as bleeps on a tape-recorder. In **whole interval** recording, the behaviour is recorded only if it occurs throughout the whole interval and with **partial interval** if the behaviour occurs during a portion of the interval, which can be specified. **Frequency within interval** is where the behaviours occurring within each interval are counted and in **momentary time sampling** the behaviour is recorded only if it is observed at a specified moment within the interval, usually at the beginning or end. There are several advantages to interval-recording systems in addition to providing some idea of the sequence in which the behaviour occurred: by dividing the time into units, any disagreements between observers can be pinpointed, thereby increasing the possibility of obtaining reliable data; estimates of both frequency and duration can be made; it is possible to observe several behaviours at the same time and, with the exception of 'frequency within interval', it can be used for recording behaviours that do not have clear onsets or endings, such as the sort of head and upper body movements that are often visible during conversations. Part of the difficulty with using the various systems of interval recording is that the estimates are often biased. Mathematical formulae, however, have been produced which estimate the error produced by partial-interval, whole-interval and momentary time-sampling procedures when used to estimate duration (Ary, 1984).

**Ratings** can be used for measuring the qualitative aspects of behaviour, such as 'appropriateness of verbal content' in the speech of schizophrenic patients, or 'degree of anxiety' shown by students giving presentations. Whereas with checklists, the only judgements the observer has to make is whether or not a particular behaviour belongs in a predetermined category, ratings require the observer to make a subjective evaluation about the behaviour in question. There are a number of ways of reducing the subjectivity of qualitative ratings: points along an evaluation continuum can be explicitly defined to provide evaluation guidelines; ratings can be made 'blind' by observers who do not know the subjects nor preferably the aims of the research and, of course, through the construction of clear, comprehensive descriptions.

# 14.9   The observer

The very fact that someone knows they are being observed, either by another person or by a camera or tape-recorder, can affect the way in which they would normally behave in a given situation. This is known as **observer effect** or **reactivity** and can present a threat to the validity of the data. It is necessary to be aware of this when planning to use observational methods as there are a number of things that can be done to reduce reactivity. Observers and/or equipment can be placed as unobtrusively as possible; you can even try to hide. If you cannot hide you could at least try to make sure your dress and behaviour attracts as little attention as possible; blend in with the surroundings. You may be able to get your subjects to habituate to your presence so they no longer take any notice of you. Subjects may also behave differently if they know precisely what you are observing and why. It is probably better to tell them only in the broadest terms. You could also tell your subjects that you are going to observe them but not tell them exactly when. Finally you could resort to deception and not tell your subjects you are observing them at all but this approach may have serious ethical implications which should be thoroughly explored and considered before deciding to go ahead with it.

Reactivity can modify not only the behaviour of the subjects under observation, it can have an effect on the observers as well. This often takes the form of **observer bias**. If you are committed to the experimental hypothesis of the project (which you may well be if it is your own project) this may well influence your perceptions of events. You may, quite unwittingly, 'see' events that conform to your theory and miss others that do not. Bias is even more likely to creep in if you are making ratings of qualitative aspects of behaviour which calls for observer interpretation. Observer bias therefore clearly reduces the reliability of the data and every attempt should be made to minimise it.

One way of doing this is to get someone else, who does not have the full details of the project and is 'blind' to your hypothesis, to observe with you for a proportion of the observations. This is obviously much easier if you are observing from video-recordings. Inter-observer agreement can then be calculated and there are a number of statistics available for this purpose. Cohen's Kappa is probably the most commonly used index of inter-rater reliability (see Bellack and Hersen, 1988). It should be noted, however, that when observers know that this sort of reliability check is being made on them, they tend to reach a higher level of agreement than when they are unaware that checks are being made. If you are using ratings perhaps you could get an independent observer to make them, or better still, a panel of, say, three people which could, depending of how they were selected, reduce the possibility of cultural or sex bias. This would only probably be feasible with recorded material.

A rather more straightforward threat to reliability of observational data comes from the understandable limitations of the observers themselves. They get tired. They may have other things on their minds. Boredom may set in. This is not such a problem with recorded observations. You can always come back to them. You can also check on the reliability of your observations yourself by taking measures of the same subject at different points in time, this time calculating intra-rater reliability. If you are observing in the field, then it is important that you are not tired and that the period of observation is consistent with your attention span. Concentration does improve with practice so, if you can, have a few 'practice runs' which can act as training sessions. Observers employed on large-scale projects usually undergo a period of training during which reliability checks are made which act as feedback. Finally, if you are designing you own (or working on someone else's) project using observational data, try to make sure it is something that interests you and has some meaning for you. Your interest will then be sustained and you will hopefully be rewarded by a supply of rich and high-quality data.

## 14.10   Conclusion

Systematic observation may seem a good deal more complicated, time-consuming and challenging than some other forms of data collection. It can also be a good deal more interesting. In this chapter the methods have been presented and discussed with reference to quite complex lengthy sequences of behaviour. You may, however, be interested in only one or two behaviours or units of behaviour emitted during a short time period (see project below). This makes it much more manageable and possible in terms of a student project. The methods and principles are exactly the same.

## 14.11   Project

Your project is to devise and test an observational system to measure the interest shown in a particular exhibit in a museum. First of all, you need to conduct some informal observation by visiting a museum, selecting two or three exhibits and making some informal observations. You will, of course, take detailed notes. Alternatively, if you do not have the time to make an actual visit, for this project you could use your imagination and construct several 'scenarios'. For example,

A woman (in her early 30s approximately) accompanied by two boys aged about 8 and 10 years approaches the exhibit. She glances at it then looks down at a catalogue and starts to read aloud from it. The older-looking boy wanders off and meets a similar-aged boy a few yards away. After about 40 seconds, the woman stops reading and turns to the boy by her side (who in the meantime has been looking alternately at the exhibit and the older boy who wandered off). She then addresses the younger boy, initially looking at him, then they both look at the exhibit, the woman pointing at it with her finger. They are then joined by the older boy, his friend (?) and a man, also in his early 30s. The woman addresses the man, looking at him as she does so. The older boy interrupts and takes the catalogue from her and proceeds to read it, etc.

First you need to decide what you are going to observe and at what level. If it is molar, namely 'taking an interest in . . .', how are you going to define it? If molecular, which specific behaviours? Again, you will need to provide definitions. Who is the target for the observation? How are you going to collect the data? What system of measurement are you going to use? Having done this, you are now ready to go and try it out.

## 14.12  Further reading

Bellack and Hersen's (1988) *Behavioral Assessment: A Practical Handbook* is a good general guide to assessing behaviour and the book's Chapter 5, in particular, expands on what is presented here. Hutt and Hutt's (1970) *Direct Observation and Measurement of Behaviour* is another good guide that takes a more ethological approach to observation.

# 15   Interviewing

*Glynis M. Breakwell*

## Contents

## 15.1   When to use interviews

Interviewing is an essential part of most types of social research. This chapter describes how interviewing is done in a research context. The skills needed are similar to those required when interviewing is used in other contexts such as selection or appraisal procedures, but there are differences. Research interviews require a very systematic approach to data collection which allows you to maximise the chances of maintaining objectivity and achieving valid and reliable results. Interviews can be used at any stage in the research process. They can be used in the initial phases to identify areas for more detailed exploration. They can used as part of the piloting and validation of other instruments. They can be used as the main vehicle of data collection. They can be used once findings have been compiled to check whether your interpretations of other data make sense of the sample which was involved. The interview is a virtually infinitely flexible tool for research. It can encompass other techniques – for instance, as part of an interview, a self-completion questionnaire can be administered or psychophysiological measurements can be taken. Also it can be placed alongside other data elicitation procedures – for example, it can be used in tandem with ethnography or participant observation.

No method of collecting information is free of pitfalls. This chapter will present both the strengths and weaknesses of the interview method. When all the problems surrounding question construction, the biases introduced by the researcher and the interviewee, and the inadequacies of the available media of communication and recording mechanisms are taken into account, the method still has much to recommend it. Like any method, it has to be used with care and in the full knowledge of its limitations.

## 15.2 Asking questions

Having specified the research questions, you need to translate them into a form that can be used with your interviewees. This translation process is often troublesome because the way that the research question can be operationalised in a series of questions posed to a sample is severely limited by the level of the capacities and cooperation of the respondents. In its entirety, the series of questions asked in an interview is usually called the **interview schedule**. Interviews use many question-and-answer formats which range from the totally structured to the totally unstructured. Few real interviews fall at either of the poles of this continuum between fixed and absent structure.

**Structured interviews** involve a fixed set of questions which the researcher asks in a fixed order. Commonly, respondents are asked to choose an answer from a fixed series of options given by the researcher. The options may include rating scales. This type of interview structure yields information which is easily quantified, ensures comparability of questions across respondents and makes certain that the necessary topics are included. However, like all pre-structured data elicitation techniques it leaves little room for unanticipated discoveries. People often feel constrained because they are not free to give the information which they feel is important. You may miss salient issues in this way.

In **unstructured interviews**, the researcher has a number of topics to cover but the precise questions and their order are not fixed, they are allowed to develop as a result of the exchange with the respondent. Open-ended answers allow the interviewee to say as little or as much as he or she chooses. Comparability across respondents is sacrificed for the sake of personal relevance. It would be wrong, however, to think that the flexibility of the unstructured interview of necessity permits a deeper analysis than the structured interview. In both cases, the richness of the data is determined by the appreciation that the researcher has of the topic.

Analysis of unstructured interviews is time-consuming and difficult but not inevitably qualitative. Content analysis will provide categorical data which are open to quantification (see Chapter 18). There are now sophisticated software packages which, given the word-processed transcript of an interview, will count the incidence of certain phrases or words for you, taking the pain out of content analysis. However, many people who use unstructured interviews shun all quantification. They believe that by immersing themselves in the data they can understand the key themes which emerge. These they believe can be illustrated through taking direct quotes from transcripts and linking these in a coherent description of the themes. Ideally, the quotes allow the interviewees to speak for themselves, telling their own story. The researcher acts as the editor only insofar as quotes must be chosen. Chapter 16 describes one of these approaches further.

Whether you use structured or less unstructured interviews there are a number of guidelines to follow in formulating questions and in asking them. Questions *should not*:

- Be double-barrelled – for example: 'Do you think whaling and seal culling should be banned?' A 'No' answer could mean no to either whaling or seal culling or both.
- Introduce an assumption before going on to pose the question – for example: 'Do you think that the terrible cruelty of whaling has been adequately reported in the press?' This question assumes that whaling is seen to be cruel by the respondent. The assumption may or may not be true and makes interpretation of any response indeterminate.
- Include complex or jargon words – for example: 'Do you think you are eco-conscious?' This might be inadvisable unless you checked that the respondent shared your definition of eco-consciousness.
- Be leading – for example: 'I suppose you know what eco-consciousness is?' Some people might say no to the question in that form but the pressure is on them to say yes.
- Include double negatives – for example: 'Do you think now that not many people would not understand the term eco-consciousness?' Could you be sure what a no response meant?
- Act as catch-alls – for example: 'Tell me everything you know about the Green movement and how it has influenced you?' After the silence, it is unlikely you will get anything useful without a series of further prompt questions.

Avoiding these traps in formulating the questions may seem relatively easy. However, a surprising number of experienced researchers fall into them. There is a further set of problems which also need to be tackled. An interview schedule needs to be looked at in its entirety. Getting the individual questions right is vital but they also have to be ordered appropriately. A good interview schedule has a rhythm to it which takes the respondent through what appears to be a set of issues which are sensibly related. Interviews cannot jump, without explanation, from one topic to another. Even if it is not the real rationale for the research, the respondent has to be given some notion of why the questions are being asked and must feel that the sequence of questions makes sense. If the schedule fails to do this, respondents can become confused, suspicious and, sometimes, belligerent. Jumps between topics can be covered by short but apparently reasonable explanations. For instance, often at the end of an interview it is necessary to get data which will allow socioeconomic status to be calculated, respondents sometimes fail to see why this is relevant to the views they have just been offering you. The switch to questions about their occupational status or educational qualifications can be made if you use a link explanation such as: 'As a matter of routine we collect information on what jobs our interviewees do, I hope you do not mind me asking you . . .'. If the respondent then queries the relevance of the questions, it can be helpful just to add 'occasionally, we find differences between the views of people who have different jobs'. The key thing in constructing link explanations is that they should not suggest what you expect people to say in answer to the next set of questions.

When designing the interview, you should also include clear guidelines to the interviewer on how to conclude the interview. Some debriefing may be needed. If a cover story has been employed, this may need to be explained. Often respondents want the interviewer to tell them immediately what their answers reveal about them. The interviewer has to be ready with a response which is non-committal and not likely to cause offence. It is best to anticipate this request for immediate analysis by stating at the end that you cannot say anything about individuals or that the findings will take a long time to produce. Whatever strategy you choose to adopt at the end of the interview, it is good practice to be consistent across respondents.

Since there are so many problems in getting the individual questions, the order in which they are asked and the links between them absolutely right, interview schedules need to be piloted. In the same way that you would pilot a questionnaire (see Chapter 12), an interview schedule must be tested and refined. There is no required routine for piloting an interview schedule. The following stages are, however, frequently used.

In **Stage 1** test whether your explanation for the interview is understood by a small sample drawn from the same population as you intend to interview. Normally, understanding in this context is ascertained by having this pilot sample explain the interview back to you in their own words. They can also be asked to tell you about any doubts or queries they might have about the interview. Getting the explanation for the interview right is fundamentally important. Not only will it influence the data you get from the people you manage to interview, it is very likely to have a big impact upon whether people are willing to be interviewed at all. The most successful explanations are those which emphasise the significance of the research, the significance of the particular individual's participation in it, the confidentiality of all data, and the possibility of withdrawing from the interview if at any point the person wishes to do so. At the pilot stage, you may wish to try alternative types of explanation in order to test if they will influence response rates.

In **Stage 2** use the same pilot sample to test comprehension of particular questions which you know have not been used with this population before or which you feel are difficult (for example, possibly ambiguous, lacking relevance, advanced vocabulary, etc.).

In **Stage 3** amend the introduction and questions in the light of stages 1 and 2. Surprisingly, researchers often go through the motions of piloting and then ignore what they find. This is a form of intellectual arrogance and research hypocrisy. There is no point in doing the pilot work if you do not respond to the information it gives you and then check by further piloting that your changes were the correct ones.

With a new subsample, in **Stage 4** test the revised explanation and all questions for comprehension. This should be a complete run through of the entire interview schedule. It is still possible to make changes at this point. It is better to fine-tune the questions in the course of the pilot work at this stage than to get into a never-ending cycle of re-sampling in order to test out small refinements of the schedule.

In **Stage 5** with a new subsample, use the interview schedule to establish whether the answers you are getting are the ones which interest you. This stage moves away from testing comprehension to being genuine data collection. Nevertheless, even if the schedule is working as you wished, the data from this stage should not be collapsed with data later collected from the main sample since this would change the sample structure (obviously, this warning only matters if your sample structure is important to you). Assuming that the schedule is performing as you expected, it is possible at this point to proceed to the main study.

Properly conducted pilot work pays off, minimising the chances of finding midway through the study that a vital issue has been ignored or that certain components of the sample cannot understand batches of questions. Of course, to be maximally useful, the pilot work must be conducted on a subsample which is thoroughly representative of the sample you will ultimately use. Rigour in choosing the subsample for pilot work is important and often missing. It should be noted that piloting is just as important for unstructured interviews as it is for structured interviews. The unstructured interview, despite not having a fixed list of questions in a fixed order, must be informed by a thorough appreciation of which routes of questioning are likely to be productive, which sorts of questions make sense, and so on. It is impossible for the researcher to achieve that understanding without preliminary pilot work (or its equivalent). In the absence of good piloting, unstructured interviews can all too easily lose sight of the main research issue they were addressing.

There are traps lurking for you when you formulate questions but there are also traps waiting for you when you ask them. In order to avoid them, there are a few golden rules which should be followed. First, be thoroughly familiar with the interview schedule before you start. Second, ask all questions of all respondents, even if you think you know what some of them will say. Give all respondents an equal hearing. Third, know what each question is meant to tap and if you are failing to get relevant material probe further. Probes (for example, non-committal encouragements to extend answers using eye contact, glance, repetition of the answer, gentle queries like 'I'm confused here') should be non-directive. Prompts (which suggest possible answers to the interviewee) should only be used if they are deployed consistently to all. In pursuing a point it is important not to seek or give unrelated or irrelevant information. It is essential to avoid offering advice or counselling as part of a research interview unless this has been explicitly agreed in advance. If the interviewee does become upset or aroused the researcher should ensure that this is acknowledged and should not leave until the interviewee is calmed. The researcher handling sensitive subject matter should be sure to have information ready which will tell the interviewee where advice can be found. Four, whatever technique you use, be consistent in recording answers. Five, an answer in a face-to-face interview has both verbal and non-verbal components. It is sometimes useful to encode non-verbal aspects of the answers even when visual recording is not used. They can change the underlying message substantially.

Of course, interviews do not have to be face-to-face. Increasingly researchers are using telephone interviewing. Telephone interviewing seems to yield similar data to face-to-face interviews. Telephone interviewing is cheaper and faster than other methods. Computer-assisted telephone interviewing (CATI) can be used. This involves the interviewer being linked to a computer which cues the questions to be asked and allows answers to be inputted directly. There is no evidence that the vocal characteristics of the interviewer influence refusal rates, but more experienced interviewers do have better success rates. Since interviewers can be all located in one place using a bank of telephones, it is easier to monitor their performance and to assess problems with the interview schedule.

The telephone interview does have its drawbacks. People are unwilling to talk on the telephone for very long periods. A maximum of 15 minutes has been suggested for the standard interview. Anything longer needs to be timetabled in advance. Answers to open-ended questions also seem to be truncated on the telephone. People are faster in their responses and silences seem to be avoided. Complex questions (or those with a large number of response options) prove more difficult to understand on the telephone and this means that question structuring needs to be tailored specifically for the telephone administration. Response rates are lower (on average 7–10 per cent lower than face-to-face approaches) and are worse on evening and weekend calls. This compounds a further problem: in the United Kingdom about 80 per cent of households have telephones. By sampling in this way, you selectively exclude lower-income groups or mobile subgroups from your sample. On balance the scales weighing the pros and cons of telephone interviewing seem nowadays to be tipping increasingly in its favour.

It should be acknowledged that interview questions do not have to be addressed to one person at a time. It is possible to conduct group interviews. Chapter 18 addresses some of these issues with regard to focus groups and consequently the peculiarities of group interviewing will not be considered here.

# 15.3   Interviewing difficult people

There are some categories of people who are particularly difficult to
interview effectively. These include children and the very elderly. There
are a number of hazards to watch out for especially when dealing with
children. Some of them clearly apply when dealing with other respondents
who may feel themselves to be in a less knowledgeable or powerful
position relative to the researcher.

Young children are often unwilling to assert themselves or to contradict
an adult. They will, therefore, answer questions in a way they think you
want them answered. Of course, later, in the teenage period they may
relish contradicting adults which results in a totally opposite bias in
information derived from interviews. Either way, it is important to guard
against giving them clues about what you expect them to say. They have to
be encouraged to disclose their own opinion. This can be achieved by
reassuring them that you are really only interested in what they think and
that there are no right or wrong answers. Any approach which looks like a
test should be avoided since this will either silence them or release a store
of responses which they think adults would like to hear. There is a strong
**acquiescence response bias** in children: children tend to say 'yes', irrespective of the question or what they think about it. Questions should be posed
so that they are not open to a yes/no response. For instance, 'Did you want
to do that?' would become 'How did you feel about doing that?'

Besides the acquiescence bias which is most marked when they are eager
to please, children exhibit a preference for 'don't know' responses.
Children say 'don't know' for a variety of reasons: they aren't interested in
answering; they don't understand the question either conceptually or its
vocabulary; they think you expect them not to know; they do not wish to
admit what they know; they are too shy to say more; they don't know how
to explain what they know; and, they really do not know. Consequently,
'don't know' is a response which needs cautious treatment. It is sensible
never to base a conclusion on 'don't knows', especially the conclusion that
children 'don't know'.

Children, like some elderly people, are relatively easily distracted. They
pay attention to unpredictable aspects of the interview situation or the
questions. They can become fascinated by your pen, the lorry loading
outside the window or an itch in their nose. Besides being disconcerting to
the interviewer, it can result in time-wasting and irrelevant information. To
retain their attention, an interview must be full of different topics and
changes of pace, with verbal questions giving way to visual materials (for
example, cartoons or objects) and responses perhaps being in the form of
some physical activity (for example, the child illustrates what he or she did
in the situation you are talking about or draws a picture which depicts his
or her feelings). A quiet location, not overlooked, and free of strong
emotional connotations (for example, not the headteacher's office where

the child was recently severely reprimanded) can improve concentration. However, it would be foolishly optimistic to expect to get more than 15 minutes' worth of good answers from young children even in optimal conditions. Therefore, it is important to keep the interview short.

Young children, like any novice to a linguistic community, tend to interpret questions literally. Metaphors, similes and analogies should all be excluded from questioning. Any phrasing of the question which relies upon an underlying set of assumptions about cultural or social mores must be carefully checked so as to ensure that children of the age group actually understand these assumptions. Essentially, any question such as 'When do you think your sister has been as good as gold?' tell you as much about what the child knows of the aphorism as what he or she thinks about her sister's activity.

Children have quite different priorities to those of adults. They may not understand that the implicit rule of the interview is that one person asks questions and the other person answers. They may wish to ask as well as answer questions. Particularly, they are likely to be curious about you, whether you are new, why you are there, all sorts of personal details. Responding to these questions briefly, without showing any exasperation is the best tactic. For the child who gets into the infinite regress of 'Why?' questions, the best strategy is to distract them with a new topic.

Very often children explain what other people do in terms of their own feelings or characteristics. They find it difficult to see the world through another person's eyes (what is called taking the role of the other). This is one aspect of childhood egocentricity (something which returns in another form in some very elderly people). It means that it is important that you check when accepting an answer that the child is actually focusing upon the right subject. For instance, you might ask a child 'Why did your mother shout at you last night?' The child might say 'She was sad'. It would be necessary to check whether the sadness mentioned referred to the feelings of the mother or the feelings that the child experienced.

Children, and other categories of people who have some vocabulary deficits, may hesitate in answering questions. The pauses which ensue introduce a pressure upon the researcher to jump in to offer suitable words. In essence, this means that the researcher answers for the respondent. This is a temptation which must be resisted.

Some groups of people, and children and the elderly are among these, are often interviewed in an institutional setting (for instance, the school or hospital). This entails taking them away from the normal activities of the institution, interviewing them and then returning them. Once back, they are liable to talk about the interview with other inmates who will subsequently be interviewed. This introduces the possibility of a feedback loop with early interviewees acting as informants for later interviewees. There is a very real prospect for the gossip about the interview to result in rumour and lead to a distorted expectation of what the interview entails.

The later interviewees may develop a distorted picture of what you are doing. This needs to be controlled. You can ask later interviewees what they have heard and what they expect and then clarify any misconceptions.

It can be especially difficult to keep accurate records of what an interviewee is saying if you are reliant upon notetaking when the responses are perhaps self-contradictory and the interviewee requires coaxing. The notetaking is also disruptive since a child interviewee may lose interest in the moments it takes you to get your notes in order. It is best to have someone else record the interaction or, if possible, use audiotaping.

The chief hazards in interviewing children, can be summarised: the tendency to say 'yes'; the tendency to say 'don't know'; susceptibility to distraction; literal-mindedness; different priorities; egocentricity; the urge to prompt; feedback loops; and recording problems.

## 15.4   Validity and reliability of interview data

There is no evidence to suggest that in any generic manner interviews as a data elicitation technique yield data which are less valid or reliable than other methods. There are artefacts intrinsic to the interview method which affect the validity and reliability of the data it produces but these tend to be common to many methods.

Like any self-report method, the interview approach relies upon respondents being able and willing to give accurate and complete answers to questions posed no matter what their format. Yet respondents may be motivated to lie. They may dislike or distrust the researcher. They may wish to sabotage the research. They may be too embarrassed to tell the truth. Even if they wish to cooperate, they may be unable to answer accurately because they cannot remember the details requested or because they do not understand the question.

You can overcome some of these difficulties by constructing a systematic set of questions which at the same time as helping the respondent to remember or to understand will provide evidence of consistency (or not) across responses. Having a pattern of questions which allows for internal consistency checking offers you one way of assessing the validity of the data. If a respondent is inconsistent in the pattern of answers, you may wish to extend the questioning to achieve clarification or you may choose to exclude that data from the analysis. Of course, consistency of response does not guarantee accuracy but inconsistency certainly entails some inaccuracy. The other way to establish the validity of interview data is by complementing it with other types of data. You might use observation, diary techniques, or experimental procedures in addition to the interview.

Collecting such ancillary data may not be necessary for the entire sample. To assure you that the interview is effective it may be sufficient to take additional evidence from only a subsample of respondents.

There is a common belief in the research community that the validity of data collected in interviews improves if you can talk to the person repeatedly. It is thought that interviewing someone on several occasions increases their openness and honesty. Of course, since only people who have a positive attitude towards the research are likely to agree to be interviewed repeatedly it is possible that the apparent power of repeated interviewing to induce frankness is an artefact of the sample bias which develops in any panel study because of differential dropout (see also Chapter 7).

Like any method where the researcher is an overt participant in the data collection process, interviewing involves **researcher effects** (elsewhere labelled experimenter effects). In an interview the characteristics of the researcher (for example, demeanour, accent, dress, gender, age, etc.) will influence the respondents' willingness to participate and to answer accurately. Various effects have been catalogued: people engage in more self-disclosure to an interviewer who they think is similar to themselves; people of both sexes of all ages are more likely to be willing to talk to a middle-aged woman rather than a man irrespective of his age about sexual matters; people are more likely to comply with requests for information from someone who speaks with a received pronunciation accent than a regional accent; and so on.

It is evident from the research which has focused on interviewer effects that the characteristics of the interviewer interact with the subject matter of the interview to determine how the interviewee will respond. An interviewer characteristic which is not salient in one interview will become important in another. For instance, the fact that the interviewer and interviewee are of different religious backgrounds may be unimportant when the topic of the interview concerns responses to traffic noise, but the religious differences may encroach if the topic was responses to the conflict in a province torn apart by religious rivalry.

Such **interviewer effects** cannot be eliminated but steps can be taken to control for them. One way to do this entails having the same interviewer conduct all interviews. This serves to hold constant the stimulus provided by the interviewer. This will not wipe out the possibility that the same interviewer has different effects across interviewees as a result of some complex interaction between their characteristics and those of the interviewer. In any case, using a single interviewer may be impractical in any large-scale study. Another way to tackle the problem is to use many interviewers and randomly allocate them to respondents. This way allows you to eradicate any strong effects of any one interviewer. It also allows you to analyse the extent of interviewer differences. The interview data collected by each interviewer are compared with those collected by others.

Any systematic differences can be identified, attributed to some characteristic of the interviewer, and, if sensible, some weighting procedure can be used to moderate the data.

Sometimes, interviewer effects are countered in a different way which uses matching procedures. For instance, if interviewer gender is thought to be the biggest potential bias, the research director might use a pool of interviewers who were all female or all male. Alternatively, in such a situation, interviewer gender might be matched to interviewee gender. The matching approach can only be used if you know which interviewer characteristics are likely to have a significant effect upon the interviewees.

Interviewer effects do not simply occur because the respondent reacts to some attribute of the interviewer. It is also possible that they occur because the interviewer reacts to some characteristic of the respondent and this influences how questions are asked or how responses are recorded. Since the interviewer may be completely unaware that this is happening, controlling it is notoriously difficult. Clearly, following the guidelines described above which emphasise consistency in question presentation will reduce the problem, but in unstructured interviews the effect can be considerable. In large samples, with large numbers of interviewers and assuming the bias is randomly distributed relative to the research question, the effect should become less important statistically. It is where the bias introduced by the interviewer is pertinent to the research issue or where the interviewer conducts large parts of the study that the problem is significant.

Good initial training of the interviewers will serve to heighten their awareness of their own prejudices, etc., that are relevant to the research topic. This may reduce the likelihood that they will be completely oblivious to biases which they are introducing. Therefore, it makes sense, when using a team of interviewers, to include a procedure for debriefing the interviewers. This would include a component which allowed them to express any doubts they had about their conduct of particular interviews in a systematic manner (perhaps as a written comment required after each interview). Where any doubt was expressed by the interviewer, that interview or set of interviews could be compared with data from interviews with other similar individuals in the sample to explore if there were apparent inconsistencies. This process might result in some interviews being excluded from subsequent analysis.

The best way to exclude interviewer bias from the recording of responses is to use some mechanical method for recording them. Audiotaping is cheap and easy. Videotaping captures the fuller range of information (for example, non-verbal communication). Either way, the record is permanent and open to verification by other researchers. There is no good evidence to show that audiotaping constrains what respondents are willing to say. Even videotaping has now lost its power to intrude as many people have access to the technology.

# 15.5 Analysing interview data

People using interviews as a research tool often find that they collect an enormous amount of information and then do not know how to interpret it. The problem is obviously less acute if you use fully structured interview schedules since then response variety is constrained. In a structured interview data are usually already framed ready for analysis. With unstructured or semi-structured interviews, there are some guidelines which could focus your activity.

First, allow your research questions to act as a prism through which you view the data collected. Content analysis (described in Chapter 18) can be used to reduce the data to manageable proportions. Content analysis can be supplemented with systematic quotations from the interviews to illustrate conclusions. There will be problems in deciding which categories to use in the content analysis. You are trying to generate slices of meaningful information and knowing where to cut into the flow of information is tricky. It may be necessary to try out several cutting positions before you find one which reveals interesting results. Also, remember that some of the best researchers rely on spotting what is omitted from what the respondent says in order to draw conclusions. It is sensible to stand back occasionally from the attempt to impose order (which is essentially what a content analysis does) and search for the disorderly elements, the discord which shows important differences. Look for themes which you expected to find but which are surprisingly absent. This may guide you to a new perspective. Sometimes people fail to say what they treat as common knowledge or very obvious. Many of the most central understandings in a community are unspoken because they are taken for granted. If you are driven by a simplistic approach to your content analysis you will misinterpret these apparent absences.

Second, your analysis should be open to verification as far as possible. You should provide a description of the data on which you base your conclusions which is good enough for someone else to repeat what you have done and check your conclusions. You may wish to include estimates of **inter-rater reliability** to establish that your interpretations of the data are not idiosyncratic. In the interests of verification, you should always keep raw data for a significant period after you publish or report on it.

Where interviews are recorded (by audio or video) it is possible to transcribe the tapes and use these transcriptions as the basis for analysis. Usually, it is easier to content analyse from the transcripts since moving backwards and forwards in the text is easier than doing so on the tapes. The transcripts can include systematic records of the non-verbal communication involved (a system of notation is available). Transcription is sadly a slow and expensive business and it may be necessary to be selective about which elements of the interviews you choose to get transcribed fully. It takes about seven hours of transcription for every one hour of recorded speech. Selection can be driven by theoretical concerns. Initial selections can always be revised later. The tapes are available as the complete and permanent record and they can always be re-examined.

'Authenticate interpretations' is a dictum which has helped many researchers. Taking the conclusions back to the interviewees (or some subset of them) to check whether they make sense has become a popular pastime. There are, of course, difficulties in knowing what to do when the interviewees do not agree with your conclusions. Who is right and at what level becomes an interesting issue.

Following these guidelines will help you to produce a relevant and focused analysis of the interview material. If there is a single thing to remember when using interviewing it is that data elicitation is a technique which can deliver the broadest possible variety of data types. The analysis you choose must match the measurement level of the data and be sensitive to your sample structure but there is usually more than one way to examine the data. Try multiple techniques in the analysis. See whether they lead you to the same conclusions. Only stop the analysis when you are satisfied that you understand the data fully.

## 15.7   Further reading

The following two texts give a more thorough overview of interviewing techniques: Breakwell's (1990) *Interviewing* and Brenner et al.'s (1985) *The Research Interview: Uses and Approaches*.

# 16 Discourse Analysis

*Adrian Coyle*

## Contents

## 16.1 Introduction

Discourse analysis is a field of enquiry that traces its roots to various domains such as speech act theory, ethnomethodology, conversation analysis and semiology. It owes a particular debt to post-structuralism which holds as its central tenet that meaning is not static and fixed but is fluid and provisional. However, discourse analysis does not fit easily within any particular disciplinary boundaries. Indeed, it does not even fit within a unitary framework as the term 'discourse analysis' has been applied to diverse analytic approaches that are often based upon very different assumptions and are sometimes downright hostile to each other. This makes it difficult to provide an account of the commonalities of discourse analysis except in the broadest terms and any representation of the field will inevitably please some and enrage others.

The popularisation of discourse analysis within social psychology can be dated to the publication in 1987 of Potter and Wetherell's classic text *Discourse and Social Psychology: Beyond Attitudes and Behaviour*. This work urged a radical reformulation of the issues that social psychology has traditionally addressed. Social psychologists have long worked with linguistic and textual material in the form of spoken responses within interview settings and written responses to questionnaire items. The question then arises as to what status should be accorded to this material. It is generally assumed that language is a neutral, transparent medium, describing events or revealing underlying psychological processes in a more or less direct, unproblematic way. The possibility of self-presentational and other biases occurring within this material may be acknowledged but it is assumed that these can be eradicated or at least minimised by refining methods of data generation and collection.

## 16.2   Assumptions and applications of discourse analysis

Discourse analysis sees language not as simply reflecting psychological and social life but as constructing it. It rejects the idea that there are objective truths existing 'out there' that can be accessed if the appropriate scientific methods are employed. Instead, language in the form of **discourses** is seen as constituting the building blocks of 'social reality'. The analysis of discourse emphasises how social reality is linguistically constructed and aims to gain 'a better understanding of social life and social interaction from our study of social texts' (Potter and Wetherell, 1987:7).

This emphasis on language as a constructive tool is one of the key tenets of discourse analysis. The person producing a discourse is viewed as selecting from the range of linguistic resources available to them and using these resources to create a version of events. The person may not be able to articulate the constructive process in which they are engaged but this does not mean that it does not exist. It simply highlights the extent to which the constructive use of language is a fundamental, taken-for-granted aspect of social life. Discourse analysis does not use people's language as a means of gaining access to their psychological and social worlds. Instead, it focuses on the language itself and examines how people use language to construct versions of their worlds and what they gain from these constructions. Within psychology, it thereby helps to negate the cognitive reductionism that characterises much of what passes for social psychology and offers the possibility of a truly *social* psychology.

It can be difficult to specify exactly what discourses are because, although they are generally thought of as broad patterns of language use within spoken or written material, a variety of meanings have been ascribed to the term 'discourse'. The diversity found among definitions of discourse is not helped by the cachet which the term has acquired in a range of post-structuralist domains in recent years. This sometimes seems to provoke writers to frame their work in terms of discourse or to invoke the term regardless of whether or not this is appropriate.

It may be useful to consider various definitions of 'discourse' and of related ideas to try to divine some basic commonalities. Foucault emphasised the constructive potential of discourses and saw them as 'practices that systematically form the objects of which they speak' (1972:49). In the same vein, Parker offers a succinct definition of a discourse as 'a system of statements which constructs an object' (1992:5). He outlines seven key criteria and three auxiliary ones to permit the recognition of discourses. Drawing on the work of Gilbert and Mulkay (1984), Wooffitt defines their key concept of the linguistic repertoire as 'a set of descriptive and referential terms which portray beliefs, actions and events in a specific way' (1993:292). People are said to use these repertoires to construct versions of the world 'for specific social purposes in specific social settings' (1993:294). This definition could just as easily be applied to discourse. Potter and Wetherell (1987) prefer the term 'interpretative repertoires' rather than 'discourses'. They regard interpretative repertoires as linguistic phenomena which have a certain coherence in terms of their content and style and which may be organised around one or more central metaphors. However, for the purposes of this chapter, the term 'discourse' will be retained because it remains the standard term that is applied to the subject matter of discourse analytic study. This definitional survey is hardly exhaustive but, amalgamating the ideas raised, it suggests a definition of discourses as sets of linguistic material that have a degree of coherence in their content and organisation and which perform constructive functions in broadly defined social contexts.

So where do analysts turn in their search for discourses? In the words of Marin, discourses are '*carried out* or *actualized* in or by means of texts' (1983:162, original emphasis). All spoken and written material (and indeed the products of every other sort of signifying practice too) can be conceptualised as a *text* and subjected to discourse analysis, in the same way that within traditional scientific paradigms, almost anything can be construed as data and analysed. Texts and discourses are to the discourse analyst what data are to the empirical scientist. This means that discourse analysis can be applied in a wide range of research settings. However, some analysts choose to focus particularly on discourses which reproduce social relations of dominance and which oppress – see, for example, Wetherell and Potter's (1992) work on racism. The practicalities of this approach have been outlined by Van Dijk (1993) in his account of 'critical discourse analysis'. Discourse analysis can reveal the constructed nature and the implications of oppressive discourses and can emphasise that alternative non-oppressive discourses can be constructed in their place.

Discourse analysis assumes that all linguistic material has an **action orientation**, that is, it is used to perform particular social functions such as justifying, questioning and accusing, and it achieves this by employing a variety of rhetorical strategies. Key tasks that discourse analysts set themselves are to identify what functions are being performed by the linguistic material that is being analysed and to consider how these functions are performed. This entails a close and careful inspection of the text. In this process, some discourse analysts are concerned with the fine grain of talk. These writers tend to adopt and adapt the approaches of conversation analysis in their work – see Heath and Luff (1993) and Wooffitt (1992) for concise accounts of conversation analysis. Generally, though, discourse analysis is more concerned with the social organisation of talk rather than with its linguistic organisation. This approach involves looking at what discourses are shared across texts and what constructions of the world the material can be seen as advocating. However, the two approaches are not mutually exclusive and a global analysis may be grounded in a fairly detailed consideration of a text.

Concerted efforts have been made to fashion a distinctively psychological version of discourse analysis and to construct it as more than simply an alternative set of analytic tools. This has resulted in what has been termed 'discursive psychology', the central tenets of which have been expounded by Edwards and Potter (1992). In the past, discourse analysis has been applied to such domains of social psychology as attitudes, social representations and the self (Potter and Wetherell, 1987). More recently, it has attempted to expand its range of application and has challenged traditional conceptualisations of the psychology of memory (Edwards et al., 1992).

## 16.3  Sampling discourse

In the following sections the practicalities of conducting discourse analysis are explored, taking as an example a study conducted by the author. This study analysed an attempt to construct an alternative to the traditional condemnatory Christian discourse on homosexuality in a workshop for members of a predominantly lesbian and gay church. In order to conduct an analysis of discourse, texts are required in which discourses may be discerned. These texts may take many forms. For example, the analyst may use recordings of interactions in natural settings, transcripts of interviews conducted on the research topic or excerpts from writing on the topic. In the study under consideration, the text was obtained through tape-recording and transcribing workshop proceedings, having obtained the permission of the workshop facilitator and participants. Accurate transcription is a lengthy process which is made even more laborious if the transcriber wishes to include every 'um' and 'uh' uttered by the speakers and to measure pauses in speech production. This sort of detailed approach is less often seen in discourse analysis than in conversation analysis.

Within traditional approaches to sampling in psychological research, the emphasis is placed on securing as large and representative a sample as possible. Within discourse analysis, if interview material is used as a source of data, there is no necessity to sample discourse from a large number of people. If newspaper reports of a particular event are to be used, it is not necessary to collect all reports from all newspapers on that event. The analysis stage of qualitative research is almost always more laborious and time-consuming than the analysis of structured data so the researcher must beware of ending up with a mountain of unstructured data to sift through. What is important is that sufficient discourse is gathered in order to discern the variety of discursive forms that are commonly used when speaking of or writing about the research topic. This may be possible from an analysis of relatively few interview transcripts or newspaper reports, especially where common discursive forms are under consideration. In this case, larger samples of data add to the analytic task without adding significantly to the analytic outcome. Where an analysis is purely exploratory and the analyst has little idea in advance of what the analytic focus might be, larger samples of data are required. Hence, in the study that will be considered here, the entire workshop proceedings were transcribed because the specific analytic focus had not been determined in advance.

## 16.4   Techniques of discourse analysis

While it is easy to expound the central theoretical tenets of discourse analysis, specifying exactly how one goes about doing discourse analysis is a different matter. On being asked how to do discourse analysis, a colleague once replied 'discourse analysis is what you do when you say you're doing discourse analysis'. A perusal of the range of approaches adopted to discourse analysis suggests that there might be some truth in her jesting comment. There is no rigid set of formal procedures to guide discourse analysis. It has been contended that the key to analysing (ideological) discourse is scholarship rather than adherence to a rigorous methodology (Billig, 1988). The emphasis is placed upon the careful reading and interpretation of texts, with interpretations being backed by reference to linguistic evidence in the texts. The first step is said to be the suspension of belief in what is normally taken for granted in language use (Potter and Wetherell, 1987). This involves seeing linguistic practices not as simply reflecting underlying psychological and social realities but as constructing and legitimating a version of events. The key to analysis is held to be the development of an 'analytic mentality' which takes the form of 'a repertoire of craft skills acquired through practical experience' (Wooffitt, 1993:291).

Discourse analysis is not simply another research method but is based on an epistemological viewpoint that differs radically from those underpinning most other approaches to psychological research. It is, therefore, not surprising that it also has a very different way of proceeding methodologically. At times, however, one cannot help feeling that a more systematic approach would be enormously beneficial to those entering the field for the first time. It is all very well to suggest that to conduct discourse analysis, one needs to develop 'a sensitivity to the way in which language is used', especially to the 'inferential and interactional aspects of talk'

(Widdicombe, 1993:97). However, it is unclear exactly how this sensitivity is developed and systematised.

Parker (1992) and Potter and Wetherell (1987) attempt to fill this gap. The former offers a 20-step guide to conducting discourse analysis and the latter suggest a loose 10-stage approach, with two stages devoted to the analytic process. This process begins with what is termed **coding**. By this is meant the process of examining the text closely. If the research focus has been specified in advance, instances of the research focus are identified at this point. It is worth being as inclusive as possible and noting what appear to be borderline instances of the research focus. This makes it possible to discern less obvious but none the less fruitful lines of enquiry. The coding process is more complex if the research focus has not been determined in advance. In this case, it is necessary to read and reread the text, looking for recurrent discursive patterns shared by the accounts under analysis. It is at this stage that Widdicombe's (1993) notion of sensitivity to the way in which language is used is important. Hypotheses about which discourses are being used in the text are formulated and reformulated. This can be a very frustrating stage as hypotheses are developed, revised or discarded as the linguistic evidence needed to support them proves not to be forthcoming. It is important that the analyst should remain open to alternative readings of the text and to the need to reject hypotheses that the text fails to support.

Once the broad discourses within a text have been identified, a useful strategy for the next stage of analysis involves reading the text mindful of what its functions might be. Any text has an action orientation and is designed to fulfil certain functions, so the question is what functions are being fulfilled by this text and how is it fulfilling them? The formulation of hypotheses about the purposes and consequences of language is central to discourse analysis. However, identifying the functions of language is often not a straightforward process because these functions may not be explicit. For example, when someone asks you to do something, they may phrase it not as an imperative ('do the washing up') but as a question to which the expected answer is 'yes' ('would you like to do the washing up?').

In seeking to identify discursive functions, a useful starting point is the discursive context. It can be difficult to divine function from limited sections of a text. A variety of functions may be performed and revisited throughout a text, so it is necessary to be familiar with what precedes and follows a particular extract in order to obtain clues to its functions. Furthermore, as Parker and Burman (1993) note, the analyst needs to be aware of broader contextual concerns such as cultural trends and political and social issues to which the text alludes. As they pointedly put it, '(i)f you do not know what a text is referring to, you cannot produce a reading' (1993:158).

Another analytic strategy that may be helpful is to examine a text mindful of what version of events it may be designed to counteract. Any version of events is but one of a number of possible versions and therefore must be constructed as more persuasive than these alternative versions. Sometimes alternative versions will be explicitly mentioned and counter-acted in a text but on other occasions they will be implicit. If analysts are sensitised to what these alternative versions might be, they may be well placed to analyse how the text addresses the function of legitimating the version constructed therein.

In analysing function, it is useful to become acquainted with the ways in which various features of discourse are described in the discourse analytic and conversation analytic literatures. These discursive features are fre-quently employed to perform specific rhetorical functions. Therefore, if analysts are able to identify these features, they can then examine the text mindful of the functions that these features typically perform. For example, the use of terms such as 'always', 'never', 'nobody' and 'everyone' may represent what has been called **extreme case formulations** (Pomerantz, 1986). These take whatever position is being advocated in the text to its extreme and thereby help to make this position more persuasive. For those interested in becoming acquainted with these technical features of discourse, Potter and Wetherell (1987) and Wooffitt (1993) outline some of the basics but the best strategy is to examine a range of studies which have used discourse analytic and conversation analytic approaches.

According to Potter and Wetherell (1987), one means of elucidating the functions of discourse is through the study of **variability** in any discourse. The fact that discourse varies appears a common-sense statement. If we were analysing discourse from different people about a particular object, we would expect variations related to whether individuals evaluated the object positively or negatively. However, variation also occurs within an individual's discourse, dependent upon the purposes of the discourse. It has been claimed that, in their search for individual consistency, main-stream approaches to psychology have sought to minimise or explain away intra-individual variation (Potter and Wetherell, 1987). Discourse analysis, in contrast, actively seeks it out. As variability arises from the different functions that the discourse may be fulfilling, the nature of the variation can provide clues to what these functions are. Examples of how variation can be used to discern the functions of discourses are provided by Wetherell and Potter (1988). The process of discourse analysis therefore involves the search for both consistency (in the identification of discourses) and variability (in the analysis of discursive functions).

## 16.5 Working with data

In order to provide some insight into the basics of analysing discourse, a broad preliminary analysis will be presented of some aspects of the proceedings of a workshop which attempted to challenge the traditional Christian discourse on homosexuality. This discourse is based on interpretations of Biblical texts and centres around notions that same-sex sexual activity is sinful and unnatural. One denomination that has tried to counter and reinterpret it has been the Metropolitan Community Church (MCC). The majority of MCC's clergy and congregations in Europe and North America are gay or lesbian. This denomination has reinterpreted those Biblical passages that are customarily seen as referring to and condemning homosexual activity and, by extension, gay men and lesbians. The essence of the alternative discourse that it offers is that the Bible contains no unequivocal prohibitions against same-sex sexual activity and that a belief in God, the authority of the Bible and homosexuality are entirely compatible. MCC has attempted to propagate its alternative discourse through its congregations and publications and by offering courses and workshops on its Biblical reinterpretations. The following analyses are based on a transcript of one such workshop conducted at MCC in East London by a senior figure in MCC's theological college in Europe, an American who will be referred to as 'David'.

Given that the workshop ran for an entire day, the transcript of the proceedings was very lengthy. This transcript was read and reread closely looking for broad recurrent discursive patterns. One which was discerned was the establishment of warrant or legitimacy by the facilitator for his reinterpretation of the traditional discourse. The attempt to ensure that one's version of events prevails against competing versions is a common feature of accounts. This aspect of the proceedings was therefore selected as a potentially interesting analytic focus. The analysis that follows is not designed to be comprehensive but rather to demonstrate some basic aspects of the analytic process in simple terms. For examples of more complete, complex and polished analyses, the reader is referred to the journal *Discourse & Society*.

The principal strategies that David used during the workshop to establish warrant were expositions of his scholarship; self-construction as a benign teacher or guide; tales of his personal experiences with the traditional discourse; and assurances of his honesty. These were juxtaposed and interwoven to create a powerful cumulative warranting effect.

At several points during the workshop, David emphasises his Biblical scholarship, particularly his skills in Biblical languages. For example, at different points he says:

> What I'm going to say to you has very sound academic structure, foundation. I don't intend to overwhelm you with the academics of it, which can be quite boring. I do have the academic background and the study in the original languages to support what I'm going to say.

> The Bible was written in ancient languages. The Old Testament is written in Hebrew with some Aramaic in the Book of Daniel and one of the other prophets. The New Testament is written in Greek, in koine Greek which was the common language of the people. Greek is a very complex language with balanced clauses and classic literary Greek is great fun to translate which is where I started my Greek studies. The New Testament Greek is sort of common street slang language sometimes and is great fun – the koine Greek.

The use of this strategy establishes credibility and validity specifically for the reinterpretations of Biblical passages that he will expound later, and generally for any other pronouncements that he will make. If his views are regarded by his audience as informed opinions, underpinned by scholarship and expertise, they are more likely to prevail than if they are seen as uninformed speculation. However, a heavy emphasis on scholarship may risk alienating the audience if they are made to feel inadequate in comparison or if they assume that what will be said will be 'over their heads'. This possibility is counteracted by the way in which David presents his learning. He reassures his audience that 'I don't intend to overwhelm you with the academics of it, which can be quite boring'. One could fill in the unspoken 'to the layperson' at the end of this utterance, which constructs David as the possessor of privileged, expert insight into the material that he is about to address.

Within the second extract he also creates the impression that he wears his learning lightly and points to the enjoyment he derives from it ('Greek is a very complex language . . . the koine Greek'). The juxtaposition of the account of the complexity of classic literary Greek (complete with the introduction of the quasi-technical term 'balanced clauses') and the description of it as 'great fun' further stresses David's scholarship. Note how the notions of complexity and fun are accompanied by terms of emphasis ('very complex'; 'great fun'). Their presence draws attention to the fact that these notions are carrying out important work in this extract. Whatever the public perception of classic literary Greek might be, it is unlikely that fun features significantly. While it takes a high level of intellectual capacity to become proficient in as complex a language as Greek, one would imagine that an even more rarefied level of operation would be required to find it fun.

Note also how the range of David's learning is stressed here. Not only is he skilled in 'classic literary Greek' but also in the 'common street slang language . . . the koine Greek', which is again described as 'great fun'. Mark the judicious use of the technical term 'koine Greek'. David provides a description of what this means, so one could ask what function the use of the technical term serves. It adds nothing in terms of meaning and could easily have been omitted, so it may be seen as performing an explicitly rhetorical function. This is an example of an occasion when the analyst needs to be mindful of potential alternative versions of the text. It may be that the use of the term again stresses David's expertise by giving an example of the privileged knowledge to which he has access.

Although David bases his warrant largely on his scholarship, he appears to belittle this scholarship at one juncture. However, the way in which he elaborates his point means that he ends up emphasising his scholarly skills. He says:

> At that point there came in hand . . . a book by an Anglican clergyman called *Homosexuality and the Western Christian Tradition* by Derek Sherwin Bailey. He wrote this as a part of the Wolfenden report and it was published as you see in

1955 and he was saying, only with all the basic academic apparatus that I didn't have and with all of the scholarly qualifications, the very same thing that I had discovered and I was quite bowled over by it.

This is a clear instance of variability in the account that David is providing of himself. We have seen how earlier he assiduously emphasised his scholarship, yet here he actively denies it. What clues does this variability provide to the function of this description? Although he underplays his 'academic apparatus' and 'scholarly qualifications', he claims that, independently, he reached the 'very same' conclusions (note the emphasising 'very') as Bailey. He exalts Bailey's standing by associating him with the Wolfenden report, on which was based the 1967 law reform decriminalising consensual private sexual activity between men aged over 21 years. This interpretation is founded on an understanding of the context which David is evoking, which underlines how important it is for the analyst to be familiar with the context in which the text under analysis is located. The rhetoric in the extract implies that underlying whatever formal academic training David has is an inspired mind that enabled him to reach the same conclusions as such an intellectually esteemed figure as Bailey. His humility at this discovery is conveyed by his reaction to it ('I was quite bowled over by it'). That this reaction is expressed in folksy terms again underlines his construction of himself as an ordinary person. Two conflicting self-constructions are thus offered in tandem. The function they serve is to reassure the audience that David possesses the formal scholarship and the creative thinking necessary for the expression of informed opinions, while downplaying any threat that this scholarship may present.

The theme of not overwhelming the audience with scholarship recurs at several points in the text. Having constructed himself as gatekeeper to a privileged realm of knowledge, David proceeds to represent himself as cutting a careful path through academic irrelevancies for the workshop participants. For example, while distributing handouts on the principles of Biblical interpretation, he says:

> These are just some basic, a basic approach for example. It's very helpful to have access to the original languages either directly or through the work of others. There are very fine books where they are attempting to–to interpret the Greek and the Hebrew in a popular way without overwhelming you with technical things, and to have access to that scholarship is very helpful if you can't do it yourself.

This extract constructs the audience as lacking knowledge of and scholarship in Greek and Hebrew and so they need to be directed to popularised texts that will not overwhelm them. Such a rhetorical construction is not without its dangers, as it may appear condescending to the audience. This possibility is offset somewhat by the use of the phrase 'if you can't do it yourself'. Although the audience's lack of knowledge and competence is strongly implied, the use of this conditional phrase hedges the implication to some extent. The extract also implicitly constructs David as a knowledgeable and benign teacher or guide, furnishing his audience with the

tools necessary for reinterpreting the traditional discourse but not overwhelming them. The way in which the extract cited earlier was constructed
tallies with this interpretation of David as teacher:

> The Bible was written in ancient languages. The Old Testament is written in
> Hebrew with some Aramaic in the Book of Daniel and one of the other
> prophets. The New Testament is written in Greek, in koine Greek which was the
> common language of the people.

The extract is constructed in a didactic fashion. It begins with a straightforward statement of 'fact'. David then elaborates this statement in a more
specific way, incorporating technical terms ('Old Testament', 'Hebrew',
'Aramaic', 'Book of Daniel') and introducing and explaining a more
inaccessible term ('koine Greek').

As Gergen put it, 'one may justifiably make a claim to voice on the
grounds of possessing privileged . . . experience' (1989:74). David invokes
this warranting strategy when he uses various powerful rhetorical devices
to construct an emotive testimony of his personal involvement in the
arguments that he will advance, saying:

> I have a very personal stake in this material. I came out of a church which taught
> me that God does not love gay and lesbian people, that God condemns us out of
> hand, and it was a very conservative church in the United States. I was married. I
> have three children. When my wife and I separated, the minister who succeeded
> me at that church used the scriptures to take my children away. I mean to take
> their minds away, convincing them that I was going to go to hell because I'm gay
> and I haven't seen two of my three children in twelve years and I have a very
> personal stake in what the Bible says.

The deeply personal emphasis within this extract acts as a counterbalance
to any connotations of objectivity that the emphasis on scholarship may
have created. This extract sees David's first explicit statement of his sexual
identity which may be viewed as another convention of warrant. He
establishes warrant for his deconstruction of the traditional Christian
discourse on homosexuality and for the need to offer an alternative
discourse because he, as a gay Christian, has suffered personally and
grievously at the hands of those who wield the traditional discourse.
Furthermore, David's disclosure of his sexual identity forges a connection
between himself and his audience, most of whom had earlier disclosed
their sexual identities as gay or lesbian. This connection is achieved
through the statement 'I came out of a church which taught me that God
does not love gay and lesbian people, that God condemns us out of hand'.
The clause 'that God condemns us out of hand' restates and emphasises the
point made in the clause 'that God does not love gay and lesbian people'.
However, its more important function is that, in replacing 'gay and lesbian
people' with 'us', David explicitly discloses his sexual identity as gay and
constructs a commonality of oppression between himself and his audience.
The workshop participants are thereby incorporated into his personal
testimony of having been oppressed by the traditional discourse, which

imparts legitimacy to the need to rework it, not just for David's sake but for the sake of all present.

Powerful though the relating of personal experience may be as a warranting device, it may also have the opposite effect. As a gay Christian, David may be seen as having a vested interest in seeking to alter the traditional Christian discourse on homosexuality. This unspoken version of events is counteracted by a fourth strategy that he uses to establish warrant, namely his self-construction as 'honest David'. He employs this device at the beginning of the workshop and again when discussing a gospel text. At the outset, he says:

> Whatever your questions are, if I don't have an answer, I won't try to bluff you. I'll tell you I don't know, cos I'm not in the business of trying to sell you a bill of goods that I can't support.

Later, he examines two verses from Matthew's gospel and two from Isaiah which refer to eunuchs. He talks of how these passages have been unjustifiably used by gay apologists to assert that sexual outcasts in general and gay men and lesbians in particular will have their place in the Kingdom of Heaven. He claims that there is insufficient evidence to support such an assertion, saying:

> It's far more honest to say we're not really sure than to try to sell a bill of goods or try to read into it . . . If we could make a case that based on the Isaiah prophecy that these people who were sexual outcasts would be gathered in and we could make that connection and jump to Matthew and then to us it would be wonderful . . . but if we're really going to be honest, it's not there, and I don't I don't see an honest connection.

The strategy of taking material that appears to support his argument and rejecting it on the basis of its unjustified interpretation is a powerful warranting device. It suggests that he has not simply amassed material regardless of how tenuously it supports his argument. Rather, it suggests that he has applied his scholarship to Biblical material and has selected those passages that can justifiably be interpreted as indicating that same-sex sexual activity is not prohibited by the Bible. The Biblical interpretations that he will offer are thus warranted in advance. David is constructed as a rigorous and honest interpreter, thereby offsetting any suspicion of bias in the interpretations that he will provide.

## 16.6   Evaluating discourse analytic work

The discourse analyst is sometimes accused of 'putting words into the mouths' of those whose discourse is being analysed and of unnecessarily complicating apparently straightforward speech acts. Yet, post-structuralist writers, with their contention that meaning is not fixed or stable, have noted how language use may have consequences that the speaker did not intend. The speaker's rhetoric may invoke discourses and ideologies of which they may not even have been aware. For example, in their analysis of talk about community care policies, Potter and Collie (1989) point out how the notion of community care invokes a reassuring community discourse, centred around images of neighbourliness, close ties and social support. This poses problems for those who wish to criticise community care, as, in naming it, they end up invoking these positive associations and thereby undermining their arguments. As individuals may not be aware that their language creates such effects, the method sometimes advocated for evaluating qualitative analyses which involves asking those who produced the data to comment on the analyses is inappropriate for discourse analysis. Those who produced the texts that have been analysed may complain 'we never meant that' but this does not invalidate the analysis. The analyst is engaged in elaborating the perhaps unintended consequences of the language that was used, tracing the ripples that linguistic material creates in the pool of meaning into which it is tossed.

This does not mean that analysts are free to posit whatever interpretations they please. In order for discourse analysis to be taken seriously, there must exist criteria which allow the quality of an analysis to be evaluated. Discussions about the evaluation of psychological research generally focus on concerns about reliability and validity. These criteria are based on the assumption of scientific objectivity, which in turn assumes that researcher and researched are independent of each other. With discourse analysis, this cannot be the case. Analysts who demonstrate the contingent, socially constructed, rhetorical nature of the discourse of others cannot make an exception for their own discourse. Like the person whose discourse they are analysing, analysts draw upon available linguistic resources to construct a purposeful version of the discourse under analysis. This reflexivity bridges the chasm that is classically created between researcher and researched and makes it impossible to assess an analysis of discourse using traditional evaluative criteria. Potter and Wetherell (1987) suggest four alternative criteria. The most convincing are that an analysis should impart coherence to a text – showing how the discourse fits together in its content, functions and effects – and should be fruitful, that is, should provide insights that may prove useful in the analysis of other discourses.

This evaluative aspect of discourse analysis and indeed of qualitative research in general requires further development. However, the method of reporting discourse analytic studies could potentially provide a useful means of evaluating them. Alongside textual interpretations, the analyst should try to present as much of the relevant text as possible, demonstrating how analytic conclusions were reached with reference to the text. Readers can thus judge for themselves whether the interpretations are warranted and can offer alternative interpretations. Parker and Burman (1993) claim that the recognition of the constructed nature of an analysis undermines any attempt to privilege a particular interpretation. Consequently, they fear that discourse analysis is in danger of slipping into the hedging relativism of liberal humanism. However, the presentation of significant amounts of raw data helps to overcome this danger because they permit interpretations to be debated so that coherent and convincing interpretations can be achieved. The only problem with this is that the submission guidelines of most academic psychology journals make it difficult to present large amounts of raw data in research reports. At present, relatively few journals cater exclusively or primarily to discourse analytic work, the notable exception being *Discourse & Society*. As the acceptability (or at least the tolerance) of discourse analysis increases within psychology, it is to be hoped that journals adopt a more open attitude to discourse analytic research and that it becomes easier to access and disseminate this work.

## 16.7   Problems with discourse analysis

In the short time since it was formally introduced to social psychology, discourse analysis has made tremendous strides in terms of its epistemological development and its influence on the discipline. However, as with any evolving field, it is not without its problems. Some of these were noted earlier, such as the lack of systematicity in techniques of discourse analysis, even though many analysts have argued against the possibility of a 'step-by-step' approach. Parker and Burman (1993) identify no less than 32 problems with discourse analysis, some of them more commonly encountered and more serious than others. For example, while they agree with the emphasis on the linguistic construction of social reality, they also believe that there is a need to hold on to some idea of language representing things that have an existence independent of language. Otherwise, they fear, the focus of interest shifts away from what is being accounted for and towards the account itself. In a similar vein, moving beyond psychology, they point out that, in analyses of power, discourse analysis encourages an over-attention to how imbalanced power relations are reproduced in language and an underemphasis on the endurance of such power relations independent of language.

Within discourse analytic literature, there is a tendency to reify discourse. One sometimes gets the impression that discourses are somehow embedded in the text and that the analyst plays the role of the linguistic archaeologist, simply chipping away the surrounding linguistic material to excavate and reveal the discourses. As Parker and Burman (1993) note, this reifying tendency leads to discourses being represented as static and unchanging. To counteract this, they urge discourse analysts to study the fluctuations and transformations of discourses. Furthermore, the archaeological model of discourse analysis is inappropriate because any discourse analysis involves interpretation by the analyst and is constructed from the analyst's reading of the text. As has already been noted, this means that a discourse analytic report can itself be seen as a text which attempts to construct a particular view of social reality and which can itself be subjected to discourse analysis. While the constructed and reflexive nature of discourse analysis and related pursuits has been acknowledged and indeed celebrated (see Ashmore, 1989), a more than technical response to this insight has yet to be produced. This may be due to the potential for a serious consideration of reflexivity to unsettle, destabilise and subvert social scientific enquiry, as taken-for-granted 'truths' are exposed as arbitrary (Pollner, 1991). However, once the constructed nature of all texts has been highlighted, it is not sufficient for discourse analysts to bracket this insight and carry on as if their analyses are somehow exceptions to the rule.

These problems are not life-threatening for discourse analysis. They merely represent the developmental troubles of a domain which, while no longer in its infancy, still has work to do on its theory and practice. As the key discourse analytic figures within psychology extend and refine their ideas and as the body of research work grows as more psychologists turn to discourse, there is every reason to believe that this developmental work will be forthcoming. During this process, it is to be hoped that discourse analysis will continue to develop and to offer a radical challenge to mainstream approaches to psychology.

## 16.8 Project

As Potter and Wetherell note, 'our accounts of how people's language use is constructed are themselves constructions' (1987:182). The analysis of warranting strategies offered in the 'working with data' section can be applied not only to the discourse under analysis there but also to the analysis of that discourse. Go back to that section and consider how the analysis of David's discourse is legitimated. In this case, the discursive function has been identified, that is, to legitimate the analysis offered, and the task now is to examine the various ways in which this function is fulfilled. More broadly, consider how the presentation of the theoretical basis of discourse analysis in this chapter is constructed as authoritative.

## 16.9 Further reading

Potter and Wetherell's (1987) very readable and broad-ranging text *Discourse and Social Psychology: Beyond Attitudes and Behaviour* remains the obvious starting point for anyone interested in discourse analysis. Edwards and Potter's (1992) *Discursive Psychology* develops discourse analysis further and applies it to some of the central concerns of mainstream psychology, drawing on a range of empirical material. For readers who wish to gain access to a variety of discourse analytic studies, the journal *Discourse & Society* is a useful resource, as is Burman and Parker's (1993) edited volume *Discourse Analytic Research: Repertoires and Readings of Texts in Action*. Readers interested in other approaches to analysing textual material should see section 18.10 of Chapter 18.

# 17 Structuring Qualitative Data: Multidimensional Scalogram Analysis

*Margaret Wilson*

## Contents

## 17.1 Qualitative data and content analysis

Qualitative data is descriptive material. It can be written, as in accounts in newspapers; verbal, such as what people say in interviews; or visual, for example drawings or photographs. Qualitative data for psychological research may already exist in the form of records, publications and so on, or it may be collected by researchers from interviews or observations.

The first step in dealing with qualitative data is to set up some type of classification scheme. The classification of open-ended material is known as **content analysis** (see for example, Krippendorf, 1980). It may often appear that content analysis is simply a matter of counting the number of times a certain thing occurs. However, most theorists are adamant that content analysis should be viewed as a process of theory development and hypothesis testing. Developing a framework for categorising qualitative data is a time-consuming process, and requires a sound theoretical basis for the results to be meaningful.

## 17.1.1    Non-verbal behaviour

The first example is based on the non-verbal behaviour of candidates being interviewed for a job. It would be possible to video the candidates and develop a coding scheme which classified aspects of their non-verbal behaviour. In order to do this, researchers would need to have hypotheses about the types of behaviour which were relevant to what they were studying. If they were interested in how nervous the candidates were, they might hypothesise about those behaviours which might be indicative of 'nervousness'. From the literature they might hypothesise that scratching one's nose indicated nervousness. They could also hypothesise that the candidate touching his or her hair was a nervous reaction. Once the types of behaviours have been established, the researchers would watch the candidates and see whether each behaviour occurred. They might be interested in whether or not the behaviour occurred regardless of the frequency, or they might be interested in the number of times a certain behaviour occurred. The coding of behaviours turns the descriptive visual material into numbers, representing whether or not, or how many times something occurred for each candidate.

## 17.1.2    Children's drawings

The second example examines the way in which children's experiences of war are reflected in their drawings. It would be possible to take two samples of children, one comprising children who had and one comprising children who had not experienced war in their country. The children might be asked to draw a picture about war. The pictures could then be content analysed to see what features were and were not represented in them. It could be hypothesised that while both sets of children would include guns or other weapons in their pictures, children with real experiences of war would include other, quite different features. For example, war experienced children might include more realistic images such as blood and dead bodies. It could also be hypothesised that children of war would include references to themselves or people known to them, whereas children who have not experienced war would be unlikely to include representations of themselves or people close to them. In this way the researcher would set up a classification scheme to include the features to be classified in the children's drawings.

### 17.1.3 Careers in the police force

The final example illustrates the use of existing data in the form of records of people's job histories. Using this type of data it would be possible to assess the different career paths followed by a group of individuals in a particular area, for example, the police force. The researcher might hypothesise that different career experiences may be related to outcomes, such as success. The classification scheme would require hypotheses about which aspects of a person's career history might be related to success in the job. The researcher might hypothesise that the police officers' educational background was important, along with the types of work they had been involved in, how long they had spent in certain departments, and how many job changes they had made during their career in the police force. Identifying the categories on each variable which distinguish between the different career paths would provide the researcher with a framework for classifying each of the individuals being studied. It would then be possible to identify what characterised those police officers who had been promoted to senior positions.

## 17.2 Inter-rater reliability

Once the classification scheme has been established it is very important that a second, independent rater classify the material in addition to the researcher. This procedure is designed to establish the **reliability** of the classification scheme. If the scheme is reliable, it is sufficiently unambiguous that two people will be able to classify the material in the same way. Unless the scheme is tested by another rater, it may be that the classifications are open to individual interpretation, and the first rater may be imposing his or her own view of the material onto its classification.

Once a second person has classified the descriptive data, it is possible to calculate the reliability by simply assessing the number of times the raters agree as a percentage of all possible observations. The strategy for quantifying rater agreement reliability is to use Cohen's kappa coefficient (see Chapter 13). When results are presented it is important to state what the inter-rater reliability of the coding scheme is.

## 17.3 Using the data

Once the researcher has established a reliable way of classifying the material, there are a variety of ways of using the data. If it is a descriptive or 'normative' study, the classification process may well be the endpoint of the research. So referring to the hypothetical examples described above, the researcher might conclude that a certain percentage of all interview candidates display some non-verbal behaviour hypothesised to be indicative of nervousness. Or, in the second example, that children who have experienced war portray different images in their drawings than non-war-experienced children. In the final example, it might be possible to indicate whether the career paths of senior officers in the police force were characterised by consistency or variability in terms of the number of qualitative job changes. These kinds of results are certainly interesting in their own right, and in much qualitative research this is as far as the analysis goes.

However, if the study is more complex, the researchers might want to use the qualitative data further. For example it would be possible to correlate the number of nose scratches in an interview with an independent measure of nervousness, in order to confirm that nose scratching is a valid measure of anxiety in an interview. Similarly, one might suggest that children who represented members of their own family in their drawings of war may have experienced greater trauma as a result of the situation in their country. It would then be possible to relate the content of their drawings to their psychological assessment, or their progress in coming to terms with their experiences. In the final example, it would be of interest to relate the features of police officers' career histories to background characteristics in order to identify, for example, whether successful female officers follow a different career path from those of successful male police officers. It would also be of interest to establish which features of the officers' career histories were most predictive of fast promotion.

## 17.4 Multidimensional analysis

Whether the researcher stops at the point of the descriptive study, or whether he or she uses the results to examine other issues, the qualitative data described above are being used at the most simple level. It may be very interesting that most people scratch their nose when they are nervous, or that English children do not represent death in pictures of war, or that most senior police officers have a degree. But the data have so much more potential when they are analysed multidimensionally. For example, say 60 per cent of the interview candidates scratched their noses, and 60 per cent of the candidates touched their hair. Are they the same people? There may be some candidates who do both, and then there may hair touchers and nose scratchers. What makes these people different? Perhaps hair touchers are more likely to be female, while nose scratchers are male. The important issue is how each of the variables (classifications) relates to one another, and how each combination of variables relate to the items themselves, in this case the people.

Multivariate analysis becomes even more important if the researchers are intending to use the descriptive categories to take the study further. If a researcher managed to find a relationship between any one feature of a drawing and a child's psychological state they would be very lucky indeed. Similarly, it would be very surprising if any one feature of a police officer's background could be used to predict success in the force. For example, just having a degree, or just having experienced a range of police work, would be unlikely to predict future career prospects. However, if the officer had a degree, *and* had experienced many types of police work, and had risen through the ranks in a comparatively short period of time, then it might be more likely that he or she would be promoted to the most senior ranks of the force.

By taking a multidimensional approach to qualitative data it is possible to look at the relationship between the variables, and the way that they overlap. This chapter describes one particular type of multidimensional analysis which allows the researcher to examine all the relationships in the data, between the items, between the variables, and between the variables and the items in the analysis. This complex set of relationships is known as the **structure** of the data. The technique to be illustrated is particularly useful to reveal this structure in qualitative data. It is called **multidimensional scalogram analysis** (MSA).

# 17.5   Multidimensional scalogram analysis

Multidimensional scalogram analysis (MSA; Lingoes, 1968) is a technique which can be used to examine the structure of qualitative data. It allows the relationship between each of the variables or classifications, and the items themselves with respect to those variables, to be represented in one coherent visual summary.

Although MSA is only one of a number of multidimensional scaling techniques it has special properties which make it ideal for understanding qualitative data relationships. In order to explain the way that MSA works and how it can be used in qualitative research this section presents a very simple worked example. The description of MSA is intended to explain how the analysis works *conceptually*. Those interested in the mathematical background to the analysis are referred to Lingoes (1968), Guttman (1941) and Gifi (1990).

## 17.5.1   The data

The example describes the similarities and differences between a number of different occupations. In order to illustrate the use of MSA, this example will only consider six occupations, which form the 'items' for this analysis. It is therefore a very simple example which will serve to illustrate the way the analysis works. The six jobs being considered are police officer (I1), nurse (I2), psychologist (I3), surgeon (I4), barrister (I5) and teacher (I6).

First, the researcher would need to decide what the key concepts are which distinguish between the different occupations. While there could be many of these distinguishing concepts, this example will work with just four. These concepts will be the 'variables' in the analysis. The concepts or classifications used in this example are salary (V1), contact with people (V2), uniforms (V3) and training (V4).

Each of the variables will describe the differences between the occupations on that concept. The concepts can have as many categories as are required to describe the differences between the items. However, this example will keep the classifications very simple to illustrate the technique.

V1   In this case **salary** has been assigned three categories:

1   well paid
2   quite well paid
3   badly paid

V2   In terms of **contact with people** there are also three categories:

1   much contact with people
2   some contact with people
3   little contact with people

V3   The classification for **uniforms** is simply:

1   wears a uniform
2   does not wear a uniform

V4   The final classification for this analysis distinguishes the **amount of training** each job requires:

1   a lot of training
2   little training

The next stage requires the classification of the occupations on each concept to form a data matrix. The matrix has each occupation as a row of data, and each concept or variable as a column. The cells of the matrix show which category each occupation has been assigned to on each of the four variables. So for example:

| Items | Variables (Concepts) | | | |
|---|---|---|---|---|
| | V1 | V2 | V3 | V4 |
| Police officer | 2 | 1 | 1 | 2 |
| Nurse | 3 | 1 | 1 | 2 |
| Psychologist | 2 | 2 | 2 | 1 |
| Surgeon | 1 | 2 | 1 | 1 |
| Barrister | 1 | 3 | 1 | 1 |
| Teacher | 3 | 1 | 2 | 2 |

Each occupation has been classified as to which characteristic it possesses according to the four variables. Thus, reading down the column corresponding to V1 it is possible to see that nurses and teachers have been classified as badly paid (3), psychologists and police officers have been classified as quite well paid (2), and surgeons and barristers have been classified as well paid (1). The same applies to column V2 which shows that in terms of their contact with people, nurses, police officers and teachers have been classified as having much contact with people (1), psychologists and surgeons as having some contact with people (2), and barristers as having little contact with people (3). Column V3 shows whether they wear a uniform (1) or not (2). Finally, column V4 shows whether each job has been classified as requiring a little (2) or a lot (1) of training.

Having classified the occupations, the resulting data matrix summarises the distinctions between the jobs which are hypothesised to be important and shows the similarities and differences between the occupations. Reading along a line of data it is possible to see a **profile** of scores which summarises the qualities which each occupation possesses. Compare the nurse and the police officer. The nurse is (3112) and the police officer is (2112). This shows that they scored the same on three out of four of the criteria, and that they are therefore quite similar in terms of the classifications used. The thing that makes them different is the salary, police officers are quite well paid whereas nurses have been classified as badly paid. Now compare the psychologist with the nurse. The two profiles show that the psychologist (2221) and the nurse (3112) have different codings on all four variables.

## 17.5.2 The analysis

Multidimensional scalogram analysis (MSA) plots each item (in this case an occupation) as a point in geometric space. It attempts to find a configuration of points so that the plot can be divided into clear **regions** which distinguish the items on the basis of each of the variables. In effect this means that the more qualities two items have in common, the closer together they are in the plot.

Since this sounds quite complex, this example will work through this process of finding a configuration of points step by step. First, it is necessary to visualise the plot as a square 'box', and in that box are six points, one representing each of the six occupations. At this stage the points could be placed anywhere in the plot and can be visualised as 'floating' or moveable in the space (see Figure 17.1).

In order to demonstrate how regions representing each variable can be established the example will consider each variable separately. First, MSA needs to separate the occupations into three regions in the plot so that they are distinguished in terms of our first variable, that is salary. The points can be moved around so that the plot is divided into three regions, each one containing the items coded as possessing that characteristic (see Figure 17.2).

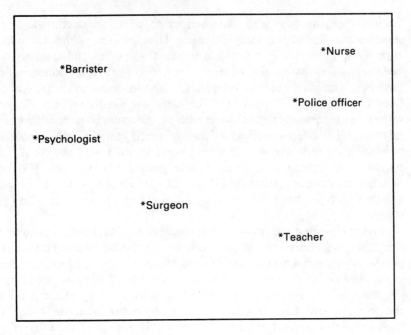

Figure 17.1 *Imaginary starting point*

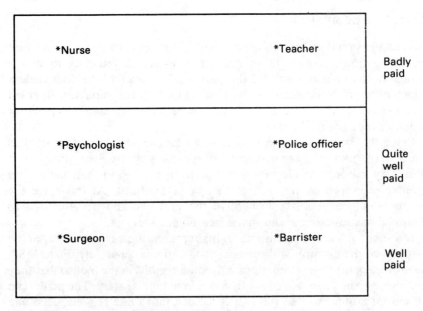

Figure 17.2 *Possible partitioning of the MSA plot according to salary*

Next the MSA needs to arrange the points again, so that the space can be divided for variable two. Once it has distinguished the occupations on variable one these boundaries cannot be crossed. So while keeping the distinctions between the occupations on variable one, the points must be rearranged so that distinctions can be made on variable two. Variable two requires that the nurse, the teacher and the police officer are in the same region of the plot because they all have a lot of day-to-day contact with people. So at this stage the existing configuration of points does not need to be changed as it is possible to draw a line diagonally, as in Figure 17.3.

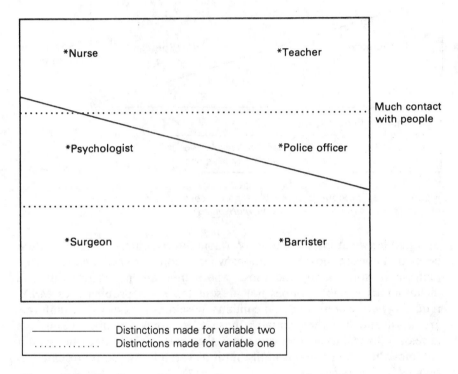

Figure 17.3   *The first partition according to contact with people*

Variable two also requires that the psychologist and the surgeon are in the same region because they both have some contact with people. In order to do this the points need to be rearranged to swap the positions of the surgeon and the barrister. This does not alter the distinction made on variable one, but allows the **partition** to be made on variable two (see Figure 17.4).

This means that the partitions generated to distinguish the occupations on variable one are still the same, but that now we can make a distinction

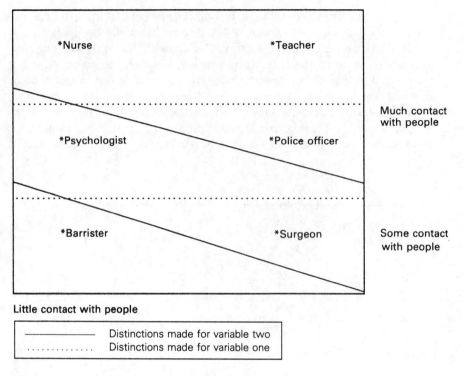

Figure 17.4 *Partitioning of the MSA plot according to contact with people (Note: barrister and surgeon rearranged)*

on variable two at the same time. Variable three requires that a distinction be made between those occupations where people are required to wear a uniform of some kind, and those where they are not. Since this is a dichotomous variable it does not present too many problems for MSA, requiring two regions, one that contains those occupations where uniforms are worn and one that contains those where they are not. Again it is necessary to maintain the distinctions that have already been made, but still move the points about until the third variable can be represented as regions in the space.

Taking the existing regions in Figure 17.4, the plot can be divided again only this time for uniforms. Looking at the data matrix, the psychologist and the teacher (no uniforms) need to be in a different region to the police officer, the barrister, the surgeon and the nurse (uniforms). This partition can be done by simply swapping the position of the nurse and the teacher. This does not alter the regions of the plot for variables one and two but allows the partition to be made for variable three, shown in Figure 17.5.

Finally, the MSA plot needs to represent the final variable, variable four, which distinguished between occupations requiring a lot of training and occupations requiring less training. This variable does not require any further alterations to the position of the points as the teacher, police officer

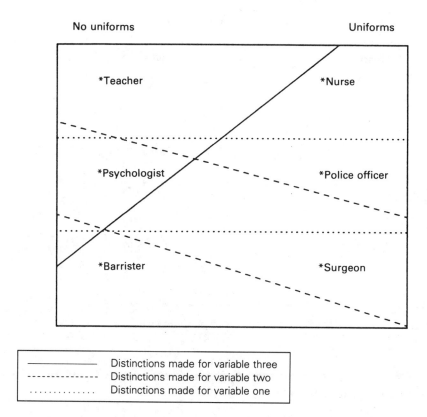

No uniforms                                                    Uniforms

*Teacher              *Nurse

*Psychologist         *Police officer

*Barrister            *Surgeon

| —————————— | Distinctions made for variable three |
| -------------- | Distinctions made for variable two |
| . . . . . . . . . . . . | Distinctions made for variable one |

Figure 17.5  *Partitioning of the MSA plot according to uniforms*
*(Note: teacher and nurse rearranged)*

and nurse (little training) can be distinguished from the other occupations (a lot of training) as demonstrated in Figure 17.6.

## 17.5.3  The coefficient of contiguity

This example has broken down the partitioning of the space into stages, one for each variable in order to describe what the analysis does. This is not the way the analysis works mathematically, but it helps to understand the analysis conceptually. In this simple example, it was possible to rearrange the points to partition the space by hand. It was possible to find a configuration of points which satisfied the ideal requirement of the analysis. That is, that the distinctions on every variable can be represented as overlapping regions in the same geometric space.

Obviously, when real data are involved it is much more complex, and less likely that all the different variables can be represented in the same space. A measure of how well the analysis has been able to achieve this solution is the **coefficient of contiguity**. A perfect solution would have a

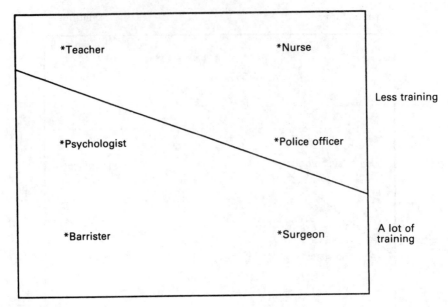

Figure 17.6   *Final MSA configuration with partitioning according to amount of training*

coefficient of +1. Most researchers using this technique would accept a coefficient of contiguity of 0.9.

### 17.5.4   Interpreting the plot

The output of the MSA provides the researcher with two types of plot. First, the overall plot shows the final configuration of points which summarises the relationships between items in the analysis (see Figure 17.7). The more similar two items are according to the classifications across all the variables, the closer together they will be positioned in the plot. This plot is comparable to the type of representations available from other MDS techniques. However, using other, more traditional techniques, it is possible to see that two items are similar across all the variables, but it is not easy to identify exactly what makes two items similar or different.

The second type of plot which MSA provides is called an **item plot**. The analysis derives one item plot for each variable. Each plot indicates the regions which correspond to the categories on each variable (see Figure 17.7). The item plots can be compared with the overall plot and with one another. In this way MSA preserves all the reasons for the similarities and differences between the items, so that it is possible to not only show that two items are similar or different, but also the *reasons why* they are similar and different.

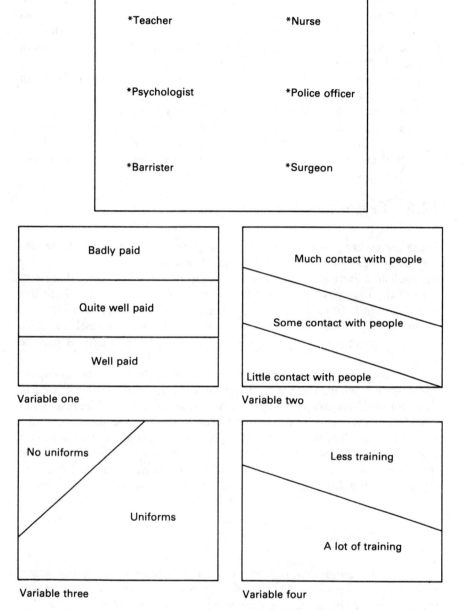

Figure 17.7  *Final configuration and item plots for the worked examples*

The results allow four important constituents of the structure of the data to be revealed:

1  The overall plot shows the similarities and differences between the items according to the variables in the analysis. This plot summarises the relationships between the items.

2   The item plots show which characteristics each of the items possesses, thus maintaining all of the original data. Comparison of the item plots to the overall plot reveals why two items are similar or different.

3   The item plots show the relationship of each variable in the analysis to the others. By comparing the way in which each item plot partitions the space it is possible to draw conclusions about the relationships between the variables themselves.

4   The most complex set of relationships portrayed by the analysis is revealed by combining all of the information from both the plots. Combinations of overlapping variables can be used to interpret the overall meaning of the similarities and differences between the items.

## 17.6   Presentation of the results

There are no hard and fast rules for presenting the findings, and the reader may come across many different ways of representing the results among the published literature. It is possible to present the overall plot, along with each of the item plots partitioned schematically, as in Figure 17.7. In this way the data relationships can be discussed and any findings of interest elaborated. The reader may be left to visualise the way in which variables combine and relate to the items, or further schematic diagrams may be presented.

The second type of presentation is to summarise the data relationships in one diagram, where the variable partitions in the item plots are used to interpret the similarities and differences between the items. The researcher would then draw partitions onto the plot to express the meaning of the similarities and differences between the items being studied. This approach is popular with authors using facet theory (see Chapter 9) and should be treated with some caution until the researcher is familiar with the different types of partitioning and their interpretative implications (see Levy, 1981).

## 17.7   Project

This project examines the different ways that daily newspapers represent a news story. It is possible to focus on whether there are any differences in the content of the reporting depending on the type of newspaper. For example, you might compare tabloids versus broadsheets, or newspapers which traditionally present a particular political bias in their reporting.

Pick a day when something of importance has happened, so that it is likely to have been reported in all of the newspapers. Start by establishing some hypotheses about the differences you would expect to find in the news coverage. Next read through the reports and start to develop a classification scheme which distinguishes between different aspects of what has been reported. Bear in mind the hypotheses you have formulated. Make sure that your categories are not too specific, and describe conceptual differences rather than specific statements. For example, if you were interested in the relationship between newspapers and the portrayal of political ideals, you might develop a classification which described whether the paper was 'supportive of', 'antagonistic towards', or 'independent about' a certain policy or action, rather than considering its specific words. Aim to develop no more than 10 classifications or variables for this example.

Code each newspaper according to the way in which its coverage is described by each of the 10 variables. Multidimensional scalogram analysis of the data will generate a plot where each newspaper is represented as a point in space. The closer together two newspapers are, the more similar will have been their coverage of the event.

Examine the plot to see whether there are any broad differences between the newspapers. For example, you might expect to find the tabloids in one region of the plot and the broadsheets in another. If you have considered a political event, you might find that the political persuasion of the newspaper is reflected in the type of coverage given.

Finally, choose a group of newspapers which are represented by points close together in the overall plot, and use the item plots to discover what it is about their coverage which makes them similar.

# 17.8   Further reading

Berelson's (1971) *Content Analysis in Communication Research* and Krippendorf's (1980) *Content Analysis: An Introduction to its Methodology* are two of the most widely cited books on content analysis, however Bainbridge's (1985) article in Brenner et al.'s *The Research Interview: Uses and Approaches* and Mostyn's (1985) article also in Brenner et al. (1985) provide more readable accounts of the procedure (see also Chapter 18).

A methodological account of MSA is provided by Zvulun's (1978) article in Shye's (1978) *Theory Construction and Data Analysis in the Behavioural Sciences*. Brown's (1985) article in Canter's (1985) *Facet Theory: Approaches to Social Research*, and Canter's (1983a, 1983b) two articles in *Environment and Behavior* and *Quality and Quantity* discuss MSA in relation to facet theory. The use of MSA in conjunction with the Multiple Sorting Procedure is outlined by Canter et al. (1985) and applications in the study of conceptual development in education, and group decision making are illustrated in Wilson and Canter's (1990) article in *Applied Psychology: An International Review* and Wilson and Canter's (1993) article in the *British Journal of Social Psychology* respectively.

# 18 Focus Groups

*Lynne J. Millward*

## Contents

# 18.1 Introduction

The focus group is a discussion-based interview that produces a particular type of qualitative data. It involves the simultaneous use of multiple respondents to generate data and it is the 'focused' (that is, on an 'external stimulus') and relatively staged (that is, by a 'moderator') nature of the focus group method that separates it from other types of group interviewing strategy. According to some, a focus group is no more than a well-targeted and -designed meeting. Yet the implications of this for psychology are not quite so simple. While the study of group processes has a rich and substantial research history, the focus group challenges the epistemological assumptions underlying much research in psychology. This lends it a rather controversial flavour.

The focus group has historical roots in sociology, being associated with research into the effectiveness of wartime propaganda (Merton and Kendall, 1946) and the social effects of mass communication generally. Yet its methodological evolution is attributable not to sociologists but to marketing consultants for whom focus groups have become central to answering the question of 'why' consumers behave as they do. For decades, the use of focus groups within the marketing context has relied on the untested assumption that generating data by focus groups is the quickest and most cost efficient means of generating consumer relevant information. Currently, the focus group method – at least in the marketing domain – has largely evolved into a 'quick and dirty' means of fulfilling client needs rather than as a sophisticated research tool. The substantial literature on how to conduct focus groups is thus mainly tied to the marketing arena (see section 18.13) rather than within a framework of social science.

In 1988 Morgan noted that 'the contribution of focus groups to social science research at present is more potential than real' (1988:75). At that time few focus group studies had been published indicating that the method could be successfully transported beyond marketing boundaries into the social sciences generally. Since then there has been an exponential rise in the number of studies employing focus group methodology. Within psychology alone, the method has gained a substantial foothold since 1988 and it is especially popular within applied psychology, particularly health psychology.

Morgan was under no illusion, however, when he noted that 'social scientists will have to work hard to adapt the focus group technique to their purposes' (1988:77–8). In this chapter, the focus group method as a data-gathering tool is considered from a distinctly psychological rather than sociological or marketing perspective. It is by no means a final statement. Secondary uses of the focus group (for example, for decision making, intervention, collective empowerment and social change) do not fall within this remit. I hope to demonstrate that focus groups not only enhance the ability of psychologists to answer research questions but that more importantly they can generate questions from new angles and perspectives. It is clear, nonetheless, that the future of focus group research in psychology will depend on how rigorously it is conducted. The issue of 'quality control' is thus central (Krueger, 1993).

## 18.2 The appropriateness of the focus group method

Used alone or in combination with other methods, the aim of focus groups is to get closer to participants' understandings of and perspectives on certain issues. It is not geared to the formal testing of hypotheses in the traditional hypothetico-deductive sense. The focus group can be used either as a self-contained means of data collection or as a supplement to other methods depending on how it fits into the overall research plan.

## 18.3 What type of evidence do focus groups yield?

From a social-psychological perspective, the focus group is 'by definition an exercise in group dynamics and the conduct of the group, as well as the interpretation of results obtained must be understood within the context of group interaction' (Stewart and Shamdasani, 1990:7). Two interrelated forms of evidence are therefore derived from focus groups: the group process (the way in which people interact and communicate with each other) and the content around which the group process is organised (the focal stimulus and the issues arising from it).

The group process can be understood on two different levels: first, intrapersonal, that is, thoughts, feelings, attitudes and values of the individual, and second, intragroup, that is, how people communicate and interact with each other within the group. Considerations of the group process are integral to the role of the moderator who will require very different skills to those of one-to-one interviewing. This is dealt with later on in the chapter. Here we need to consider the implications of the group process for the form of evidence elicited. Basically, focus groups afford rich insight into the realities defined in a group context and in particular the dynamic effects of interaction on expressed beliefs, attitudes, opinions and feelings.

One advantage of using the group as opposed to the individual as the medium of investigation is its 'isomorphism to the process of opinion formation and propagation in everyday life' insofar as 'opinions about a variety of issues are generally determined not by individual information gathering and deliberation but through communication with others' (Albrecht et al.; 1993:54). Focus groups are communication events in which the interplay of the personal and the social can be systematically explored.

This alludes to the potential of the focus group method in the investigation of social representations – their structure and processes, and identity related phenomena (Breakwell, 1993). Social representations originate in communication and interaction processes. They are forged in particular by people attempting to make sense of their lives. As such, social representations reflect and communicate identity issues and provide a basis for action.

Gervais (1993) used focus groups (among other qualitative methods) involving Shetlanders to analyse their processes of social representation in the wake of an oil spill. Each focus group comprised a natural social unit (a family, a fisherman crew, fish farmers, local council members and a group who had got together after the spill to act on behalf of the community). Evidence revealed the evolution of a collective rhetoric which maintained community integrity by minimising the impact of the crisis despite its being experienced 'like a death in the family' (engendered by the intimate relationship that Shetlanders have with their land). The rhetoric was derived from Shetlanders' representations of their identity as 'resilient' and of the archipelago as 'The Old Rock'. The focus groups thus provided the ideal forum in which the collective mobilisation of community resources and traditions could be captured and analysed in the face of crisis.

The assumption of focus groups is that people will become more aware of their own perspective when confronted with active disagreement and be prompted to analyse their views more intensely than during the individual interview. Attempting to resolve differences is one of several mechanisms whereby participants build comprehensive accounts to explain their various experiences, beliefs, attitudes, feelings, values and behaviours. Jarrett (1993), for instance, describes how in her study involving low-income Black Americans, participants were inclined to 'perform for each other'; a climate was established in which they were encouraged to discuss things with greater licence than they would otherwise. The reality created within this forum was tempered by peer pressure to 'tell it like it is' whenever idealism prevailed. In this way group pressure inhibited people from providing misleading information.

## 18.4 The focal stimuli

The 'focusing' component of focus group research – that is, its distinguishing characteristic – refers to the concrete and specific character of the discussion in relation to a particular stimulus object, event or situation. Originally the stimulus object was a form of mass media communication (for example, a film or a pamphlet). In marketing, the focus of research might be people's reactions to a particular advertising campaign or consumer product. In the social sciences, the stimulus might be a behavioural scenario (for example, a sexual encounter as a way of accessing attitudes towards safer sex – O'Brien, 1993), a concrete event (for example, driving and young people's risk taking – Basch, 1987), or even a concept (for example, household crowding and its effects on psychological well-being – Fuller et al., 1993). The range of possible stimuli is in fact quite extensive, extending to the use of projective techniques, role-play scenarios, word association exercises, sentence completion and fantasy themes – which have proven especially effective in eliciting responses from children.

## 18.5 The use of focus groups in survey design and interpretation

Although surveys and focus groups originate from different research paradigms, there is nothing inherent in the methods themselves that should prevent them being integrated into one research design. The survey method is not designed to investigate phenomena in any great depth and yet in its design must be built on some assumptions about the meaning of certain things for a particular population of people. The focus group method provides a forum in which some of these assumptions can be tested. Moreover, it can yield information about an issue or indeed, raise issues that have never been considered in relation to the topic at hand.

Specifically, the researcher can become acquainted with the phraseology and concepts used by a certain population of respondents. They can establish the variety of opinion concerning a topic, establish relevant dimensions of attitudes and identify relevant indicators for the constructs being measured. Focus groups are helpful in cross-cultural survey research where they can clarify the relevance of certain concepts and redefine them using common vernacular. They can be used to test various questionnaire items for readability, comprehension, wording, order effects and response variation.

There are other ways that focus groups might be used once the survey has been conducted. First is to assess respondents' reactions to the survey and in particular to trace the cognitive and social processes involved in answering and second, to aid in the interpretation of survey findings by exploring in greater depth the implications of certain quantitative patterns and relationships.

# 18.6 Focus group design and planning

The very first step in the design and planning process is to define and clarify the issues to be investigated in terms of the exact nature of the evidence required. Both substantive and practical considerations will influence this.

## 18.6.1 Sampling and recruitment of subjects

It is not the intention of focus group methodology to yield generalisable data, so random sampling is not necessary. None the less, it is important to employ a systematic strategy when deciding on group composition. The sample should be chosen on theoretical grounds as reflecting those segments of the population who will provide the most meaningful information in terms of the project objectives. Moreover, the participants should have something to say about the topic of interest.

The recruitment strategies employed have important consequences for the degree of cooperation and commitment generated among respondents. The time and energy invested in meeting with 'local' people and making personal contact with potential participants at the outset can facilitate group rapport and contribute substantially to this. Focus group researchers disagree on whether it is necessary to use screening procedures during the recruitment process. One argument in favour of screening alludes to differences in participant background and/or lifestyle that might inhibit the flow of discussion due to lack of common ground. Others argue to the contrary that if all participants were to share virtually identical backgrounds the discussion will be flat and unproductive. The general rule of thumb is that group members should exhibit at least some common characteristics (for example, same socioeconomic class, same age group) to facilitate the sharing of experiences.

Another argument in support of screening is based on the principle of **reactivity**. Ordinarily, the reactivity arising from the screening process is seen as a liability: participants are given the opportunity to familiarise themselves with the research issues and may therefore enter the focus group situation with prejudice and bias. However, the reactivity created by screening procedures may also afford people the opportunity to mull over the topic in advance. Effectively, the attention given to the topic may enhance rather than undermine the validity of the content generated by the discussion.

Ultimately the decision rests on determining the composition of the group which will maximise the probability of obtaining the most theoretically relevant information. Research identifying how best to construct focus groups is lacking. There is some evidence that males and females interact differently in mixed-sex than same-sex groups which has prompted some to suggest that focus group sessions should be homogeneous in terms of gender (Stewart and Shamdasani, 1990).

Knodel (1993) advocates conducting separate focus group sessions with homogeneous but contrasting subgroups defined in terms of **break characteristics**. Break characteristics are selected on substantive grounds and involve the subdivision of groups according to their potentially contrasting views and experiences concerning the issues being investigated. For example, the sample may consist of females who are subdivided by role – for example, 'housewife and mother' and 'career woman', in an investigation of social representations of women in connection with female identity. Another pertinent break characteristic might be socioeconomic class. There is a limit to the number of break characteristics that can be incorporated into any one study. Knodel suggests that they should be kept to a minimum, otherwise both the sampling and analysis process will become unwieldy and also very costly given, at the very least, one focus group conducted for each combination of break variables.

It has become conventional in the marketing context, to ensure that the focus group is comprised of strangers. Acquaintanceship can indeed inhibit the flow of discussion in certain instances. Social scientists however would argue that there are many occasions when the fact of a shared history is of interest from the point of view of the research objectives. Indeed, there are many examples of focus groups being successfully conducted with naturally occurring communities of people (for example, Gervais, 1993). Ultimately, the decision rests on determining the composition of the groups which will maximise the probability of obtaining the most theoretically relevant information.

## 18.6.2   Sample size

Sample size (not group size, note) varies widely from as small as 21 (for example, Occupational Therapy Practitioners; Llewellyn, 1991) to one rare exception of 744 (for example, Parents, Adolescents and Educators; Croft and Sorrentino, 1991). The number of focus group sessions conducted will be a function of both sample and group size. Some researchers have noted that the data generated after about 10 sessions is largely redundant. The decision rests on the type of evidence required and from whom, as well as considerations of cost in terms of time and resources.

## 18.6.3   Group size

A systematic perusal of recent focus group research in psychology yields an average of nine participants per session as conventional with a range of six to twelve which on the whole is consistent with the figures quoted in the focus group literature although some would advocate between six and eight participants as ideal (Albrecht et al., 1993). The latter is based on evidence showing that group size is inversely related to the degree of participation fostered.

There are several reasons why it is advisable to keep the groups as small as possible while still being able to elicit the breadth of responses required. Large groups are unwieldy to manage, they afford free-riding and can be apt to fragment as subgroups form. Also it may be hard to obtain a clear recording of the session: people talk at different volumes and at different distances so the discussion may be difficult if not impossible to track. It is common practice to over-recruit for each session by 20 per cent since it is inevitable that not all will actually turn up. The group size on the day will therefore vary.

## 18.6.4 Location and setting

Choice of location will need to balance the needs of the research with those of participants. It should set the tone of the research as professional and where possible on neutral ground although there are times when the sample will be hard to reach unless the research is conducted on home territory (for example, a hospital). Two prime considerations for partici-

e location should be easy to reach
ose any difficulties for participants
ation problems). Once there, the
e conducive to a smooth flowing
_ (for example, an appropriate
of refreshments, nearby toilets,
). It is also usual to supply name

between one and two hours is the
ving adults and up to a maximum
en.

**tation**

ental to the effectiveness of the
it is preferable for the moderator
project who is sensitive to the
ological rigour even if his or her
ly polished. Moreover, instances

may arise where the moderator must be someone with whom the participants can identify in order to gain their trust and commitment (for example, members of low-income ethnic minority groups). The issue is whether the moderator is able to obtain theoretically useful information. This will require more than the just the ability to manage a group: the moderator will need to be someone who can maximise self-disclosure by balancing the 'requirements of sensitivity and empathy on one hand and objectivity and detachment on the other' (Stewart and Shamdasani, 1990:69). In practice people will talk surprisingly freely about a wide variety of personal topics so long as the climate is permissive and non-critical.

The art of moderating can be termed **process facilitation**. Central to this is the concept of **participant empowerment**. Basically this means that the moderator is the facilitator of someone else's discussion. A pose of 'incomplete understanding' but not ignorance (which will appear insincere) is recommended; the moderator makes it clear that he or she is there to learn from the participants.

The best facilitator guides the proceedings in an unobtrusive and subtle way, intervening only to the extent of maintaining a productive group. For example, one or two of the more dominant group members are engaged in a heated exchange at the expense of others in the group who are obviously experiencing some discomfort. In this case the moderator would need to take active steps to defuse the situation, refocus the group and balance out the discussion process (segment 3, Figure 18.1).

There are some instances where group members may themselves take responsibility for the flow as well as the content of the discussion. This would occur when, say, someone in the group tries to reorient a discussion that has gone off track or who frequently asks others for clarification. Jarrett (1993) describes how the low-income African-American women in her study challenged each others' 'idealised accounts' (for example, as strong women who have to manage errant husbands, disobedient children and meddlesome mothers) of their housewife role. The extent to which self-management of this kind occurs depends on the climate established by the moderator at the very outset (segment 4, Figure 18.1).

Segment 1 of Figure 18.1 shows maximal direction and control of content and process. This type of moderator style is characterised by a standardised exchange of questions and answers – best suited to the highly structured one-to-one interview. Segment 2 shows high content control–low process control. This moderator style would befit only the 'expert mode' (for example, doctor–patient, teacher–pupil). It affords little if any scope for participant involvement. A norm of passivity rather than interaction is created of only talking when asked. Without participant-centred inter-action there is no focus group.

Segment 3 of Figure 18.1 shows low content control–high process control. This is the 'process facilitation' moderator style most appropriate for the conduct of focus groups. The moderator facilitates interaction participants as ideal (Albrecht et al., 1993). The latter is based on evidence showing that group size is inversely related to the degree of participation fostered.

There are several reasons why it is advisable to keep the groups as small as possible while still being able to elicit the breadth of responses required. Large groups are unwieldy to manage, they afford free-riding and can be apt to fragment as subgroups form. Also it may be hard to obtain a clear recording of the session: people talk at different volumes and at different distances so the discussion may be difficult if not impossible to track. It is common practice to over-recruit for each session by 20 per cent since it is inevitable that not all will actually turn up. The group size on the day will therefore vary.

### 18.6.4 Location and setting

Choice of location will need to balance the needs of the research with those of participants. It should set the tone of the research as professional and where possible on neutral ground although there are times when the sample will be hard to reach unless the research is conducted on home territory (for example, a hospital). Two prime considerations for participants are convenience and comfort. The location should be easy to reach and the research schedule should not pose any difficulties for participants (for example, child care and transportation problems). Once there, the conditions of the room itself should be conducive to a smooth flowing discussion and basically comfortable (for example, an appropriate ambience of informality, availability of refreshments, nearby toilets, suitable seating and table arrangements). It is also usual to supply name tags.

### 18.6.5 Length of session

Most focus group researchers agree that between one and two hours is the standard duration for each session involving adults and up to a maximum of one hour for sessions involving children.

## 18.7 Focus group implementation

### 18.7.1 Moderator style and skills

The skills of the moderator are fundamental to the effectiveness of the focus group. In the social science context it is preferable for the moderator to be someone directly involved in the project who is sensitive to the research issues and the need for methodological rigour even if his or her group management skills are not especially polished. Moreover, instances may arise where the moderator must be someone with whom the participants can identify in order to gain their trust and commitment (for example, members of low-income ethnic minority groups). The issue is whether the moderator is able to obtain theoretically useful information. This will require more than the just the ability to manage a group: the moderator will need to be someone who can maximise self-disclosure by balancing the 'requirements of sensitivity and empathy on one hand and objectivity and detachment on the other' (Stewart and Shamdasani, 1990:69). In practice people will talk surprisingly freely about a wide variety of personal topics so long as the climate is permissive and non-critical.

The art of moderating can be termed **process facilitation**. Central to this is the concept of **participant empowerment**. Basically this means that the moderator is the facilitator of someone else's discussion. A pose of 'incomplete understanding' but not ignorance (which will appear insincere) is recommended; the moderator makes it clear that he or she is there to learn from the participants.

The best facilitator guides the proceedings in an unobtrusive and subtle way, intervening only to the extent of maintaining a productive group. For example, one or two of the more dominant group members are engaged in a heated exchange at the expense of others in the group who are obviously experiencing some discomfort. In this case the moderator would need to take active steps to defuse the situation, refocus the group and balance out the discussion process (segment 3, Figure 18.1).

There are some instances where group members may themselves take responsibility for the flow as well as the content of the discussion. This would occur when, say, someone in the group tries to reorient a discussion that has gone off track or who frequently asks others for clarification. Jarrett (1993) describes how the low-income African-American women in her study challenged each others' 'idealised accounts' (for example, as strong women who have to manage errant husbands, disobedient children and meddlesome mothers) of their housewife role. The extent to which self-management of this kind occurs depends on the climate established by the moderator at the very outset (segment 4, Figure 18.1).

Segment 1 of Figure 18.1 shows maximal direction and control of content and process. This type of moderator style is characterised by a standardised exchange of questions and answers – best suited to the highly structured one-to-one interview. Segment 2 shows high content control–low process control. This moderator style would befit only the 'expert mode' (for example, doctor–patient, teacher–pupil). It affords little if any scope for participant involvement. A norm of passivity rather than interaction is created of only talking when asked. Without participant-centred inter-action there is no focus group.

Segment 3 of Figure 18.1 shows low content control–high process control. This is the 'process facilitation' moderator style most appropriate for the conduct of focus groups. The moderator facilitates interaction

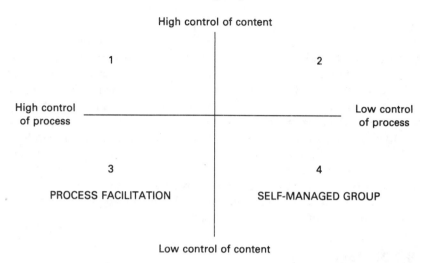

High control of content

1                                    2

High control _____ Low control
of process                           of process

3                                    4

PROCESS FACILITATION          SELF-MANAGED GROUP

Low control of content

Figure 18.1   *Four types of moderator style*

amongst the participants by ensuring that the discussion is productive (that is, all the relevant issues are covered and in sufficient depth). Control over content is minimal; only the issues to be focused on are determined in advance. However there will be occasions when the research objectives are revised in accordance with the findings derived from focus group sessions in which case the moderator should allow mainly the participants to determine the agenda.

Segment 4 of Figure 18.1 shows minimal direction and control of content and process. This segment characterises the self-managed group. The moderator may introduce the focus group session in the process facilitation mode and then work to empower the participants to take progressively more responsibility for the process as well as the content of the discussion (movement from segment 3 to segment 4). It therefore provides the opportunity to see how participants naturally organise their discussions of certain issues. The climate is also ripe for the discussion of controversial or sensitive topics that would otherwise threaten rapport if the researcher introduced them. The main disadvantage, of course, is the complete absence of standardisation thus rendering it impossible to compare findings across different focus groups within the same research project. Without prompting, some topics may never come up.

The degree of control over the structure in any one focus group session will vary along the central continuum. The less the degree of external control, the less opportunity for moderator biases to operate (for example, unwittingly leading participants into a particular area of discussion that provides validation for previous work) thereby increasing the validity of the information derived.

As well as the criterion of minimal direction, there are three additional criteria for ensuring that 'focus' is maintained: specificity, range and depth.

The first requires that minute detail is sought in people's responses and reactions to the stimulus object or event. It is the moderator's task to elicit meanings and differential responses. The second concerns coverage, the issue for the moderator being one of facilitating transitions from one area of a discussion to another and the third concerns the personal context of the response or reaction elicited by the stimulus. Eliciting in-depth responses involves expanding on responses beyond limited reports of 'positive' or 'negative', 'pleasant' or 'unpleasant' reactions. The moderator's task is to diagnose the level of depth at which participants are operating (that is, ranging from superficial description to detailed elaboration) and where necessary to shift it towards a 'deeper' level. All these criteria can be met by the moderator who is skilled in listening and questioning techniques.

## 18.7.2　Topic guide

A topic guide is necessary only to the extent that it prompts the moderator to recall the key issues to be discussed. The guide should be no more than suggestive, affording the moderator considerable latitude to improvise fruitful questions and pursue unanticipated lines of enquiry as the discussion progresses. Do not use the guide in the form of a questionnaire or interviewing straitjacket. Reliance on fixed questions may undermine the ability of the moderator to listen analytically to content of the discussion thereby overlooking the implications of what is said. Sometimes the feelings being expressed in people's comments are cloaked in abstractions and rationalisations. The moderator might form a hunch about the nature of the undercurrent and raise it in the form of tentative questions, thus creating a climate in which people are encouraged to articulate their feelings. To ward against using the guide as a script, some have advocated that the issues to be covered are instead committed to memory. The number of issues raised will depend on the extent to which the group identifies with the topic as a whole and the type of thinking the group members are required to engage in (for example, highly sensitive topics may lead quickly to emotional fatigue). It may be advisable to pretest the 'tone' of the discussion to derive clues about the appropriateness of the focus group's method for how easily or openly a topic is discussed and the range of emotions elicited.

## 18.7.3　Listening and questioning skills

The listening and questioning style of the moderator is key to determining the nature of the discussion. This will reflect in both the sequence of questions as well as how questions are worded. Leading questions – ones that prompt people to agree or confirm something that they have not actually said (for example, 'Would you agree that . . . ?') are likely to provoke people into reacting against the flow of the discussion, engendering a climate of defensiveness and/or withdrawal. Some people may need help articulating a response (for example, 'Are you saying that you feel . . . ?') but it is important not to actually lead them into saying something that they did not really mean for the sake of a response. Leading questions give the impression of being uninterested in listening to what the respondent really thinks and feels. The wording should facilitate openness. Closed questions, for example, direct people to say either 'yes' or 'no' without elaboration ('Are you happy with . . . ?') whereas open questions – ones that invite a response without specifying the particular nature of the response (for example, 'What are your thoughts about . . . ?') and probing questions – designed to elicit more specific information (for example 'Tell me more about . . .', 'Why do you feel that way?'), help create a climate of attentiveness and listening where people feel able to respond in any way they like.

Merton and Kendall (1946) distinguish questioning styles according to their degree of structure: unstructured, semi-structured and structured. The unstructured question is one which is **stimulus and response free**; the respondent is not guided on either which stimulus or aspect of a stimulus to respond to nor the type of response that is required (for example, 'What are your thoughts on recent health education campaigns emphasising safer sex?'). There are two types of semi-structured questions – **stimulus structured and response free** and **stimulus free and response structured**. In the former, the particular focus of the question is specified but the nature of the response is left completely open (for example, 'How do you feel about the emphasis on condom use in campaigns on safer sex?'). In the latter, the focus of the question is unspecified but a particular kind of response is requested (for example, 'What did you learn from the campaigns on safer sex?'). In the structured question, both the stimulus and response component are rigidly specified (for example, 'Do you think that sticking to one sexual partner is better or as good or a poorer means of practising safer sex than the regular use of condoms?'). From this you can see that the structured question exerts complete control over the respondent to answer in a particular way.

Silence is also a powerful way of getting people to talk, allowing them time to think about and formulate a response. Moderators should not be tempted to fill every single void with a question.

Different combinations of questions can be used that 'funnel' people into responding at a more concrete and specific level, that is, generally provide a series of openers which orient them into thinking about a particular issue (for example, 'Tell me about . . .') and progress to using more focused but not leading types of questions in order to obtain information in minute detail. If there is some initial reluctance to talk, 'inverted funnel' tactics can be used whereby a very specific 'factual' question is asked, the response to which is then used to motivate people gradually to talk more freely about the issue (for example, using open questions).

Skilled use of questions also requires **double hearing**. This means that the moderator should be able to read between the lines of a discussion in order to 'ferret' out only what is implied rather than relying totally on what is made explicit. By explicating the implied (for example, tentatively playing it back to respondents in the form of a clarificatory question), it is rendered legitimate (for example, it is acceptable to talk about this) and respondents may thus feel able to elaborate.

### 18.7.4   Managing transitions in the discussion

There are two types of transitions: respondent-initiated and moderator-initiated. **Respondent-initiated transitions** can be informative in that they may reflect an unwitting attempt to escape from talking about something uncomfortable. While people can never be forced to pursue something they obviously feel uncomfortable about, the moderator can at least try to uncover the reasons for and the spread of the discomfort (for example, is the discomfort shared by others and if so what is the basis of this?).

**Moderator-initiated transition** may be cued by something said or alluded to by a respondent or by a more strategic desire to revisit an issue that was side-stepped, superficially discussed or not mentioned at all. Cues originating from the respondents help maintain the flow of the discussion whereas the more stylised kind of moderator-initiated moves can interrupt the flow if not managed carefully.

### 18.7.5   Managing difficult people

Use assertive techniques to undermine the tendency of **self-appointed experts** to state opinions as fact. In particular, make it a rule that the basis for strong opinions must be explained to the group thereby using the group process to deal with them.

If someone is hostile to the extent of intimidation it may be advisable to discretely ask this **hostile member** of the group to leave at the most opportune time (for example, coffee break).

A skilful use of questioning can encourage otherwise **silent members** to contribute. And if there is a **talkative member**, lever the energy of this person by playing the reactions of the group against him or her.

## 18.8   Collecting the data

Focus groups usually generate qualitative data in the form of transcripts produced from audiotape or videotape. By videotaping the focus group sessions observational data can also be extracted (such as, non-verbal communication) as well as the content of the discussion. However, this might be outweighed by the effects on the interaction and communication process created by the presence of the equipment. This may render the situation more formal than is conducive to relaxed and open discussion especially if two sets of equipment are used to capture it from different angles. The audiotape limits the form of data to the content of the discussion but can be supplemented by observations of process made by the moderator. It is unlikely, however, that the moderator will be in a position to observe, take notes and concentrate on facilitating the process of discussion unless co-moderation is possible. The presence of a separate observer/co-moderator may, however, have the same alienating consequences as video equipment. It also adds to the cost of running the focus groups. Most researchers rely on audiotaped recordings of the discussions supplemented by a few general fieldnotes.

Whatever the type of recording used it is crucial to first obtain the consent of the participants by explaining the purpose of the recording and assuring them of confidentiality. Once agreed, the logistics of using the tape-recorders needs to be considered (such as, how many and where best positioned). The larger the group the less easy it is to get a clear recording using one tape-recorder alone. The ground rule established at the outset that everyone should speak loudly and clearly enough to be picked up by the microphone does not always work.

## 18.9    Transcription

It has been said that the analysis of transcriptions is one of the most challenging aspects of the focus group method. If each session lasts about two hours, 40–50 pages of transcription are yielded. If 20 sessions are conducted overall that's 1000 pages of transcription to analyse.

Transcription is a purely mechanical task. Its time-consuming and laborious nature, however, has often led researchers to analyse the content directly from the tape which entails transcribing only those most illustrative comments. Since the purpose of a focus group is to gain insight into how respondents represent a particular issue as a whole and on a collective rather than individual basis, it is important to capture the entire character of the discussion, warts and all. Any form of editing during transcription is therefore undesirable.

## 18.10    Content analysis

This discussion of content analysis as it is used to analyse transcription data is equally applicable to other types of data that can be reduced to textual form (for example, discourses and historical materials). Content analysis can even be used to analyse non-textual data such as works of art and architecture. However, most psychological applications are concerned with analysing material that can be presented to content analysts as texts (Holsti, 1969).

Content analysis comprises both a mechanical and an interpretative component (Krippendorf, 1980). The mechanical aspect involves physically organising and subdividing the data into categories while the interpretative component involves determining which categories are meaningful in terms of the questions being asked. The mechanical and interpretative are inextricably linked in a cycling back and forth between the transcripts and the more conceptual process of developing meaningful coding schemes.

There are three main forms of content analysis; qualitative, quantitative and structural.

## 18.10.1   Qualitative content analysis

This type of content analysis tends to be more subjective and less explicit about the processes by which interpretation of the target material occurs. The emphasis is on meaning rather than on quantification.

Initially the system of classification may be derived from the research question and the topic guide used by the moderator during process facilitation. Additional conceptual codes may arise from a closer examination of the data as a whole. Coded segments may include long exchanges, phrases or sentences. The transcripts are cut and then sorted. Codes can also be developed to signal useful quotations. Following this a grid which tabulates code on one axis and focus group identifier on the other is developed that provides a descriptive overview of the data. The aim is to be able to find quotations to illustrate particular themes or strands of meaning within the transcript. With this form of content analysis the aim is not normally to put numbers to the data.

Computer assisted approaches to data reduction which are designed to organise textual data can make at least the mechanics of the task much more manageable. The most well known of these is a software package called The Ethnograph (Seidel et al., 1988). Coding is performed on the transcript and the segments coinciding with each code are then sorted so that all units of data relating to a particular theme can be readily assembled and retrieved.

Chapter 16 on discourse analysis also deals with many related issues so they will not be dealt with further here.

## 18.10.2   Quantitative content analysis

This type of content analysis can be used to generate numerical values from the target material. These might be frequencies, rankings or ratings.

However, the process by which these values are generated may include elements of qualitative analysis so the qualitative/quantitative distinction is far from clear cut. Quantitative content analysis is slightly mislabelled anyway as it is less a type of analysis than a way of producing data which can then be statistically analysed, that is, the output of the content analysis is not the end of the analysis as a whole.

The first stage involves the selection of the material to be analysed – **the universe of material**. Clearly, in the case of transcripts of focus groups this will be all the material that has been collected while running the groups. More generally, the universe of material refers to all the material that is potentially available for analysis. Indeed, the initial definition of the universe of material is common to all forms of content analysis.

The second stage involves the selection of some **unit of analysis**. The units of analysis are the discrete bits of information that will be assigned to categories in the subsequent analysis. A unit of analysis (or coding unit) can be a word, a theme, a character, an item, time spent on a topic, etc.

When the unit of analysis is a word then content analysis may become a relatively simple exercise of counting the occurrences of particular words or types of words (for example, active vs. passive constructions). Although this approach has some advantages, in particular that it can be easily computerised, it is limited in that the meaning of a word can change depending upon the context. A more subtle, though potentially less reliable, approach is to identify themes.

A **theme** is a statement or proposition about something. Sometimes themes can be identified by the presence or absence of specific words (for example, self-referential statements may be identified by the presence of 'I' and 'me'). However, the identification of themes will often require some interpretative action on the part of the coder(s).

In order to conduct a thematic content analysis one needs to generate a **coding frame**. The coding frame is a set of categories into which instances will be allocated. The categories should be **exhaustive** (that is, all instances can be assigned to a category) and **exclusive** (that is, all instances should be assigned to only one category). The coding frame can be developed either on the basis of the substantive content of the target material (for example, categories could be different types of environmental issue) or on the basis of theoretically determined categories (for example, internal and external attributions). To some extent, a theoretically derived coding frame is more analytic while a content derived coding frame is more descriptive. Of course, different coding frames may be applied to the same material.

Thematic content analysis requires an assessment of the reliability of the coding. This is typically done by using more than one coder to code the same material. Inter-rater reliability is then assessed by computing an agreement index such as Cohen's Kappa.

The output of a content analysis is often the frequency of occurrence of the different coding categories, for example, how many times does a particular coding category appear in a transcript (or text, etc.) – quantification of the material. Comparisons between different source materials may then be assessed. However, it is possible to evaluate the content along ordinal dimensions. This increases the scope for statistical analysis of the data. Ranking may be used when a number of instances are being analysed, for example, one could rank focus groups on the degree to which group members used personalised examples to illustrate points in their arguments. Rating scales may also be used in some cases.

## 18.10.3   Structural content analysis

This type of content analysis involves the development of a representation of the relationships between elements in the target material. In order to do this both qualitative and quantitative aspects of the data have to be considered.

Structural content analysis is appropriate for the analysis of complex systems of which naturally occurring focus groups are an excellent example. Variants of this approach, such as cognitive mapping (Axelrod, 1976), have often been applied to aspects of decision making. As well as being relevant to decision making this approach is useful for investigating belief systems and social representations. Structural content analysis involves some of the same processes and techniques as are used in quantitative (and qualitative) content analysis. However, the rules governing the relationships between response categories also need to be defined. This allows both qualitative and quantitative aspects of the target material to be represented.

These relational rules will vary depending upon the research aims. Research on political decision making, for example, might examine belief systems about crime and what should be done about it. As well as being able to examine the effects of group contexts on the expressed beliefs one can compare the belief systems of members of different parties (or other groups), and explore change in the belief systems over time. Relational rules would relate to covariation and potential causality – for example, does the political make-up of the group influence the way crime is discussed? Do expressions of particular policies tend to come from people who believe in certain classes of causes of crime? etc.

Content analysis is not without its problems. It is heavily reliant on the multiple judgements of a single analyst. As the analyst may be (unknowingly or otherwise) keen to find support for a particular view of the data it is advisable to involve independently two or more people in the coding of the transcripts so that the reliability of the analysis can be systematically assessed.

Other problems include concentrating only on what is mentioned. Sometimes what is not mentioned or strategically side-stepped by the group may be as important. If it does not appear in the transcript it cannot be content analysed. Also, talking about themes in the data in isolation may side-step the complex totality in which themes are embedded. In the focus group the content is generated by communication and interaction in the collective sense. Structural content analysis may go some way to dealing with this problem though the techniques of structural analysis are relatively underdeveloped and where they are developed they tend to be tailor-made to deal with very specific problems.

## 18.11   Other forms of analysis

Researchers working within the framework of discourse analysis have established specific procedures for handling textual data, which are beyond the scope of this chapter. From this perspective the focus group method is a particularly apt medium for the analysis of the collective functions of discourse generated therein (see Chapter 16).

Fantasy Theme Analysis is a form of discourse analysis but one which is based on an entirely different set of epistemological assumptions (Bormann, 1972). It is concerned with how communication affords dramatisation (for example, story telling) which in turn creates social realities for people. Dramatisation is of interest only in the collective sense as providing insights into the cultural, emotional and motivational style of a particular community or population of people. The focus group method provides the ideal forum for the investigation of 'dramatised communication'. A detailed consideration of how to conduct fantasy theme analysis can be found in Bormann (1972).

## 18.12   Project

Your remit is to conduct research on the family, in particular to identify representations of the family and various family roles and the implications of these for social influence processes within the family. To do this, you need to carry out the following:

1   Determine your sample composition.
2   Determine your focus group composition.
3   Plan your recruitment strategy.
4   Produce a topic guide.
5   Conduct a real focus group.
6   Transcribe and analyse the data.
7   Identify various lines of supplementary or follow-up research.

## 18.13   Further reading

Several books have recently appeared which cover focus group methods. Stewart and Shamdasani's (1990) *Focus Groups: Theory and Practice* is a clear explanation of these methods as is Morgan's (1993) recent *Successful Focus Groups: Advancing the State of the Art*. Krueger's (1988) *Focus Groups: A Practical Guide for Applied Research* is a very down-to-earth and pragmatic handbook on the do's and don'ts.

# 19  Diary Techniques

*Glynis M. Breakwell and Peter Wood*

## Contents

## 19.1  What are diary techniques?

Any data collection strategy which entails getting respondents to provide information linked to a temporal framework is essentially a diary technique. The record of information in relation to the passage of time is referred to as the diary. In fact, this record may be unlike anything that would be recognised as a traditional diary purchased in a stationery shop and would not necessarily involve a *daily* record of events, the frequency of entries differs according to the research purpose. Diary techniques can be used with virtually any type of data. For instance, though they often involve self-report, this is not inevitable and they can focus on information about other people. The diary does not have to be the product of one person. Sometimes multiple authors are active in producing it (there are even institutional or corporate diaries with anonymous, committee author-ships). Diaries can involve various media of report (most obviously verbal or written records but also photographic or video descriptions). Nowadays, researchers will use multimedia diary records. The diary techniques allow the medium of the record to be chosen so as to best suit the topic and the type of respondent studied.

The reports required can differ substantially in the amount of structure imposed by the researcher and the flexibility permitted the diarist. Some demand very detailed accounts of one type of behaviour. For instance, consumer researchers may wish to know how often certain women purchase eco-labelled products. They can find out something about this by asking them to keep shopping diaries in which they simply have to tick their purchases against a checklist on a daily or weekly basis. In such diaries, entries are carefully pre-structured. If, however, the object was broadly to understand more about eco-friendly behaviour, the research might ask each of these women to describe in the diary what she thought she had done during that period which had some bearing on environmental conservation.

The breadth of the subject matter for diary records is as big as the imagination of the researcher. They may entail reports of actions, thoughts, or feelings as well as accounts of physical or social context. An interesting example of unusual subject matter for a diary comes from the work of Freud on the interpretation of dreams. He compiled records of his own dreams by writing down what he remembered of them as soon as he awoke each morning.

Diary studies can use reports which are specially elicited or can be analyses of spontaneously generated records of information over time. So, for instance, a researcher attempting to identify the way military leaders make decisions under stress may ask a sample of such leaders to produce diaries during an operation specifically for the study, or alternatively may consider it more useful to analyse the published diaries of senior army commanders. The value of historical diary material has recently become more accepted by psychologists who now recognise that it is one way to test claims that psychological processes are socioculturally specific.

Since it is simply a data collection strategy, the diary can be used as part of any type of research design. Diary techniques have been used in experimental and quasi-experimental research designs as well as in single case studies, large-scale surveys and ethnographies.

The time period over which the diary is drawn can vary widely from a few hours to several years and there may be similar variability in the periodicity of entries, which can range from every few minutes to every few months.

## 19.2  The pros and cons of the diary approach

Since diary techniques have no simple uniform guise, it is not easy to draw up simple lists of the pros and cons associated with them as a research method when exploring psychological processes. Some forms of diary technique have some types of advantage and disadvantage; other forms have different costs and benefits. It is, however, possible to give general indications of the strengths and weaknesses of this approach to data collection.

The diary approach can be used to great effect because respondents are typically familiar with the notion of what a diary is. When you ask someone if they will keep a diary of activities of a specific kind every day over a fortnight, the person understands the task. You may need to refine that understanding through careful instructions, but you have the advantage that the respondent has some initial appreciation of what you want. This may be very helpful if you are dealing with individuals who are especially anxious, suspicious or ignorant about psychological assessments.

The diary approach can be particularly useful, and cost-effective, when you want data from the same person over a considerable period of time and/or very frequently. Given appropriate instructions, respondents can be generating information for long periods without the need for the researcher to be in contact. They can be given the diary to complete and only recontacted at the end of the study.

Of course, the greatest advantage of the diary approach is that it yields information which is temporally ordered. It tells you the sequence of events; giving you the profile of actions, feelings or thoughts across time. There are other ways of doing this but they tend to involve greater intervention by the researcher and consequently higher potential interference with the sequence under consideration.

Diaries are often used in order to access so-called 'intimate' information (for example, about sexual behaviour) in the belief that iterative self-reporting, mostly without any interpersonal interaction, will engender self-revelation and honesty. Whether this assumption is valid has not been established. It is, however, true that the range and variety of personal information elicited in a diary can be very great. This makes it a valuable tool when first formally exploring an area of psychological processes.

Diaries can be used to map the variety of human experiences salient in a domain. In doing this, it is sometimes useful to use spontaneously generated diaries. Just because a diary was not produced specifically for your research does not mean that it is not useful to your research. There are essentially two types of spontaneously generated diaries: those produced for private consumption and those produced for public consumption. Both types can be useful for the psychological researcher. They differ significantly in two ways: their accessibility and their veracity. The accessibility difference is evident. Getting hold of diaries which have not been produced for publication can be difficult for obvious reasons: you are unlikely to know of their existence and even if you do, you are unlikely to get permission to use them. The veracity difference is more contentious. Diarists writing for public consumption are subject to a variety of pressures which may lead to misrepresentation of events or their sequencing. In the simplest terms, diarists who seek publication of their diaries are unlikely to wish to represent themselves negatively. They will wish, most probably, to justify or excuse themselves. Questions concerning their accessibility and veracity obviously limit the real usefulness of spontaneously generated diaries for psychological researchers. However, it must be added that published diaries are one of the few sources of data giving a historical perspective on psychological processes. If, for instance, a researcher wishes to examine whether questions of identity processes which are pertinent in the latter twentieth century were salient in the nineteenth century, one of the rare ways of tackling the question will be through a systematic analysis of diaries produced in that period.

The advantages of the diary approach can be summarised, therefore, in a few key words: familiarity; cost-effective sampling of information; sequencing data; intimacy; exploration; spontaneity; and historicity.

The potential disadvantages of the diary approach can be ameliorated and are not inevitable. They should nevertheless be summarised before examining the ways to overcome them. Control over the data elicited is always difficult to achieve. Clearly, if you use spontaneously generated diaries you have no real control over what data is provided. These diaries inevitably involve self-selection of material by the diarist. Even if you use diaries which you request, your level of control is suspect. You can, of course, ask for specific categories of information. However, getting people to remember to make entries at the right time about the right things can be difficult, even when they have goodwill towards the research and every intention of complying with your instructions.

The diary technique is plagued by a further lack of control. Diary studies suffer significant problems with dropout: respondents do not always continue to provide information throughout the designated period. This problem of 'sample maintenance' often can be exacerbated by poor initial recruitment into the study. Completing a diary (especially over any lengthy period) can be seen as onerous and will result in people being unwilling to join the study in the first place. This combined with subsequent potentially high dropout rates is likely to mean that the sample is highly biased by the end of the study.

Another disadvantage of the diary approach harks back to the issue of veracity. Getting the respondent to tell you the truth may be difficult but, more importantly, you may never be able to ascertain whether they did or not. It may be necessary, if you are very concerned with verifying of data, to use other methods alongside the diary approach.

Like any intrusive research technique, the diary when initiated by the researcher may produce data affected by 'reactance'. The very fact of having to produce the diary may alter the behaviour, thoughts, feelings, and so on, which are recorded. An example of this effect comes from Freud's dream diaries. As he got into the habit of recording the dreams, he found that he 'dreamed more often' (that is, tended to wake at a point in the sleep cycle when he was more likely to recall his dreams). The extent of reactance is essentially unassessable and may vary over time through-out the period of the research, thus influencing results in a non-constant fashion. It is clear, however, that if we require individuals to make large numbers of entries, or write extensively about events, then the action 'diary filling in' becomes a significant element of everyday behaviour.

The disadvantages of diary techniques can be summarised in a few key words: control of content; dropout; poor recruitment; veracity and verification; and reactance.

## 19.3   Getting the best out of diary techniques

The advantages of the diary approach can, obviously, be enhanced and the disadvantages minimised by careful construction of the research. First, it is obviously important to choose the right recording medium for your type of respondents. Respondents lacking the necessary level of literacy should not be asked to produce written diaries (this might include the young, the ill-educated, and anyone who for physical reasons – for example, poor eyesight – might find the task impossible). Alternative recording forms such as audiotaping should be considered.

Second, respondents should be given very comprehensive and comprehensible instructions on how to complete the diary. Pilot work should be used to establish that the instructions are understandable. These instructions should emphasise the importance of accuracy and offer assurances of confidentiality and anonymity where appropriate. They should indicate that entries need to be made regularly at the times specified and explain that entries made retrospectively, relying on memory, are subject to distortions which detract from the value of the information. The possibility of reactance should be described to the respondents in simple terms so that they are on guard against it.

Third, the diary format should be straightforward and uncluttered. With written diaries the print quality of the booklet is important as a cue to the professionalism of the research. Layout is vital for the written diary. Respondents have to be given enough room to provide their answers. Figure 19.1 is an example of a diary layout which might be used in a piece of research designed to establish how unemployed men spend their time. The format imposes a clear structure on the record, indicating which types of activity should be reported and what the unit of report is to be (that is, length of time).

Four, no matter how clear the diary format and instructions are, there will be respondents who fail to understand. It helps to give respondents an example of a completed entry to the diary so that they can see what they are supposed to be doing. It is also desirable that the respondent should be 'talked through' the diary. This will allow you to cue and target appropriate recording. As a general rule, therefore, diary-placement would normally involve a personal contact by a member of the research team, rather than sending diaries by post.

MONDAY

Please enter today's date here:

Please enter in the table below how much time (in minutes) you spent in the twenty-four hours between twelve midnight Sunday and twelve midnight Monday doing each of the things listed.

Number of minutes

Sleeping
Physical exercise (e.g. walking, football)
Doing housework (e.g. cooking, cleaning the
    house, washing clothes)
Looking for a job
Watching TV
In the public house
House maintenance (e.g. painting, decorating)
Gardening

Figure 19.1   *Example page of a diary*

Five, problems with 'sample maintenance' are reduced if you can ensure relatively frequent contact with respondents. This is particularly important in the early stages of a diary study. As with direct observation (see Chapter 14) there will inevitably be queries about category definitions (what, for example constitutes a 'leisure activity'?), questions about the boundaries between various activities, the level of detail required and so on. It may be useful to provide respondents with a telephone number, so that they can contact you to resolve such queries fairly quickly. If this is not done then they may abandon the recording because they are in a state of uncertainty about what to record, or perhaps even worse, make up their own decisions about what should be recorded and thus provide large numbers of entries that are useless for your analysis.

A postcard or telephone call occasionally (for example, birthday or Christmas cards) for long-term diary studies have been shown to improve sample retention. Requiring diaries to have frequent entries also seems to improve sample maintenance. Material incentives (such as small payments) tend to have a good effect upon retention. Along these lines, researchers have used lotteries to encourage both joining and remaining in studies. The prospect of winning something has been shown to incite initial interest but, once the outcome of the lottery is known, some researchers have found large-scale dropout. One answer seems to be to operate with repeated lotteries but this practice is less effective now as the general public have become sensitised to the technique.

Six, in order to maximise initial response rates and to retain the sample subsequently, it has been shown that it is best to start with relatively brief diaries. If you need to collect lengthy diaries, it seems to be most effective to introduce the respondent to the process by first using a short diary. They can be weaned from the short to the long version more easily than persuading them to start from scratch on a lengthy diary.

Finally, there have been various ingenious techniques used to ensure that people remember to make entries when they are supposed to do so. One involved giving respondents a radio-paging device and asking them to make their entries when it bleeped. Another involved enlisting the help of other members of the family to remind the respondent at meal times.

## 19.4 Analysing diary data

Since the forms of data yielded by diary studies vary widely many analytic approaches are possible. The initial decision that you take concerning the amount of structure which you impose upon the record will affect all subsequent decisions. If you leave the diarist free to choose what is recorded you are virtually sure to need to conduct a content analysis before doing any further data processing. The procedures involved in content analysis are described in Chapter 18. Having done the content analysis the data can be subjected to either a qualitative or quantitative description (see Chapter 2 for further details).

Content analysis, when tied to simple quantification, is most likely to result in a matrix which tells you how many people report each category of behaviour or event and how often these occurred. This may be all you need to do, but that is unlikely. A major feature of a diary technique is that it gives you data which are ordered over time. To take advantage of this you need to use analyses which allow you to map sequences or patterns in the data across time.

One way to do this with non-parametric data is to use an analysis which identifies whether within the sample there are groups of respondents whose sequences of entries are similar or different from the patterns of other groups. So for instance in a sample of 25 men completing diaries for the first three months of a period of unemployment, there might be 10 who spent most of their time in job-search for the first month, house-maintenance for the second and watching television for the third. Another ten might focus on housework in month 1, job search in month 2 and television watching in month 3. The remaining five might concentrate on television watching in month 1, job search in month 2 and television-watching again in month 3. The analysis would show the range of profiles that exist in the sample. It would also show whether the distribution of individuals across the profiles deviates significantly from that which might be expected to occur by chance. Profiles exemplified by either more or less of the sample than would be expected by chance are worth exploring further since these may be indicative of 'types' or 'anti-types' of response. The task of the psychologist then would be to explain the origin of these 'types'. One statistical technique which will allow you to identify these profiles is called configural frequency analysis (see for example, von Eye, 1990). There are, of course, many other mechanisms for structuring qualitative data (see for example, Chapter 17).

When you use highly structured entry formats in the diary the range of analytic approaches available is very broad. There is no reason why the diary should not include standard questions with response categories such as those used in a questionnaire. In this case, you would be able to use all of the techniques described in Chapter 12.

In choosing analytic approaches the vital thing to remember is that you are using them merely as tools that will give you answers to the questions you posed at the start of the research. Amid the flood of data which a diary technique can generate, it is easy to lose sight of your original objectives for the research. You can get lost in the minutiae of the specific life stories. The process of analysis should be one which allows you to see genuine patterns within these data. Thus it is vital to choose analytic tools which give you relevant answers and which are appropriate for the type of data you have.

## 19.5 Conclusion

It should be clear that the diary technique is potentially extremely useful as a means of collecting psychological and behavioural data. As with other methods it has both advantages and disadvantages. Before embarking on a diary study you should ask yourself a number of questions. First, a blindingly obvious one, 'Do I *really need* to collect data on a continuous basis over time?' Second, although we should always have a clear idea of our research objectives, this is particularly so when using diaries. The reason for this was mentioned earlier. Diaries can be a very rich source of data, and unless we have a clear view of the purpose of the study, the unwary researcher can be overwhelmed by the volume of data generated. Finally, do not be seduced by the apparent simplicity of the technique. The quality of the data will be directly related to the amount of time which has been spent in the development of the instrument and the care which is invested in its subsequent placement and maintenance.

## 19.6 Project

Examine Figure 19.2 and list the elements which make it a poor format for a diary. The diary can be assumed to be designed for 16–21-year-old unemployed women with low educational attainment. The researcher's objective is to establish how the respondent's attitude towards being unemployed changes over time and in relation to the level of social support she receives.

The unemployment effects diary

This is a weekly diary. Write in the matrix below firstly the people that you have had positive contacts with during the week, on a day-by-day basis. Use the following codes to indicate your relationship with the people concerrned:

1 Friend
2 Family
3 Neighbour
4 Social worker

In the second column in the table write how you felt each day.

|  | PEOPLE CONTACTED | EMOTIONS |
| --- | --- | --- |
| MONDAY | | |
| TUESDAY | | |
| WEDNESDAY | | |
| THURSDAY | | |
| FRIDAY | | |
| SATURDAY | | |

Figure 19.2 *A diary project*

Revise the format to improve it. Describe what forms of analysis you would use in order to achieve the researcher's objective.

## 19.7 Further reading

Perhaps not surprisingly given the novelty of diaries in psychological research, there are few general texts on the topic; most discussion of the technique is associated with particular instances of diary research. If you come across a diary study in your chosen research area, by all means be guided by precedent, however you should not feel obliged to copy existing procedures.

# 20   Ethnographic and Action Research

*David Uzzell*

## Contents

## 20.1   Introduction

Most psychological research has the goal of getting as close as possible to the mental processes and products which structure and guide human action and give it meaning. Psychological research methods try to minimise the distance and distortions between what is in the head with its representation to the researcher. In our choice of research method we are often presented with many dilemmas. One such dilemma is do we use a nomothetic or idiographic methodology? A **nomothetic methodology** is one in which we collect data from a large number of people (for example, through questionnaire surveys) and by some process of averaging purport to generalise with some degree of confidence to a larger population and thereby imply a wider validity. An **idiographic methodology** (for example, in-depth interviews), on the other hand, often captures the richness and complexity of the phenomenon under investigation but at the risk of basing conclusions on a small number of potentially atypical cases.

The use of a nomothetic methodology such as questionnaire surveys on, say, attitudes to the environment allows the collection of a large quantity of data but at the expense of a detailed insight into the complex and often contradictory ways people think about issues. A questionnaire, for example, channels responses along a predetermined route with very little opportunity for the individual to say 'Yes, but . . .', to elaborate on exactly what they mean or to contextualise their responses. When asked, for example, how concerned they are about environmental problems many people may respond positively. They may be concerned but what does this mean in terms of behaviour? We know from research that attitudes are not always a predictor of behaviour – what people say they do and what they do are often very different things. Would this information in any case lead to usable and actionable conclusions for policy and decision makers? This type of problem raises a rather more fundamental issue which serves to distinguish ethnography from many other approaches in psychology. The meaning and significance of the social world being investigated is defined by the researcher, not the respondent.

It should be emphasised from the outset that ethnography is not a single method. Many of the methodologies described in this book could be used by the ethnographic researcher – direct observation (Chapter 14), interviewing (Chapter 15), discourse analysis (Chapter 16), diary techniques (Chapter 19) and even questionnaire surveys (Chapters 8 and 12). What distinguishes ethnographic research is its purpose – **cultural description**. Spradley defined ethnography as a 'culture-studying culture. It consists of a body of knowledge that includes research techniques, ethnographic theory, and hundreds of cultural descriptions. It seeks to build a systematic understanding of all human cultures from the perspective of those who have learned' (1979:10–11). This last point is crucially important for it stresses that unlike other areas of social science research where the researcher attempts to explain human action in terms of psychological theories such as attribution theory, ethnographic research lays emphasis on the actor's understanding and theorising about their actions. In other words, the view is not the outsider looking in, but the insider looking around.

It might also be useful to think of the distinction between the ethnographic approach and other types of research in psychology and the social sciences as a distinction between a quest for questions and a quest for answers. Within psychology, we know (or we think we know) what questions we are trying to answer. In ethnographic research we are interested in the questions people are answering themselves about their life, their relationships and their environment by their actions. They may be questions which are unarticulated because they are part of the taken-for-granted world. Nevertheless, by their actions people are responding to the situations, rules and relationships in which they find themselves. Ethnographic research often starts with observation and description, for it is in the process observing that situation-specific questions emerge. In Spradley and Mann's (1975) closely observed study of life in Brady's Cocktail Bar, they found that cocktail waitresses learn very quickly that a good waitress is not one who serves customers well but one who knows how to please the bartenders. Making the bartender's job easy is essential not only to ensure a trouble-free life, but because of the status hierarchy the waitresses need the approval and praise of bartenders.

## 20.2   What is ethnography?

Werner and Schoepfle propose that 'Ethnography is description' and that 'description must closely resemble the original cultural reality. The resemblance must be good enough that the natives are able to recognise in it familiar features of their own culture' (1987:24). Goetz and LeCompte have defined ethnography as the 'analytic descriptions or reconstructions of intact cultural scenes and groups. Ethnographies recreate for the reader the shared beliefs, practices, artifacts, folk knowledge, and behaviours of some groups of people' (1984:2). For Hammersley and Atkinson, however, it 'is simply one social research method, albeit a somewhat unusual one, drawing as it does on a wide range of sources of information' (1983:2).

Goetz and LeCompte (1984) suggest that ethnography is a process, a way of studying human behaviour, and that ethnographic methodologies have four characteristic features. First, they aim to elicit phenomenological data – that is, they aim to represent the worldview of those individuals or groups under investigation. Although other methodologies in psychology seek to do this, where ethnography differs from other methodologies is that the representations of the world are structured by the participants, not by the researcher. It is the participants' structuring of the world in which the researcher is interested.

In an **ethogenic approach**, for example, the researcher is interested in how participants theorise about their own behaviour, rather than imposing theory onto the behaviour. Marsh et al. write that the ethogenic approach 'is based on the idea that human social life is a product of an interaction between sequences of actions and talk about those actions. Everything can be redone by talk' (1978:21). They argue that since the same skills and social knowledge are involved in the creation of both action and accounts of that action, then the researcher has two mutually supporting and confirmatory ways of revealing the underlying system of social knowledge and belief. Marsh et al. go on to argue that the best (but not the only) authorities as to what action is and means are the actors themselves. This is not to say that such accounts are in any sense 'true'. Marsh et al. demonstrate quite clearly in their multimethod study of football hooligans that the rhetoric and ritualisation of aggression does not reflect 'reality' in any documentary sense, but the accounts by the football supporters serve to confer on the football supporters' world structure, meaning and status. 'Hooliganism', rather than being seen as mindless and irrational aggression, can be reinterpreted as rational and rule-bound from the perspective of the 'hooligans'.

Another important aspect of Marsh et al.'s (1978) study is that it demonstrates that the social situations or context in which action takes place is fundamental to the analysis of the behaviour, illustrating Spradley's comment above. The social context is not ignored as if it were irrelevant or interfering noise but is crucial to the explanation of behaviour both by the researcher and the actors themselves.

Second, ethnographic techniques are empirical and are almost without exception employed in naturalistic settings. The researcher is interested in how individuals and groups behave in their own real-world setting unmanipulated by the researcher. Ethnographic research has been undertaken in an extensive range of situations (Hammersley, 1990) and has been concerned with a substantial number of social issues (Burawoy et al., 1991).

Third, ethnographic research attempts to present the totality of the phenomenon under investigation. The context is as important as the action. The temporal and environmental factors and the social/cultural and economic context are not noise but fundamental contributory explanatory variables. Behaviour is seen to have a history and an anticipation of the future. Finally, given the kind of picture painted here of ethnographic research, it will not come as a surprise to find that not only does one find a variety of methods and techniques used in ethnographic research but any one study will invariably be multimethod.

## 20.3 Ethnography: journalism or science?

An accusation sometimes levelled at psychology is that so much psychology is just 'common sense' (Wegner and Vallacher, 1981). A criticism that is similarly directed at ethnography is that it is just journalism. Perhaps its extensive use of qualitative data, its employment of illustrative quotations, and the strong 'human interest' focus makes such a misunderstanding inevitable. But there are important differences between ethnographic research and journalism. Any social scientific account of human action, if it is to be of worth, has to be based on sound research, systematic data collection, reliable and valid data. Perhaps most importantly, it has to be theory-driven. In the case of ethnography the emphasis may, at least in the early stages, be descriptive but even description is theory-driven however slightly articulated the theory. One aim of collecting ethnographic data is to assist in the development and verification of theory in order to account for human behaviour. This is not the aim of journalism.

There is a long tradition of ethnographic research in the social sciences, with many notable studies dating back to the 1920s and the Chicago school of human ecology (Zorbaugh's (1929) *The Gold Coast and the Slum*, Wirth's (1928) *The Ghetto* and later, Whyte's (1943) *Street Corner Society*). Park (1967) believed that urban areas and communities constituted large-scale social laboratories and could be studied like any scientific phenomena. Thomas argues that 'Ethnography . . . respects the same basic rules of logic, replication, validity, reliability, theory construction, and other characteristics which separate science from other forms of knowledge' (1993:16).

A further distinction between journalism and ethnography is that journalism is typically concerned with news: the reporting of the atypical events of everyday life – the unusual, the non-routine, the breaking of tradition. Much ethnographic research is concerned with precisely the opposite – revealing the routine and the 'paramount reality' of the everyday world of individuals and groups (Berger and Luckmann, 1971).

## 20.4   Problems in ethnography

So much of what is cultural is hidden and is rarely made explicit. It exists between the lines and in the assumptive world of both the researcher and the researched. Murray Parkes, describing the concept of the **assumptive world**, writes:

> A man is tied to his assumptive world. By learning to recognise and act appropriately within his expectable environment a man makes a life space of his own . . . the assumptive world not only contains a model of the world as it is . . . it also contains a model of the world as it might be. (1971:104).

Young and Kramer describe the assumptive world as 'multidimensional; it includes perceptions of the world, evaluations of its aspects, a sense of relatedness to them, and recurrent demands that they are acted upon. These dimensions interact to generate preferred states of the world and "calls to action" ' (1978:239).

Ethnographic approaches present a particular set of problems for the researcher. In the process of trying to understand the assumptive world of individuals and groups we have to try to break free from our own assumptive world. In the process of description and interpretation there is always a danger that our viewpoint will be ethnocentric. However hard we try, it is difficult to describe or analyse outside our own cultural references and worldview. Werner and Schoepfle (1987) suggest that we should keep two separate records – the **journal** – which is the ethnographer's account (that is, texts that are the product of the ethnographer's mind), and the **transcript** text which is the product of the respondent's mind. Although the term respondent is used here, it denotes the person providing ethnographic data in whatever form. It is not necessarily interview data as typically implied by that term: it could be text material. Some psychologists often use the generic term 'subjects' but this implies a certain relationship between researcher and researched which is questionable. Some ethnographers use the label 'natives', but outside certain contexts this may be equally inappropriate.

Allied to this problem is the reduction of what Werner and Schoepfle (1987) call 'semantic accent' – the confusion of respondents' meanings with the ethnographer's meanings. One word may be the same but the meanings may be different. Therefore we think we know what an individual means when in fact they may mean something very different.

It was suggested at the beginning of this chapter that the attraction of the ethnographic approach is that it reduces the distance from respondents' meanings, understandings and world-view to our own understandings. With each description and analysis we inevitably translate others' meanings and world-views into our language – the language of the social scientist. However hard we try to retain the fidelity and verisimilitude of the original there is not only a mutation in meaning, but probably also in richness and complexity. This can be illustrated if we think of the problem of research methods which attempt to understand the past.

No historical account can ever capture what is the infinite content of an event. Most of the information generated by an event – whether it is at the individual or group level, or whether it is cognitive, affective or behavioural information – is not recorded. That which is recorded is also only a record of the past and can only be verified through other accounts of the past. Lowenthal (1985) argues that what is now known as the past was not what anyone experienced as the present. There is a sense in which we know the past better than those who experienced it. We have the benefit of hindsight and we know the outcome of the story: 'Knowing the future of the past forces the historian to shape his account to come out as things have done'. Historical knowledge, however well authenticated, is subjective and subject to the biases of its chronicler who in turn is subject to the psychological processes of selective attention, perception and recall. Finally, there is the temporal equivalent of the problem of ethnocentricity. It is very difficult to view and understand the world outside the framework of our twentieth-century beliefs, values and attitudes.

The touchstone of scientific endeavour is reputedly the replicability of the investigation. When one is working within a naturalistic setting with social groups engaged in everyday actions, one cannot guarantee that a research exercise and its results can be repeated. Reality is not stable. As the Greek philosopher Heraclitus argued 2500 years ago, the essence of the universe is change – you cannot step into the same river twice, for the second time it is not the same river. It is doubtful whether you can even step into the same river once as it changes while one is stepping. This would suggest that a thing never *is* because it is always changing into something else. Although this is particularly relevant to ethnographic methodologies it ought to be seen as no less of a problem in all psychological research.

In ethnographic research it is impossible to duplicate naturally occurring events in all their complexity and their history because the river has flowed on, but this does not necessarily invalidate the findings. One should remember that many important events take place on unique occasions and for this reason one must separate statistical or scientific significance from behavioural significance. The significance of an event is independent of its probability of occurrence. Events are behaviourally significant when something happens which makes a difference to the values and behaviour of the individuals or groups affected, or when behaviour departs significantly from a previous steady state. There have been many one-off events which have brought about behavioural changes for individuals and the communities in which they live. In the absence of replication, multimethod and confirmatory data sources (see Chapter 2) become all the more important.

In experimental psychology the researcher attempts to control as many of the experimental variables as possible. Any change in the dependent variables can be attributed to purposeful manipulation of the independent variables. But in naturalistic or field settings the researcher only has limited opportunities to manipulate the independent variables. Furthermore, the contextual variables such as place and time (what in many experimental situations would be called 'noise') are not only equally likely to have an effect, but one is also interested in them in their own right. They may be an important source of data contributing to the explanation of behaviour.

## 20.5   Action research

In the traditional model of research, the researcher is often conceptualised as a dispassionate chronicler of social activity akin to what Bannister and Fransella described as the 'stereotypical Victorian physicist who seems to be our current ideal' (1971:193). Furthermore, we like to believe that the researcher is an invisible filter allowing through information which they perceive to be important and relevant. At least two objections can be raised regarding the researcher simply as a chronicler of social activity.

First, research methods such as questionnaire surveys serve to distance researchers from the very people they are trying to get closer to in order to understand their world. In the process by which researchers collect information they move through a number of stages which increasingly serve to distance them from the individuals and communities they are studying. For example, hypotheses about communities and the activities of social groups will be formulated. The decisions social scientists then take as to how they will test these hypotheses are crucial, because they will have an important influence on everything else that follows. If a survey approach is to be used, *which* questions are asked and *how* those questions are phrased and structured will be conditioned by the subsequent statistical analysis. Therefore, the nature and form in which information is collected will be determined not by their meaningfulness to the respondents but by the way the information is to be treated statistically. For this reason, once the questionnaire is designed we are talking to processed people, that is, people who are answering our questions in our terms. Furthermore, the way in which we collect data will also have a highly significant effect on the degree to which the research will allow a critical analysis of the phenomenon under investigation (Habermas, 1979).

Second, the researcher's role, especially those researchers working in the community and on issues of public policy, is a political one. However objective we try to make research techniques, researchers will always be there with their values, perceptions and interventions. Researchers are intermediaries as they stand amid the research methods on the one side and the individual, the community and society on the other. The researcher's position is essentially a political one because the techniques used will affect the relationships they have with the community. In addition to the implications of the research for public policy which will have political implications in a more conventional sense, the relationships formed in the course of the research raise questions of power, influence, control, responsibility, accountability and even 'the public interest'.

Some have argued that the relationship between researcher and researched can become mechanistic, authoritarian, if not ethically highly suspect (Argyris, 1970; Haney et al., 1973). The goals and methods of the research are defined almost totally by the researcher. The 'subject' is seen to be able to offer little or nothing to the research design because the researcher is seen as a skilled technician who knows how best to collect information. The 'subject' is expected to conform to the goals of the researcher and unquestioningly comply with all instructions.

Warr (1977) maintains we have to earn the right to become involved in people's lives. There are costs in all research, and if a researcher is to intervene in an individual's life, then that person must see that the research has relevance for him or her. Warr amplifies this point when he writes 'I have quite often met objections to a research proposal on the grounds that the potential participants are tired of University researchers taking up their time and then disappearing to their ivory towers: nothing has changed and the participants have gained nothing' (1977:4).

It is doubtful whether researchers are seen by groups as the dispassionate unbiased observers we have deceived ourselves into believing for so long. Because we have been inculcated with a natural science model of research, we have deluded ourselves into believing that our role is a neutral one (Murphy et al., 1984). For many groups, our role is not neutral however hard we try to suggest that it is. One only has to read Roy's (1965) account of his attempted study of industrial conflict in which he mistakenly assumed interviewees understood his role to see the disturbing result of such a misunderstanding.

If research is to really benefit the communities whom it is at least partially intended to serve, then should we not be giving our techniques and disciplines away as George Miller suggested a quarter of a century ago (Miller, 1969)? This might be achieved in any number of ways. Research in community psychology has for many years sought to devise ways in which people, organisations and communities can mobilise psychological theory and practice to take control over their own affairs. The community self-survey may be one way whereby communities, with the assistance of social scientists, are made responsible for the collection and analysis of information about their community and which in turn might lead to a more insightful understanding of the phenomena we are trying to study. Fetterman (1993) suggests that through 'empowerment evaluation' evaluators can teach people to conduct their own evaluations, thereby demystifying and desensitising evaluation and making it an accepted part of programme planning. It is within the context of issues such as these that some researchers have turned to action research strategies. This is also one of the interfaces between ethnography and action research.

## 20.6   The researcher as an agent of social change

Action research is not just an alternative way of collecting data. The premisses and relationships upon which the methods are based are very different from conventional social research techniques. Action research has its origin in the writings of Kurt Lewin (1952) who believed that in order to gain insight into a process one must create change and then observe its variable effects and new dynamics. The use of this approach in research probably reached its apogee in the 1960s and 1970s when government research funding and policy was more liberal and participatory. Action research methodologies have been employed in many different areas of social investigation such as public policy (Lovett, 1975), police management (Horton and Smith, 1988), industrial organisation and management (Whyte, 1991), and community development (Lees and Smith, 1975). One area where it continues to be influential is education (Elliot, 1991; Zuber-Skerritt, 1992).

Approaches to action research vary – there is not just one way of doing it. Rapoport (1972) identifies four types of action research (diagnostic, participant, empirical, experimental), but what is common to each is that, 'Action research is a type of applied social research differing from other varieties in the immediacy of the researcher's involvement in the action process' (1972:23). Carr and Kemmis (1986) distinguish between three types of action research (technical, practical and emancipatory), with the authors arguing that only the last is 'true' action research. Central to all though is the idea that the researcher moves from the role of being solely a chronicler of social activity to that of an agent of social change. Doing the research is integral to taking action, because action is part of the research and research part of the action: they are two sides of the same coin.

Action research can take many forms including education and training, facilitation, advocacy and decision making. In action research, the researcher acts as a facilitator or resource, providing information which helps those making decisions come to an informed choice over alternative courses of action. The researcher becomes part of the decision-making machinery, so that research findings are in the form of shared experience which creates a knowledge which may not be so readily communicable in conventional academic terms.

Zuber-Skerritt (1992) identifies five defining characteristics of action research which serve to distinguish it from orthodox social science methodologies. First, it is practical in that the research should not only lead to theoretical and disciplinary advances but will also have practical consequences for all the participants. Second, it is participative and collaborative, thereby attempting to overcome the unequal power relationship between researcher and researched to which reference was made earlier. Third, it is emancipatory, liberating those involved with the research from traditional 'subject' roles and placing them in positions of influence both in respect of the research and subsequently in terms of their actions and daily lives. Fourth, it is interpretative whereby the perspectives and interpretations of all the participants have validity, rather than just seeing the researcher's expert opinion as dominant and 'correct'. Finally, it is critical as all the participants engage in a critical analysis of their situation, possible courses of action and constraints on action, which may as a consequence lead to a change in both their situation and themselves.

Action research has some features in common with participant observation (see Chapter 14), but the relationship between researcher and researched is different in several important respects. In participant observation, those being observed reveal themselves to the observer, but the observer does not reveal him- or herself to them. In action reseach the researcher acts as a fully participating member of the group, and so the relationship is more honest and open. As Rowan states, the participant observer 'can often remain unchanged and unchallenged by his experience which thus becomes of one-way benefit to him and his sponsor' (1974:93). The sort of role outlined here has the flexibility to accommodate changes in the research, researcher and the community which inevitably and unavoidably take place in the life history of a research project.

One implication of using a technique such as action research in, for example, a community context is that the researcher can become actively involved and help shape the future of voluntary and community groups. One might be able to help them towards an effectiveness they might not otherwise have achieved, or which could have taken much longer. Such groups may well give the researcher insights into the research problem and an understanding which might never have emerged had more conventional research practices been adopted. It is a two-way interaction with mutual benefits.

One important issue concerns interviewer 'effects' or **contamination**. It is sometimes argued by critics of this approach that by being involved one will not only influence community group activities but also any attitudinal or behavioural information which one is collecting for the study. Ultimately this would mean that the researcher does little more than monitor him- or herself. The type of researcher described here is an activist who is most effective when being only an encourager, and not adopting manipulative or doctrinaire positions. It also has to be recognised that whichever type of study is being undertaken there will always be experimenter effects. The important point is to be aware of them and, if possible, control for them.

## 20.7  Change

A common theme running through this account of both ethnographic research and action research is the idea of change. One aim of ethnographic research is to record processes of change – not stability. Conventional approaches to social science invariably take people's behaviour at a static moment in time, with little regard to the fact that people are constantly changing in response to changing situations. Researchers who takes a static view of a social group's activities would surely not fail to realise that in their own research they are continually developing and refining their ideas and theories about those whom they are studying. As the social scientist is continually developing, so too is the community. In understanding change, action research is a particularly apposite strategy as development is part of the research process. At the same time, the researcher plays an active role in becoming a change agent by informing, encouraging and supporting the community group, and studying and interpreting their actions in the light of the interventions. The important point to make about the researcher's role as an agent of social change is that they are still a researcher, but a fully participating one.

Data collection methodologies such as questionnaire surveys and interviews can be planned with a relatively high degree of precision in terms of time management. The process of designing, piloting, modifying and administering a questionnaire can be planned to take place over a set number of weeks or months. Likewise, the processing of the data in terms of cleaning, coding and analysing can also be anticipated with a reasonable degree of accuracy. This is less the case for action (and ethnographic) research where one is following the life history of events.

Some events may take place over a day, a week, a month or even several years. For example, one event in which the author participated took over two years to play itself out (Uzzell, 1988). This involved an attempt by a community group to receive statutory recognition in local government by becoming a Parish Council. The application for Parish Council status involved organising a community-wide survey of attitudes towards local government and the establishment of a Parish Council, the analysis and interpretation of the data with community leaders, presenting the findings to the local authority and lobbying for change. Initially the application was rejected and so an appeal was made to the Boundary Commissioners who instituted an Inquiry at which barristers representing local commercial interests, trades organisations and senior local authority officers opposed the community group. Throughout the two-year period the author was involved at every stage from the design and analysis of the community survey to making representations to the Boundary Commissioners' Inquiry.

## 20.8   Conclusion

Having read this far through the book the reader should be alert to the dangers of assuming that there is only one appropriate model of scientific activity and one appropriate role for the researcher. The question is not how flawed is action research because of the researcher's involvement, or how reliable is ethnographic research because of the 'noise' and confounding variables, but rather are we not deluding ourselves into believing these same processes are not operating in other, more conventional research strategies?

Some researchers will feel unhappy with the roles implied by these types of research methodologies, either for professional or personal reasons. It is not everyone's preference to make these kinds of interventions or to engage in these kinds of relationships. Likewise, it should be emphasised that both ethnographic and action research strategies are not appropriate for all types of research. The goals and objectives of the research, as well as the constraints which inevitably operate in any research, should determine the type of research strategy adopted. But in coming to any decision about the most appropriate methodology to use it should be remembered that as there is not one model of science, so there is not one model of the researcher.

## 20.9   Further reading

Whyte's (1991) *Participatory Action Research* and Elliot's (1991) *Action Research for Educational Change* are both excellent general introductions to action research. For ethnographic texts Hammersley's (1990) *Classroom Ethnography* and Werner and Schoepfle's (1987) *Systematic Fieldwork: Volume 1 Foundations of Ethnography and Interviewing* are both worth investigating.

# 21   Historical Analysis in Psychological Research

*Jonathan Chase*

## Contents

## 21.1   Introduction

Historical material is an important data source for psychologists but its under-representation in theory development may be a function of at least two factors. On the one hand, much psychological theorising posits universal processes and researchers often implicitly assume these processes will be ahistorical. On the other hand, historical data are often assumed to be inherently unreliable and invalid. While the focus of this chapter will be on how historical data can be used to develop theory it is necessary to consider some theoretical issues as well.

One of the defining features of data generated on current phenomena is that the data source can be interacted with or acted upon by the researcher. Experimental methodology depends upon controlling some variables and manipulating others. In surveys and questionnaires the respondent is specifically asked about target behaviours. The conditions under which historical materials are produced are generally removed from the researcher in time. It often appears to be this inaccessibility of the past (but not of the material produced per se) which leads to historical material being ignored and devalued.

In order to use historical data one has to identify the conditions under which the material was generated. From the perspective of the researcher these are 'natural' conditions, that is, they have not been determined by the researcher. These conditions need to be specified and selected so as to provide theoretically relevant data (that is, they vary systematically according to theoretical concepts). The fact that the conditions are determined by the researcher (to some extent at least) in the present but not in the past, is irrelevant.

## 21.2   Why use historical data?

Historical analysis and material can have a variety of functions for psychologists. Some of these functions are described in the following paragraphs.

An awareness of historical phenomena may help in the generation of theory. Typically, particular salient events are seen as problematic and requiring explanation. For instance, the Holocaust as an event has stimulated a number of psychologists (and other social scientists) to try to develop theory explaining it (see for example, Adorno et al., 1950). Theories of intergroup behaviour, of discrimination, and of helping behaviour have all been developed directly in response to knowledge of this particular historical event.

Historical material can be used to test existing theories. For instance, Lord and Hohenfeld (1979) used archived statistics about baseball players' performances to test hypotheses derived from equity theory. The theory would predict that players who could not look forward to having their contracts renewed (that is, their teams were not committed to them financially or otherwise) would feel undervalued and would not play as well once they knew they were not wanted. Using archive game statistics it was possible to show that 'unwanted' players played less well once they knew they were on their way out of the team.

Another example of how one might use historical material would be to look for historical evidence with which to test competing hypotheses.

Social Identity Theory (Tajfel, 1982), for instance, suggests that members of similar groups will be more in conflict with one another than will be members of dissimilar groups. This is due to a need for positive distinctiveness, which is lacking between similar but present between dissimilar groups. Psychodynamic theories suggest that early socialisation leads to the presence of inhibitions against the expression of negative feelings towards in-group members which, in its turn, leads to more negativity and, therefore, conflict between members of dissimilar groups.

Thus, one has a null hypothesis – that levels of similarity/difference and cooperation/competition will be unrelated and two alternative hypotheses deriving from different theories. The first states that levels of similarity/ difference will be positively related to those of cooperation/competition. The second states that levels of similarity/difference will be negatively related to those of cooperation/competition. The derivation of the hypotheses from psychological theory defines the research as psychological rather than historical (in disciplinary terms) even though the data will have to be generated from histories and historians.

Of course, historical data can be used to illustrate the operation of psychological processes and historical events can be analysed with regard to psychological theory. For instance, it has been argued that the behaviour of the two sides (mainly German and mainly French/British) on the Western Front in the First World War can be explained with reference to the Prisoners' Dilemma and Games Theory as an exchange process. The battlefront conditions (trench systems, weapons capacities), the belief systems of the general staff (current military thinking, assumptions about 'human nature') and of the other ranks (motives), as well as the structure of the military system (chain of command, communication channels) can all be assessed. The behaviour of the armies can be described at various levels (for example, army, subgroup, individual or headquarters, support, front). This assessment then allows one to describe the possible actions of different groups and the distribution of the outcomes of those actions. Essentially, it is argued that the soldiers at the front (on both sides), who can be conceived of as the main consumers of actions (that is, they are the target of small arms fire and of artillery fire) had a common interest in *not* shooting at each other. Therefore, informal ceasefires tended to develop. In technical terms, there was a reiterated, reciprocal exchange (of munitions) in which cooperation (not firing) dominated competition (firing). Psychology provides a set of theoretical concepts but history provides the content. The historical event is analysed in psychological terms.

Historical data can give access to phenomena that are not readily amenable to other types of investigation for practical, ethical and other reasons. Aggression and conflict are examples of this. While some experimental work is possible it is neither practical nor ethical to attempt to create a war. Of course, researchers can (and should) opportunistically investigate wars as they happen. Fortunately, these are not frequent events. However, there is a wide range of data about wars that have already happened. These data include 'expert' analyses of various aspects of the conflict as well as official records, personal records, artefacts, etc. Another example is that of Janis (1972) who developed a theory of groupthink using a number of personal accounts of the Bay of Pigs episode produced by senior US government officials.

Many phenomena are emergent, that is, they are new events, modes of interaction, social structures, etc. Due to their novelty, the actual emergence of the phenomenon is not noted until after the event itself. Thus, data are often not collected at the time the phenomenon first appears. Research on HIV/AIDS is an example of this. HIV/AIDS was first noticed in the press in the early 1980s; however, psychological research on people's attitudes towards, and representations of, HIV/AIDS did not really get going until the mid-1980s. Thus, data on the initial representational processes were missing. A historical analysis of newspaper and other media sources may usefully augment the data collected through surveys, etc. (see for example, Markova and Wilkie, 1987).

Many psychological theories are about social structure and changes in social structure. A historical awareness is needed in order to describe adequately social structure. Historical data have been used in the development of a number of psychological theories. For instance, McClelland (1961) used historical data derived from a variety of sources (such as, folk tales, stories, pictures on vases, etc.) to test his theory that levels of need for achievement (n_achievement) are related to a variety of economic indicators.

## 21.3   Some theoretical issues

Gergen (1973; Gergen and Gergen, 1984) in a now well-known challenge to the psychological establishment, argues that social psychology is really a form of history. Social psychological processes, he suggests, are time-bound and reactive to knowledge about these processes. If someone says to you that a particular social psychological theory would predict that you would do 'X', knowledge of this may lead you to deliberately choose to do 'Y' instead. The historical nature of social psychology therefore means that the search for regularities and universal laws of behaviour is misguided. Research on contemporary phenomena produces knowledge that is descriptive of that present but not explanatory of the past nor predictive of the future.

Gergen is not explicit about the limits of either the historicity or the reactivity of these phenomena. Just how transient is any given social psychological phenomenon? To what extent does reflexivity really allow one to react to the knowledge that one's own behaviour is a function of some process? Which behaviours and when? Realistically, Gergen could not be expected to answer all these questions himself so it is incumbent on psychologists generally to concern themselves with these challenges and acknowledge that the phenomena they study may 'only' be transient and tied to a particular time and culture. These questions concern the nature of the relations between structure, process and content and require investigation across time to answer them.

## 21.4 Methodological issues

This section deals with issues that need to be considered when thinking about using historical data.

### 21.4.1 Timeframe

One important parameter is the timespan of the phenomenon that is under investigation. Some processes are very rapid while others are very slow. Some phenomena may also vary at different rates. For instance, self-esteem may vary as a consequence of events across a short timespan – for example, success or failure in achieving immediate goals. However, it may also vary systematically across longer timespans – for example, changing status of particular social groups within society.

Awareness of a historical context is probably best obtained from secondary sources, usually history books. Analysis of primary sources is also needed for the examination of psychological and social processes. The generation of evidence differs between psychology and history, however. Historical data depend upon material surviving an arbitrary selection process. While such data are limited by this contingent and erratic survival and are therefore second best to prospectively gathered data, second best is better than nothing at all. Sometimes historical data are the only, or the greater part of, the available data. Palaeontology, although similarly dependent upon an arbitrary and partial fossil record, is a major source of data used in the development and testing of evolutionary theory. It is worth noting that evolutionary theory is one of the most successful theories developed in the last two centuries.

### 21.4.2 Historical data sources

Lowenthal (1985) suggests that there are three main sources of historical data. These are the following:

1 Memory: data produced from living human subjects at the time of research.

2   Historical sources (these are often seen as the strictly historical data sources): this category includes any stored representational information – for example, writing, painting and pictures, film, video- and audio-tape, CD-ROM, computer disks, etc. In this paper these sources will be referred to as representational sources because the essential defining feature is the symbolic or representational meaning and not the actual physical structure of the object or data source.
3   Artefacts: any other physical products of human activity – for example, buildings, tools, commodities, etc.

In the context of this chapter, historical data will denote all three of these types of information. Like all sources of data, each of these sources has its particular characteristics which constrain the information that is gathered. Generally, data become more limited and limiting as one moves from memory to representational to artefactual data sources. While memory may seem to be better than representational or artefactual sources, memory is an account of a past produced in the present and, thus, may be affected by factors in the present. Representational and artefactual data sources are actually produced in what is now the past. The different types of data give access to different (although sometimes overlapping) populations. Memory potentially allows access to any living person. Representational sources give access to a population, both living and dead, that had the skills and opportunity to create a record of their beliefs and behaviours. For some cultures and societies such people are typical, while for others they are more rare and, therefore, less representative. Artefactual data provide access to the most distant past and, possibly, the potentially widest population. Each of these data sources will be considered in more detail.

Another way to consider this issue is to discriminate between the use of historical analysis of events and of people. Examples of events include general processes, such as industrialisation, as well as particular ones, such as the emergence of HIV/AIDS. These phenomena are present in the world at large and not just in the minds of individuals. The analysis of people refers to phenomena such as cognitive processes, the self and identity processes. Although these phenomena are supposed to effect external reality they, themselves, are (usually) conceptualised as residing within individuals. To some extent, this reflects the differences between psychology as the study of external, observable behaviour and psychology as the study of the internal, private mind.

This distinction between events and people may relate to differences in the historical materials used. For the former, one may tend to use secondary sources, that is, history books and historians. For the latter, one may tend to use primary sources, that is, material produced in the past. Of course, history books, typically secondary sources, can be used as primary sources as they, themselves, are produced at a specific time. For example, the writing of a history of an area or of a group may be a part of the process by which a social representation of a social identity develops, that is, it may act to define the social group.

### 21.4.3  Sampling frames

A sampling frame needs to be developed. This should specify some time period or periods (for example, one could select two periods of 20 years, one at a time of social flux and another at a time of social stability) and some definition of group (for example, size, continuity, etc.). It should also specify the source – such as history books, expert judgement – of the data.

The next step is to generate a number of measures on which to characterise the sample. The emphasis in the selection, development and operationalisation of these measures should be on psychological factors rather than their historical relevance and meaningfulness, though the latter does also need to be considered.

The historical sources (whether they be people, books, or whatever) are then used to identify instances falling within the sampling frame and characterise these, or a subset, according to the previously defined measures. This would produce a data set amenable to statistical analysis testing the hypotheses (for example, the Lord and Hohenfeld (1979) baseball example above).

## 21.5  Time-series analysis

This is a general type of analysis of change across time (see also Chapter 7). It often makes use of data that have not been gathered with the specific research question in mind. Time-series analyses have often been used to try to examine the effects of a change in government policy or some other relatively identifiable event. For instance, data about vehicle-related accidents have been analysed to assess the effects of compulsory seat-belt wearing and other safety devices. It has been argued (Wilde, 1986) that people have an optimum level of risk. When a safety device makes a behaviour, such as driving, safer then people adjust their behaviour to return to the same level of risk as before (this has been called risk homeostasis). The rates and types of accidents before and after the introduction of these devices or policies can be compared. A number of studies have used archival data in order to test this hypothesis (see for example, Evans, 1986). Of course, in this instance the dataset is very good. The events – vehicle-related accidents – are relatively well defined and recorded. Evans found that the data did not support the risk homeostasis hypothesis and that driver responses to any particular change in safety were more varied than the hypothesis would suggest.

In some cases it is possible to identify a control group made up of people who did not experience the target event but are similar to those who did.

Where this is possible one can be more certain in the attribution of causality for the observed findings.

The recording of data which are to be used in the time-series analysis is a central issue. The ideal is that the recording of events is representative of their actual occurrence. However, recording rates often vary for reasons other than variation in the events themselves. Crime statistics are a notorious example of this. The recorded rate of different types of criminal behaviour may vary for all sorts of reasons including government policy, police procedure, public awareness of, and concern about, particular crimes as well as changes in the actual events. These factors may change not just the apparent rate of the events but the way in which these events are defined. Obviously, as the length of time analysed increases it becomes more likely that changes in the recording of events will have happened.

Time-series analysis can be used on any type of data. However, it is vital to consider how the variables to be measured are operationalised. When some form of statistical or bureaucratic record is used then this task is relatively simple. The recording categories are likely to reflect the official categories. In these cases the data are already partially cooked, as it were. Campbell and Beets (1978) reviewed a number of studies on the relationship between the lunar cycle and behaviour. Rates of hospital admissions, suicides, and homicides were sampled and examined but did not to appear to vary as a function of the stage of the lunar cycle. Campbell (1969) analysed the number of speeding violations, for which there are official records, before and after a change in state policy. In many other cases the data are present in a more raw state. In these cases the reliability of the data can be evaluated through cross-referencing (that is, using multiple sources) and through calculating inter-rater reliability in much the same way as is done in content analysis.

# 21.6 Research using memory, representational and artefactual data sources

## 21.6.1 Research using memory data sources

Using people's memories and memory processes as the data source has the advantage, compared with other historical data sources, of allowing some manipulation of the conditions under which the memory is at least accessed. This section will concentrate on everyday memory, that is, on how memory functions in 'real life'.

Autobiographical memory focuses upon the way in which an individual stores and recalls his or her personal past. The social context and the function of these memories can also be examined. Autobiographical memory may provide both individuation and definition to the person. On the one hand, the recall of specific events and experiences deriving from that individual's unique perspective upon the world differentiates that person from others. On the other hand, these experiences can be shared with other people and provide commonality and, perhaps, shared identity. Coyle (1992) shows how the story a person tells about him- or herself serves both personal and social identity functions. In particular, memory is important in regard to continuity of the self. Recent research suggests that autobiographical memory is not ordered in a strictly chronological way (Conway, 1990). Instead, autobiographical memory has a hierarchical structure. Neisser (1986) suggests that this is a consequence of the hierarchical structure of events (namely, that events are nested within other events). Routine experiences are not individually stored. Information about the structure of autobiographical memory is useful when, for instance, one needs to distinguish between memory effects and conscious self-presentation or when the veridicality of a memory is at issue.

Varying the subject group compares the memories (in regard to content and structure) of individuals selected from different groups. For instance, a comparison could be made of the memories of people from different cohorts (a cohort is a set of individuals born within a certain time). Older and younger people could be asked to remember public and private events. A comparison of the different ages' memories could be used to assess change and stability in what is considered to be an aspect of one's private self and what is considered to be part of one's public self.

## 21.6.2   Research using representational data sources

Representational historical data is probably the type most people think of when considering some form of historical analysis. It is certainly one of the most commonly used data sources in explicitly historical analyses.

Representational, and artefactual, data can be considered to be available data – that is, data that are present in the environment and do not need to be generated intentionally by the researcher. Available data have the advantage over generated data of not being directly susceptible to researcher-derived effects (such as, demand characteristics, leading questions, etc.). Available data, however, have the disadvantage of being produced for reasons other than the researcher's. Thus, historical material should not be taken as a necessarily 'true' or accurate account of events, thoughts, feelings, or any other phenomena. An implication of this is that the researcher should try to gain some understanding of the constraints surrounding the production of the material and of the motives and intentions of the material's producers.

Within the general class of representational data there are many different data sources. These include the following:

1   Media records: there are many archives of media products such as newspapers, magazines, television programmes, etc. Some of these go back 200 years or more.

2 Books: these include novels, plays, poems and stories as well as more factual accounts such as diaries, autobiographies, biographies and histories. Books provide access up to about 500 years ago, although the number of books and their accessibility decreases prior to this point. This source would also include history books.

3 Manuscripts: prior to printing there are handwritten documents and records going back to Sumer (2000 BC). Again access is limited.

4 Official records: many bodies produce records of various events. This includes national and local government records (for example, unemployment figures, parish records, court records, records of parliamentary debates, etc.). Carroll et al. (1982) examined parole board decisions using both archival data and questionnaires in order to identify the most valid predictors of recidivism. Other agencies, such as companies, charities, etc., also have records that may be used. Many sporting associations record a variety of statistics about teams, individual players, etc. The extent of these records varies greatly.

5 Data archives and journals: this is an often neglected data source, at least as far as historical analyses are concerned. One advantage of these sources is that the conditions under which the data were generated may be more explicitly recorded.

6 Visual records: these include pictures, paintings, cartoons and prints.

This list of historical material includes very varied material. Some of it is already present in a numerical form (for example, various official statistics). This tends to obviate the need to reduce the material into numbers. However, many of these sources are essentially qualitative rather than quantitative in nature. Although such material can be analysed qualitatively in a manner akin to literary criticism (that is, without further data reduction) a more systematic, explicit and 'objective' analysis may be desirable.

## 21.6.3 Research using artefactual data sources

Artefactual data are similar in many respects to representational data. Both are available rather than generated data and both are amenable to content analysis. Thus, most of what has been said of representational data is also true of artefactual data.

There are many different types of artefact that can be used as a source for the generation of data. These include the following:

1 Buildings: public and private buildings can be examined. Analysis may be at the level of individual buildings (such as, the structure) or of a group of buildings (such as, the relationship between different buildings).

2 Monuments: this includes monuments, gravestones and mausoleums, statues, and other constructions. (As there is a strong representational

element to monuments one might include them under the representational heading.) For instance, one could examine changes in gravestones to explore representations of death.

3 Artefacts: these include tools, furniture, toys, etc. The range of artefacts is huge and expanding.

4 Clothes: clothing includes any covering for the person. Clothing may be used to identify and define social group membership. The boundaries of social groups may be clarified through members of different groups wearing different clothes. Clothes may also make salient a content of the identity.

Artefactual data can be analysed in a similar manner to representational data – that is, through content analysis. However, it can also be examined in other ways. Behaviour may result in traces, marks, abrasions, etc. on the material of the artefact. These can be recorded and used as an index of behaviour. For instance, one can infer which books (and which parts of books) are read from an examination of the condition of the books' spines.

## 21.7   Content analysis

One of the most commonly used forms of analysis for representational material is **content analysis** (Holsti, 1969). In principle, content analysis can be used on any form of representational material, that is, verbal, textual or pictorial sources are all amenable to content analysis. Content analysis, in general, is a way of systematically and, usually, explicitly examining representational material and deriving quantitative and qualitative measures from that material. Content analysis is a very broad label which, in fact, covers a range of quite different techniques. A general discussion of content analytic techniques appears in Chapter 18.

## 21.8   Secondary analysis and meta-analysis

One often neglected data source for historical analysis is past research. The advantage of this as a data source is that the conditions under which the data were generated will be more controlled and explicit. Thus, differences in these conditions can be, at the least, consciously acknowledged and, at best, corrected for. However, from the perspective of the new researcher this material is available and not generated data. This is in contrast to strictly longitudinal research where data from previous sampling phases have been generated by the same researcher (or research team).

While it is standard practice to cite the date of a piece of research when mentioning the research the implications of that are often forgotten. The research is carried out both on a particular set of subjects (that is, is culturally specific) but also at a specific time. Therefore, a series of studies using similar methodology may provide a series across time. A meta-analysis of the different research projects may then be undertaken to explore change across time. At its simplest these might be analysed through a PsycLit search of the abstracts of papers, etc. More complex analyses may be carried out, this is often called a meta-analysis, research integration or quantitative review.

There are obvious data sources of this type, such as British Social Attitudes (BSA) surveys. The advantages of such survey series are that they will show greater consistency in terms of both content and style of data generation. Public opinion surveys are another rich source of data. Even if the surveys used have been carried out independently one can still construct a series from them. However, one needs to be more concerned about the definitions of the target concepts as these are more likely to vary between independent surveys than those that are designed as a series. For instance, Bakvis and Nevitte (1987) used data from three Canadian national election surveys to test a theory about post-materialist values (Inglehart, 1981). In general, they found that Inglehart's generational explanation for post-materialism was not very well supported by the data; instead, changes across the individual life-cycle were better explanations. However, post-materialism was found to be multidimensional and to include both private needs and public values. Private needs, such as self-actualisation and economic security, were subject to life-cycle effects while public post-materialist goals were subject to generational effects.

Typically, differences in the definition and operationalisation of concepts may be addressed through some kind of weighting of the variables. In the same way, the size of an effect can be coded rather than simply its presence or absence. In this context, meta-analysis provides a systematic and quantitative assessment of a number of pieces of research. Meta-analysis may be deployed to other ends than for a historical analysis. In fact, most meta-analyses are carried out in order to examine the importance of particular variables – for example, Shapiro and Shapiro (1982) examined the efficacy of psychotherapy. However, by including the temporal sequence of a set of studies one can explicitly analyse change across time. Chapter 25 gives more details on the techniques of meta-analysis.

## 21.9   Conclusion

This chapter has discussed some of the sources of historical data and different ways of analysing these data. I hope to have demonstrated that historical analysis may be a rich and varied resource for the psychologist and one that can be used in many ways.

It has not been the intention to set historical analysis in opposition to other types of analysis. History relates to the past which is only one dimension of time. At the theoretical level this temporality, often treated as process, dynamic, or dialectic, must be a basic assumption of social scientists. Historical analysis is one way of practically including and exploring temporality. However, again practically speaking, the generation of data in the present offers many advantages (as well as being a historical resource for subsequent researchers). Temporal questions can be researched using longitudinal designs and longer-term research programmes as well by using various types of historical analysis. A plurality of methods rather than a dominance of one is the ideal to be aimed for.

## 21.10 Further reading

Axelrod's (1976) *Structure of Decision* is a clear account of the analysis of textual material for the development of representations of individual and group belief systems. Barnes and Stearns's (1989) *Social History and Issues in Human Consciousness: Some Interdisciplinary Connections* brings together both historians and psychologists to consider how mind is affected by history and how mind affects history. Middleton and Edwards's (1989) *Collective Remembering* includes a variety of approaches, both methodological and theoretical, to the study of social memory.

# 22 Using Computer Simulation to Define and Explore Theories in Psychology

*Peter Simpson*

## Contents

## 22.1  Introduction

Training in the use of the computer forms an essential part of most contemporary degree courses. In psychology the computer is most often used to carry out statistical analyses. Computers can also be used to present words, text, graphics and sounds. They can be used in experimental procedures, psychometric testing, questionnaire studies, psychophysics, psychoacoustics, etc.

In these applications it is possible to integrate the control and presentation of material with response recording and data analysis. Of course it remains possible to carry out a significant range of statistical analyses using pencil, paper, a calculator and graph paper. But access to a computer-based resource enables the user to conduct a range of analyses, and especially those which are complicated and arduous to perform, on data stored in magnetic form within the computer or on disks.

During the last 40 years computers have also been used to test models of psychological processes expressed in the form of computer programs. This work has been carried to specify and test the viability of a number of theories relating to psychological functions and to create systems which display artificial intelligence. This chapter describes the role of simulation in scientific investigation and what is involved in programming a computer to carry out this process. The argument is illustrated by reference to studies using the computer which have extended our understanding of psychological processes.

## 22.2    Understanding through simulation

In the seventeenth century, the philosopher Descartes proposed that scientific enquiry involves the analysis and synthesis of phenomena. In the case of psychology, the term phenomena encompasses the concept of behaviour exhibited by humans and other animals. The behaviour of interest to the psychologist could involve the occurrence of a coordinated motor response or the appearance of a syntactic feature in language. It might entail the expression of an attitude or knowledge within or in response to a language statement. It might involve the generation of a solution to a problem or task which allows us to infer states of understanding or misunderstanding.

Within Descartes' scheme, the first step is analysis. This involves the creation of a simplified description, or model, of a phenomenon and identification of the variables that produce the phenomenon. If the phenomenon of interest is still present in the simpler model, then you have identified the key variables contributing to it. This assumption can be tested through the process of synthesis which will test the adequacy of our understanding. There are three types of synthesis. In the physical sciences it has proved possible to test by means of **direct synthesis**. The chemist can synthesise compounds – for example, penicillin, solvents, hormone preparations, etc. – which were originally extracted from natural sources. If the synthetic compounds produce the same effects as the original natural products we can take that as evidence of the acceptability of the original analysis.

In those parts of psychology which can use the experimental method, the test by synthesis takes the form of a **synthesis by prediction**. If our analysis of the important variable is correct, then the behaviour of interest will change as the variables are manipulated. In practice our analysis may have led to proposals not only about what variables are controlling the phenomenon but also to proposals about the independence, or dependence, of the variables in controlling the phenomenon. These relationships can be tested or explored by use of the synthesis by prediction procedure.

A third type of synthesis involves the creation of a model, called **synthesis by model**. In this case we test out understanding of a phenomenon by constructing a model. We build into the model the elements we think are important and also our conception of the way these elements interact to produce the phenomenon. This approach is especially attractive when the phenomenon of interest reflects the action of a number of variables and component processes linked to subsystems. Models of weather patterns, economic processes and artificial intelligence systems capable of language understanding, reasoning and planning have been investigated.

Since the late 1950s computers and programming languages which lend themselves to use in describing and testing of theories in psychology have become generally available. Using this kind of method potentially involves two of the types of synthesis described by Descartes. Using a simulation procedure embodied in a computer program it is possible to carry out synthesis by prediction and synthesis by model.

The origins of work on computer simulation arose in the context of engineering rather than psychology. The stimulus for this work was the need to design computers which could carry out symbolic manipulation tasks which matched the capacity of humans (Minsky, 1968). The criterion for evaluating their design and content was the degree to which the performance of the computer program could match the performance known to arise from the human cognitive system.

Whether or not the means by which the artificial intelligence program achieved its performance parallels the processes underlying human performance remains a key question for philosophers (Searle, 1990). However, from the perspective of the engineer and systems analyst, the important part of the hypothesis under test relates to the specification and organisation of the functional elements involved in a system. These properties are independent of how the functions are embodied in a biological or electronic substrate (Simon, 1981).

## 22.3 Computer simulation: metaphor, analogy or hypothesis?

Craik (1967) presented a 'Hypothesis on the nature of thought' which argued that mechanical and psychological systems share properties which make them capable of reasoning. The key element is the generation of an internal representation which forms the basis of reasoning, deduction, inference, etc. The symbols or states in this internal representation can be realised in mechanical, electromechanical, solid state physics or biochemical form.

Craik's argument may not find easy acceptance because at a concrete level the appearance and performance of mechanisms, electronic and biological systems, are obviously different. However Simon (1981) has argued that the success of the scientific thought arises from the creation of an abstract account of the phenomena of interest. This account can be independent of an understanding of the detailed processes which cause those phenomena. Thus we accumulated a great deal of knowledge of the gross physical and chemical behaviour of matter before we had knowledge of molecules. Similarly we had a great deal of knowledge about molecules before we had an atomic theory, and so on. These developments were possible because the behaviour of a system at each descriptive level depended on only a very approximate, simplified, abstracted characterisation of the system at the level next beneath it.

According to Simon, artificial systems and adaptive systems, which include both psychological and biological systems, have properties which make them particularly susceptible to simulation using simplified models. Resemblances in the behaviour of these systems without identity of the inner (that is, underlying) systems are particularly likely if the aspects of behaviour in which we are interested arise from the organisation of the parts making up the inner system, independently of all but a few properties of the individual components. For example, in structural engineering we may need only to know about the tensile and compressive strength of a material and not its chemical properties or origins to predict its behaviour and design a structure.

Given these considerations, taken together with the abstract character and symbol manipulation capacity of the computer and the ease with which it is possible to generate functional descriptions, then the computer provides a powerful medium in which to express and test theories.

## 22.4   The practice of computer simulation

Emphasis has been placed on the use of the computer as the medium for defining and testing theory and understanding. In this role the computer is used as a tool in the process. Thinking and imagination are essential in the generation of schemes of understanding and theories relating to the phenomena of interest. Indeed investigation through simulation may be achieved through the process of a thought experiment alone in combination with externalised reasoning aids – schematic diagrams, flow diagrams, logical formulae, etc.

If thought experiments can be considered as a form of simulation why do we need to resort to simulation using a computer? How can a simulation ever tell us anything that we do not already know? Surely a simulation is no better than the assumptions built into it and the computer can only do what it is programmed to do. Simon (1981) considers that while both these assertions are true, they distract from the fact that simulation can provide new knowledge. Even if we start from the correct premisses, it may be difficult to discover what they imply. This problem is especially marked when the system under investigation involves a number of variables which may interact. Constructing and running a simulation is a means to uncovering these details.

Miller et al. (1984) have described stages in the construction of theory in cognitive science. This is a discipline which draws on the techniques of linguistic and semantic analysis, psychological experimentation and artificial intelligence. They suggest that computer simulation is a technique best used at the midpoint between initial theory formulation and the development of explicit process models. Both Miller et al. and Simon suggest that clarification of the scope and problems of a theory can be achieved in the middle stage even though the system underlying the theory is poorly understood. Simon's account of the role of abstraction in theory formation, reviewed earlier, provides a rationale for this view.

## 22.5  Understanding case studies in simulation

Thus far, the principles underlying investigations using computer simulation have been described. It is appropriate to consider specific case studies. Unfortunately we now encounter a significant communication problem with respect to computer models. Miller et al. (1984) argue that it is very difficult to understand how a simulation model works without gaining experience in constructing models of this type. Having access to appropriate computing resources and training may also be necessary.

The problem is compounded by dialect variations in computer programming languages which occur even if they nominally are the same language. Furthermore, it is generally very difficult to infer the properties of the theory which are embodied in a computer program from the listing of the program statements. This problem arises from the nature of the relationship between the surface form of a computer language and its meaning in relation to the processes they refer to (Strachey, 1966). This point is amplified below in the section on communicating with computers.

One solution to this communication problem is for the author of a computer model to explain the theory underlying its construction in verbal form – that is, by using natural language. But this medium for explanation is open to lack of clarity, imprecision and fuzzy thinking and/or description. Moreover, the means by which elements of a theory are implemented can use procedures which are ad hoc and independent of any theoretical principles which guide the construction of the model under investigation.

Miller et al.'s (1984) observations suggest that it is crucial to learn about simulation and the use of programming languages in relation to concrete tutorial examples. Clocksin's (1987) and Scott and Nicholson's (1991) accounts of the use of the language Prolog use this tactic. Similarly in Winston and Horn's (1984) textbook explanation of the features of the language LISP is linked to worked examples. Naylor (1983) presents a number of programming case studies which model expertise in the BASIC programming language. It should be noted, however, that teaching material designed to develop skills in using a programming language are not explicitly concerned with promoting skills in the use of computer simulation as a research tool.

## 22.6   Communicating with computers

In order to use a computer as a medium for computer simulation, the user must learn to use the operating system and an appropriate language to specify the actions required of the computer. Computer languages can vary in their complexity and their expressive power. Languages also differ in their semantics. For example Prolog is a **declarative language**. Using Prolog, a program can be built by writing down statements in formal logic which specify facts and relationships. This language is best suited to applications that require symbolic computation. Prolog contrasts with procedural languages like Basic, Fortran or Algol 68. The writing of a program in Prolog is not like specifying a procedure or algorithm. Another language built for symbol manipulation is the language LISP. Advocates of this language argue that many psychological functions are easily realised in LISP (Winston and Horn, 1984).

Strachey (1966) reviewed the skills required to become an effective programmer. He argued that it was necessary for the user to understand the meaning, that is, the semantics of the instruction language as well as its form, that is, the syntax. Strachey's perspective is further clarified by Winston's commentary on representations (Winston, 1984). A language representation is a set of syntactic and semantic conventions that make it possible to describe things – with a particular interpreter in mind of course. The syntax of a representation specifies the symbols that may be used and the way those symbols may be arranged. The semantics of a representation specifies how meaning is embodied in the symbols and the symbol arrangements allowed by the syntax.

With this perspective in mind, the programmer must translate the description of the theory relating to the system or process under investigation into instructions in a computer program. This operation will involve consideration of how the elements in a theory can find expression in the semantics and syntax of the programming language. The form of the programming language may have its origins in mathematics, logic or symbolic information processing. Thus the choice of the computer language used to create the simulation can play a major role in the translation of the theory into program form and potentially the results obtained from the simulation.

The hope is that the initial stage of analysis leads to an account of the phenomena at a level of abstraction (Simon, 1981) which allows the theory to be expressed in an accurate form within the programming medium for investigation by simulation.

# 22.7   Studies in reasoning and language understanding

Two investigations will be now described to illustrate the form that a computer simulation can take. Both studies are relatively old since they date from 1968 and 1972. However, the time since their first publication has allowed the ideas they contain to be assimilated and evaluated. Both studies have explored concepts which are relevant to psychological issues.

The first study is Evans's (1968) study which involved the generation of a program to solve Geometric Analogy test questions. The test material was taken from an educational testing context. The figures used in the traditional Geometric Analogies test utilise a small set of geometric figures and relationships in their construction. The task is primarily concerned with the perception of relationships rather than the perception of the meaning or the significance of the stimuli. Investigations of language understanding using computer simulation have modelled the processes underlying the perception of meaning and significance. Obermeier (1987) has summarised the various approaches to natural language processing.

Scores on geometric analogy test items have long been used as an index of intellectual performance. In consequence Evans could compare the program's performance with the performance level and errors observed with human solvers. The stimulus for the study, however, was the need to devise an artificial intelligence program which could reason with visual representations.

The system described by Evans (1968), and summarised by Minsky (1968), involved four stages. After the initial 'perception' of the individual test figures, descriptions of the geometric figures (taken singly and in pairs) were generated at three levels. At the first level the description specifies the object properties and relationships of each element in the test figures. At a later stage, descriptions are generated which represent the differences, transformations and equivalences existing between the various test figures pairs. The transformation rules governing the changes which occur between pairs of figures are systematically compared to determine the best answers for each analogy problem.

Evans's investigation suggests that solving geometric analogy test problems depends on the ability to form (that is, generate) and compare abstract descriptions. This insight emerged in the context of generating a theory about the representations and process leading to the choice of the analogous pairs. Some of the programming techniques and representations used to achieve a working program seem unlikely candidates for a psychological theory of task performance. However, the overall organisation of the program and characterisation of the intermediate representations are independent of the programming medium used. The principles used in the program were sufficiently compelling for Sternberg (1977) to draw on the Evans model for his work on modelling geometric analogies performance. Subsequent work by Winston (1984) on a model of inductive concept learning with pictorial concepts shared a number of the organisational and process features found in the Evans program.

By working with a computer simulation technique, Evans was able to formalise aspects of a process of visual reasoning which it is difficult to formalise from direct experience on this kind of task. The work carried out by Evans, Winston and others suggests that common processes underlie performance on tasks which are traditionally regarded as distinct and separate. These investigations show that pattern recognition, inductive learning and simple analogy involve common processes and representations. The insight gained from this family of programs indicates the possibility of shared principles and processes. Thus a number of distinct phenomena can be explained within a common framework.

One very significant study of language understanding was conducted by Winograd (1972). His work brought together a number of elements to create a model and a system which carried out an integrated process utilising syntactic, semantic and pragmatic knowledge. His program had three components. A **syntactic parser** which embodied a large-scale grammar of English, **semantic routines** which interpreted the meaning of words and sentence structure, and a **cognitive deductive system** to explore consequences, plan and carry out commands and find answers to questions. When interpreting sentences Winograd's system worked from the analysis of syntax to semantics to action. However, the system allowed interaction between representational domains to, for example, resolve structural and referential ambiguity.

The criterion used by Winograd to evaluate the system's capacity to understand language was based on an operational definition of understanding. The system's capacity was tested in terms of its ability to answer questions and carry out actions in a simulated block world. On these criteria, the program proved an impressive performer.

Following its initial publication, Winograd's model was subject to scrutiny and comment. Objections were raised with regard to the type and scope of the model of grammar used in the system. Others have considered that the blocks world in which the program acted placed serious limits on the generality of the study and Winograd's demonstration. It is evident that the scope of the 'real world knowledge' available to the system was limited. In effect the program operated in a very specific and concrete conceptual 'world'. Thus it is was not capable of the elaborative inferences which contribute to our comprehension of language.

Winograd has continued to develop his ideas about language under-standing, in particular with regard to communication between persons and the issues of shared knowledge and understanding. See Winograd's (1980) paper reproduced in Aitkenhead and Slack (1994) for details.

As noted earlier a number of criticisms were made of Winograd's (1972) work. Of course unlike many accounts of traditional psychological theor-ies, the description provided by Winograd was sufficient to allow detailed analysis and commentary. This feature can be considered as one of the strengths of the method of investigation through simulation. However, it is easy to get distracted by the details of the implementation and forget the overall principles and organisation which guided the design of Winograd's scheme. Simon (1981) would, of course, argue that these features are the key aspects to consider.

Winograd (1980) lists four features of his model which involved concep-tual and technical innovations in modelling the language understanding process. The model used a reasoning formalism based on the 'procedural embedding of knowledge'. Knowledge of language form, semantics and pragmatics were expressed as procedures. The states of knowledge involved are implicit in the processes carried out. At any point in the interpretative process, the particular steps in the procedure which operates on a sentence will reflect the general syntactic properties of language and the particular structure and lexical content of the sentence under interpre-tation. The adaptive quality of this process is illustrated in the case of morphemic analysis in Winograd (1971).

Within Winograd's model, meaning was based on an imperative as against a declarative process. The meaning of a sentence was represented as a command to the program to do something rather than as a fact about the world. Thus a statement about ownership of an object was represented as a program which added information to the database of the system. In effect language statements result in the initiation of action within the system. The representation for the meaning of words and idioms was also based on procedures which operate to build representation structures corresponding to the sentence. This feature enabled the program to deal with features like pronouns.

Finally the program included an explicit representation of the cognitive context. In order to resolve the reference for a phrase, the program must decide on the basis of a representation of conceptual focus or a recency criterion specific to the context of the sentences preceding the current phrase. This knowledge obviously lies outside the category of general facts about the objects within the domain considered.

The significance of these features for the development of a process model of language understanding can only be assessed in relation to theory and findings in this area. A number of specific aspects of Winograd's (1972) implementation have proved difficult to extend to other language under-standing phenomena. Nevertheless the range of the phenomena his system exhibited is impressive. The clarity with which he was able to describe the properties and operation of the elements included in the system make it possible to specify how the model might be extended. This is not always the case for verbal descriptions of a theory.

## 22.8   Conclusion

Using a computer to test and explore theory in psychology forces the investigator to express the theory in a form compatible with the programming medium, that is, programming language to be used. That language must have a semantic structure which is compatible with the states and processes envisaged in the theory. In practice the need to express the theory in program form may shape and hopefully clarify the theory. This aspect of creating and using simulation programs has elements of the chicken and egg problem!

As Miller et al. (1984) have noted, the use of simulation for investigation only becomes appropriate when sufficient facts about a phenomenon have been accumulated and a theory or theories have been formulated. If the theory predicts that a phenomenon reflects interactions between sub-components of a system, then simulation can provide a powerful investigative technique. Working with a simulation technique brings the user into contact with concepts from computing and mathematics, representation theory and systems analysis. These concepts have proved to be fruitful additions to psychological theory.

## 22.9   Further reading

An inexpensive set of edited readings in cognitive science which includes papers in both psychology and artificial intelligence can be found in Aitkenhead and Slack (1994) *Issues in Cognitive Modelling*. Detailed discussions of theory and method used in work carried out within a computational framework are reported in Kintsch, Miller and Polson (1984) *Methods and Tactics in Cognitive Science*. Herbert Simon provides a clear account of investigation through simulation in Simon (1981) *The Sciences of the Artificial*. Waltz (1982) gives a well-illustrated review of work in artificial intelligence extending over 30 years in his article 'Artificial intelligence' in *Scientific American*.

# PART IV

# 23 Bivariate Statistical Analyses

*Chris Fife-Schaw*

## Contents

## 23.1 Introduction

In a book on research methodology it is not possible to avoid a discussion of statistical techniques or approaches to data analysis. Teachers of statistics around the world know how the topic strikes fear into the hearts of many a psychology student yet, most of the ideas underlying these analyses are very straightforward. Many people see statistical formulae and assume that they will not be able to understand them yet the vast majority involve no more than being able to add, subtract, multiply or divide numbers and being able to put numbers in rank order.

In this chapter I will attempt to explain the ideas underlying some commonly used tests with reference to as few formulae as is possible. There is not enough space in this book to provide full explanations of all bivariate tests so you will need to look at a statistics book at some point. However, the aim is to explain the logic of common bivariate statistical tests in the hope that when you do look at the statistics text it will make more sense to you. You should make sure you have read Chapter 4 on levels of measurement first as I will assume you are familiar these issues. Before looking at any bivariate analyses you should be aware of some key concepts that many texts take for granted that you understand.

## 23.2 Some basic definitions

*Population*: The collection of all individuals of interest in a particular study. More abstractly it is the set of all 'units' of analysis defined by your problem area. For example, all people resident in the United Kingdom, all people with a particular disease, all females, etc. Unfortunately, the term **population** is also used in a more specific way to refer to a population of scores. The **sample** you draw will provide you with a **sample of scores** from the **population of scores**. This can be confusing since the population of scores probably does not exist in any real sense – for example, you get test scores from your sample but as the rest of the population has not taken the test their scores exist only at a kind of abstract, 'as if' level.

*Sample*: Set of individuals selected from a population and intended to represent the population under study. Usually it is impractical to study everybody in your target population so you have to draw a sample. See Chapter 8 for a discussion of sampling issues.

*The case or unit of analysis*: As psychologists we are interested in people and this means that for many applications the **case** or **unit** of analysis is the individual respondent or subject. We assign individuals to conditions, say, and measure their responses. You should be aware that statistical tests do not require that the case be a person. The case could be a household or a rat or a stick or anything that could reasonably provide data.

*Data*: measurements or observations. A **data set** is a collection of measurements.

*Raw score*: An original measurement or observed value (a datum). A value before some form of manipulation has been done.

*Variable*: A characteristic or condition that changes or has different values for different individuals (for example, height, hair colour, score on a test).

*Parameter*: A value that describes a population. It could be a single measurement (for example, mean score on a mathematics ability test) or derived from a set of observations *drawn from the population* (for example, mean maths score of all females who are above average on an English test). There is a convention in text books that population parameters are indicated by using Greek characters (for example, $\sigma$, $\mu$).

*Statistic*: A value that describes *a sample*. This can be a single measurement (for example, mean maths score of the people in your sample) or derived from a set of observations (for example, mean score of the females in your sample). Often a statistic is the best estimate you have of a population parameter since you may not be able to test everybody in your target population. All sorts of numerical values that summarise your sample data are statistics. These could be means, medians, percentages, correlations, *t*-values, *F*-ratios, etc.

*Descriptive statistics*: Summarise raw scores – for example, average, percentage, variance, etc.

*Inferential statistics*: These are techniques for using sample data to make statements about the population that the sample came from. Most of the time you are interested in using **inferential statistical techniques** to tell you how justified you are in concluding something about the population based on the data provided by your sample.

Most psychologists collect data from samples of people. We rarely have access to the total population of people who we might have been interested in studying. Say, for instance, you were conducting an experiment to assess the impact of two teaching methods on mathematical ability in children. The chances are you would set up the two teaching schemes in local schools and test the children's ability before and after the schemes were put in place. Obviously, in the long term you would like to be able to recommend one scheme as being more generally useful than the other, as you would like your research to have an impact on children's education generally. However, you cannot test all children in the country on one or other of the methods, you have to draw a sample of children and then extrapolate the findings from your sample to what you think you would have found if you had tested all children.

This process of extrapolating from findings based on sample data is referred to as **statistical inference**. You try to infer something about the population from your sample. Analytical procedures that allow this sort of extrapolation are called **inferential statistics**.

*Test statistic*: Most inferential statistical tests produce a number which has to be compared with some criterion value to determine its **statistical significance**. A *t*-test produces a '*t*' statistic, a Kendall's tau ($\tau$) correlation produces a 'tau' statistic, etc. These summarise something about the *relationship* between your variables.

*Statistical significance*: This is the probability of having observed a test statistic as large as you have if there was, in fact, no relationship between the variables in question. Statistical significance, probability and hypotheses are considered in more detail later in the chapter.

*Substantive significance*: This is not to be confused with statistical significance. Psychology journals are packed with statistically significant findings but this does not necessarily mean that the findings are psychologically or theoretically important. As we will see later, it is possible to get a statistically significant result associated with a relationship between variables that is so small that it is of no substantive significance at all.

*Measurement error*: As discussed in Chapter 4, all measures of psychological constructs contain errors that are attributable to the measurement tool itself. With the exception of a small class of sophisticated multivariate analyses (for example, LISREL), common inferential statistical procedures do not allow for this kind of error. Even if a statistical test is highly appropriate for the data you have, poor quality measures with unknown amounts of measurement error, could invalidate any conclusions you might wish to draw from your test. You must always seek to minimise measurement errors.

*Sampling error*: When you calculate a statistic based on sample information it is likely that your sample is not absolutely representative of the population. In fact, it is highly unlikely that any sample statistic will exactly match the population parameter. So, there is something called **sampling error** which we need to know about whenever we want to make general statements about the population. Most of the time, the bigger your sample in relation to the size of population, the smaller the size of the sampling error.

*Random sampling*: The way you draw your sample from the population of interest should be by true random selection if at all possible. Non-random selection processes are likely to introduce biases into your parameter estimates. Many popular inferential statistical techniques assume that you have obtained your sample using random sampling procedures.

In practice, psychologists often use non-random samples of convenience (for example, students, attenders at the local clinic, etc.) or implicit quota designs (see Chapter 8). Much has been written on the relationship between inferential statistical procedures and sampling procedures and those interested in techniques of estimating the impact of sample designs, known as **design effects**, should consult Moser and Kalton (1971).

## 23.3   What are bivariate statistical analyses?

In the remainder of this chapter the focus is on the use of inferential statistical procedures since, as researchers attempting to explain human behaviour generally, we are rarely interested in merely describing our sample. We would like to make theoretical claims that apply to all people in a given population.

This chapter deals with analyses that involve two variables. These analyses can be broken down into two broad categories: first, tests that look for *differences between groups*, as defined by one variable, on scores on another variable and, second, tests that detect an *association* or correlation or relationship between scores on two variables. Chapter 24 will discuss analyses that deal with more than two variables at a time, which are called **multivariate analyses**.

## 23.4   Classical bivariate designs

Much of this book has been concerned with explaining common research designs and, at the risk of repeating material you may already have read, the following, prototypical approaches commonly require bivariate analyses. It is important to understand the relationship between research design and the types of statistical procedures which are appropriate for use with them.

### 23.4.1   Experimental designs

In experiments an **independent variable** is changed or altered while changes in a **dependent variable** are observed. To be sure of a cause and effect relationship between the two variables, the experimenter tries to exclude the effects of all other variables by randomly assigning people to **conditions** or **treatments** (values of the independent variable) and by controlling or holding constant other things that might affect the results. It is possible to have more than one independent variable but we will deal with that in Chapter 24.

The independent variable is a variable that is controlled or manipulated by the experimenter. It always has at least two levels of treatment or condition. Usually it is a categorical/nominal level variable and normally you have an expectation that the independent variable causes changes in the dependent variable. Levels of the independent variable are often referred to as conditions or treatments. For example, no drug treatment vs. low-dose treatment vs. high-dose treatment; teaching method A vs. teaching method B.

The dependent variable is the variable that is affected by changes in the independent variable. The putative outcome of your manipulation of the independent variable. It is never thought of as influencing the independent variable.

In its most basic form an experiment will randomly allocate people to one of two conditions of the independent variable, say, people taught statistics by 'Method X' and a control condition of people who are exposed to no statistics classes. We let a period of time elapse so that Method X can have some impact and then we test both groups at statistics, our dependent variable. This is referred to as an **independent groups** or **between-groups** design since none of the subjects appear in both groups and we are interested in differences between groups.

This design is acceptable but there may be problems if, by chance, when randomly allocating people to the two groups, we allocate people who are already better at statistics to the Method X group. This would make it more likely that we would get higher statistics scores for the Method X group. To get over this we could simply measure everyone's statistics ability first, then expose them to Method X and then retest their statistics ability. This is called a **repeated measures** or **within-subjects** design. This latter design does not get over the problem that statistics ability might improve over time without help from Method X, but it does get over the problem of randomly allocated subjects being different before the experiment took place. Chapter 5 deals with more complex experimental designs.

It is important to know about whether you have independent/between-groups design or repeated measures/within-subjects design when selecting an appropriate statistical test.

## 23.4.2 Quasi-experimental designs

These are similar to true experiments except that the levels of the independent variable are not under the control of the experimenter. For example, if you wanted to see whether school-based anti-smoking campaigns had an effect on smoking behaviour you could not randomly allocate children to the schools that either would, or would not, have the anti-smoking intervention.

Quasi-experiments are often the best you can hope for as you do not always have any real ability to control the independent variables. There is always a possibility that any effects you show are due to unforeseen **confounding variables**. For example, smoking rates might already be different in the schools you studied; your campaign might have no effect but schools will show a difference in smoking rates after the intervention. Your 'control' school might choose to run its own anti-smoking campaign which would be another kind of confounding variable (see Chapter 7 for more on quasi-experimentation).

Relationships between supposed independent and dependent variables in most questionnaire surveys are only tested within this quasi-experimental framework. If you conduct a survey and want to see what effect various background factors (such as, social class, amount of education, etc.) have on test scores, again you cannot randomly allocate people to different levels of class or educational experience. This is important because some survey analyses are written up to read *as if* they were true experiments.

### 23.4.3   Correlational and observational designs

These look to see if there is any systematic relationship between two variables. The aim is only to show that levels of one variable are associated with levels of another. There are no independent and dependent variables as such as no causal relationship can usually be inferred from correlational analyses even if you have a good hunch that there is one.

For example, if you found that the size of car engines seemed to increase with the aggressiveness of their owners, as measured on a personality test, you could draw at least three conclusions: first, it could be that aggressive people buy fast cars to express themselves; second, it could also be that owning a fast car gradually makes you more aggressive; or third, something else that you have not measured causes both the buying of fast cars and the development of aggressive personalities. You cannot sort this out with a correlational or observational study but you can at least show that there is a relationship and that it is not zero.

A notable exception to this is when the temporal ordering of events is not in question. For instance, the number of cigarettes smoked when someone was aged 20 might be highly correlated with levels of tar found in the lungs at age 50. It seems *unlikely* that levels of tar at age 50 *caused* levels of cigarette smoking at an earlier age (though even here, the possibility of a third, unmeasured variable influencing both variables still cannot be ruled out).

Note that all three of these general approaches concern the relationship between two variables. These designs can be made multivariate by incorporating additional variables, but for the present purposes we will deal with these prototypical cases. The experimental, and to a lesser extent, quasi-experimental designs tend to require analyses that look at differences between groups (the independent variable) in scores on some outcome (the dependent variable). Correlational or observational approaches require analyses that detect associations between variables where neither variable is necessarily the dependent nor independent variable (they could be but it is not necessary that they are).

## 23.5   Theories and hypotheses

This section spells out some aspects of classical hypothesis testing. This view of how to conduct good research is only one of a number views but it is the currently dominant view in psychology. It owes a lot to the theorising of Karl Popper (1968) and is sometimes called the Hypothetico-Deductive Model. It is also a form of positivism and assumes that there is a reality and some form of truth out there waiting for us to find it. Chapter 2 discusses this and alternative perspectives and if you are in any doubt about what is said here, refer back to that chapter.

### 23.5.1 Theories

These are statements about the underlying mechanisms of behaviour. The how and why of behaviour. To satisfy Popper it is essential that these are stated in such a way as allows the potential of them being shown to be wrong. Theories that could never, in principle, be shown to be wrong are not part of good science. They become acts of faith. Theories should generate specific **hypotheses** that can be tested. If these prove false then the theory can be questioned then modified or rejected.

### 23.5.2 Hypotheses

These are predictions about the outcomes of experiments or studies. Usually one does this by formally expressing a theoretically generated prediction, or an educated guess, about how an independent variable will affect a dependent variable. Conventionally we deal with two sorts of hypothesis when we do any inferential statistical tests. These are the **null hypothesis** and the **alternative hypothesis**.

### 23.5.3 The null hypothesis

This is what we actually test and it appears slightly odd at first sight. The null hypothesis in an experiment is the statement that: the independent variable has *no effect* on the dependent variable at all *in the population*. In a correlational study the null hypothesis would normally be that two variables are not associated, or uncorrelated, with one another *in the population*. Note that what happens in the *sample* is not what we are really interested in. The null hypothesis is often referred to as $H_0$.

### 23.5.4 The alternative hypothesis

This is usually our 'hunch' hypothesis, that the independent variable does indeed affect the dependent variable *in the population* or that two variables are correlated with one another *in the population*. However, this is only one hypothesis in a range of possible alternative explanations about what really affects the dependent variable and we cannot treat our preferred alternative hypothesis as absolutely true. This is in part because we normally draw on data from a sample rather than from the whole population.

For example, say you wanted to prove the hypothesis that 'all people have two hands' and you draw a sample of one person. If that person had two hands that would not prove that all people had two hands. Some people that you have not sampled might have more hands or, more likely, fewer. If the sample person had one or none, however, then you would have to throw out your hypothesis; it would definitely be wrong.

It is easier to show that a hypothesis is false than it is to show that a hypothesis is true. Indeed, there is a philosophical argument that we can only ever prove that something is not true – we can never show that something is always absolutely true. The alternative hypothesis is referred to as $H_1$.

## 23.6   Type I and Type II errors

### 23.6.1   Type I error

This has occurred when you reject a true null hypothesis. This is where you conclude that the independent variable did affect the dependent variable when, in fact, it did not. This can happen when, for instance, by chance you allocate people who were already high scorers to one condition and low scorers to another. When you test the dependent variable, the differences between the conditions is due to the fact that the people were different before you started *not* because the independent variable had any effect. In terms of correlational analyses, Type I errors occur when you say that the two variables were related to one another when, in fact, they were not.

Publishing findings with Type I errors in them could mislead people into doing more research on a dead-end topic or making serious life-threatening decisions based on the inaccurate conclusions in your paper.

### 23.6.2   Type II error

This occurs when you fail to reject a false null hypothesis. You conclude that the independent variable has no influence on the dependent variable when it actually does. This happens sometimes because the size of the treatment effect is very small and hard to notice in your sample. It can also happen when you get the opposite of the example given for Type I errors. Here, by chance, you allocate people who were already high scorers on the dependent variable to the treatment condition that actually lowers scores and vice versa. The effect of the experiment is to level up the two groups so that there is now no difference between treatment groups on the scores and you accept the null hypothesis of 'no differences' between groups. In fact, the independent variable had a big effect but your sampling obscured this. One solution for this example is to adopt repeated measures designs so that you know how people scored before and after the experiment.

With correlational designs Type II errors have occurred when you conclude that there is no relationship between your two variables when, in fact there is. If you can publish such 'non-findings' at all, then it may discourage people from investigating a potentially important effect.

The aim is always to minimise the probability of these two types of error occurring.

## 23.7   Probability

Probability ($p$) is the likelihood or chance that something will happen. Where a number of possible outcomes could occur, the probability of any particular outcome is a proportion based on the following:

If there are a range of possible outcomes A, B, C, D, etc.

$$\text{Probability of outcome A} = p(\text{A}) = \frac{\text{number possible A outcomes}}{\text{total number of outcomes}}$$

Probabilities always vary between 0 and 1. The sum of the probabilities of all possible events (A, B, C and D above) must always add up to 1.

$p = 1$      if something *always* happens. For example, the probability of picking a Joker out of a pack of 52 Jokers.

$p = 0$      if something *never* happens. For example, the probability of picking a Joker out of a pack of cards with no Jokers in it.

Some examples:

$p = 0.5$      for example, the chance of an unbiased coin coming up heads. Another way of saying this is a '1 in 2 chance'.

$p = 0.25$      for example, the chance of picking a diamond card from a pack of 52 playing cards. Another way of saying this is a '1 in 4 chance'.

The most common application of probability notions in psychology is to decide how likely it is that your *sample based* test statistic is found to be as big as it is by chance, assuming that your null hypothesis was, in fact, true. As an example, if there really was no real difference between people who had received a medical treatment and those who had not, then could it be (or rather, how likely is it) that the observed improvement in the treatment group was as big as it was just by chance?

Let us say we have a new treatment under test, and our null hypothesis is that mean scores of our cognitive test (the dependent variable) will be no different from that found in untreated subjects. In other words, our null

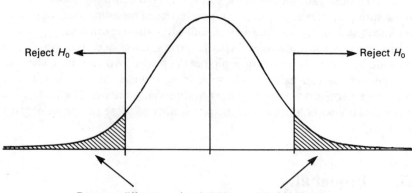

Extreme differences (probability = alpha) if $H_0$ is true.
Possible but quite unlikely group differences.

Figure 23.1 *A sampling distribution of* differences *between group means under the assumption that the null hypothesis is true*

hypothesis is that the population mean for treated subjects is the same as that for untreated subjects.

Figure 23.1 is a frequency distribution of all the possible *differences* between treatment and control group means that would be obtained if you repeatedly drew new samples and calculated the means for each new sample. This is called a **sampling distribution**. You do not have to create this distribution yourself, this is simply shown here to explain the logic of hypothesis testing.

The shaded areas, known as **critical regions**, contain 'extreme' or very unlikely outcomes. They are still possible means even if our null hypothesis is true. The proportion of sample means falling into the critical regions gives you the probability of observing a mean that, or more extreme, if $H_0$ is true.

By convention, if the probability of observing a mean as different from that predicted by the null hypothesis (under the assumption that the $H_0$ is true) is less than $p = 0.05$ (alternatively, 1 in 20 or 5 per cent) then you reject the null hypothesis. If the probability is not less than 0.05 then you do not reject the null hypothesis. This $p = 0.05$ figure, called an **alpha criterion**, is the maximum probability of making a Type I error.

In the above example we have looked at the difference between group/ treatment means observed in your sample and what would have been predicted under $H_0$. The same logic applies to designs concerned with associations between variables, too. When you are interested in correlations your null hypothesis is usually (though not always) that there is no (zero) correlation between the variables. As with the means, you look to see how likely it is that, using sampling, you would have observed as large a correlation between the two variables if it were actually zero. Again you could create a sampling distribution of correlations and look to see if your observed correlation fell into the critical region where you would reject the null hypothesis.

Most inferential statistical techniques, whether concerned with means or correlations or some other test statistic, use sampling distributions to determine whether the observed value falls into a critical region. Sometimes these sampling distributions make reference to population parameters and assume you have drawn random samples from the population and sometimes the sampling distributions are constructed out of the range of possible outcomes given the particular experiment or study you are doing (see section 23.8).

The 0.05 probability figure is only a convention and there are times when you would not be happy to reject the null hypothesis at this level. When people are conducting particularly controversial research, like trying to prove the existence of clairvoyance (if true it would undermine some existing laws of physics) it is usual to adopt a more strict alpha criterion. This has the effect of making all your analyses more conservative. You are free to set the alpha criterion at any value you like but you must declare it and be prepared to have to convince others that you are justified in doing this. This may be very difficult to do.

### 23.7.1   One- vs. two-tailed tests

When hypothesis testing you must decide whether you are going to make a one- or two-tailed test of the null hypothesis. In a one-tailed test, you reject the null hypothesis if the difference between the observed mean, say, and that predicted under $H_0$ is relatively small but is in a *previously specified direction*. A two-tailed test requires a somewhat larger difference but is independent of the direction of difference.

This distinction is best illustrated by an example. Say you had a wonder drug that was supposed to influence cognitive performance. If you had a strong theory about the action of this wonder drug which said that it would increase scores on the cognitive test, then if you observed no difference between treatment and control groups *or* you found that the drug group scored less then you would have disconfirmatory evidence for your theory. In this case your *null hypothesis* would be that drug treatment scores would be the same *or less* than those of the controls. This would be a one-tailed test.

In most psychological research, our theories are generally less well specified and we would be interested in differences in either direction. Big drops in score would be just as interesting as big gains. We would not wish to ignore a big drop in scores by doing a one-tailed test. This time our null hypothesis would be that treatment and control group means would be the same. Figure 23.2 illustrates the point.

In this figure we can see that the shaded areas in the tails of both distributions occupy 5 per cent of the total areas under the curves and thus

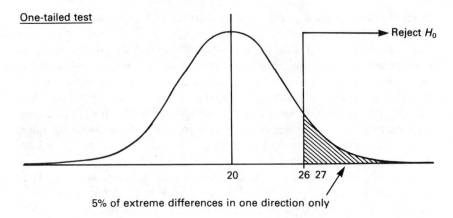

<u>One-tailed test</u>

→ Reject $H_0$

20          26 27

5% of extreme differences in one direction only

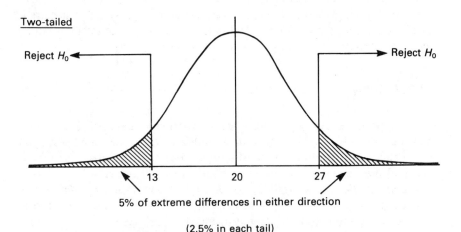

<u>Two-tailed</u>

Reject $H_0$ ←          → Reject $H_0$

13          20          27

5% of extreme differences in either direction

(2.5% in each tail)

Figure 23.2  *Sampling distributions of* differences *between group means: critical regions for one- vs. two-tailed hypothesis tests*

5 per cent of all sampling means. In this hypothetical example, the one-tailed critical value is 26 so any observed mean for the drug group greater than 26 would lead us to reject $H_0$. For the two-tailed test any value greater than 27 or less than 13 would lead us to reject $H_0$. Notice that when doing a two-tailed test you have to get a bigger difference between the two group means to reject $H_0$. This makes the two-tailed test inherently more conservative (less prone to Type I error) and this is partly why psychology journal articles contain more two-tailed tests.

The same logic applies to tests of hypotheses of association. If you have a strong hypothesis that two variables will be positively (or, alternatively, negatively) correlated then you can specify a one-tailed test. In most psychological applications you will be interested in strong relationships regardless of whether they are positive or negative and so two-tailed tests may be more appropriate. Use the less conservative one-tailed test only when you have a very strong hypothesis that specifies the direction of the expected effect.

## 23.7.2 Statistical power

The point of all research in the hypothetico-deductive tradition is to reach the correct conclusion about the research hypotheses. The previous sections looked at the Type I and Type II errors and the probability of making Type I errors. Statistical power is associated with the tests you use and is the probability that the test will correctly reject a false null hypothesis. This is the test's power to detect an effect when there really is one there to detect.

Most textbooks refer to the probability of making a Type II error (the probability of accepting a false null hypothesis) as $\beta$ (Greek letter beta). Since the sum of the probabilities of all possible events must add up to 1, the probability of rejecting a false null hypothesis, the power of your test, is:

Power $= p$ (rejecting a false $H_0$) $= 1 - p$ (accepting a false $H_0$) $= 1 - \beta$

While this formula is very simple, settling on a single value for $\beta$ is not straightforward. Although people often talk of this or that test as being more powerful than another, power depends on a number of factors that vary for each application. There is no single figure that always applies to each particular type of test.

One factor is the size of the **treatment effect** (see also **effect size**, Chapter 25). Put simply, if your independent variable has an effect on the dependent variable (that is, $H_0$ is false) but the size of this effect, the treatment effect, is small, it is going to be harder to detect this effect. Thus you will need a more powerful test to detect the effect (with a given size of sample) than would be the case if the treatment effect was strong. If the treatment effect is large, detecting it will not be difficult. A second factor is the level you set for the alpha criterion. Setting a smaller level will make it less likely that you will reject a true null hypothesis but it will also now be harder to reject a false hypothesis all other things being equal.

A third factor is sample size. As the sample size gets larger and approaches the size of the population so you will increase the statistical power of your test. If there really is a treatment effect ($H_0$ is false) in the population, you are more likely to find it in a larger sample than with a small one. Note, however, that power is about the ability to reject a false $H_0$ and is not about the size of the treatment effect. You might add more and more subjects to your study to increase statistical power but this will not change the absolute magnitude of the treatment effect or its substantive significance.

As an example, you might have invented an expensive intervention programme to improve scores on IQ tests. Let us assume that it does work but, though you do not know it yet, it only improves IQ by one point (IQ scores often have a mean of 100 and standard deviation of around 15). You set up a controlled experiment with 10 subjects getting your programme and 10 control subjects. You carry out the appropriate test and it would lead you to accept the null hypothesis and you make a Type II error.

Disappointed but not deterred, you realise that you did not have enough statistical power, so you re-run the study with sample sizes of 1000. You now have a lot of power and your test correctly leads you to reject the null hypothesis. The intervention programme has a statistically significant effect on IQ scores. However, in practical terms, this effect is too small to justify the expense of the programme and people may well question the importance of being able to improve IQ by a point. Beware confusing statistical significance with substantive significance.

It is possible to use **power tables** to estimate the size of sample you would need to achieve a test with a given power as long as you can make some reasonable estimate of the likely size of the treatment effect (effect size). When designing a study it makes good sense to use such tables to work out in advance how many subjects you need rather than to conduct a study only to find out later that you had very little chance of detecting the effect because you did not have enough statistical power because you did not approach enough subjects (see Kraemer and Thiemann, 1987).

## 23.8   Parametric vs. non-parametric tests

The final major distinction you need to be aware of before selecting a statistical test is whether you can do a parametric or non-parametric statistical tests. A good number of the well-known statistical tests such as the *t*-test, the product moment correlation and analysis of variance (ANOVA), make assumptions about the distribution of scores in the populations. The common assumptions are that the scores are normally distributed (have the classic 'bell-shaped' curve) in the population or that the distribution of (hypothetical) sample means is normally distributed. Also they assume that you have drawn a random sample from this population of scores. Some parametric tests assume that the variances of population scores are the same in your treatment groups. Tests that involve these assumptions are called **parametric tests**, they make use of assumptions about the population parameters and the nature of the distribution of scores in the population.

If, as is often the case, your own data do not satisfy these assumptions then you should use the **non-parametric** alternatives to the parametric tests. These do not make the same assumptions about the distributions of scores in the population and so violating these assumptions is not a problem. Sometimes you will see these tests called **distribution-free tests**. These sorts of test are also especially appropriate for use with ordinal and categorical measures where the mean is not an appropriate measure of central tendency. To truly establish the normality of a distribution you would need to be able to estimate its mean and variance and thus it is difficult to establish this assumption with ordinal and categorical data. This is not to say that there are no parametric procedures appropriate for such measures but these require additional special assumptions to be met and will not be considered here.

Hypothesis testing with non-parametric tests proceeds by creating sampling distributions that apply specifically to your study. In essence, most work by calculating all possible values of the relevant test statistic given your study's data, design and null hypothesis. Then they look to see whether your observed value of the test statistic is relatively extreme and therefore unlikely to have occurred by chance if your null hypothesis were true. While not identical to the procedures used with parametric tests, I hope you will appreciate that the basic logic of hypothesis testing remains the same as described earlier in this chapter. Statements about differences in the population can only be made if you have used random sampling procedures.

Parametric tests, if appropriate for your data, should be chosen in preference to their non-parametric equivalents since they tend to be more powerful and are thus better able to detect treatment effects if they really exist. See Chapter 4 for a discussion of violations to the levels of measurement assumptions of parametric tests.

## 23.9 Choosing a statistical test

Most statistics textbooks give you tree diagrams like the ones at the end of this chapter (see Figures 23.4 and 23.5) that help you decide which statistical test you should use. However, you need to know the following before you can use such trees.

First, are you interested in looking for relationships (for example, correlations, associations) or differences (for example, between groups)? Second, if you are interested in differences then you should identify which variable is the dependent (outcome) measure and which is the independent variable. Third, if you are interested in tests of association and you have normally distributed interval or ratio scale measures, produce a scatterplot (a graph) of scores on one variable against scores on the other. Figure 23.3 shows some hypothetical scatterplots. You should decide whether the relationship between the two variables looks linear or monotonic. Graphs ('a') and ('b') in the figure show linear, 'straight line' relationships between

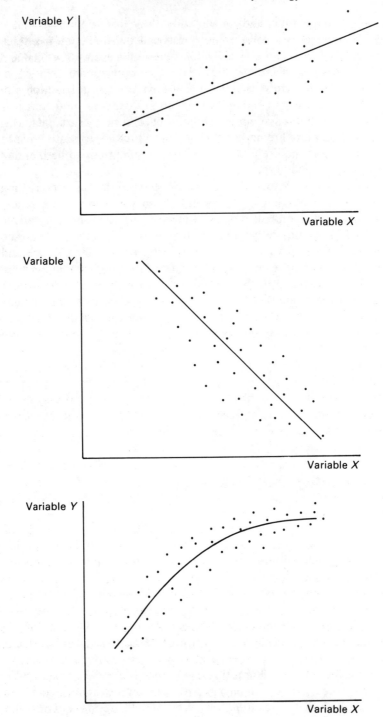

Figure 23.3 *Scatterplots showing linear and monotonic relationships between two variables*

the $X$ and $Y$ variables. Graph ('a') shows a positive linear relationship; higher scores on $X$ seem to be associated with higher scores on $Y$. Graph ('b') shows a negative linear relationship; higher scores on $X$ are associated with lower scores on $Y$.

A relationship is considered to be linear if you could reasonably draw a straight line through the points. Straight lines have been added to graphs ('a') and ('b'). If there was a perfect relationship between $X$ and $Y$ then all the points would lie on a straight line. As the relationships are not perfect you observe an elliptical distribution of observations around the 'best-fit' straight lines.

I hope you can see that it would not be possible to do this with graph ('c') since changes at higher scores on variable $X$ do not seem to be associated with big changes in $Y$. Lower down the scale, changes in $X$ are associated with bigger changes in $Y$. This is a monotonic relationship. Monotonic relationships are ones where increases in one variable are always associated with increases (or, if a negative relationship, decreases) in the other variable but the rate of change is not constant or linear. Graph ('c') shows a positive monotonic relationship.

If the scatterplot looks 'U' shaped or 'n' shaped or has several peaks, you will not have a simple relationship between the two variables. You will have to consult a statistics text and look at the possibility of carrying out a mathematical transformation of one, or both of your variables.

Fourth, what is the level of measurement of each variable? When testing for an association the choice of test will depend on the levels of measurement of both variables. When testing for differences between groups or conditions, the level of measurement of the *dependent* variable is crucial for test selection.

Fifth, if you have interval level or ratio scale measures and you think you may be able to do a parametric test, you must ask whether the variables are likely to be normally distributed in the population and whether you have been able to sample at random from the population.

As noted earlier, many psychological studies rely on convenience samples so, in such cases, you will not have met the random sampling assumption. In practice, the use of parametric tests such as the $t$-test, is acceptable as long as subjects are **randomly assigned** to treatment conditions (see Minium et al., 1993). The justification of this is technically complex but boils down to the fact that, in most cases, the conclusion drawn from the $t$-test is the same as would have been achieved if the most appropriate statistical model had been used. However, results from your convenience sample are not sufficient for making generalisations about the population; you will need further evidence to support those conclusions.

In practice you are also unlikely to have access to information about the distribution of scores in the population so you will only be able to look at the distributions of scores in your sample data. There is much written about how **robust** parametric tests are to violations of the normality assumption (see Blalock, 1988). Although there are dissenting voices, there is now some consensus that minor deviations from normality will not unduly undermine the value of many common parametric tests. So, if your sample data appear normally distributed then it is probably safe to assume you have satisfied the normality assumption. If, however, you have multiple modes ('peaks') in your sample data or the distributions are skewed or it otherwise looks severely non-normal, then use the non-parametric equivalent test. When in doubt, do both types of test and rely on the non-parametric test if the two tests do not lead to the same conclusion.

Finally, when group difference testing you must know if independent (separate) samples provide scores or whether the samples are either matched so that each respondent (case) is paired off with another respondent assumed to be alike on some basis, or each respondent provides more than one score on a measure. This simply refers back to your research design. If you have two or more separate groups or con-ditions and each respondent (case) provides a single score you have what is often referred to as **independent groups**. If your respondents provide two or more scores on a measure, say before and after an intervention, the design is a repeated measures one. In this example, each respondent's before and after scores are matched together for the purposes of the test. Studies involving matched samples are possible but relatively rare.

Unfortunately, statistical texts have yet to reach a consensus in the terminology to be used to deal with test selection. This is partly because authors want to provide decision trees that are appropriate for all possible applications of tests and thus they need to use abstract terms. Here, since this chapter has only discussed the two most common types of bivariate test (tests of difference and tests of association), we can hopefully adopt more simple terminology.

Figures 23.4 and 23.5 give examples of **decision trees**. Figure 23.4 should be used when you wish to look for differences between groups or differences between conditions/treatments. Figure 23.5 should be used when you are looking at the relationship between two variables.

Let us assume you had two groups of people, those with maths GCSE and those without, and you wanted to see if their scores on a statistics test were different. This is a quasi-experimental research design. Let us assume the scores are on a ratio scale (number of items correct) and in your sample data, the scores appear to be normally distributed in both groups. This requires a test of differences so you would look at Figure 23.4.

The first question you are asked is how many groups or conditions/treatments you have. You have two, so you move up the tree to the next question which asks what type of design you have. Here, your two groups are independent of one another (you cannot both have and not have maths GCSE) so you move along and up again. This leads you to the independent groups *t*-test which is a parametric test. As you have a normally distributed

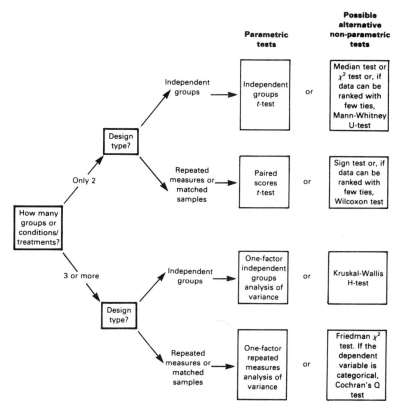

Figure 23.4  *Simplified decision tree for tests of differences between groups or treatments/conditions*

interval level you can use the *t*-test. Were you unable to satisfy these parametric assumptions you could use the Mann-Whitney U-test providing there were not too many people who had the same score on the test.

Using another example, let us assume you had measured attitudes towards death metal music on a seven-point, strongly-in-favour to hate-it scale, and you had asked people to tell you how many times they had been to church in the last month. You want to know if church-goers like death metal. Using Figure 23.5 you are first asked how many variables are dichotomous (have two categories only). Neither of your measures is dichotomous so you move up to the question that asks if both variables are on interval or ratio scales. Your church attendance measure is on an interval scale but strictly speaking the attitude measure is an ordinal one so you move down the 'no' branch. The next question asks if both variables are ordinal or you have a mix of ordinal and interval/ratio. Here the answer is 'yes' which leads you to the box containing Kendall's tau, a non-parametric correlation coefficient.

Both decision trees have been much simplified for the sake of clarity and there are a range of tests that could also have been included. However, for

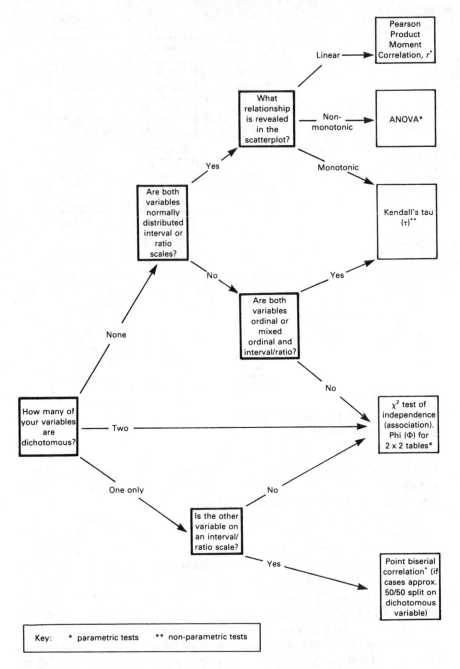

Figure 23.5 *Simplified decision tree for tests of association or relationship between two variables*

most basic bivariate tests of either difference or association, these decision trees will lead you to an appropriate analysis.

# 23.10  Conclusion

The aim of this chapter has been to describe the logic underlying hypothesis testing with simple bivariate statistical tests and give some guidelines on how to select appropriate tests. In the space of one chapter it is not possible to describe individual tests but I hope you now have a better understanding of what they can do for you. To keep matters simple I have dealt with the two most popular classes of bivariate tests; those that test hypotheses about differences between samples and those that test for associations between variables. There are other kinds of bivariate test such as tests for trends or tests of differences in dispersion, for example. These are less common applications within psychology but most standard texts deal with these issues.

# 23.11  Further reading

Minium et al.'s (1993) *Statistical Reasoning in Psychology and Education* is very good for explaining the reasons behind various statistical procedures and is clear and accessible. Blalock's (1988) *Social Statistics* is a more technical though still reasonably accessible text which has become something of a classic in the social sciences. While it does not take a psychologist's perspective it does deal with some useful procedures in considerable depth.

Finally, Kraemer and Thiemann's (1987) *How Many Subjects? Statistical Power Analysis in Research* is an easy to understand text on how to calculate statistical power and thereby estimate the numbers of subjects that will be needed for a study. Of the books available on this topic this is by far the easiest to use.

# 24  Introduction to Multivariate Data Analysis

*Sean Hammond*

## Contents

## 24.1  Background

When we collect information based upon a large number of variables such data are termed **multivariate**. This is in contrast to data from one variable (univariate) or two variables (bivariate) (see Chapter 23). By convention, data from more than two variables are known as multivariate data.

Obviously multivariate data can convey more information about a sample of people than univariate or bivariate data. As undergraduates most of us learn the standard univariate and bivariate statistical approaches to data analysis but we are rarely taught the more sophisticated methods of multivariate data analysis in any great detail. This is a shame because most of the more interesting research questions we might ask in the social sciences are multivariate by nature.

A common problem that faces research psychologists is the one where we are interested in looking at the differences between two or more groups of people and we have a number of measures (dependent variables) on which to compare them. The temptation is to carry out a separate statistical test of group difference for each dependent variable. This commonly involves the multiple use of the *t*-test or one-way ANOVA. There are two major problems with this approach.

First, we have the problem of 'weighing the odds' in favour of a significant result. As discussed in Chapter 23, statistical tests are commonly interpreted by probability estimates. What this means is that if we carried out 100 *t*-tests using random data, we would expect to obtain five *t*-values with an estimated probability less than or equal to 0.05. In other words the more tests we carry out the greater the chance we have of obtaining a statistic that will be interpreted as significant. This will lead us to a **Type I error** (see Chapter 23).

One way around this problem is to apply an adjustment to the probability level that we use to signify a significant statistic. A commonly used method is known as **Bonferroni adjustment** and simply involves dividing the traditional probability level by the number of dependent variables. Thus, if you were looking for a probability of 0.05 or less before deciding that the result was significant, and, if you had five dependent variables, you would divide 0.05 by five giving you the probability 0.01. You would then only describe statistics with a probability of 0.01 or less as statistically significant. Other methods of adjusting the probabilities for multiple statistical tests exist (Holm 1979; Sidak 1967) but the Bonferroni method is the simplest to apply.

However, this only gets around one of the problems of multiple statistical tests. Another, more difficult problem is the one of relationships between the dependent variables. Let us consider a simple example in which an educational psychologist is comparing persistent truants to non-truant children on three variables: IQ, Scholastic achievement and Reading ability. They might easily find that the *t*-tests for each variable are statistically significant at the 0.01 level. This may lead them to assume that the two groups differ on three distinct variables. However, another interpretation may be that the two groups differ in reading ability and the other two dependent variables merely reflect this since reading is fundamental to both scholastic achievement and the successful completion of an IQ test. Thus, the IQ measure and the achievement ratings may be highly correlated with the reading test and the fact that they also show significant *t*-tests is an artefact of this relationship. What is needed in this situation is a method of data analysis that takes the relationships between the variables into account. We will return to this example later when we describe the technique known as Discriminant Function Analysis.

It should be apparent from the preceding chapters that the nature of the research question will dictate the data analytic strategies used. Multivariate data analysis techniques can be grouped according to the research question being posed. For the purposes of this chapter we will categorise available methods under the following headings:

1  predicting outcomes
2  examining differences between groups
3  exploring underlying structure
4  fitting our measurements to theoretical models.

Some of the methods appropriate for each type of question will be discussed and then we will look at the special case of categorical data. Clearly, in the space of one chapter it will not be possible to give a comprehensive review of multivariate methods, and a number of books that attempt to do this are reviewed at the end of the chapter. What this chapter aims to do is to act as an initial pointer to the new researcher who is looking for a data analytic method to fit his or her research questions.

## 24.2  Making predictions

One common question that is often asked is 'how can we use our data to make predictions?' For example, we may have carried out a piece of research showing that self-efficacy is related to recovery time after a hospital operation. We may need to answer the question 'how can we predict recovery time if we know a patient's self-efficacy level?' Typically, this kind of question is addressed by a class of multivariate methods known as **regression procedures**. We will describe the most common form of regression analysis starting with the special bivariate case where we have one predictor and one dependent variable. We will then develop our arguments to include the multivariate situation.

### 24.2.1  Simple regression

As an example of simple regression we will consider the problem of predicting scholastic achievement from IQ. In Figure 24.1 we see the relationship between IQ score and reading ability represented in a scatterplot. We can see that the relationship is a positive one such that an individual with a high IQ will tend to have a high scholastic achievement. Thus if we know an individual's IQ score we can make a guess at their likely scholastic achievement score. In fact, we can do better than that, we can estimate the scholastic achievement score statistically.

To do this we first calculate the position of the regression line. This is the straight line that passes through the scattered points such that the distance

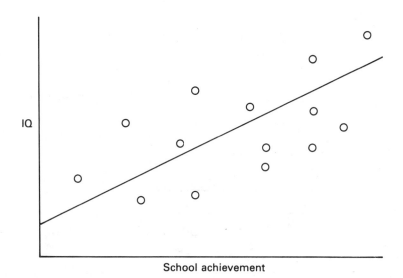

School achievement

Figure 24.1   *Scatter plot of IQ against school achievement*

from the points to the line is minimised. The slope of the line is calculated as the parameter beta (β) and the intercept (that is, the point at which the line cuts across the X-axis) is estimated as parameter alpha (α). Given a new individual with a known IQ (X) we can then estimate the Achievement Score (Y) by using the following formula:

$$Y = X\beta + \alpha \qquad (24.1)$$

Thus, β is a weight which is applied to our predictor variable to predict optimally our dependent or criterion variable. The parameter α is simply a scaling parameter to transform the scale of the predictor variable to that of the criterion variable (IQ score to Scholastic achievement score). This estimate is only accurate if the points in the scatter plot are close to the regression line since we are using this line as our 'model' of how the two variables are related. If all the points in the plot lie on the regression line we will have an absolute correlation coefficient of 1.00 and we will have a perfectly accurate estimate. The product moment correlation coefficient refers to a relationship represented by the product of the moments around the regression line. Thus, whenever the correlation is less than 1.00 and greater than −1.00 we have some inaccuracy in our prediction.

Let us think of this correlation between IQ and Scholastic achievement in another way. Figure 24.2 shows a schematic representation of the relationship in which each variable is conceptualised as a ball of variance. Where a correlation exists two variables are said to covary, this is represented by an overlap between the two variables. In Figure 24.2 we see that the correlation between IQ and Scholastic achievement is 0.60, the squared correlation (0.36) represents the proportion of covariance or overlapping

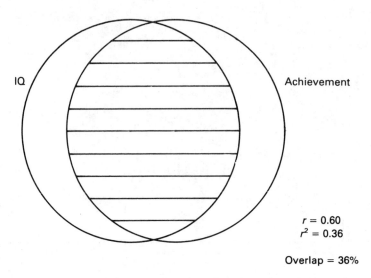

Figure 24.2   *Schematic representation of a correlation between two variables*

variance between the two variables. This tells us that 36 per cent of the variance of Scholastic achievement is shared with IQ and the remaining 64 per cent is unique or residual. Note that where correlations are concerned we assume that each variable has been standardised to have a mean of zero and variance of 1.00. This is done automatically when we calculate the product moment correlation. Thus, if two variables have a perfect correlation of 1.00 or −1.00, they will be represented as two perfectly overlapping spheres in which 100 per cent of the variance is shared.

## 24.2.2   Multiple regression

From this analysis we might be tempted to say that scholastic achievement is a function of IQ. However, we have to be very careful about making causal judgements. Causality can only be shown if three features are true:

1   A is related to B.
2   A precedes B.
3   The relationship between A and B is not due to their joint relationship with C.

We have demonstrated point 1 and we may theoretically argue that point 2 holds but point 3 remains a problem. This latter point tells us to beware of confounding variables. Let us consider one such variable, reading ability. Figure 24.3 shows a schematic representation of the relationships between the three variables scholastic achievement, IQ and reading ability. The first thing to notice is that when we look at IQ and reading ability together we

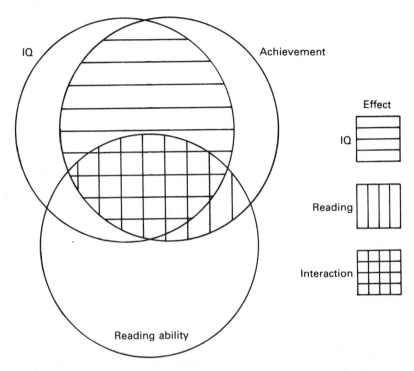

Figure 24.3   *Schematic representation of a correlation between three variables*

notice that we have accounted for a greater proportion of scholastic achievement than with IQ alone. We also note that some of the covariance between IQ and achievement is also shared by reading ability. If we were to take only the covariation unique to IQ and achievement and exclude that (cross-hatched) part we would be partialing out the effect of reading ability. This would result in what is known as the **partial correlation**. Note that since we are talking about proportions of variance, of course, we are describing the squared partial correlation. Thus, while the correlation of IQ with achievement is 0.60 when we partial out the effect of reading ability we may find that the resulting partial correlation becomes 0.50.

The multiple regression method utilises this notion of partitioning of variance to find the optimal prediction of one variable (achievement) given a number of predictors (IQ, reading ability). The fundamental idea is to account for as much of the variance of the criterion variable as possible. We have seen that the variance of the criterion variable, achievement, can be partitioned into that which is accounted for by IQ, reading ability, the interaction or overlap of the two and that which remains which is commonly termed the residual or unique variance.

Of course, these schematic representations of the process are rather simple. In practice we do not use such graphical methods for analysing our

| Predictor | r | Beta |
|-----------|------|------|
| IQ | 0.60 | 0.45 |
| Reading | 0.60 | 1.34 |

Multiple $r = 0.80$
Multiple $r$ squared $= 0.64$

Figure 24.2  *Multiple regression with two predictors*

data but rather resort to sophisticated mathematical estimation methods. This essentially involves the generation of a composite variable consisting of the relevant parts of the predictor variables plus a rescaling coefficient. This composite is constructed in order to produce a maximal correlation between it and the criterion variable. This composite variable represents the estimate of the criterion variable given the predictor variables. Beta weights for the predictor variables are calculated as in the bivariate case. The predicted value is then calculated by:

$$Y = \alpha + X_1\beta_1 + X_2\beta_2 + . . X_n\beta_n \qquad (24.2)$$

The size of the beta weight indicates the relative weight of the standardised predictor variable in question. Variables with greater weights are more relevant to the prediction equation. In our example, we see the results of the regression analysis for our example. Here we see that reading ability is the most important variable in predicting achievement.

It is possible to carry out a **stepwise regression** in which the computer program (no one does multiple regression by hand any more) will select the best combination of predictors for accounting for the criterion variance. One procedure is to use all the possible predictors and take them out one at a time until a more parsimonious but almost equally accurate solution results (**step-down method**). Alternatively, the program could select the predictors one at a time to build up the solution (**step-up method**). Most programs now include a method that combines both strategies (**stepwise method**). Personally, I have always found the step-down method to be most useful although it is really a matter of individual preference.

The multiple regression analysis also provides a multiple correlation coefficient which represents the correlation between the composite of predictor variables and the criterion variable. The composite is simply an estimate of the criterion variable estimated by formula (24.2). Thus, if we manage a perfect prediction $Y$ (from formula 24.2) will be identical to the criterion score for every individual. The multiple correlation between $Y$ and the criterion variable will be perfect and will produce a coefficient of 1. The statistical significance of the multiple $r$ is estimated by carrying out an analysis of the ratio of accounted for variance over the residual variance. This is exactly equivalent to the ANOVA test which provides an $F$ statistic.

## 24.2.3 Further issues in regression

The procedures we have been talking about here have a number of strict assumptions. First, they are parametric methods. The use of the product-moment correlation always assumes that the variables in question have a relatively normal distribution and that the relationships between the variables are assumed to be linear. If the variables cannot be assumed to be normally distributed it may be appropriate to use a non-parametric correlation coefficient as a starting point. The only non-parametric **product-moment** correlation is **Spearman's rho** which is essentially a Pearsonian correlation on the data after the data have been transformed into ranks. However, if this is done it is important that the researcher realises that he or she is simply predicting the **rank order** of the criterion variable and not the actual value.

In addition, it is important that a relatively large sample size is used so that the sampling error, which inflates the correlation coefficient, is minimised. This would normally mean that a multiple regression should only be attempted with a sample size in excess of 200 (Thorndike and Hagen, 1977). If the sample size is smaller the reliability of the result may be open to question. However, in the research process there may be times where it may be interesting to carry out the analysis on smaller samples. When reporting a regression analysis it is important to indicate the sample size.

Another problem with the multiple regression method is that it loses accuracy when the predictor variables are highly correlated with each other. This situation is known as **multicollinearity** and it causes difficulty when estimating the beta weights. In order to mitigate this problem techniques exist such as **ridge estimation** or **stein type estimation**. These are not commonly available on the most widely used computer packages so it is a good policy to take care that your predictors are reasonably independent of each other by examining the simple correlations between your variables before proceeding.

Other methods of regression analysis exist for cases where non-linear relationships are assumed although these non-linear methods are theoretically and mathematically complex. Methods also exist for categorical data – these methods include **logistic regression, logit and probit analysis**. Detailed discussion of these methods is beyond the scope of this paper but the interested reader is referred to Clogg and Shockey (1988) and Haberman (1978; 1979).

One situation that we have not touched upon is the case where the researcher has more than one criterion variable as well as a number of predictor variables. In this case, one set of variables is being used to predict responses on another set of variables. The method used in this case is known as **canonical variate analysis**. Again this brief chapter cannot do justice to this method and the interested reader is referred to the excellent introductory treatment in Hair et al. (1992:ch. 5).

# 24.3   Examining differences between groups

We now turn to the second of the research questions we may need to ask. The focus of this question is the difference between two or more groups. Typically, this question demands that we specify a particular representative parameter of each group and compare that. More often than not this parameter is the mean, although tests exist to compare medians and variances as well. Traditionally, when we are faced with the question of group difference we will look to the set of techniques known as the Analyses of Variance (ANOVA) in which means are compared (see Chapter 23). In this case we have at least one variable that is measured on the nominal level. The nominal variable represents the group membership. For example, we may be interested in truancy from school and one of our variables will be coded 1 if the child in question is a regular truant and 2 if not. The number we give to each group is arbitrary since all we are conveying by this level of measurement is the group membership for each individual and the number simply serves as a name (hence nominal).

As with regression we will begin by describing how group differences may be viewed in the simple bivariate situation and show how this can be generalised to the multivariate case. We will then turn to the situation where we have one independent variable and a number of dependent variables.

## 24.3.1   Analyses of variance

Let us assume that we have one dependent variable and one independent variable and that the independent variable is categorical. For the purpose of demonstration we will look at the case where the dependent variable is IQ score and the independent variable is truancy. We are interested in group differences and group membership is represented by the categories of the independent variable (1 = a truant, 2 = not a truant).

In order to see whether the two groups are different in IQ we would normally perform a $t$-test in which the two means are compared. The $t$-test is actually a special case of the one-way ANOVA when there are just two groups to compare. If we carry out an ANOVA on this data the resulting $F$ statistic will equal the square of the $t$ statistic obtained by a $t$-test. This approach to testing group differences appears quite straightforward and entirely different in concept and approach to the correlational methods we have just discussed. However, this difference is more apparent than real.

In Figure 24.5 we see a schematic diagram of the problem. Note that it looks almost identical to Figure 24.1 where we were discussing correlation. In fact, the principles are essentially the same. We are interested in finding out how much of the dependent variable's variance can be accounted for by variation in the independent variable. This partitioning of the variance is

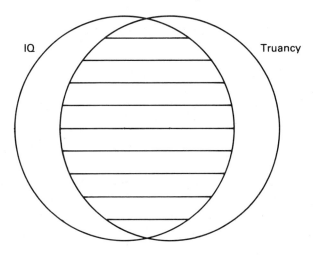

Figure 24.5   *Schematic representation of the effect of IQ on truancy*

| Source of variation | SS | DF | MS | *F* |
|---|---|---|---|---|
| Truancy | 10.00 | 1 | 10.00 | 4.00 |
| Residual | 120.00 | 48 | 2.50 | |
| Total | 130.00 | 49 | | |

Figure 24.6   *Summary for a one-way ANOVA*

where Analysis of Variance gets its name. The terminology differs somewhat from that of correlation. We talk in terms of the mean squares rather than variance but the concepts are essentially the same. In Figure 24.6 we show the ANOVA summary table. This tells us a few things about Figure 24.5. The mean square (MS) column informs us that a large amount of the variance of IQ has been accounted for by truancy. This **accounted for variance** is greater than the residual or error variance. The statistic *F*, which tells us whether there are differences between the mean scores of the two groups is a ratio of accounted for variance and the residual variance represented by the truancy MS and residual MS respectively. Because this example involves just two groups, the resulting *F* statistic of 4.00 is exactly equivalent to a *t*-test statistic of 2.00.

Let us now move on to consider the multivariate situation where we have more than one independent or 'group' variable. To illustrate this let us assume that we have simply added the independent variable of sex into the study. We are now interested in seeing whether IQ differs between truants and non-truants as well as females and males. We may also be interested in the additional information of the interaction between sex and truancy in respect to IQ.

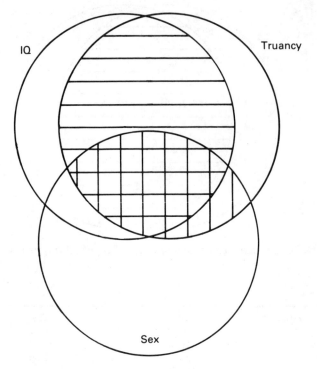

Figure 24.7  *Schematic representation of the effect of IQ and sex on truancy*

| Source of variation | SS | DF | MS | F |
|---|---|---|---|---|
| Truancy | 8.40 | 1 | 8.40 | 3.76 |
| Sex | 6.20 | 1 | 6.20 | 2.78 |
| Truancy by sex | 1.60 | 1 | 1.60 | 0.72 |
| Residual | 113.80 | 46 | 2.23 | |
| Total | 130.00 | 49 | | |

Figure 24.8  *Summary of a two-way ANOVA*

Figure 24.7 represents this situation schematically. Here, we have two independent variables accounting for a substantial amount of the IQ variance. The part at which they both intersect represents the interaction between truancy and sex. The results may look something like Figure 24.8. The largest effect is that of truancy and this is statistically significant at the 0.05 level. Neither the sex effect of the interaction between sex and truancy account for a statistically significant amount of IQ variance.

The ANOVA procedures are extremely flexible and they can be adapted to analyse data derived from a very wide variety of research designs (see Chapters 2, 5 and 6). It is beyond the scope of this brief chapter to go into all the possible design variations and the interested reader is referred to the comprehensive treatment of Winer (1971).

## 24.3.2  Discriminant analysis

So far in this section we have discussed the situation where there is one dependent variable and a number of independent variables. At the beginning of this chapter we alluded to this situation in discussing multiple significance tests where we have a large number of dependent variables and we wish to see how our groups differ on them. This is essentially a problem of group discrimination. In other words we are using our dependent variables to allow us to discriminate between the groups. The method most often employed in this case is Multiple Discriminant Function Analysis. Our treatment here must be very brief but should it whet a reader's appetite for more information, the short book by Klecka (1980) is a more comprehensive though very readable account.

Let us take the example mentioned at the beginning of this chapter. We are interested in seeing how truants and non-truants differ on the three variables, IQ, scholastic achievement and reading ability. The technique of discriminant function analysis begins by forming a composite of the dependent variables such that this composite variable will maximally discriminate between the groups. This composite variable (or function), as in the case of multiple regression, is made up by weighting the dependent variables. A simple analysis of the group differences on this composite variable is then carried out. If there are just two groups this analysis is equivalent to a simple *t*-test and, as developed by Harold Hotteling, is known as Hotteling's *t*-test. Where there are more than two groups a large number of alternative tests are possible but they mostly use the chi-squared statistic to test for significance.

The result of our example may look like Figure 24.9. Here we see that the multiple *t*-tests suggest that all of the variables differentiate the two groups significantly (the t values all exceed 1.96). The multivariate test tells us that the two groups can indeed be discriminated but when we look at the weights on the discriminant function it is apparent that reading ability is the important variable and that the other two have little or no relevance. This tells us that the discriminant function (composite) is essentially one of reading ability. When we look at the group means on this function we see that the truant group has a low score while the non-truant group has a high score (we have already observed that this difference is statistically significant).

However, IQ and scholastic achievement also have significant bivariate *t*-test statistics and we are now saying that they have no relevance. This is because we can now see that they are largely made up of reading ability. In *t*-tests

|  | Control Group mean | Phobic Group mean |  |
|---|---|---|---|
| IQ | 101.23 | 94.20 | t = 3.56 |
| Reading | 100.83 | 82.63 | t = 5.62 |
| Achievement | 104.10 | 88.55 | t = 5.44 |

Discriminant function weights

|  | Raw | Standardised |
|---|---|---|
| Reading | 1.342 | 0.723 |
| Achievement | 0.344 | 0.251 |
| IQ | −0.033 | −0.116 |

Group means

|  |  |
|---|---|
| Phobic | −1.562 |
| Control | 1.621 |

Figure 24.9   *Discriminant analysis on data from the school example*

other words reading is necessary to perform well on the IQ test and it is also an essential part of scholastic achievement. The discriminant analysis has shown us that it is reading problems that discriminate the truant group from the non-truant group. This gives us the potential for remedial intervention which may not have been the case had we assumed that truancy was largely a function of IQ.

This is a very simple example of discriminant function analysis and it is often the case that we are trying to discriminate between more than two groups. In this case, the analysis will generate more than one function. The maximum number of functions will be one less than the number of groups or one less than the number of dependent variables whichever is the smaller. Each function can be assessed for statistical significance, usually by a chi-squared statistic, and they are always presented in descending significance. When multiple functions exist they must be interpreted by examining which variables have been weighted the most in forming them. The group means (sometimes called **centroids**) on the function are then examined to see how they discriminate the groups.

One of the uses that discriminant analysis is sometimes put to is to classify new cases where the group is unknown. Suppose we have a new child at our school, we have their IQ, reading ability score and scholastic achievement record and we wish to predict whether he or she will become a truant or not. We can use the weights generated in our discriminant function analysis to estimate this child's score on the function. This allows us to estimate the probable group that the child belongs to. In this way we can see that discriminant function analysis serves the function of a multiple regression analysis when the criterion variable is a nominal group membership variable.

Discriminant function analysis is a very useful method but it does have a number of strict assumptions. Most importantly, an assumption of normal distributions among the discriminating variables is made. This is also true for the traditional ANOVA procedures but it is rather more critical with discriminant function analysis.

As with multiple regression the larger the sample size the more reliable the results. There are no easy 'rules of thumb' in discriminant analysis as there are with regression. Certainly, each group should be large enough to enable us to argue that they are representative of the population of such people. As a general rule it would be inadvisable to carry out a discriminant function analysis with less than 30 subjects in each group although much larger samples should be aimed for.

The discussion so far has assumed that the discriminating variables are measured at the interval level. Procedures for carrying out discriminant analysis on categorical data do exist but they are not readily available in existing computer packages. The interested reader might consult Anderson (1972) for a mathematical description. Alternatively, a technique mentioned later in this chapter, named correspondence analysis, might prove useful.

One situation that we have not mentioned is the one in which we have a number of independent variables as well as multiple dependent variables. The typical method of data analysis in this case is the **multivariate analysis of variance (MANOVA)**. MANOVA is simply a generalisation of ANOVA and discriminant function analysis combining the generation of composites with variance partitioning. The procedure is extremely complex and general and it can be shown that multiple regression and canonical variate analysis are also special cases of the MANOVA model. Most psychological researchers come across MANOVA when they are trying to carry out a simple ANOVA analysis with repeated measures using a computer package such as SPSS. This simply shows that nearly all ANOVA designs are a special case of MANOVA, which in this case is just the name of the program subroutine and not the specific analysis method.

For any reader who has an interest in the statistical models underlying these methods the MANOVA is a fascinating model and an excellent introductory account is provided in Marascuilo and Levin (1983).

## 24.4 Exploring underlying structure

A very common research question concerns the underlying structure of our data. Often in multivariate research we are interested in finding out whether our variables imply the existence of some superordinate structure.

For example, questions in a scale designed to measure extroversion and neuroticism are assumed to have a structure comprising two underlying traits. Alternatively, a group of 20 symptoms from a checklist might be expected to be clustered into two groups relating to psychological and physical symptomatology. In each of these cases we are interested in examining the underlying *structure* of our observed variables.

One of the main reasons for examining the underlying structure of our data is so that we can describe what is being observed in a more parsimonious way. Thus, we can describe the 20 symptoms mentioned above in terms of only two superordinate variables, psychological and physical symptomatology.

The underlying structure of a group of variables is implied by the interrelationships that exist between them. This means that for nearly all of the methods described below the first step is the calculation of intervariable associations. These are usually, but not always, correlation coefficients. The table of all intervariable correlation coefficients is known as the correlation matrix and it is the structure implied by this matrix that is to be explored.

Although we are addressing the exploration of underlying structure, it is important to realise that no good research is entirely exploratory. The selection of the variables will have been informed by some theoretical position. The fact that we are looking at the structure implies that we have reasoned grounds for such a tactic. In other words, we will usually have some a priori expectation, at least in broad terms, of what we will discover. This expectation need not be formally stated but it will be useful to use as a yardstick when we have to interpret our analyses.

In this section, I will briefly describe three methods for analysing multivariate structure: these are the factor analyses, cluster analyses and multidimensional scaling analyses. We will then turn to the issue of **confirmatory** or **restricted** analyses.

### 24.4.1  Factor analysis

One of the most widely used approaches for exploring the underlying structure of a set of variables is factor analysis. Factor analysis is a global term describing a wide variety of different techniques developed primarily as a means of examining the existence of underlying latent traits. This means that the use of factor analysis cannot ever be said to be purely exploratory since the most basic assumption of this method is that the structure may be described in terms of one or more bipolar constructs.

As with nearly all methods for examining structure, factor analysis begins with the calculation of the intervariable correlation matrix. It is most important to note that almost all factor analysis methods require that these correlations are product-moment estimates or direct estimates of covariance.

The analysis proceeds to identify the set of underlying linear traits that are best implied by the intervariable relationships. In fact, the analysis generates underlying composite variables in much the same way that regression and discriminant analysis do. These composites are then identified and interpreted by observing their correlations or regression weights with each variable included in the analysis.

The factor analysis treats the correlation matrix as a ball of intervariable variance and it extracts chunks of variance to represent each underlying factor sequentially. These 'chunks' get smaller as each factor is extracted. The mathematical terminology for these chunks is the **eigen value**. Thus, the first factor extracted has a relatively large eigen value and each successive factor is built around a smaller chunk of variance or eigen value than the preceding one.

As an example, let us look at a questionnaire study on environmental concern. A short 20-item checklist taken from Ashford (1994) was administered to 311 university students. Each item concerned an environmental issue such as 'global warming', and 'threat to sea mammals', and the respondents were asked to indicate the degree of concern they felt for that issue on a five-point rating scale. It was expected that the resulting 20 variables would be described by three underlying factors relating to global, local and wildlife concerns. A $20 \times 20$ correlation matrix was generated and a factor analysis was performed. The three eigen values extracted were 8.76, 2.93 and 1.71. The resulting structure is reported in Figure 24.10. Here we see that each factor is represented as a column of numbers. Each number is known as a loading and describes the weight that each item has on the factor in question. What we can immediately see is that the large (or salient) loadings on factor 1 belong to items associated with global issues. Factor 2 has high loadings from items relating to wildlife while factor 3 appears to be associated with local issues. Note that some items have quite large loadings (here we take 0.35 or above as salient) on more than one factor. Thus, 'Transport congestion' is seen as relevant to both local and global issues. These items are known as **factorially complex**.

Factor analysis is essentially a descriptive method. This means that the usefulness of the technique is a function of how interpretable the solution is. However, there are a number of pitfalls in factor analysis that this simple example has not highlighted.

The first problem is deciding how many factors to extract. In this example we extracted three factors because we had good reason (from Ashford's work) to expect this solution. Often, we do not have an a priori expectation of the appropriate number of factors. Indeed, the technique allows the researcher to extract as many factors as there are variables which would be unhelpful. The researcher has to have some broad expectation of the number of potential factors before embarking on a factor analysis. A number of strategies for deciding on the number of factors has been proposed but none are without limitations.

| Variable | I | II | III |
|---|---|---|---|
| Global warming | **.88** | .01 | −.26 |
| Ozone layer | **.91** | .03 | −.28 |
| Water pollution | **.61** | .17 | .12 |
| Air pollution | **.69** | .12 | .14 |
| Factory farming | .29 | **.49** | .09 |
| Endangered wildlife | .17 | **.81** | −.12 |
| Threat to forests | .11 | **.45** | −.15 |
| Overpopulation | **.45** | .17 | .15 |
| Acid rain | **.60** | .17 | .21 |
| Threat of nuclear power | **.53** | −.02 | .28 |
| Fossil fuels | **.48** | −.13 | .37 |
| Cruelty to animals | −.12 | **.81** | .09 |
| Trade in rare animal products | −.06 | **.89** | .01 |
| Litter | −.20 | .26 | **.71** |
| Transport congestion | **.51** | .02 | **.36** |
| Waste disposal | **.47** | .03 | **.43** |
| Building on green belt land | .12 | **.41** | **.40** |
| Food contamination | .22 | .01 | **.69** |
| Noise nuisance | .01 | .03 | **.81** |
| Threat to sea mammals | .05 | **.78** | .02 |

Factor correlation matrix:

| | | | |
|---|---|---|---|
| Factor 1 | 1.00 | | |
| Factor 2 | .40 | 1.00 | |
| Factor 3 | .30 | .31 | 1.00 |

Figure 24.10  *The factor structure of 20 pro-environment behaviours*

One of the most commonly used criteria is also one of the worst and this is to extract only as many factors as have eigen values greater than or equal to one. This method will usually extract more factors than appropriate and so it has some value as a means of identifying an upper bound. Despite its use in common practice and its occasional recommendation in the literature the researcher is strongly advised to avoid the use of this criterion for deciding the number of factors. The advice we present here is to use **interpretability** as the criterion for selecting the number of factors. This means that the researcher identifies the minimum and maximum number of factors and carries out an analysis for each potential solution. The solution which makes the most theoretical sense is the most appropriate. Clearly, this method involves an element of subjective interpretation but it assumes that the researcher is in tune with the theoretical underpinnings of the data and that the interpretation is properly detailed in the dissemination of results. To find out more about alternative methods to aid in deciding the number of factors the researcher is referred to works by Cattell (1978), Harman (1976) and McDonald (1985).

Another bone of contention in factor analysis is the issue of rotation. This is where the initial factor loading matrix is transformed to aid in interpretation. Essentially, this involves moving the variance around to overcome the artefact where successive factors contain less variance than those preceding them. There are two types of rotation (although there are many techniques) termed orthogonal and oblique. Orthogonal rotation involves a transformation that forces the underlying factors to be uncorrelated with each other. Oblique rotation, on the other hand allows the factors to be correlated. Some authors advise the researcher to use orthogonal rotation (Child, 1990) because it is supposed to be 'simpler'. Indeed, orthogonal rotation, using the VARIMAX technique, is the default option on many computer programs. However, psychologists rarely deal with constructs that are unrelated to each other. In our example, it would be odd if concern for global issues were not correlated with concern over other environmental issues. If we were to use orthogonal rotation in this case we would be imposing an unnecessary artefactual restriction on our data. In Figure 24.10 we also see the correlations between the factors which indicate a high degree of relationship.

Factor analysis is a huge topic but anyone wishing to use the method should take the time to find out about the various controversies and pitfalls that attend it. Factor analysis is widely used but is also very widely misused and many poor factor analytic studies succeed in being published. If a study reports extracting factors with eigen values greater than one and then carries out VARIMAX rotation, the chances are that it is an ill-considered and opportunistic analysis. When writing up a factor analysis the author should justify the use of factor analysis, the number of factors extracted and the rotational strategy employed.

A final point worth highlighting is the need for a good sample size. Since the factor analysis is a variance partitioning method we need a sample size that allows for a minimum of sampling error. To produce a reliable factor solution it is advisable that a sample size of 200 plus is used where possible. As a general rule it is also recommended that there are at least four times as many subjects as variables. Of course, smaller samples can be used although the reliability of the solution may be questionable; however, there is one very definite requirement of sample size and that is that there are more subjects than variables. This latter stipulation is necessary to justify the matrix algebra that underlies the method.

## 24.4.2 Cluster analysis

Factor analysis is widely used but, as we have seen, it is not without limitations. An alternative method of exploring underlying structure which may be more supportable with the data psychologists often handle is termed cluster analysis (Blashfield and Aldenderfer, 1988).

The basic premiss of cluster analysis is that the variables can be grouped into discrete clusters. Thus in our environmental concerns example we might expect the variables to group into three discrete groups representing global concerns, local concerns and wildlife concerns. Unlike factor analysis, we do not expect these clusters to represent an underlying bipolar trait ranging from high to low concern but simply as a descriptive set of categories. These clusters can be represented as simple nominal categories or as hierarchical arrangements in which all variables belong in one superordinate (general concern) cluster which may be broken down into more and more clusters.

Cluster analysis is often used to cluster people rather than variables. Commonly, this involves a variety of clustering methods termed **partition-ing** or **non-hierarchical** methods. These methods usually require the user to tell the program how many clusters are expected. The program then places objects (people or variables) into the relevant clusters according to the similarity they have with each other. The idea is that objects within a particular cluster will be more similar to each other than to objects in other clusters.

The hierarchical methods generally start by placing each of the objects into its own unique cluster and then, by examining the similarity of the objects, merges the two most similar into a new cluster. The resulting $N-1$ clusters are then examined and another merger occurs. This continues until only one cluster remains.

Unlike factor analysis, cluster analysis does not place a great many demands upon the researcher and it is accessible to a wider range of data types. Like factor analysis it relies upon the relationships between the objects to describe the underlying structure. However, factor analysis is a variance partitioning method which means that the measure of intervari-able relationship must be a measure of covariance or correlation. Cluster analysis, in contrast, can start from any symmetrical measure of associa-tion. This means that it may be carried out using data which do not allow the use of product-moment correlations. For example, Kendall's tau ($\tau$) or Goodman-Kruskal's gamma ($\gamma$) for ordinal variables may be used and if skewed dichotomies exist non-parametric association coefficients such as Jaccard's index or Yule's $Q$. More commonly, cluster analysis uses the simple euclidean distance coefficient.

As an example of a hierarchical cluster analysis we will use the data already used in the factor analysis above. A summary of the results is presented in Figure 24.11. This figure presents a dendogram showing the hierarchical structure of the 20 environmental concerns. It is clear immediately that there are three distinct clusters that appear to overlap well with the factor solution of Figure 24.10.

As with factor analysis, cluster analysis presents the user with the problem of specifying the number of clusters to use in describing the data structure. Again, the best way to address this problem is to develop a

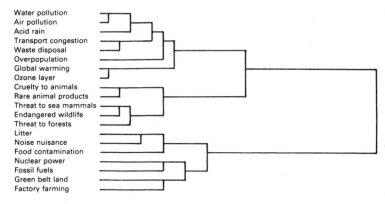

Figure 24.11  *Hierarchical cluster analysis dendogram of*
*20 pro-environmental behaviours*

sound theoretical justification for the solution chosen. A number of less subjective methods have been developed but, as with factor analysis, these operate outside the substantive context of the research. One strategy that I have employed with some success is to generate a series of cluster solutions using different methods of clustering. The solution which shows the most agreement across methods is the solution that may have greatest reliability. However, this procedure still requires that the researcher has some idea of the upper and lower bound for numbers of clusters.

Another problem with cluster analysis is the interpretation of the clusters. This is particularly a problem when people rather than variables have been clustered because we do not necessarily have a simple label we can apply to each person in our sample as we do for the variables.

A common strategy in identifying clusters of people is to carry out a non-hierarchical partitioning cluster analysis and then to treat the cluster membership as a criterion variable in a subsequent discriminant function analysis. In this way each cluster may be defined by the composite functions that discriminate them. When clustering people in this way the usual focus of the study is to identify some kind of typology and this is perhaps the simplest way of distinguishing between factor analysis and cluster analysis. Factor analysis assumes an underlying trait model while cluster analysis assumes a simple type model.

### 24.4.3  Multidimensional scaling

We now move on briefly to describe another method that offers yet another way of examining data structures. Parametric methods for multi-dimensional scaling (MDS) grew originally out of early work on factor analysis. However, in the 1960s and 1970s a series of non-parametric methods became available and it is these so called non-metric methods that we commonly refer to when using the term MDS.

The basic idea of MDS is to represent data spatially by plotting variables as points in $n$-dimensional space. The distance between the points represents the similarity of the variables. Thus, if variable $X$ is highly correlated with variable $Y$ then these two variables will be situated close together on the plot. The advantage of MDS is that the structure of the data can be examined in a number of ways. For example, we can examine the regionality of the space by identifying regions occupied by a particular group of variables. Alternatively, we can examine the shape of the plot for example, do the variables arrange themselves in a straight line or a circle?

Non-metric MDS has very few assumptions and is appropriate for most forms of data (Chapter 17 describes a variation of this method for use with qualitative data). Because MDS solutions may be interpreted very broadly it makes them an ideal choice when carrying out entirely exploratory work. They are particularly effective for theory building since the method does not tend to impose a model on the data that may influence the interpretation as the linear factor model does. However, this may also be seen as a problem because it means that interpreting MDS solutions is often a somewhat arbitrary and subjective affair. As we have stated above there is no replacement for some kind of a priori expectation in interpreting structure, but when these expectations do not include underlying linear traits or discrete groupings, MDS is a useful method. The combination of facet theory (see Chapter 9) and MDS is a very potent research strategy since it merges the strict conceptualisation of the research topic with a flexible and open-ended data analytic technique.

In order to demonstrate an MDS analysis the same environmental concern data were used. A two-dimensional plot is reported in Figure 24.12. In this plot we can see the three regions of global, local and wildlife concern emerging. It is also worth noting the almost circular structure that emerges.

Apart from the necessary subjectivity in interpretation MDS has a problem in common with factor analysis and cluster analysis, that of choosing the number of dimensions to present the data in. It should be apparent that the maximum dimensionality we can expect will be one less than the number of variables. Thus, two variables only need one dimension (a straight line) to represent them (see Figure 24.13(a)), while three variables only need two dimensions (see Figure 24.13(b)) although they can be represented in less (see Figure 24.13(c)).

When we have 20 variables the maximum dimensionality is 19. However, it would be impossible for most researchers to conceptualise a 19-dimensional space. Even the most able of researchers cannot think in terms of more than four dimensions and even that is not simple. Three dimensions is about all any of us can hold in our heads spatially. This means that MDS, in order to be readily interpreted must squash the variables down into, at most, four dimensions. This 'squashing' results in pressure as our recalcitrant variables want to express their true dimensionality and push against the constraints imposed by the MDS. This pressure is

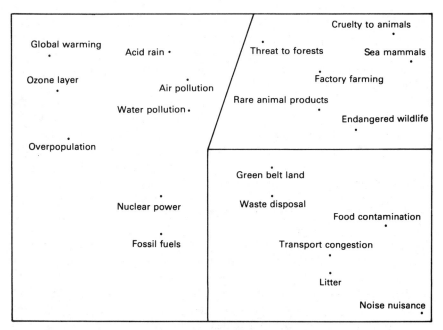

Figure 24.12 *Multidimensional scaling analysis of 20 environmental concerns*

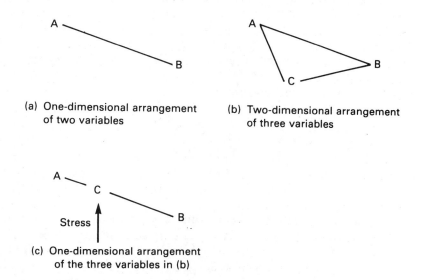

Figure 24.13 *The dimensionality of three variables*

measured by an index known variously as the **stress** or **alienation** coefficient. This ranges between 0 and 1 and the smaller this coefficient is the less pressure and the better the data fit the MDS solution. Unfortunately, there is no hard and fast rule which says what is a 'good' stress measure. In our example the stress was 0.15 which would normally be considered reasonable for 20 items. Advice on the size of the stress ranges widely from the very strict (Kruskal, 1964) to the more laissez-faire (Shye, 1988).

The only advice I can give here is to suggest that interpretability is the first and most important criteria. Clearly, if you find you can interpret a solution but the stress is very high, say 0.60, then you will need to question the tenets of your interpretation since the data do not appear to fit very well.

### 24.4.4 The myth of confirmatory methods

So far we have been concerned to describe three methods for exploring the underlying structure of your data. It should be clear that, despite the use of the term 'exploratory' the effective use of these methods requires that the researcher has some theoretical expectations of what they might find. Indeed, carrying out a factor analysis without understanding that the result will suggest underlying linear structure would be a waste of time and may result in the researcher thinking that they have discovered something that they themselves imposed on the solution. Nevertheless, these methods may still be used in an exploratory way since the researcher may not have a formalised set of hypotheses but rather a number of broad expectations.

There now exists an increasing interest in approaches claiming to be confirmatory as opposed to exploratory. Essentially, what this means is that the researcher is asked to generate a formal model of the relationships between the variables. This model is then tested for fit to the empirical data resulting in a statistic evaluating the degree of misfit to the model. This statistic is usually a chi-squared one. The most useful of these approaches grew out of factor analysis and came to be called variously linear structural relations analysis or covariance structure analysis. A number of computer programs now exist for carrying out these analyses (LISREL, COSAN, EQS). It should be mentioned that a number of 'confirmatory' methods have also grown out of MDS, but it is the factor analytic methods that have seen the most widespread use.

The most immediate limitation with these methods is that they are generally built around a strict linear (or at least polynomial) model. This means that if we wanted to test the hypothesis of a circumplex model of our data (meaning that the variables form a circle in an MDS plot) we would have to represent it formally in linear form. The second limitation is that the statistics which supposedly tell us whether the data fit the model are severely problematic and are sample size dependent. This suggests that a large sample size will almost inevitably produce an inflated chi-squared statistic which means that the data do not fit the model. A number of coefficients for fit which do not have this drawback have been proposed but they generally do not allow statistical inference to be made so they take on the status of the stress coefficient in MDS.

A third and altogether more important limitation with these methods is that although they are termed confirmatory methods, they confirm nothing. Simply finding that the data do not contradict a model does not confirm that model. Note that these methods work by constraining the freedom of the data parameters to emerge in a way that contradicts the model. Remember too, that for each model there are a large number of competing models that may fit the data as well or better. Typically, these models are not tested. This coupled with the weakness of the 'confirmatory' statistics does not support the extravagant claims that are sometimes made about the use of these methods.

I do not wish to appear to be advising against the use of these methods since they can be extremely useful in the appropriate context. I have found them especially useful when examining measurement models. However, a better term to describe such methods is as 'restricted' rather than 'confirmatory'. This is because the data are constrained to fit, as best as possible, the model in question. Once this terminological problem is resolved we can get back to the basic issue in the multivariate analysis of intervariable relationships. This is to apply a method which is appropriate to the nature of the research question and is justifiable for the data being analysed. Certainly, in many cases a restricted analysis is appropriate. Confirmation, on the other hand, comes with replication and the cumulation of research findings (see Chapter 2).

# 24.5 The special case of nominal data

So far we have been concentrating our description on variables derived from continuous measures. However, psychological researchers commonly have to deal with categorical data. Increasingly, with the growth of the content analysis of qualitative data there is a demand for multivariate procedures for handling categorical measures.

Traditionally, group differences with categorical variables have been analysed by chi-squared methods. In fact, these methods can be readily generalised to the multivariate situation as long as there are not too many variables. The result is a nominal equivalent of the ANOVA termed **interaction structure analysis** (ISA) which derives from the partitioned chi-squared model of Lancaster (1969). However, there is very little about the technique in the literature and very few computer programs exist to help the researcher. Interested readers are referred to Lautsch and von Weber (1990) or von Eye (1990).

A more common strategy is to apply the more general **loglinear methods**. These methods allow the researcher to test differences between groups analogously to ANOVA and also to test predictive models analogous to regression models. A treatment of loglinear methods is beyond the scope of this chapter and the interested reader is referred to Everitt (1977).

When the research question involves the examination of underlying structure special methods exist for categorical variables. However, these techniques are not widely available on computer packages as yet. One useful technique is known variously as **correspondence analysis** or **optimal scaling**. This is essentially a **principal component analysis** (similar to factor analysis) of categorical data but it produces a graphical output much like MDS. In addition to exploring structure it may also be used as a form of discriminant analysis for categorical data. Interested readers should consult Greenacre (1984) or Weller and Romney (1990) or Gifi (1990) for a more comprehensive mathematical account. The MDS methods described in Wilson's chapter are based on a similar mathematical premise as correspondence analysis.

A number of methods also exist for examining typologies of respondents measured on categorical variables. The interested reader should look up references to **latent trait analysis** (Clogg and Stockley, 1988) and **Configural Frequency Analysis** (von Eye, 1990).

## 24.6  Conclusion

None of the methods reported here are typically carried out by hand with the exception of the ANOVAs, although even these are rarely carried out without the use of a computer. The use of computer programs for data analysis has liberated researchers from the toil of data analysis and so, presumably, generated more time for thought and consideration of the research process. Unfortunately, the other side of this coin is that researchers have been provided with a host of very sophisticated methods for analysis of their data and there is a temptation to throw the data into the computer in the vague hope that the analysis will tell us something. There is certainly emerging a class of research in which the researcher has taken very little time to understand the basic principles and logic of the methods used. Such work is increasingly managing to emerge in the research literature despite the best efforts of journal reviewers and its presence, at best, fails to add much to the body of psychological knowledge and at worst, sets a precedent for the rest of us to misuse the powerful and often mathematically complex techniques that are increasingly available to us.

This chapter is certainly neither sufficiently comprehensive nor sufficiently detailed to convey the full range and limitation of multivariate data analytic methods. The purpose here has been to give the new researcher some feel for the basic classes of methods that exist. It is fervently hoped that student researchers will seek out more detailed and critical sources before embarking on their analysis. I finish on a plea that if you are considering a multivariate analysis you will make the acquaintance of the method, its logic, its assumptions, its controversies and its theoretical underpinnings. The unquestioning use of user-friendly computer programs with their host of default options is becoming a significant source of suboptimality in psychological research.

## 24.7 Further reading

An excellent introduction to multivariate data analysis is to be found in Hair et al.'s (1992) *Multivariate Data Analysis*. This provides detailed examples of a number of the most commonly used techniques. Another very useful reference book is Nesselroade and Cattell's (1988) *Handbook of Multivariate Experimental Psychology*. This is now in its second edition and provides a series of review chapters by different authors on a variety of data analytic methods. If the reader is looking for a reasonably accessible introduction to the statistical background to the methods discussed here, then Marascuilo and Levin's (1982) *Multivariate Statistics in the Social Sciences* is a good starting point.

# 25 Meta-analysis

*Peter Wood*

## Contents

## 25.1 Literature reviews as 'meta-analysis'

Take one step forward all those people who have ever had to write a research report, a thesis or a dissertation. Few people who have studied or worked in the behavioural sciences will be left unmoved by such an order. Conducting and writing-up research is considered by all educationalists to provide training in numerous valuable skills which go far beyond the exercise itself.

So we have all done it – so what? Well you may be surprised to learn that if you have 'done it', then you've also conducted a 'meta-analysis'. In its most general sense, meta-analysis is no-more-nor-less than the business of describing, synthesising and analysing research findings in a particular field. So, that second chapter of your dissertation, which was probably headed 'previous research' or 'literature review', and which involved you spending hours in the library and wading through all those expensive photocopies was a meta-analysis.

## 25.2 Objectives of reviewing research

When you've stopped congratulating yourself for something you did not know you had done, let us ask ourselves a simple question – why did you do a literature review? Well, leaving aside the trite answer ('because my supervisor told me to'), the reasons which spring to mind include the following:

1 To ensure that your chosen research problem is clearly defined and set within an established context.
2 To examine what researchers have previously found about the chosen topic.
3 To try to draw some broad, overall conclusions from previous research.
4 To derive a theoretical stance, either based upon earlier findings or on the current most successful theory.

None of these activities is easy. Although databases have made access to references wonderfully simple, the choice of keywords and search strategy have become crucial. Thoughtless use of either can lead to the novice researcher deciding to pursue a different career. (Use 'stress' as a keyword in PsycLit and it will come up with more than 27,000 references!)

Let us suppose we do not have the problem of too many references, but that our chosen topic has generated a 'reasonable' number. What a reasonable number is will depend mainly on how narrowly we have defined our topic and also upon the context. An undergraduate dissertation for example would be expected to look at the major papers in the area, whereas a Ph.D. thesis would attempt a comprehensive review. There is no answer to the unspoken question 'How few papers can I use in my literature review?'

## 25.3 Difficulties inherent in reviewing

There is no getting away from the fact that if you are going to achieve any of the goals set out in section 25.2, you are actually going to have to *read* all this previous research. We are all prone to that sense of glowing achievement that stems from successfully photocopying a core article, brought on no doubt by the belief that by some magical process of osmosis, the very act of photocopying has imparted knowledge of the contents. No, that will not do – we have to read and inwardly digest what researchers have done. We have to know which variables have been used, how they have been defined, which measures were employed, the context of the research, the sample used, the method of analysis.

The reason we must go through this procedure is that all of these things (and others not mentioned) may have a profound effect on the findings and conclusions. In this respect the social and behavioural sciences stand in contrast to the physical sciences, where in many cases research is based upon standardised techniques and measures conducted on well-established samples under controlled conditions.

If the object of a literature review were merely to describe research which had previously been conducted, then the process we have described so far sounds fairly straightforward. This is hard work, but not intrinsically difficult. Description, however, is not what it is all about. Our goal is to synthesise, to draw together results from disparate sources, to interpret their findings and to integrate them into broad conclusions. This is where it all gets a bit tricky, for even a cursory review of literature in a given field will often find it littered with contrasting and contradictory findings. Explanations for differing results may seem equally reasonable and the theoretical implications drawn may appear equally attractive. In such circumstances, how can we go about integration? – draw general conclusions? The strategy adopted by many researchers is simply to side-step the issue and conduct a 'pseudo-synthesis'. Such reviews are peppered with such phrases as 'in contrast, Strabismus and Myopia (1982) found', or 'on the other hand Toast-Rack (1976) concluded that', or 'contrast this result with Probocis et al. (1989)'. Such reviews, while not valueless, are really little better than annotated bibliographies.

If this approach exemplifies the 'could-do-better' end of the scale, what does a 'proper' reviewer do that is different? Perhaps the most important thing is to offer *reasons* why findings may differ, and to suggest research which may help *resolve* such differences. They will also identify why some research findings are more significant (in the non-statistical sense) than others and which ones make important theoretical contributions. It will be readily appreciated that reviews of this type are immensely valuable, not only in saving time and effort for less gifted researchers, but also in summarising the current state of knowledge, and stimulating fresh directions for research. It will also be appreciated why not everyone is good at this exercise. Synthesis and integration of this nature demands the highest levels of cognitive ability. You will find literature reviews which achieve these standards appear in prestigious journals across the psychological literature.

Even the best literature reviews as just described are not above criticism, however. Inevitably the interpretation of findings, the insights derived, the manner in which conclusions are drawn, are all dependent on the judgements of a single individual, the reviewer (or at best a small group of reviewers). In other words, such opinions fall squarely into the category of **subjective judgements**. If we disagree with a viewpoint, we may quite validly say – 'my (subjective) opinion is as good as their (subjective) opinion'. It is of no help to counter this statement with the indisputable fact that many major literature reviews are published by researchers who are exceedingly eminent in their field. Sadly, the history of science teaches that these individuals are no less prone to bias, selective inclusion of evidence, and misinterpretation of research findings. Indeed, since most eminent researchers often have a long-standing association with a particular theoretical standpoint, or line of research, it could be argued that they will have to work *harder* to maintain a suitably unbiased view. The foregoing is not intended, in any sense, to question the academic standards of any literature reviewer, but merely to illustrate the fact that even the best literature reviews are *subjective*.

## 25.4 Quantifying the review process

So far we have talked exclusively about literature reviews in their most familiar form. We have discussed their aims, their value and their disadvantages. Because of this, the reader may be assuming that 'literature review' and 'meta-analysis' are the same thing. This is not the case. What we have described up to this point should more accurately be called **narrative literature reviews** and these form only one of a range of meta-analysis techniques. All the alternative meta-analysis techniques have been developed in an attempt to bring the same standards of scientific rigour to the literature review as exist for individual studies (Wolf, 1986). In other words, to move away from the possible biases and subjectivity which are acknowledged to be present in narrative reviews. Guzzo et al. (1987) suggest that we may think of meta-analysis techniques as being on a **continuum of quantification**. At one end (least quantified) rests the narrative review in the form already discussed. Moving along the scale we may conduct what is often called a 'box score' review. To do this one constructs a table in which counts are made, based upon the frequency with which studies in the research literature support (or refute) a particular finding.

Yet further along our scale we could include techniques for combining and cumulating significance levels reported in individual studies. Using these methods it is possible to estimate the probability associated with research findings (Guzzo et al., 1987)

At the 'most quantified' end of the continuum are a group of statistical techniques which have, over the last 15 or so years, become known by general usage as **meta-analysis**. It is these techniques which we will concentrate on for the remainder of this chapter.

## 25.5   The rationale of meta-analysis

That meta-analysis has become associated with one particular set of techniques is largely due to a seminal paper by Glass (1976). In this, he categorised three levels of analysis:

1   Primary analysis: the original analysis of the data from a research study.
2   Secondary analysis: the re-analysis of original data from a research study using different statistical techniques, perhaps to examine alternative questions or explanations.
3   Meta-analysis: the statistical analysis of results from a large number of individual research studies so as to integrate their findings.

The word statistical is important here. It is Glass's position that 'The findings of multiple studies should be regarded as a complex data-set, no more comprehensible without statistical analysis than would be hundreds of data points in a single study' (Glass et al., 1981:12). So each *study* in a meta-analysis is equivalent to a *subject* in a primary analysis. The requirement for statistical meta-analysis techniques was in response to the perceived subjective nature of traditional narrative reviews. An additional consideration was the very large number of studies which have been conducted. Hunter et al. (1982) suggest that 'In many areas of research the need today is not additional empirical data but some means of making sense of the vast amounts of data that have accumulated' (1982:27). Not only were statistical meta-analysis techniques seen as offering a more objective means of integrating the findings of previous research, but in doing this they move literature reviews closer to the standards of scientific enquiry and repeatability which are applied to the individual study.

More specifically, meta-analysis is thought to address a number of particular problems to which narrative reviews are prone:

1   It is suggested that narrative reviews are often not comprehensive. There is a danger that a reviewer may, for a variety of reasons, only include a subset of studies in the review.
2   There is a tendency in narrative reviews to concentrate on whether particular hypotheses are supported by significance tests in each individual study. In so doing, such reviews overestimate the accuracy and importance of significance tests on small samples, and underestimate the importance of the *size* of any effect.
3   We have already noted that there are many conflicting results in psychology. Narrative reviews have great difficulty in dealing with these differences. Elaborate explanatory frameworks may have to be constructed to synthesise such results. Meta-analysis suggests that in the majority of cases the results of primary research studies are distorted by many artefacts (Hunter and Hirsh, 1987). It is failure to take these errors into consideration which leads to the wide discrepancy in findings within a given topic area.

4  Because the procedures for integrating research findings have not been agreed or made explicit, the conclusions from narrative reviews may be difficult to replicate.

## 25.6  General principles underlying the statistical procedure

Meta-analysis incorporates a wide variety of statistical techniques which vary in complexity. All, however, follow similar principles and offer a quantitative method of cumulating research findings. Having first collected the relevant studies, the findings of each analysis are then treated so that they may be expressed as a common statistic. It thus becomes possible to examine this statistic across the range of studies. In the most commonly used meta-analytic techniques, the common metric selected is an **effect-size** measure, in other words an index of how important or powerful the relationship between the variables is. In addition to using a common metric, the most frequently used meta-analytic techniques use further statistical treatments so as to correct for major artefacts which will include sampling error, error of measurement and range restriction.

At this point it is worthwhile describing the procedures involved in meta-analysis. The best known are those by Glass et al. (1981) and Hunter and Schmidt (Hunter et al., 1982). Both are presented below.

The stages involved in Glass's procedure are as follows.

1  Select the independent and dependent variables of interest.
2  Identify, locate and obtain all relevant and usable studies containing information of interest.
3  Code each study for characteristics which might be a predictor of study outcomes, that is, might relate to the size of effects obtained. Typically these might include differences in subject's age, sex, length of treatment, etc.
4  Calculate estimates of the effect-size for the variable pairs (independent–dependent) of interest. (Glass (1977) has derived formulae for converting statistics used in primary analysis to a common effect-size metric.)
5  Calculate the mean and standard deviation of effect-size across studies.
6  Examine those study characteristics identified in (3) above, which correlate with study effects.

Hunter and Schmidt's method may be regarded as an extension of Glass's in that it incorporates steps to correct for study artefacts. The first four stages are essentially the same and are not repeated.

5  Calculate the mean effect-size across studies. The effect-size for each study is then weighted by its sample size.

6   Calculate the variance of effect-size.
7   Determine the extent to which differences in variance of effect-size are due to sampling errors, errors of measurement and range restriction.
8   If a large percentage of the variance across studies can be attributed to the artefacts above, it is concluded that the average effect-size is an accurate estimate of the relationship between the variables.
9   If, on the other hand, a large proportion of the variance is unaccounted for, then study characteristics are examined to determine their correlation with effect-size (as with Glass's procedure).

It will be noted that the procedures are similar in terms of the emphasis they place on the importance of effect-size, but differ in relation to correcting for study artefacts. In fact the central importance of these corrections to the Hunter and Schmidt method would lead them to recommend not undertaking stage (3) (coding for study characteristics) *before* estimating the proportion of variance attributable to the artefacts. The procedures described are of course a simplification, and the reader should consult Hunter et al. (1982) for a full description.

Although the methods outlined are not in themselves intrinsically difficult, the reader may be unfamiliar with the manipulations at some of the stages.

## 25.7   Significance levels, effect-size and common metrics

Hypothesis testing by assessing significance levels is one of the most familiar procedures in primary analysis of psychological data. Having decided a priori upon the acceptable level, calculated the appropriate statistic, and consulted the relevant table, the significance level associated with the particular result can be reported. If our test statistic reaches or exceeds our set level then 'a significant relationship' can be reported; if not then we must accept the null hypothesis. It is clearly important to know whether or not any difference we may discover, between say control and experimental groups, could have arisen by chance. However, it has been appreciated for many years that significance level alone is an inadequate study outcome. This is particularly true in areas of applied psychology, where the findings of research studies may have policy implications. So, for example in human factors, it is insufficient to know that workstation A is 'significantly better' than workstation B at the 5 per cent level, or in personnel psychology that selection method 1 is significantly better than selection method 2, or in clinical psychology that two treatments provide significantly different outcomes. In such settings what may be of more importance is the *magnitude* of the effect between the two. It is not difficult to see why this should be so. In the real world resources are always finite. Policy decisions must be made on the basis of utilitarian and efficiency considerations. Clearly a Rolls-Royce might be assessed as 'a significantly better' car than a Mini, but if our purchasing decision is based on rational considerations, the important factor is 'how much better?' If the purchase-price ratio is 20 to 1, is it 20 times better? Clearly the effect-size, that is, magnitude of the difference, assumes considerable importance in policy situations.

While effect-size is universally used in meta-analysis, there is some general debate concerning whether effect-size or significance level is the more meaningful (Chow, 1988). However, as Mullen (1993) points out, the two aspects are mutually dependent. Any significance level can be expressed as a function of effect-size, and vice versa. The relationship is illustrated below:

$$\text{Significance level} = \text{Effect-size} \times \text{Sample size}$$

$$\text{Effect-size} = \text{Significance level/sample size}$$

Clearly, if we are intending to compare findings across many studies, which will inevitably report different statistics, we need a 'common currency' as the basis for calculation.

Different meta-analysis techniques may utilise different common metrics. Glass et al. (1981) calculate an effect-size statistic $d$ where

$$d = \frac{(\text{Mean of expt. group} - \text{Mean of control group})}{\text{Standard deviation of control group}}$$

Robust strategies for estimating means and standard deviations may need to be applied in certain circumstances. These might involve the 'Jacknife' (Miller, 1974), the 'Bootstrap' (Efron, 1979) or subsampling procedures (Hartington, 1969). Hunter and Schmidt, on the other hand, consistently use the Pearson Product Moment Correlation, $r$, as the expression of effect-size. Alternatively some researchers suggest the use of Fisher's $Z$ as a measure of effect-size (Mullen, 1993).

Wolf (1986) provides useful tables of formulae for converting the most common test statistics, $t$, $F$, $X$ to $r$ and $d$. Care must be exercised when making such conversions to include only those test statistics which compare pairs of variables, that is, only for comparing two group means, or statistics with one degree of freedom.

## 25.8 The effect of study artefacts

Hunter and Schmidt's meta-analytic procedures are firmly rooted in the conceptual approach that unaccounted for errors in individual research studies are the underlying reason for the many conflicting results in psychology. Their analysis procedures correct for three major sources of error, sampling error, measurement error and range restriction, although they have identified nine artefacts which may distort study findings (Hunter and Hirsh, 1987).

Sampling error is present in all studies, although the larger the sample the less the error. It arises because the sample sizes used in individual research studies are small in relation to the population. This is particularly true in psychological research, where sample sizes are most often in the range 50–500. When we average effect-size measures (correlations) in a meta-analysis, we also average sampling errors. Thus if we cumulate 40 studies each with a sample of 100, then the averaged correlation will have sampling error as if our sample had been 4000.

Correcting for the variance in our cumulated effect-size measure is a little more complex. In calculating variance we must first calculate deviation scores. Some will be positive and some negative. Squaring the deviations to calculate variance eliminates the sign, and therefore stops errors from cancelling themselves out. The effect of this is, of course, to increase the magnitude of the variance (since negative deviations will not be represented). So in cumulating across studies we will produce a variance which is greater than the 'true' variance for our cumulated sample. Hunter and Schmidt, however, point out that this is a systematic change, and the effect of sampling error on variance is to add a known constant, which they call the 'sampling error variance'. This constant can be subtracted from the observed variance, and the difference is then an estimate of the required variance of the effect-size measure for the cumulated sample.

As with sampling error, measurement error is endemic in psychological research. Many psychological constructs may be measured in a variety of ways. For any given subject, measurement error is randomly distributed. Our observed score will be made up of the 'true' score plus error:

$$\text{Observed score} = \text{True score} + \text{error}$$

Error can of course be a negative value, so for an observed score of 100, error might be plus or minus one yielding a true score of 99 or 101. The true score is unknowable. When we correlate scores across subjects, the previously random effects of measurement error have a systematic effect, in that they cause the correlation to be lower than it would have been if we could correlate 'true' scores. By utilising the reliability for each measure, Hunter and Schmidt have developed a formula **for correction of attenuation**, that is, correcting for error of measurement.

Similarly with **range restriction**, that is where the range of values presented on the independent variable varies between studies, this will also affect correlations produced. Given that one has the standard deviation of the independent variable, Hunter and Schmidt use a range correction formula to project all correlations to the same reference standard deviation.

Of necessity the above explanations are considerably oversimplified and many aspects have been omitted. The reader is referred to Hunter et al. (1982) for a full description of the rationale and methods used.

While providing a simple description of these artefacts we have not yet answered the question posed in the heading to this section. Hunter et al.

observe that 'In many [meta-analysis] studies we have found no variance in results across studies once artefacts such as sampling error have been eliminated' (1982:164). Over a series of 152 meta-analyses, the average amount of variance accounted for by the three statistical artefacts discussed above was 72 per cent.

## 25.9 Some criticisms of the procedure

This chapter began by discussing narrative reviews and the criticisms which may be levelled at them. The statistical methods of meta-analysis which have been described clearly offer an alternative, quantitative method of achieving the same objectives. We may validly ask whether this new methodology answers the criticisms or, indeed, has problems of its own.

Since all such reviews begin by definition with the research literature, this is a good place to start. The first stage is to define 'the relationship of interest'. Guzzo et al. (1987) have pointed out that while narrative reviews may be open to accusations of reviewer bias, meta-analytic procedures may fare no better. While meta-analysis emphasises that *all* studies relevant to a particular topic should be included, this leaves unspecified how to define the boundaries of this domain. Decisions about which studies to include are what Guzzo et al. label 'Judgement Calls', that is, subjective. The requirement to include all studies has certainly led to some earlier meta-analyses being criticised for lack of focus, and the charge that 'apples were being counted with oranges' (Eysenck, 1978). More recently emphasis has shifted to a more careful definition of the relationship to be tested. It is unlikely that such boundary questions are capable of satisfactory resolution. However, reviews of *all types* should include an explicit definition of the criteria on which studies have been selected.

Meta-analysis, of course, concerns itself with studies reported in the research literature. However, it is widely acknowledged that published work represents only a proportion of the research studies which are conducted; many potentially useful studies never get published and remain stored in people's offices. This problem is often referred to as the **file-drawer problem**. Does this matter? It has, in the past, been argued that journal reviewers are not only more likely to favour research which is methodologically sound, but also studies which show significant results. Rosenthal (1979) has attempted to address this problem by deriving formulae for assessing how many non-significant studies you would need to find in order to show that there was actually no relationship between the variables. Hunter et al. (1982) suggest that any difference in findings between unpublished and published research is mainly due to differences in methodological quality.

Considerable debate has surrounded the issue that, even within the domain of published research, not all studies will be methodologically sound. The question arises as to how methodologically flawed research should be treated. It has been argued that narrative reviewers, on detecting weak studies may tend to exclude them, while meta-analysis, with its injunction to include all studies may include them. Hunter et al. suggest caution in deciding whether or not to exclude studies, since it is impossible to know when such flaws may lead to biased findings. Others adopt the view 'Garbage in . . . Garbage out' (Eysenck, 1978). The issue is not resolved.

A category of studies which will be completely excluded by meta-analysis are those which have collected qualitative research data. The nature of meta-analysis demands that research findings be expressed in terms of a quantitative statistic, which can thus be converted into an effect-size estimate. This is probably not a serious restriction since the areas of psychology where meta-analysis has had most impact, particularly organisational psychology, are primarily based on quantitative measures. In other areas of psychology where a mix of quantitative and qualitative measures are used, this may prove a more fundamental limitation, since meta-analysis could only be applied to a restricted, non-representative, subset of studies.

It must be clear from the procedures outlined in section 25.6, that the techniques used in meta-analysis demand the presence of particular descriptive statistics in the reported results of each individual study. In a perfect world this would, of course, be the case. However, in the real world of research literature it is far from true. While higher standards of result-reporting may in future be insisted on, it is an unfortunate fact that much research conducted prior to 1976 does not report appropriate statistics. This means that even quantitative studies of this type will be excluded from the analysis. Guzzo et al. (1985) and Stone (1986) both report having to exclude some 50 per cent of studies in a meta-analysis for this reason. In some cases it may be possible to make estimates of the required statistic based upon those results which are reported. However, this cannot be regarded as a defensible procedure.

While correction for artefacts, as proposed by Hunter et al., may be impossible, the majority of primary analyses will provide a statistic from which an effect-size estimate may be calculated. There is, however, no agreed procedure as to how this should be done, although the range of methods appear conceptually similar. One potentially more serious problem which can arise is how to calculate effect-size in a research study which produces multiple results (longitudinal data for example). The formulae used for cumulation assume that values are statistically independent. Hunter et al. discuss this application and suggest ways of dealing with it. However, their explanations go beyond the scope of this chapter.

Some critics have suggested that meta-analysis produces a spurious simplification of results by its concentration on overall effects, at the expense of possible interaction or mediating variables. It is, of course, a fundamental precept of the Hunter et al. method that such interaction effects should only be explored once statistical artefacts have been corrected. In contrast, Glass's method prescribes utilising pre-coded characteristics once mean effect-size has been calculated. The problem remains, however, that decisions must be made as to which characteristics should be coded – that is, which might reasonably be considered as possible interaction variables. Yet another 'Judgement Call' arises here, since by coding for very large numbers of possible interaction variables and exhaustively testing against each one, we naturally increase the likelihood of throwing up interaction effects which have occurred by chance. On the other hand, the perhaps more defensible approach of using relevant theory and specific hypotheses as a means of selection, while minimising the chance of Type I errors (false positives) is also less likely to uncover new and unsuspected relationships. This difficulty is not restricted to meta-analysis however.

## 25.10  Conclusion

This chapter has given a brief, and perforce simplified overview of the place of meta-analysis in psychological research. The stance is adopted that meta-analysis is a generic term for all types of formal research literature review. Over recent years, the term 'meta-analysis' has come to be used as a shorthand for the statistical meta-analysis techniques which have been described here. Terminological confusion is not eased by the fact that Hunter and Schmidt's methods were originally labelled, **validity generalisation**, which is now considered to be a special application of meta-analysis.

As a conceptual approach and set of statistical techniques, meta-analysis has had a meteoric rise in popularity since 1976. A large range of psychological journals now publish articles based on such analyses. A comprehensive bibliography would run to many pages.

It is probably sensible to group our concluding remarks under a number of points.

1   There is still a place for narrative reviews of the psychological literature. Although quantitative meta-analyses call for a comprehensive inclusion of research studies, the number of studies which 'include themselves out' (to misquote Cecil B. de Mille) because they do not report suitable statistics, or because they provide qualitative data, means that for some topics meta-analysis would be operating on only a restricted subsample of research findings.
2   Meta-analysis is an important and powerful technique when properly applied which may have a far-reaching impact in psychology. In applied fields of psychology, education, clinical, organisational, validity-generalisation results may come to have important policy implications.

3   Many of the early criticisms of meta-analysis were based on misconceptions of how it worked. For an informative and interesting debate on many of the issues the reader should consult Schmidt, Sackett et al. (1985).

4   While adopting quantitative statistical methods for reviewing research literature, meta-analysis is not devoid of 'Judgement Calls', that is, steps where subjective judgement is required.

5   Although it is early days, meta-analysis may have more utility in synthesising research findings and identifying gaps in knowledge, than in theory generating and testing.

6   Quantifying the previously unquantified can confer a spurious validity in the mind of the reader. This is not a criticism of meta-analysis but a general comment on the bias many people have when confronted by numbers (Strube and Hartman, 1982). When new statistical techniques are developed we must learn to be 'consumers' of them.

7   This chapter was written and based on a (non-quantitative) review of the literature.

Finally the most apposite comment would seem to be that by Green and Hall (1984:52) : 'Data analysis is an aid to thought, not a substitute'.

## 25.11   Project

Conducting a full meta-analysis goes beyond the scope of what might be expected for students of this book. However, it is well worthwhile attempting two of the initial stages of such a study. These are:

1   Defining the relationship or hypothesis to be tested. Select two variables which you know to have been of interest to psychologists. An example might be the effect of goals upon performance. Now answer the following questions:
    (a)   Which hypotheses have been tested?
    (b)   How have the dependent and independent variables been operationalised?

2   Conduct a literature search using your selected hypothesis. Examine the variety of statistics which have been employed, the strength or significance of any relationships which have been found. Using a subsample of studies (say about 10), convert the study statistics into a common metric.

## 25.12   Further reading

Three inexpensive books provide a particularly clear exposition of meta-analytic techniques. These are: Wolf (1986) *Meta-analysis: Quantitative*

*Methods for Research Synthesis*, which gives a broad introduction to the range of research synthesising methods and supplies the relevant formulae for all the common procedures. Hunter et al.'s (1982) *Meta-analysis: Cumulating Research Findings Across Studies* introduces the concepts underlying validity generalisation and provide numerous worked examples. Rosenthal's (1991) *Meta-analytic Procedures for Social Research* is a particularly well-balanced account of the advantages and disadvantages of using a variety of research synthesising procedures.

# References

Adorno, T.W., Frenkel-Brunswick, E., Levinson, D.J. and Sanford, R.N. (1950) *The Authoritarian Personality*. New York: Harper and Row.

Aitkenhead, A.M. and Slack, J.M. (1994) *Issues in Cognitive Modelling*. Hillsdale, NJ: Lawrence Erlbaum Associates.

Albrecht, T.L., Johnson, G.M. and Walther, J.B. (1993) 'Understanding communication processes in focus groups', in D.L. Morgan (ed.) *Successful Focus Groups: Advancing the State of the Art*. London: Sage.

Anastasi, A. (1990) *Psychological Testing*. New York: Macmillan.

Anderson, J.A. (1972) 'Separate sample logistic discrimination', *Biometrika*, 59: 19–36.

Andreassi, J.L. (1989) *Psychophysiology: Human Behaviour and Physiological Response* (2nd edn). Hillsdale, NJ: Lawrence Erlbaum Associates.

APA (1992) *APA Ethics Code*. Washington DC: American Psychological Association.

Arber, S. (1993) 'Designing samples' in N. Gilbert (ed.) *Researching Social Life*. London: Sage.

Argyris, C. (1970) *Intervention Theory and Method: A Behavioural Science View*. Reading, MA: Addison Wesley.

Ary, D. (1984) 'Mathematical explanation of error in duration recording using partial interval whole interval, and momentary time sampling', *Behavioral Assessment*, 6: 221–8.

Ashford, P. (1994) *Proenvironmentalism: Identity and the Media*. Unpublished Ph.D. thesis. University of Surrey.

Ashmore, M. (1989) *The Reflexive Thesis: Wrighting Sociology of Scientific Knowledge*. Chicago: University of Chicago Press.

Atkinson, J.W. (1958) *Motives in Fantasy, Action and Society*. New York: Van Nostrand.

Axelrod, R. (ed.) (1976) *Structure of Decision*. Princeton, NJ: Princeton University Press.

Baer, D.M., Wolf, M.M. and Risley, T.R. (1968) 'Some current dimensions of applied behaviour analysis', *Journal of Applied Behaviour Analysis*, 1: 91–7.

Bainbridge, L. (1985) 'Inferring from verbal reports to cognitive processes', in M. Brenner, J. Brown and D. Canter (eds) *The Research Interview: Uses and Approaches*. London: Academic Press.

Bakvis, H. and Nevitte, N. (1987) 'In pursuit of postbourgeois man: postmaterialism and intergenerational change in Canada', *Comparative Political Studies*, 20(3): 357–89.

Bandura, A. and Walters, R.H. (1963) *Social Learning and Personality Development*. New York: Holt.

Banks, M., Bates, I., Breakwell, G., Bynner, J., Emler, N., Jamieson, L. and Roberts, K. (1992) *Careers and Identities*. Milton Keynes: Open University Press.

Bannister, D. and Fransella, F. (1971) *Inquiring Man: The Theory of Personal Constructs*. Harmondsworth: Penguin.

Barlow, D.H. and Hersen, M. (1973) 'Single case experimental designs: uses in applied clinical research', *Archive of General Psychiatry*, 29: 319–25.

Barlow, D.H. and Hersen, M. (1984) *Single Case Experimental Designs*. New York: Pergamon Press.

Barnes, A.E. and Stearns, P.N. (eds) (1989) *Social History and Issues in Human Consciousness: Some Interdisciplinary Connections*. New York: New York University Press.

Basch, C.E. (1987) 'Focus group interview: an underutilized research technique for improving theory and practice in health education', *Health Education Quarterly*, 14(4): 411–48.

Bates, P. (1980) 'The effectiveness of interpersonal skills training on the social acquisition of moderately and mildly retarded adults', *Journal of Applied Behaviour Analysis*, 13: 237–48.

Beattie, G. (1983) *Talk: An Analysis of Speech and Non-Verbal Behaviour in Conversation*. Milton Keynes: Open University Press.

Bellack, A.S. and Hersen, M. (1988) *Behavioral Assessment: A Practical Handbook* (3rd edn). New York: Pergamon Press.

Bellack, A.S., Hersen, M. and Himmeloch, J.M. (1983) 'A comparison of social skills training, pharmacotherapy and psychotherapy for depression', *Behaviour Research and Therapy*, 21: 101–7.

Berelson, B. (1971) *Content Analysis in Communication Research*. New York: Free Press.

Berger, P. L. and Luckmann, T. (1971) *The Social Construction of Reality*. Harmondsworth: Penguin.

Bergin, A.E. and Strupp, H.H. (1972) *Changing Frontiers in the Science of Psychotherapy*. New York: Aldine.

Billig, M. (1988) 'Methodology and scholarship in understanding ideological explanation', in C. Antaki (ed.) *Analysing Everyday Explanation: A Casebook of Methods*. London: Sage.

Birnbaumer, N. and Ohman, A. (eds) (1993) *The Structure of Emotion*. Berlin: Hogrefe and Huber.

Blake, R. and Hiris, E. (1993) 'Another means for measuring the motion aftereffect', *Vision Research*, 33: 1589–92.

Blalock, H.M., Jr. (1988) *Social Statistics* (2nd edn). Singapore: McGraw-Hill.

Blascovich, J. and Kelsey, M. (1990) 'Using electrodermal and cardiovascular measures of arousal in social psychological research', in C. Hendrick and M.S. Clark (eds) *Research Methods in Personality and Social Psychology*, Newbury Park, CA: Sage.

Blashfield, R.K. and Aldenderfer M.S. (1988) 'The methods and problems of cluster analysis', in J.R. Nesselroade and R.B. Cattell (eds) *Handbook of Multivariate Experimental Psychology*. London: Plenum Press.

Blum, G.S. (1949) 'A study of psychoanalytic theory of psychosexual development', *Genetic Psychology Monograph*, 39: 3–99.

Borg, I. (1977) 'Some basic concepts in facet theory', in J.C. Lingoes, E.E. Roskam and I. Borg (eds) *Geometric Representations of Relational Data*. Ann Arbor: Mathesis.

Borg, I. (ed.) (1981) *Multidimensional Data Representations: When and Why*. Ann Arbor: Mathesis.

Bormann, H. (1972) 'Fantasy and rhetorical vision: the rhetorical criticism of social reality', *Quarterly Journal of Speech*, 58: 396–407.

Boulton, M. (ed.) (1994) *Challenge and Innovation: Advances in Social Research on HIV/AIDS*. Brighton: Falmer Press.

BPS (1993) *The BPS Code of Conduct, Ethical Principles and Guidelines*. Leicester: The British Psychological Society.

Breakwell, G. M. (1990) *Interviewing*. London: BPS/Routledge.

Breakwell, G.M. (1993) 'Integrating paradigms', in G.M. Breakwell and D.V. Canter (eds) *Empirical Approaches to Social Representations*. Oxford: Oxford University Press.

Breakwell, G.M. (1994) 'The echo of power: an integrative framework for social psychological theorising', *The Psychologist*, 7(2): 65–72.

Breakwell, G.M. and Canter, D.V. (1993) *Empirical Approaches to Social Representations*. Oxford: Blackwell.

Breakwell, G.M. and Fife-Schaw, C.R. (1992) 'Sexual activities and preferences in a UK sample of 16–20 year olds', *Archives of Sexual Behavior*, 21: 271–93.

Breakwell, G.M. and Fife-Schaw, C.R. (1994) 'Using longitudinal cohort sequential designs to study changes in behaviour', in M. Boulton (ed.) *Challenge and Innovation: Advances in Social Research on HIV/AIDS*. Brighton: Falmer Press.

Brenner, M., Brown, J. and Canter, D.V. (eds) (1985) *The Research Interview: Uses and Approaches*. London: Academic Press.

Brown, J. (1985) 'An introduction to the uses of facet theory', in D.V. Canter (ed.) *Facet Theory: Approaches to Social Research*. New York: Springer-Verlag.

Bryant, P. E. (1990) 'Empirical evidence for causes in development', in G. Butterworth and P.E. Bryant (eds) *Causes of Development*. New York: Harvester Wheatsheaf.

Bryant, P. and Bradley, L. (1985) *Children's Reading Problems*. Oxford: Blackwell

Burawoy, M., Burton, A., Ferguson, A.A., Fox, K., Gamson, J., Gartrell, N., Hurst, L., Kurzman, C., Sabinger, L., Schittme, J. and Shiori, U. (1991) *Ethnography Unbound: Power and Resistance in the Modern Metropolis*. Berkeley, CA: University of California Press.

Burman, E. and Parker, I. (eds) (1993) *Discourse Analytic Research: Repertoires and Readings of Texts in Action*. London: Routledge.

Butcher, B. and Dodd, P. (1983) 'The Electoral Register: Two surveys', *Population Trends*, 31: 15–19.

Cacioppo, J.T. and Tassinary, L.G. (1990) *Principles of Psychophysiology: Physical, Social, and Inferential Elements*. Cambridge: Cambridge University Press.

Campbell, D.E. and Beets, J.L. (1978) 'Lunacy and the Moon', *Psychological Bulletin*, 85: 1123–9.

Campbell, D.T. (1969) 'Reforms as experiments', *American Psychologist*, 24: 409–29.

Campbell, D.T. and Fiske D.W. (1959) 'Convergent and discriminant validation by the multitrait-multimethod matrix', *Psychological Bulletin*, 56: 81–105.

Campbell, D.T. and Stanley, J. (1966) *Experimental and Quasi-Experimental Designs for Research*. Chicago: Rand McNally.

Canter, D.V. (1983a) 'The purposive evaluation of places: a facet approach', *Environment and Behavior*, 15(6): 659–98.

Canter, D.V. (1983b) 'The potential of facet theory for applied social psychology', *Quality and Quantity*, 17: 33–67.

Canter, D.V. (ed.) (1985) *Facet Theory: Approaches to Social Research*. New York: Springer-Verlag.

Canter, D., Brown, J. and Groat, L. (1985) 'A multiple sorting procedure', in M. Brenner, J. Brown, and D.V. Canter (eds) *The Research Interview: Uses and Approaches*. London: Academic Press.

Carlson, J.G., Siefert, A.R. and Birnbaumer, N. (1993) *Clinical Applied Psychophysiology*. London: Plenum Press.

Carr, W. and Kemmis, S. (1986) *Becoming Critical: Education, Knowledge and Action Research*. London: Falmer Press.

Carroll, J.S., Wiener, R.L., Coates, D., Galegher, J. and Alibrio, J.J. (1982) 'Evaluation, diagnosis, and prediction in parole decision making', *Law and Society Review*, 17: 199–228.

Cattell, R.B. (1978) *The Scientific Use of Factor Analysis*. London: Plenum Press.

Cattell, R.B. (1981) *Personality and Learning Theory, Vols I and II*. Berlin: Springer.

Child, D. (1990) *The Essentials of Factor Analysis*. London: Cassell.

Chow, S.L. (1988) 'Significance test or effect size?' *Psychological Bulletin*, 103(l): 105–10.

Christensen, L. B. (1988) *Experimental Methodology* (4th edn). Boston: Allyn and Bacon.

Clocksin, W. (1987) 'A Prolog primer', *BYTE*, 12(9): 147–58.

Clogg, C.C. and Shockey, J.W. (1988) 'Multivariate analysis of discrete data', in J.R. Nesselroade and R.B. Cattell (eds) *Handbook of Multivariate Experimental Psychology*. London: Plenum Press.

Cohen J. (1960) 'A coefficient of agreement for nominal scales', *Educational and Psychological Measurement*, 20: 37–46.

Conway, M.A. (1990) *Autobiographical Memory: An Introduction*. Milton Keynes: Open University Press.

Cook, T.D. and Campbell, D.T. (1979) *Quasi-Experimentation: Design and Analysis Issues for Field Settings*. Chicago: Rand McNally.

Coombs, C. (1983) *Psychology and Mathematics*. Ann Arbor: University of Michigan Press.

Cornsweet, T.N. (1962) 'The staircase-method in psychophysics', *American Journal of Psychology*, 75: 485–91.

Cornsweet, T.N. and Teller, D.Y. (1965) 'Relation of increment thresholds to brightness and luminance', *Journal of the Optical Society of America*, 55: 1303–8.

Coyle, A. (1992)' "My Own Special Creation"? The construction of gay identity', in G.M. Breakwell (ed.) *Social Psychology of Identity and the Self Concept*. London: Surrey University Press.

Craik, K. (1967) *The Nature of Explanation*. Cambridge: Cambridge University Press.

Croft, C.A. and Sorrentino, M.C. (1991) 'Physician interaction with families on issues of AIDS: what parents and youth indicate they desire', *The Journal of Health Behavior, Education and Promotion*, 15(6): 13–22.

Cronbach, L.J. (1951) 'Coefficient alpha and the internal structure of tests', *Psychometrika*, 16: 297–334.

Cronbach, L.J. (1971) 'Test validation', in R.L. Thorndike (ed.) *Educational Measurement*. Washington: ACE.

Cronbach, L.J. (1990) *Essentials of Psychological Testing* (5th edn). New York: Harper & Row

Cronbach, L.J., Gleser G.C., Nanda H. and Rajaratnam, N. (1972) *The Dependability of Behavioral Measurements: Theory of Generalizability for Scores and Profiles*. New York: Wiley.

Crowne, D.P. and Marlowe, D. (1964) *The Approval Motive: Studies in Evaluative Dependence*. New York: Wiley.

Dale, A., Gilbert, G.N. and Arber, S. (1985) 'Integrating women into class theory', *Sociology*, 19: 384–409.

Dancer, L.S. (1990) 'Introduction to facet theory and its applications', *Applied Psychology: An International Review*, 39: 365–77.

Davis, A. M. (1991) 'The language of testing', in K. Durkin and B. Shire (eds) *Language and Mathematical Education*. Milton Keynes: Open University Press.

Davison, M.L. and Sharma, A.R. (1990) 'Parametric statistics and levels of measurement: Factorial designs and multiple regression', *Psychological Bulletin*, 107: 394–400.

Dempster, J. (1993) *Computer Analysis of Electrophysiological Signals*. London: Academic Press.

Dodd, T. (1987) 'A further investigation into the coverage of the postcode address file', *Survey Methodology Bulletin*, 21: 35–40.

Donald, I.J. (1985) 'The cylindrex of place evaluation', in D.V. Canter (ed.) *Facet Theory: Approaches to Social Research*. New York: Springer-Verlag.

Donald, I.J. (1987) 'Place evaluation', in D.V. Canter, D. Stokols and M. Krampen (eds) *Ethnoscapes: Transcultural Studies in Action and Place*. Aldershot: Gower.

Donald, I. (1994) 'The structure of office workers' experience of organizational environments', *Journal of Occupational and Organizational Psychology* (in press).

Dunn, J. (1988) *The Beginnings of Social Understanding*. Oxford: Blackwell.

Dunn, J. and Kendrick, C. (1982) *Siblings: Love, Envy and Understanding*. Cambridge, MA: Harvard University Press.

Edwards, D. and Potter, J. (1992) *Discursive Psychology*. London: Sage.

Edwards, D., Potter, J. and Middleton, D. (1992) 'Toward a discursive psychology of remembering', *The Psychologist*, 5: 441–6.

Efron, B. (1979) 'Bootstrap methods: Another look at the Jacknife', *Annals of Statistics*, 7: 1–26.

Elliot, J. (1991) *Action Research for Educational Change*. Milton Keynes: Open University Press.

Erdberg, P and Exner, J.E. (1984) 'Rorschach assessment', in G. Goldstein and M. Hersen (eds) *Psychological Assessment*. New York: Pergamon Press.

Evans, L. (1986) 'Risk homeostasis theory and traffic accident data', *Risk Analysis*, 6: 81–94.

Evans, R.I., Rozelle, R.M., Mittelmark, M.B., Hansen, W.B., Bane, A.L. and Havis, J. (1978) 'Deterring the onset of smoking in children: knowledge of immediate physiological effects and coping with peer pressure, media pressure and parent modelling', *Journal of Applied Social Psychology*, 8(2): 126–35.

Evans, T.G. (1968) 'A program for the solution of geometric-analogy intelligence test questions', in M. Minsky (ed.) *Semantic Information Processing*. Cambridge, MA: MIT Press.

Everitt, B.S. (1977) *The Analysis of Contingency Tables*. London: Chapman and Hall.

Exner, J. (1986) *The Rorschach: A Comprehensive System* (2nd edn). Chichester: Wiley.

Eysenck, (1978) 'An exercise in mega-silliness', *American Psychologist*, 33: 517.

Eysenck, H.J. and Eysenck, S.B.G. (1975) *Manual for the Eysenck Personality Questionnaire*. London: Hodder and Stoughton.

Eysenck, H.J. and Eysenck, S.B.G. (1976) *Psychoticism as a Dimension of Personality*. London: Hodder and Stoughton.

Fetterman, D.M. (1993) *Speaking the Language of Power: Communication, Collaboration and Advocacy*. London: Falmer Press.

Fife-Schaw, C.R and Breakwell, G.M. (1992) 'Estimating sexual behaviour parameters in the light of AIDS: a review of recent UK studies of young people', *AIDS Care*, 4(2): 187–202.

Fisch, B.J. (1991) *Spehlmann's EEG Primer* (2nd edn). Amsterdam: Elsevier Science.

Fleiss, J.L. (1971) 'Measuring nominal scale agreement among many raters', *Psychological Bulletin*, 76: 378–82.

Forgays, D.G., Sosnowski, T. and Wrzeniewski, K. (1992) *Anxiety: Recent Developments in Cognitive Psychophysiological and Health Research*. New York: Hemisphere Publishing Corp.

Foucault, M. (1972) *The Archaeology of Knowledge*. London: Tavistock.

Freeman, P.R. (1973) *Table of d' and β*. Cambridge: Cambridge University Press.

Fried, R. and Grimaldi, J. (1993) *The Psychology and Physiology of Breathing*. London: Plenum Press.

Fuller, T.D., Edwards, J.N., Vorakitphokatom, S. and Sermsri, S. (1993) 'Using focus groups to adapt survey instruments to new populations: experience from a developing country', in D.L. Morgan (ed.) *Successful Focus Groups: Advancing the State of the Art*. London: Sage.

Gage, N.L. (1963) *Handbook of Research on Teaching*. Chicago: Rand McNally.

Gale, A. and Eysenck, H.O. (eds) (1993) *Handbook of Individual Differences: Biological Perspectives*. Chichester: John Wiley.

Gaskell, G., Wright, D. and O'Muircheartaigh (1993) 'Reliability of surveys', *The Psychologist*, 6(11): 500–3.

Gergen, K.J. (1973) 'Social psychology as history', *Journal of Personality and Social Psychology*, 26: 309–20.

Gergen, K.J. (1989) 'Warranting voice and the elaboration of the self', in J. Shotter and K.J. Gergen (eds), *Texts of Identity*. London: Sage.

Gergen, K.J. and Gergen, M.M. (eds) (1984) *Historical Social Psychology*. Hillsdale, NJ: Lawrence Erlbaum Associates.

Gervais, M.C. (1993) 'How communities cope with environmental crises: the case of the Shetland oil spill', Paper presented at the BPS Social Psychology Section Annual Conference, Jesus College, Oxford, September.

Gescheider, G.A. (1985) *Psychophysics* (2nd edn). Hillsdale, NJ: Lawrence Erlbaum Associates.

Gibson, K. and Peterson, A.C. (1991) *Brain Maturation and Cognitive Development*. Chicago: Aldine de Gruyter.

Gifi, A. (1990) *Nonlinear Multivariate Analysis*. Chichester: John Wiley.

Gilbert, G.N. and Mulkay, M.J. (1984) *Opening Pandora's Box: A Sociological Analysis of Scientists' Discourse*. Cambridge: Cambridge University Press.

Glaser, B.G. and Strauss, A.L. (1967) *The Discovery of Grounded Theory*. Chicago: Aldine.

Glaser, R. (1963) 'Instructional technology and the measurement of learning outcomes', *American Psychologist*, 18: 519–22.

Glass, G. (1976) 'Primary, secondary and meta-analysis of research', *Educational Research*, 5: 3–8.

Glass, G. (1977) 'Integrating findings: the meta-analysis of research', *Review of Research in Education*, 5: 351–79.

Glass, G., McGraw, B. and Smith, M.L. (1981) *Meta-analysis in Social Research*. Beverly Hills, CA: Sage.

Goetz, J.P. and LeCompte, M.D. (1984) *Ethnography and Qualitative Design in Educational Research*. London: Academic Press.

Goldberg, D. (1972) *The Detection of Psychiatric Illness by Questionnaire*. London: Oxford University Press.

Gratch, H. (1973) *Twenty Five Years of Social Research in Israel*. Jerusalem: Jerusalem Academic Press.

Green, B. and Hall, J. (1984) 'Quantitative methods for literature review', *Annual Review of Psychology*, 35: 37–53.

Green, D.M. and Swets, J.A. (1966) *Signal Detection Theory and Psychophysics*. New York: Wiley.

Greenacre, M.J. (1984) *Theory and Application of Correspondence Analysis*. New York: Academic Press.

Gronwall, D.B. and Wrightson, P. (1974) 'Recovery after minor head injury', *Lancet*, ii: 1452.

Groves, R.M. (1989) *Survey Errors and Survey Costs*. New York: Academic Press.

Gulliksen, H. (1950) *Theory of Mental Tests*. New York: Wiley.

Gutride, M.E., Goldstein, A.P. and Hunter, G.F. (1973) 'The use of role-playing and modeling to increase social interaction amongst asocial psychiatric patients', *Journal of Consulting and Clinical Psychology*, 40: 408–15.

Guttman, L. (1941) 'The quantification of a class of attributes: a theory and method of scale construction', in P. Horst (ed.) *The Prediction of Personal Adjustment*. New York: SSRC.

Guttman, L. (1953) 'What lies ahead for factor analysis?', *Educational and Psychological Measurement*, 18: 497–515.

Guttman, L. (1991) *Chapters from an Unfinished Textbook on Facet Theory*. Jerusalem: Hebrew University Press.

Guttman, L. and Guttman, R. (1976) 'The theory of generality and specificity during mild stress', *Behavioral Science*, 21: 469–77.

Guzzo, R.A., Jackson, S.E. and Katzell, R.A. (1987) 'Meta-analysis analysis', *Research in Organizational Behaviour*, 9: 407-42.

Guzzo, R.A., Jette, R.D. and Katzell, R,A, (1985) 'The effects of psychologically based intervention programs on worker productivity', *Personnel Psychology*, 38: 275–92.

Haberman, S.J. (1978) *The Analysis of Qualitative Data. Volume 1*. New York: Academic Press.

Haberman, S.J. (1979) *The Analysis of Qualitative Data. Volume 2*. New York: Academic Press.

Habermas, J. (1979) *Communication and the Evolution of Society*. Boston: Beacon.

Hair, J.F., Anderson R.E., Tatham R.L. and Black, W.C. (1992) *Multivariate Data Analysis*. New York: Macmillan.

Hall, J.L. (1981) 'Hybrid adaptive procedure for estimation of psychometric functions', *Journal of the Acoustical Society of America*, 69: 1763–9.

Halliday, A.M., Butler, S.R. and Paul, R. (1987) *A Textbook of Clinical Neurophysiology*. Chichester: John Wiley.

Hambleton R.K., Swaminathan H. and Rogers H.J. (1991) *Fundamentals of Item Response Theory*. London: Sage.

Hammersley, M. (1990) *Classroom Ethnography*. Milton Keynes: Open University Press.

Hammersley, M. and Atkinson, P. (1983) *Ethnography: Principles in Practice*. London: Tavistock.

Haney, C., Banks, C. and Zimbardo, P.G. (1973) 'Interpersonal dynamics in a simulated prison', *International Journal of Criminology and Penology*, 1: 69–97.

Harman, H. (1976) *Modern Factor Analysis*. Chicago: University of Chicago Press.

Hartington, J.A. (1969) 'Using subsample values as typical values', *Journal of the American Statistical Association*, 64: 1303–17.

Harvey, L.O., Jr. (1986) 'Efficient estimation of sensory thresholds', *Behavior Research Methods, Instruments and Computers*, 18: 623–32.

Heath, C. and Luff, P. (1993) 'Explicating face-to-face interaction', in N. Gilbert (ed.) *Researching Social Life*. London: Sage.

Henkel, R.E. (1975) 'Part-whole correlations and the treatment of ordinal and quasi-interval data as interval data', *Pacific Sociological Review*, 18: 3–26.

Holm, S. (1979) 'A simple sequentially rejective multiple test procedure', *Scandinavian Journal of Statistics*, 6: 65–70.

Holsti, O.R. (1969) *Content Analysis for the Social Sciences*. Reading, MA: Addison-Wesley.

Horton, C. and Smith, D. (1988) *Evaluating Police Work: An Action Research Project*. London: Policy Studies Institute.

Hunter, J.E. and Hirsh, H.R. (1987) 'Applications of meta-analysis', in C.L. Cooper and I.T. Robertson (eds) *International Review of Industrial and Organizational Psychology*. Chichester: Wiley.

Hunter, J.E., Schmidt, F.L. and Jackson, G.B. (1982) *Meta-analysis: Cumulating Research Findings Across Studies*. Beverly Hills, CA: Sage.

Hutt, S.J. and Hutt, C. (1970) *Direct Observation and Measurement of Behaviour*. Springfield, IL: Charles C. Thomas.

Inglehart, R. (1981) 'Post-materialism in an environment of insecurity', *American Political Science Review*, 75: 880–900.

Israel, J. (1972) 'Stipulations and construction in the social sciences' in J. Israel and H. Tajfel (eds) *The Context of Social Psychology*. London: Academic Press.

Janis, I. (1972) *Victims of Groupthink*. Boston: Houghton Mifflin.

Jarrett, R.L. (1993) 'Focus group interviewing with low-income minority populations', in D.L. Morgan (ed.) *Successful Focus Groups: Advancing the State of the Art*. Newbury Park, CA: Sage.

Jaskowski, P. (1993) 'Selective attention and temporal-order judgement', *Perception*, 22: 681–9.

Jennings, J. and Coles, M.G. (eds) (1991) *Handbook of Cognitive Psychophysiology: Central and Autonomic Nervous System Approaches*. Chichester: John Wiley.

Johnson, C., Wood R. and Blinkhorn, S. (1988) 'Spurious and spuriouser. The use of ipsative personality tests', *Journal of Occupational Psychology*, 61(2): 153–62.

Kelly, G.A. (1955) *The Psychology of Personal Constructs, Volumes 1 and 2*. New York: Norton.

Keppel, G. and Saufley, J.R. (1980) *Introduction to Design and Analysis: A Student's Handbook*. San Francisco: W.H. Freeman.

Kerlinger, F.N. (1973) *Foundations of Behavioural Research* (6th edn). London: Holt, Rinehart and Winston.

King-Smith, P.E., Grigsby, S.S., Vingrys, A.J., Benes, S.C. and Supowit, A. (1994) 'Efficient and unbiased modifications of the QUEST method: theory, simulations, experimental evaluation and practical implementation', *Vision Research*, 34: 885–912.

Kintsch, W., Miller, J.R. and Polson, P.G. (1984) *Methods and Tactics in Cognitive Science*. Hillsdale, NJ: Lawrence Erlbaum Associates.

Kirchner, R.E., Schnelle, J.F., Domash, M.A., Larson, L.D., Carr, A.F. and McNees, M.P. (1980) 'The applicability of a helicopter patrol procedure to diverse areas: a cost benefit evaluation', *Journal of Applied Behaviour Analysis*, 13: 143–8.

Klecka, W.R. (1980) *Discriminant Analysis*. London: Sage.

Kline, P. (1988) *Psychology Exposed: Or the Emperor's New Clothes*. London: Routledge.

Kline, P. (1993) *Handbook of Psychological Testing*. London: Routledge.

Kling, J.W. and Riggs, L.A. (eds) (1972) *Experimental Psychology* (3rd edn). London: Methuen.

Klopfer, W.G. and Taulbee, E.S. (1976) 'Projective tests', *Annual Review of Psychology*, 27: 543–68.

Knodel, J. (1993) 'The design and analysis of focus group studies: A practical approach', in D.L. Morgan (ed.) *Successful Focus Groups: Advancing the State of the Art*. London: Sage.

Koocher, G.P. (1977) 'Bathroom behaviour and human dignity', *Journal of Personality and Social Psychology*, 35: 120–1.

Kraemer, H.C. and Thiemann, S. (1987) *How Many Subjects? Statistical Power Analysis in Research*. Newbury Park, CA: Sage.

Krippendorf, K. (1980) *Content Analysis: An Introduction to its Methodology*. Beverly Hills, CA: Sage.

Krueger, R.A. (1988) *Focus Groups: A Practical Guide for Applied Research*. Newbury Park, CA: Sage.

Krueger, R.A. (1993) 'Quality control in focus group research', in D.L. Morgan (ed.) *Successful Focus Groups: Advancing the State of the Art*. London: Sage.

Kruskal, J.B. (1964) 'Nonmetric multidimensional scaling: a numerical method', *Psychometrika*, 29: 1–27.

Kuder, G. and Richardson, M. (1937) 'The theory of the estimation of test reliability', *Psychometrika*, 2: 151–60.

Labovitz, S. (1975) 'Comment on Henkel's paper: the interplay between measurement and statistics', *Pacific Sociological Review*, 18: 27–35.

Lancaster, H.O. (1969) *The Chi-Squared Distribution*. New York: John Wiley.

Latane, B. and Darley, J.M. (1970) *The Unresponsive Bystander: Why doesn't he help?* New York: Appleton-Century-Crofts.

Lau, R.R. and Russell, D. (1980) 'Attributions in the sports pages', *Journal of Personality and Social Psychology*, 39: 29–38.

Lautsch, E. and von Weber, S. (1990) *Konfigurationsfrequenzanalyse*. Berlin: Volk and Wissen.

Lees, R. and Smith, G. (1975) *Action Research in Community Development*. London: Routledge and Kegan Paul.

Levy, S. (1976) 'Use of the mapping sentence for coordinating theory and research: A cross cultural example', *Quality and Quantity*, 10: 117–25.

Levy, S. (1981) 'Lawful roles of facets in social theories', in I. Borg (ed.) *Multidimensional Data Representations: When and Why*. Ann Arbor: Mathesis Press.

Levy, S. (1990) 'Values and deeds', *Applied Psychology: An International Review*, 39: 379–400.

Levy, S. (1994) *Louis Guttman on Theory and Methodology: Selected Writings*. Aldershot: Dartmouth.

Lewin, K. (1952) *Field Theory in Social Science*. London: Tavistock.

Light, R.J. (1971) 'Measures of response agreement for qualitative data: Some generalisations and alternatives', *Psychological Bulletin*, 76: 175–81.

Lingoes, J.C. (1963) 'Multiple scalogram analysis: a set theoretic model for analysing dichotomous items', *Educational and Psychological Measurement*, 23: 501–24.

Lingoes, J.C. (1968) 'The multivariate analysis of qualitative data', *Multivariate Behavioral Research*, 3: 61–94.

Lingoes, J.C., Roskam, E.E. and Borg, I. (eds) (1977) *Geometric Representations of Relational Data*. Ann Arbor: Mathesis.

Llewellyn, G. (1991) 'Adults with an intellectual disability: Australian practitioners' perspectives', *Occupational Therapy Journal of Research*, 11(6): 323–35.

Lord, F.M. and Novick, M. (1968) *Statistical Theories of Mental Test Scores*. Reading, MA: Addison-Wesley.

Lord, R.G. and Hohenfeld, J.A. (1979) 'Longitudinal field assessment of equity effects on the performance of major league baseball players', *Journal of Applied Psychology*, 64: 19–26.

Lovett, T. (1975) *Adult Education, Community Development and the Working Class*. London: Ward Lock.

Lowenthal, D. (1985) *The Past is a Foreign Country*. Cambridge: Cambridge University Press.

McClelland, D.C. (1961) *The Achieving Society*. New Jersey: D. Van Nostrand Company.

McDonald, R.P. (1985) *Factor Analysis and Related Methods*. Hillsdale, NJ: Lawrence Erlbaum Associates.

McGrath, J.E. (1967) 'A multifacet approach to classification of individual, group, and organisation concepts', in B.P. Indik and K.F. Berrien (eds) *People, Groups, and Organisations*. New York: Columbia University.

Marans, R.W. and Spreckelmeyer, K.F. (1986) 'A conceptual model for evaluating work environments', in J.D. Wineman (ed.) *Behavioral Issue in Office Design*. New York: Van Nostrand Reinhold.

Marascuilo, L.A. and Levin, J.R. (1983) *Multivariate Statistics in the Social Sciences*. Monterey: Brooks/Cole.

Marcus, A.C. and Crane, L.A. (1986) *The Validity and Value of Health Survey Research by Telephone: A Review of the Literature Concerning Four Methodological Issues about Health Survey Research*. Jonsson Comprehensive Cancer Center, Univ. of California, Los Angeles/The Commonwealth Fund, New York.

Marin, L. (1983) 'Discourse of power – power of discourse: Pascalian notes', in A. Montefiore (ed.) *Philosophy in France Today*. Cambridge: Cambridge University Press.

Markova, I. and Wilkie, P. (1987) 'Representations, concepts and social change: The phenomenon of AIDS', *Journal for the Theory of Social Behaviour*, 17: 389–409.

Marsh, P., Rosser, E. and Harré R. (1978) *The Rules of Disorder*. London: Routledge and Kegan Paul.

Matlin, M.W. and Foley, H.J. (1992) *Sensation and Perception* (3rd edn). Boston: Allyn and Bacon.

Merton, R.K. and Kendall, P.L. (1946) 'The focused interview', *The American Journal of Sociology*, 51(6): 541–57.

Middlemist, R.D., Knowles, E.S. and Matter, C.F. (1976) 'Personal space invasion in the lavatory: suggestive evidence for arousal', *Journal of Personality and Social Psychology*, 33: 541–6.

Middleton, D. and Edwards, D. (eds) (1989) *Collective Remembering*. London: Sage.

Milgram, S. (1974) *Obedience to Authority*. New York: Harper and Row.

Mill, J. S. (1874) *A System of Logic*. New York: Harper.

Miller, G.A. (1969) 'Psychology as a means of promoting human welfare', *American Psychologist*, 24: 1063–75.

Miller, J.R., Polson, P.G. and Kintsch, W. (1984) 'Problems of methodology in cognitive science', in W. Kintsch, J.R. Miller and P.G. Polson (eds) *Methods and Tactics in Cognitive Science*. Hillsdale, NJ: Lawrence Erlbaum Associates Publishers.

Miller, R.G. (1974) 'The Jacknife: a review', *Biometrika*, 61: 1–15.

Minium, E.W., King, B.M. and Bear, G. (1993) *Statistical Reasoning in Psychology and Education*. New York: John Wiley and Sons.

Minsky, M. (ed.) (1968) *Semantic Information Processing*. Cambridge, MA: MIT Press.

Mislevy, R.J. (1993) 'Foundations of a new test theory', in N. Frederiksen, R.J. Mislevy and I. Bejar (eds) *Test Theory for a New Generation of Tests*. London: Lawrence Erlbaum.

Morgan, D.L. (1988) *Focus Groups as Qualitative Research*. Newbury Park, CA: Sage.

Morgan, D.L. (1993) 'Future directions for focus groups', in D.L. Morgan (ed.) *Successful Focus Groups: Advancing the State of the Art*. London: Sage.

Moser, C.A. and Kalton, G. (1971) *Survey Methods in Social Investigation*. London: Heinemann.

Mostyn, B. (1985) 'The content analysis of qualitative research data', in M. Brenner, J. Brown and D.V. Canter (eds) *The Research Interview: Uses and Approaches*. London: Academic Press.

Mullen, B. (1993) 'Meta-analysis', *Thornfield Journal*, 16: 36–41.

Murphy, J., John, M. and Brown, H. (1984) *Dialogues and Debates in Social Psychology*. London: Lawrence Erlbaum.

Murphy, K.R. and Davidshofer, C.O. (1991) *Psychological Testing: Principles and Applications*. London: Prentice-Hall.

Naylor, C. (1983) *Build your own Expert System*. Cheshire: Sigma Technical Press.

Neisser, U. (1986) 'Nested structure in autobiographical memory', in D.C. Rubin (ed.) *Autobiographical Memory*. Cambridge: Cambridge University Press.

Nesselroade, J.R. and Cattell, R.B. (eds) (1988) *Handbook of Multivariate Experimental Psychology* (2nd edn). London: Plenum Press.

Newell, R. (1993) 'Questionnaires', in N. Gilbert (ed.) *Researching Social Life*. London: Sage.

Nitko, A.J. (1988) 'Designing tests that are integrated with instruction', in R.L. Linn (ed.) *Educational Measurement*. New York: Macmillan

Nunnally, J.C. (1978) *Psychometric Theory*. New York: McGraw-Hill.

O'Brien, K. (1993) 'Improving survey questionnaires through focus groups', in D.L. Morgan (ed.) *Successful Focus Groups: Advancing the State of the Art*. London: Sage.

Obermeier, K.K. (1987) 'Natural-language processing', *BYTE*, 12(14): 225–32.

Oppenheim, A.N. (1992) *Questionnaire Design, Interviewing and Attitude Measurement*. London: Pinter Publishers.

Park, R.E. (1967) *On Social Control and Collective Behaviour: Selected Papers*. Chicago: University of Chicago Press.

Parker, I. (1992) *Discourse Dynamics: Critical Analysis for Social and Individual Psychology*. London: Routledge.

Parker, I. and Burman, E. (1993) 'Against discursive imperialism, empiricism and constructionism: thirty-two problems with discourse analysis', in E. Burman and I. Parker (eds) *Discourse Analytic Research: Repertoires and Readings of Texts in Action*. London: Routledge.

Parkes, C. M. (1971) 'Psycho-social transitions: a field for study', *Social Science and Medicine*, 5: 101–15.

Pentland, A. (1980) 'Maximum likelihood estimation: the best PEST', *Perception and Psychophysics*, 28: 377–9.

Piaget, J. (1952a) *The Child's Conception of Number*. London: Routledge, Kegan and Paul.

Piaget, J. (1952b) *The Origins of Intelligence in the Child*. New York: Basic Books.

Pollner, M. (1991) 'Left of ethnomethodology: the rise and decline of radical reflexivity', *American Sociological Review*, 56: 370–80.

Pomerantz, A.M. (1986) 'Extreme case formulations: a new way of legitimizing claims', in G. Button, P. Drew and J. Heritage (eds), *Human Studies* (Special Issue on Interaction and Language Use), 9: 219–29.

Popper, K.R. (1968) *The Logic of Scientific Discovery*. London: Hutchinson.

Potter, J. and Collie, F. (1989) ' "Community care" as persuasive rhetoric: a study of discourse', *Disability, Handicap and Society*, 4: 57–64.

Potter, J. and Wetherell, M. (1987) *Discourse and Social Psychology: Beyond Attitudes and Behaviour*. London: Sage.

Powell, G.E. and Wilson, S.L. (1994) 'Recovery curves for patients who have suffered very severe brain injury', *Clinical Rehabilitation*, 8: 54–69.

Rapoport, R.N. (1972) 'Three dilemmas in action research', in P.A. Clark (ed.) *Action Research in Organisational Change*. London: Harper and Row.

Roethlisberger, F.J. and Dickson, W.J. (1939) *Management and the Worker*. Cambridge, MA: Harvard University Press.

Rorschach, H. (1921) *Psychodiagnostics*. Berne: Huber.

Rose, D. (1988) 'ZSCORE: a program for the accurate calculation of $d'$ and $\beta$', *Behavior Research Methods, Instruments and Computers*, 20: 63–4.

Rose, R.M., Teller, D.Y. and Rendleman, P. (1970) 'Statistical properties of staircase estimates', *Perception and Psychophysics*, 8: 199–204.

Rosenthal, R. (1979) 'The "file drawer problem" and tolerance for null results', *Psychological Bulletin* 86: 638–41.

Rosenthal, R. (1991) *Meta-analytic Procedures for Social Research*. Beverly Hills, CA: Sage.

Rowan, J. (1974) 'Research as intervention', in N. Armistead (ed.) *Reconstructing Social Psychology*. Harmondsworth: Penguin.

Roy, D.F. (1965) 'The role of the researcher in the study of social conflict', *Human Organisation*, 24: 262–71.

Rust, J. and Golombok, S. (1989) *Modern Psychometrics*. London: Routledge.

Schaie, K.W. (1965) 'A general model for the study of developmental problems', *Psychological Bulletin*, 64: 92–107.

Schmidt, F.L., Hunter, J.E., Pearlman, K., Hirsh, R.H., Sackett, P.R., Schmitt, N., Tenopyr, M.L., Kehoe, J. and Zedeck, S. (1985) 'Forty questions about validity generalization and meta-analysis (plus commentary)', *Personnel Psychology*, 38: 697–798.

Schuman, H. and Presser, S. (1981) *Questions and Answers in Attitude Surveys: Experiments on Question Form, Writing and Context*. London: Academic Press.

Scott, P. and Nicholson. R. (1991) *Cognitive Science: Projects in Prolog*. Hillsdale, NJ: Lawrence Erlbaum Associates.

Searle, J.R. (1990) 'Is the brain's mind a computer program', *Scientific American*, 262(1): 20–5.

Seidel, J.V., Kjolseth, A. and Seymour, J.A. (1988) *The Ethnograph: A User's Guide*. Littleton: Qualitative Research Associates.

Sekuler, R. and Blake, R. (1994) *Perception* (3rd edn). New York: McGraw-Hill.

Selltiz, C., Wrightsman, L.S. and Cook. S.W. (1976) *Research Methods in Social Relations* (3rd edn). New York: Holt, Rinehart and Winston.

Shapiro, D.A. and Shapiro, D. (1982) 'Meta-analysis of comparative therapy outcome studies: a replication and refinement', *Psychological Bulletin*, 92(3): 581–604.

Shaughnessy, J.J. and Zechmeister, E.B. (1994) *Research Methods in Psychology*. New York: McGraw-Hill.

Shavelson, R.J. and Webb, N.M. (1991) *Generalizability Theory*. London: Sage.

Shye, S. (ed.) (1978) *Theory Construction and Data Analysis in the Behavioral Sciences*. San Francisco: Jossey Bass.

Shye, S. (1988) *Multiple Scaling*. Amsterdam: North-Holland.

Sidak, Z. (1967) 'Rectangular confidence regions for the means of multivariate normal distributions', *Journal of the American Statistical Association*, 62: 625–33.

Simon, H. A. (1981) *The Sciences of the Artificial*. Cambridge, MA: The MIT Press.

Skinner, B.F. (1953) *Science and Human Behaviour*. New York: Macmillan.

Spearman, C. (1907) 'Demonstration of formulae for true measures of correlation', *American Journal of Psychology*, 18: 161–9.

Spencer, L., Faulkner, A. and Keegan, J. (1988) *Talking About Sex*. London: Social and Community Planning Research.

Spradley, J. P. (1979) *The Ethnographic Interview*. New York: Holt, Rinehart and Winston.

Spradley, J.P. and Mann, B.J. (1975) *The Cocktail Waitress: Women's Work in a Man's World*. New York: Wiley.

Spreen, O. and Strauss, E. (1991) *A Compendium of Neuropsychological Tests*. New York: Oxford University Press.

Sternberg, R.J. (1977) *Intelligence, Information Processing and Analogical Reasoning*. Hillsdale, NJ: Lawrence Erlbaum Associates.

Stevens, S.S. (1946) 'On the theory of scales of measurement', *Science*, 103: 677–80.

Stewart, D.W. and Shamdasani, P.N. (1990) *Focus Groups: Theory and Practice*. Newbury Park, CA: Sage.

Stine, W.W. (1989) 'Meaningful inference: the role of measurement in statistics', *Psychological Bulletin*, 105: 147–55.

Stone, E.F. (1986) 'Job-scope satisfaction and job-scope performance relationships', in E.A. Locke (ed.) *Generalisation from Lab to Field Settings*. Lexington, MA: Heath-Lexington Books.

Strachey, C. (1966) 'Systems analysis and programming', *Scientific American*, 215(3): 112–24.

Strube, M.J. and Hartmann, D.P. (1982) 'A critical appraisal of meta-analysis', *British Journal of Clinical Psychology*, 21: 129–39.

Sudman, S. and Bradburn, N.M. (1982) *Asking Questions: A Practical Guide to Questionnaire Design*. San Francisco: Jossey Bass.

Suen, H.K. (1991) *Principles of Test Theories*. London: Lawrence Erlbaum.

Sunderland, A. (1990) 'Single-case experiments in neurological rehabilitation', *Clinical Rehabilitation*, 4: 181–92.

Tajfel, H. (ed.) (1982) *Social Identity and Intergroup Relations*. London: Cambridge University Press.

Taylor, M.M. and Creelman, C.D. (1967) 'PEST: efficient estimates on probability functions', *Journal of the Acoustical Society of America*, 41: 782–7.

Thomas, J. (1993) *Doing Critical Ethnography*. London: Sage.

Thorndike, R.L. and Hagen, E.P. (1977) *Measurement and Evaluation in Psychology and Education* (4th edn). New York: Wiley.

Thurstone, L.L. (1951) 'Psychological implications of factor analysis', in M.H. Marx (ed.) *Psychological Theory*. New York: Macmillan.

Tizard, B., Blatchford, P., Burke, J., Farquar C. and Plewis, I. (1988) *Young Children at School in the Inner City*. Hove: Lawrence Erlbaum.

Townsend, J.T. and Ashby, F.G. (1984) 'Measurement scales and statistics: the misconception misconceived', *Psychological Bulletin*, 96: 394–401.

Treisman, M. and Watts, T.R. (1966) 'Relation between signal detectability theory and the traditional procedures for measuring sensory thresholds: estimating $d'$ from results given by the method of constant stimuli', *Psychological Bulletin*, 66: 438–54.

Tyrrell, R.A. and Owens, D.A. (1988) 'A rapid technique to assess the resting states of the eyes and other threshold phenomena: the modified binary search (MOBS)', *Behaviour Research Methods, Instruments and Computers*, 20(2): 137–41.

Uzzell, D.L. (1988) 'Four perspectives on political participation in the city', *Psicologia*, VI(3): 377–84.

Van Dijk, T.A. (1993) 'Principles of critical discourse analysis', *Discourse & Society*, 4: 249–83.

von Eye, A. (1990) *Introduction to Configural Frequency Analysis*. Cambridge: Cambridge University Press.

Wagner, H. and Manstead, A (eds) (1989) *Handbook of Social Psychophysiology*. Chichester: John Wiley.

Waltz, D. L. (1982) 'Artificial intelligence', *Scientific American*, 247(4): 101–22.

Warr, P. (1977) 'Aided experiments in social psychology', *Bulletin of the British Psychological Society*, 30: 2–8.

Watson, A.B. and Pelli, D.G. (1983) 'QUEST: a Bayesian adaptive psychometric method', *Perception and Psychophysics*, 33: 113–20.

Wegner, D.M. and Vallacher, R.R. (1981) 'Common-sense psychology' in J.P. Forgas (ed.) *Social Cognition: Perspectives on Everyday Understanding*. London: Academic Press.

Weller, S.C. and Romney, A.K. (1990) *Metric Scaling: Correspondence Analysis*. London: Sage.

Werner, O. and Schoepfle, G.M. (1987) *Systematic Fieldwork: Volume 1 Foundations of Ethnography and Interviewing*. London: Sage.

Wetherell, M. and Potter, J. (1988) 'Discourse analysis and the identification of interpretative repertoires', in C. Antaki (ed.) *Analysing Everyday Explanation: A Casebook of Methods*. London: Sage.

Wetherell, M. and Potter, J. (1992) *Mapping the Language of Racism: Discourse and the Legitimation of Exploitation*. Hemel Hempstead: Harvester Wheatsheaf.

Wetherill, G.B. and Levitt, H. (1965) 'Sequential estimation of points on a psychometric function', *British Journal of Mathematical and Statistical Psychology*, 18: 1–10.

White, O.R. (1972) *A Manual for the Calculation and Use of the Median Slope: A Technique of Progress Estimation and Prediction in the Single Case*. Eugene, OR: University of Oregon Regional Resource Center for Handicapped Children.

White, S. and Mitchell, T. (1976) 'Organization development: a review of research content and research design', *Academy of Management Review*, 1: 57–73.

Whyte, W.F. (1943) *Street Corner Society: The Social Structure of an Italian Slum*. Chicago: University of Chicago Press.

Whyte, W.F (1991) *Participatory Action Research*. London: Sage.

Widdicombe, S. (1993) 'Autobiography and change: rhetoric and authenticity of "Gothic" style', in E. Burman and I. Parker (eds) *Discourse Analytic Research: Repertoires and Readings of Texts in Action*. London: Routledge.

Wilde, G.J. (1986) 'Beyond the concept of risk homeostasis: Suggestions for research and application toward the prevention of accidents and lifestyle-related disease', *Accident Analysis and Prevention*, 18: 377–401.

Wilson, G.D. and Patterson, J.R. (1968) 'A new measure of Conservatism', *British Journal of Social and Clinical Psychology*, 7: 264–90.

Wilson, M.A. and Canter, D. (1990) 'The development of professional concepts', *Applied Psychology: An International Review*, 39(4): 431–55.

Wilson, M.A. and Canter D. (1993) 'Shared concepts in group decision making: a model for decisions based on qualitative data', *British Journal of Social Psychology*, 32:159–72.

Wilson, S.L. and McMillan T.M. (1993) 'A review of the evidence for the effectiveness of sensory stimulation treatment for coma and vegetative states', *Neuropsychological Rehabilitation*, 3(2): 149–60.

Wilson, S.L., Powell, G.E., Elliots, K. and Thwaites, H. (1991) 'Sensory stimulation in prolonged coma: four single case studies', *Brain Injury*, 5(4): 393–400.

Winer, B.J. (1971) *Statistical Principals in Experimental Design*. New York: McGraw-Hill.

Winograd, T. (1971) *An AI Approach to English Morphemic Analysis*. Artificial Intelligence memo No. 241, February 1971, Cambridge, MA: MIT AI Laboratory.

Winograd, T. (1972) *Understanding Natural Language*. Edinburgh: Edinburgh University Press.

Winograd, T. (1980) 'What does it mean to understand language?' *Cognitive Science*, 4: 209–41.

Winston, P.H. (1984) *Artificial Intelligence* (2nd edn). Reading, MA: Addison-Wesley.

Winston, P.H. and Horn. B.K.P. (1984) *LISP* (2nd edn). Reading, MA: Addison-Wesley.

Wirth, L. (1928) *The Ghetto*. Chicago: University of Chicago Press.

Wolf, F.M. (1986) *Meta-Analysis: Quantitative Methods for Research Synthesis*. Beverly Hills, CA: Sage.

Woodworth, R.S. and Schlosberg, H. (1954) *Experimental Psychology* (revised edn). London: Methuen.

Wooffitt, R. (1992) *Telling Tales of the Unexpected: The Organization of Factual Discourse*. Hemel Hempstead: Harvester Wheatsheaf.

Wooffitt, R. (1993) 'Analysing accounts', in N. Gilbert (ed.) *Researching Social Life*. London: Sage.

Young, K. and Kramer, J. (1978) 'Local exclusionary policies in Britain: the case of suburban defence in a metropolitan system', in K. Cox (ed.) *Urbanization and Conflict in Market Societies*. London: Methuen.

Yule, W. (1987) 'Evaluation of treatment programmes', in W.Yule and J. Carr (eds) *Behaviour Modification for People with Mental Handicaps*. London: Chapman and Hall.

Ziller, R.C. (1973) *The Social Self*. Oxford: Pergamon Press.

Zorbaugh, H.W. (1929) *The Gold Coast and the Slum: A Sociological Study of Chicago's Near North Side*. Chicago: University of Chicago Press.

Zuber-Skerritt, O. (1992) *Action Research in Higher Education*. London: Kogan Page.

Zvulun, E. (1978) 'Multidimensional scalogram analysis: the method and its application', in S. Shye (ed.) *Theory Construction and Data Analysis in the Behavioural Sciences*. London: Jossey Bass.

# Index